JIMMY ADAMSON

THE MAN WHO SAID 'NO' TO ENGLAND

JIMMY ADAMSON
THE MAN WHO SAID 'NO' TO ENGLAND

DAVE THOMAS
FOREWORD BY SIR BOBBY CHARLTON

First published by Pitch Publishing, 2014
Paperback edition 2018

Pitch Publishing
A2 Yeoman Gate
Yeoman Way
Durrington
BN13 3QZ
www.pitchpublishing.co.uk

A CIP catalogue record is available for this book from the
British Library

ISBN-13: 978-1-78531-403-2

Typesetting and origination by Pitch Publishing.
Printed in India by Replika Press

Contents

Acknowledgements

Writing this book was a labour of love but it needed help from many people.

The five grandchildren: Katie, Sarah and James Bolton; Jennie and Sam Halstead; plus nephew Mark Adamson.

Support came from five locations – Ashington, Burnley, Rotterdam, Sunderland and Leeds.

Ashington research: Alan Parker and Mike Kirkup in particular, Ken Brown, Jim Nichol, Ken Dixon, Bill Ogilvie and Alf Martin.

The Burnley chapters: *The Burnley Express*, Burnley Library, Tony Scholes, Tim Quelch, Ray Simpson, Gerard Bradley, Terry Ridout, John Lingard, Derek Gill, David Binns, Veronica Simpson, Peter Higgs, Paul Fletcher, Dave Thomas, Colin Waldron, Jim Thomson, John Angus, Jimmy Robson, Frank Casper, Elizabeth Flynn and Jimmy McIlroy.

Rotterdam research: Tony Scholes, Alfons Meijboom and Cliff Hacking.

The Sunderland chapter: Gary Rowell, Stan Ternent, Rob Mason, John Gibson, George Forster and Martyn McFadden.

The Leeds chapters: John Wray in particular, plus Paul Harrison, Paul Dews, Gary Edwards, Graeme Smith, Michael Green, Stan Ternent, Dave Merrington, Brian Flynn, Eddie Gray and Martin Dobson.

For help with pictures, Burnley FC, Sunderland FC, Gerard Bradley, Howard Talbot, Katie Bolton and Jennie Halstead, Neville Chadwick, Andrew Varley, *Football Monthly* archives and the Press Association.

For the foreword: Sir Bobby Charlton.

For reading and commenting on various draft chapters: Mike Kirkup, Alan Parker, John Gibson, Colin Waldron, Paul Fletcher, Elizabeth Flynn, Rob Mason, Dave Merrington, Martin Dobson, Eddie Gray, Gary Edwards, Chris Watson, and Peter Ellis.

Reading and checking the complete draft: Winston Sutcliffe.

My computer technician: Mrs Harriet Thomas who never grumbles when I vanish for hours into my little room.

At Pitch Publishing: Paul and Jane Camillin.

I delved into a whole host of books but the following were particularly important:

Never Had It So Good 1959/60; Tim Quelch, Pitch Publishing

Leeds And Scotland Hero; Peter Lorimer, Mainstream

Marching On Together; Eddie Gray, Hodder and Stoughton

Harry Potts – Margaret's Story; Margaret Potts and Dave Thomas, Sportsbooks

My England Years; Sir Bobby Charlton, Headline

Foreword by Sir Bobby Charlton

T HE 1950s produced so many wonderful players in an age when there were no great riches to be earned; there was no such thing as squad rotation and terms like 'transition' and 'channels' were unheard of. The pitches were frequently mudbaths, the footballs weighed a ton; we played on ice and in snow and there was minimal protection from referees from all the hardmen who plied their trade back then.

One player who strode around those pitches surviving all the bruising confrontations was Burnley's Jimmy Adamson, a tall, slim, elegant player who to my astonishment never played for England. What was all the more surprising was that the England manager Walter Winterbottom often turned to Jimmy for help with coaching. He respected him to the extent that he asked Jimmy to be assistant manager of the England team in Chile in the 1962 World Cup. And that is where our paths crossed for a lengthy period.

Our paths had crossed on the field of play many times when Burnley played Manchester United and some of the games were memorable during a period when Burnley had a wonderful team; its flowing moves orchestrated by Jimmy McIlroy and of course Jimmy Adamson.

They had players of the calibre of John Connelly, John Angus, Brian Miller and Ray Pointer, all England internationals. They won the title in 1959/60. They played in the European Cup as it was called then. They reached the FA Cup Final in 1962 and came so close to doing the double. And in that same year Jimmy was rightly named Footballer of the Year.

But in fact the paths our lives took started in the same place, in Ashington, and quite amazingly in the same part of Ashington – Laburnum Terrace. My own family later moved to Beatrice Street but it is an amazing fact that Laburnum Terrace produced not just three First Division footballers, but three Footballers of the Year. The three of us – myself, my brother Jack and Jimmy – all won this prestigious accolade.

Jimmy was offered the England managership in 1962 when Walter Winterbottom left the post. He declined the offer for various reasons which this book makes clear. He later joked that by turning it down he helped England win the World Cup, so perhaps in a roundabout kind of way I actually owe my winner's medal to Jimmy. But, many years later when Bob Lord had no further use for him, he regretted his decision to decline the offer.

In Chile I came to greatly respect him and we talked on the plane on the way back home for several hours. I wrote about that journey home and all that we talked about, as we sat together, in my own book *My England Years* in a chapter devoted to Jimmy. Later, I used to drive over the moors to Burnley to visit and talk with him again, such was the impression he made on me when he spoke of his visions and ideas for the England team and England players.

It was no surprise to me that he eventually became Burnley's manager and in the 1970s he had a brief period when although his attractive, passing team won no trophies, they came so close to becoming what he wanted them to be – 'The Team of the Seventies'. If there are reasons why that dream died, this book describes them and certainly tells of how the chairman of Burnley, Bob Lord, by decreeing that the best players should be sold to pay the bills, and eventually dismissing Jimmy, ultimately broke his heart.

He went on to Sunderland for a couple of years and then to Leeds United. But for Jimmy, football was never really the same when he left Burnley so after a tough time at Leeds he turned his back on football altogether.

His story is one of great success until the mid-70s, but this was then followed by broken dreams and frustrated ambitions. He suffered personal tragedies in his family life and for many years was estranged from Burnley Football Club because of the breakdown of his relationship with Bob Lord. It was only shortly before he died that I am happy to say that the relationship with the club was mended when he attended the unveiling ceremony of the Jimmy Adamson Suite.

He was a great footballer, a fine coach, a football visionary and I was truly saddened to attend his funeral in November 2011. I had the greatest admiration for him so it is a pleasure to provide this foreword.

Sir Bobby Charlton, 10 May 2013

Chapter 1

Fetch my luggage

I ONLY ever managed to speak to Jimmy Adamson once. It must have been sometime in 2005 and I knew that by then he rarely spoke to people about football. He'd had nothing to do with the game since the time he left Leeds United in 1980. They had joked there that he was the Yorkshire Ripper. The police used to go round the pubs of Leeds and play the infamous hoax tape of the Geordie voice belonging to the guy who claimed to be the Ripper. They would ask, 'Does anyone recognise this voice?' Voices would shout back, 'It's Jimmy bloody Adamson.' By 1980 he was none too popular at Elland Road.

The end for him came after yet another defeat when Leeds lost 3-0 to Stoke City on 6 September 1980. He'd had a year of abuse, 'Adamson out' chants, banners and demonstrations. The Stoke defeat was already the fourth of the new season in just five games. Each day he must have longed to return to the warmth and sanctuary of his home and the love of his wife, May. He kept his innermost thoughts to himself during this period and afterwards said nothing during all the years that he was out of the game. If he endured untold heartache, then he put on a brave front. If the pressure became intolerable a drink or two blurred the edges. As each Stoke goal went home he surely knew it was one more reason for the directors he could never trust to dismiss him.

The win against Norwich a couple of weeks earlier had given false hope as his arm punched the air in jubilation at the end of the game. Following that there was a home defeat against

Leicester City and more vicious fury from a seething, savage section of the crowd betraying their tribal Brigantes origins. The writing was on the wall; it was a matter of time before the curtain came down on what only a few years earlier at Burnley had seemed such a glittering managerial career following his golden years as a player.

A couple of drinks before the Stoke game would have eased his tensions, and made facing the intimidating crowd a little more bearable, but by the end he was under no illusions that this was it, the end of the line and a merciful release from an unmanageable job with its incessant demands and impossible directors. Leeds United was the Bermuda Triangle of football management and would remain so for some time to come.

He retired into a shell and avoided interviews; for consolation he enjoyed his holidays abroad, another drink or two, and he played crown green bowls. People still knocked at his door wanting to chat, or have things signed but he was frequently unavailable. Years later, by the time I decided to call it was usually his wife May who answered the door. His health was none too clever and she was protective. By this time they were almost reclusive.

It was funny the way I was asked inside. I didn't telephone first but was driving by one day while writing a book about Burnley hero Willie Irvine, and thought if I don't stop and call now, I never will. As I had been warned, it was indeed May who opened the door.

I smiled and spoke. 'I'm Dave Thomas, the guy who writes the Burnley books...'

I didn't get the chance to even finish the sentence before she broke into the biggest smile and clapped her hands. 'Ah Dave,' she spoke with clear affection, 'Come in, come in, Jimmy will be so surprised and pleased to see you.'

I knew immediately the mistake she had made. She thought I was THE Dave Thomas the footballer, the player who had joined Burnley as a young lad, and Jimmy had nurtured and coached in the late 1960s, a stunning player but had eventually been sold in 1972. Ironically, Dave had no reciprocal warm feelings for Jimmy but I kept quiet about that.

'Come in, come in,' May said again. In I went and not until I was in and the door had closed did I tell her that I wasn't THAT Dave Thomas, but only the one who wrote books and had brought one as a present for Jimmy, the anthology that featured a number of his former players – Ralph Coates, Dave Thomas, Steve Kindon, Colin Waldron and Paul Fletcher.

Mistake explained, nevertheless I was welcomed and sat for an hour or more talking about Willie Irvine and then Martin Dobson. I explained I would love to do a book about the 'Team of the Seventies'. That was the label he gave to his certainty that he was developing a Burnley team that would dominate the 1970s, but it hung round his neck like an albatross as soon as the team was relegated in 1971. The club rose again but bad results resumed in the autumn of 1975 and once again he was mocked for the claim he had made that they would dominate the decade.

They agreed I should go again and talk more. But I never did. I telephoned some weeks later to arrange another visit to the house they had, not that far from Turf Moor, just a couple of miles up the road at Pike Hill on the way to Cliviger. Further away were the moorland hills over which I often drove, bleak and desolate on some days, beautiful on others when the sun shines and utterly stunning when the winter snows fall. It was a different May who answered. 'No sorry, Jimmy is not well. We don't want to see anyone.' I sighed; the chance was gone.

I have regretted that lost opportunity ever since. There was such a legion of questions to ask about his boyhood, him and Harry Potts, him and Bob Lord, the England job, his broken dreams; for his is certainly a story of unfulfilled ambitions and hopes. And ever since then, I have written other books saying to myself that much as I would like to try and fathom out the enigma that was Jimmy Adamson, it was something that seemed to pose so many difficulties.

I would finish one book, a year later finish another and then think, 'What next?' But the Adamson idea was always shelved. How could you begin to unravel the story and the changes over time of that complicated relationship between himself, Harry Potts and Bob Lord when all of them were gone? For different reasons these three men were giants in the history of the Burnley club over something like a 20-year period. Their paths were so intertwined, and their lives so inseparable, their bonds so close that it seems impossible to accept that by the time Lord died in 1981, neither Potts nor Adamson ever spoke to him until Potts, on finding out how ill Lord was, went to visit him right at the very end.

Worse still, Adamson and Potts did not speak to each other; and Harry's wife, Margaret, disliked Adamson intensely. In fact her feelings bordered on abhorrence for the way she perceived that Adamson had betrayed Harry and stabbed him in the back ten years earlier at the beginning of the 1970s. She wrote about this in her book *Harry Potts – Margaret's Story* with total candour and obvious hurt. With Jimmy having passed away we'll never know his side of things or the reality of Margaret's accusations.

So many mysteries to delve into: when did Bob Lord first begin to plan that one day Jimmy Adamson should have the Burnley manager's job? Why did some players revere him and others quite the opposite? Why did he turn down the England manager's job in 1962? Why did Bob Lord owe him a considerable sum of money? Why did his opinion of Harry Potts turn from what was once affection and comradeship to something that bordered on disdain? When and how did the change happen between him and Bob Lord so that a deep mutual bitterness developed? Why did that bitterness last so long and to such an intense degree, until he was persuaded to attend the opening of the suite named in his honour at the club, in 2011?

Ironically, persuaded by his former players Paul Fletcher and Colin Waldron, he had agreed to visit a few years earlier than that, but the game he was to attend was on a night of monsoon rains. He sat in the boardroom with them waiting for the directors to arrive but none did and the game was postponed. For over 20 years he had not set foot in the place. He felt shunned and unwanted, his achievements neglected.

Some questions will never be answered. We miss the opportunities to talk to people and try to solve the riddles; the answers go with them when they are no longer here and then we scold ourselves for missing the chances to ask.

For years he had refused to attend any function at Turf Moor, but when he did at last attend a game there, in January 2011, to open the corporate suite named in his honour in the Jimmy McIlroy Stand, he was a resident in a care home in Burnley. His wife May and both his daughters had died and his mind was going into that faraway place where lucidity and memory largely disappear, yet he could still remember games and results from the distant past.

Sadly his daughter Julie had died in 1998 aged only 44 and his other daughter Jayne in 2005 aged only 45. Tragedy thus visited Jimmy and his wife May so cruelly. The deaths of both his daughters must have come like hammer blows. May herself then died in August 2010. His own mother had committed suicide after he had brought her to live in Burnley near him more than 50 years earlier.

It was his former player Paul Fletcher who hosted his former boss on the occasion of the opening of the suite. Paul had become chief executive at the club and for him it was just as special as it was for Jimmy. Fletcher will forever pay Adamson the hugest compliment. 'I was a Second Division player. Then I came here. Jimmy changed my life.'

Jimmy arrived along with his grandchildren and was content to stay in the background as he sat talking to Jimmy McIlroy for half an hour by the large picture windows. As he seemed to edge closer to them it was then that he was asked to step outside. The Burnley fans were rapturous as he was introduced to the crowd before the game. Dementia is so cruel but he was in a good enough state of health to be aware of everything happening, including the reception he was given by the crowd when he appeared in front of them. The wounds that went back so many years were healed that day.

'At that moment,' remembers Paul Fletcher, 'all was forgiven and he realised how wrong he had been. The club had never disliked him; it loved him.'

The chairman of the club then was Barry Kilby and he too was present. Kilby had been a young lad at Turf Moor in his teens trying to make the grade as a footballer. 'He was in charge when I was in the A team,' said Kilby. 'I remember him coming over at the training ground one day to shake my hand and wish me well. When he left in 1976 he fell out of love with the club for a while. But the wounds healed.'

That suite today is a fitting tribute. Glass cabinets line the walls and are filled with pictures, mementoes and reminders of a long and glittering career. It was the way it all ended that is such a haunting story. I looked at one photograph in particular of Jimmy and his Scottie dog in the garden of their home and looking at it you could almost sense the person. He was a family man and he and May were inseparable.

Although he captained the title-winning side of 1959/60 and went on to play in the European Cup, the peak of his career was maybe later in 1962. He was Footballer of the Year, captain of the Wembley Cup Final side, went to Chile as assistant manager to Walter Winterbottom, and was then offered the post of England manager. His star was in the ascendancy. A long, long distinguished career was in prospect. The England job was turned down and for the next 14 years his involvement at Burnley was total before it ended so abruptly. It was a swift, unexpected termination and the start of the long and acrimonious feud with the dictatorial Bob Lord, and then a bitter period when he felt that the club did not give him the recognition he deserved.

We all have pivotal moments in our lives. Sometimes they are the result of our own decisions; sometimes they are the consequences of other peoples' actions. When Bob Lord sent a director to see Adamson on a cold, bleak, Monday morning in January 1976 to ask if he would resign in exchange for a generous settlement (dismissed and sweetened in the same sentence) his life was changed forever. What he had once thought, in fact had been told was a job for life, was finished. He poured out his feelings about Bob Lord in an unpublished article that must have been written sometime in 1976. It was among his possessions and collection of old paperwork found by his grandchildren:

'I lasted for six years under Lord after expecting to be Burnley manager for a lifetime. To be fair Lord treated me well until I started disagreeing with him. Then our relationship went sour. We lived almost in each other's pockets. I planned Burnley's future on the playing side and Lord did the rest. At one time I thought we were a great team. We both made mistakes but I thought our future was healthy until the day Lord retired from his butchery business and took up football as a full-time job.

'Then things started to go wrong. I spent more of my time filling in forms and listening to Lord rather than concentrating solely on the job I was paid for. Not that I'm blaming Lord entirely for the lowly position the club were in when I left last January. But his interference didn't help. I expect any chairman to be fully informed but I don't think it's right to devote the majority of the working day to the chairman's whims.

'And he had many of those. He ruled the club with an iron fist demanding attention most of the time. My wife used to dread weekends especially when we were playing at home. Sometimes she just didn't feel like going to the game but it wasn't just a case of opting out. She had to ring the chairman's wife and report the fact that she wouldn't be there. Too many excuses were frowned upon.

'Even after a game, Lord needed his men around him – to play snooker.

'We'd troop down to the local Conservative Club, discuss the game, while Lord popped in the colours and got results that world snooker champion Ray Reardon would have been proud of. Most of us were reasonable players but somehow we always seemed to miss a crucial pot.

'That was only the start of the weekend activities. Most Sundays we were summoned to the Lord household for lunch and hours of chatter. I didn't mind the ritual but my wife hated it. But we kept going, kept eating the roast beef and Yorkshire pud, and swallowed the rest just to keep Lord happy.

'There's nothing worse than Lord when he's upset or angry. Conversation is restricted to a grunt or a sharp blast and he seems to surround everything with a deep, dark, depressive cloud. The consequences can be disastrous as I know to my cost. He starts with what I term his "pressure" system forcing people to the limit until he gets the results he wants.

'He started with me by picking up every point, scrutinising, and then trying to provoke an argument. This went on for months until our FA Cup defeat at Blackpool. Obviously this was the last straw in a disappointing season for Lord. Nobody likes going out of the Cup at the first attempt especially to a Second Division side. Burnley were no exception.

'Whilst I was out of the dressing room there were heated exchanges which finally exploded between skipper Colin Waldron and my chief coach Joe Brown. I eventually got into the dressing room and sorted out the row. It was just one of those instant flare-ups and I knew there would be no recriminations. Lord missed the Saturday snooker match for the first time in 10 years and I spent the whole of Sunday in bed. I was shattered from working a 12-hour day and suffering from an overdose of Bob Lord. I was no better on the Monday morning and I decided to take the morning off – my first in 12 years.

'But I didn't get the sleep I needed. A director called, examined the facts and then said, "Would you be willing to resign if Mr Lord paid up your contract?" Lord had the final word of course. The following day he sent for me to sack me for not reporting the Blackpool incident and not turning up for work.

'The pay-off of £25,000 softened the blow somewhat as I became another of Lord's victims.

'I'd almost walked out on him 12 months earlier after an explosive bust-up at London Airport. The club's tour of Madeira had started off badly for him. Somebody had forgotten to pick up his luggage and he had to carry it to the taxi himself. The strain must have been too much. He was grumpy for the whole train journey down to London and didn't improve when another taxi spilled his luggage into a London street.

'I'd arranged to meet the party at London Airport and Lord was in vintage form even for him. The red cheeks had exploded into a deep crimson. The chest was heaving and the hat was tilted. Then old war-horse was ready for battle and London Airport suddenly inherited a new tannoy system.

'"It's your bloody fault that my luggage was forgotten. You ought to arrange things properly," he bellowed.

'I just turned and headed back for Burnley. I didn't get far. Another director stepped in and calmed me down. It took hours for Lord to regain his composure and grunt his apologies.

'Many troubles with Lord seemed to come from tours or holidays. A couple of years ago I was lying in the sun enjoying Majorca when I got a phone call from our groundsman. He was upset and complaining bitterly that Lord had ordered him to work from 8am until 6.30pm with only an hour for lunch and no tea breaks. I didn't want to lose a highly qualified groundsman and asked him to hold on until I got back from holiday. I found that the groundsman had apparently upset the Lord family over the growing of tomatoes. In his spare time the groundsman was paid for looking after Lord's garden. On one of his weekly visits he found that two tomato plants had died through lack of water. The following day Lord informed the groundsman that he didn't want him at his home again.

'Whatever I said didn't matter. The groundsman eventually left and we had a real problem. It ended with me and my family manning the mowers at Turf Moor and the club's training ground at Gawthorpe. But we didn't mind; we thought Burnley was a family club, a place of spirit and warmth.

'It was until Bob Lord blew through and froze me out.'

Here was the man who had fashioned such a beautiful passing team in those golden seasons of the 1970s. The man who had been so elegant as a player, the captain of the title team, the 1962 Footballer of the Year, and the man who was even offered the England job and so much admired by Bobby Charlton. Yet here he was being spoken to and used as if he were some kind of lackey and lowly worker at Lord's meat factory.

There is so much angst and torment in that article. When I read it for the first time all I could think was if only I had been able to make those extra visits and spend long hours talking to him. But it was not to be.

One thing Adamson did do was to pen a few thoughts for a small booklet produced in the late 1980s to raise money for a by then financially stricken Burnley. When it was written Bob Lord had been dead for some years and the club was in an appalling state. A report in 1981 by Derek Gill into the financial and administrative state of the club was damning. In 1987 Burnley saved their league status only in the very last game of the season with a win and even then it was only preserved because Lincoln City lost. Jimmy Adamson watched all this happening and must have wondered just how the club had declined to such a desperate position, penniless and floundering in the depths of the Fourth Division. His finger pointed at Bob Lord:

'When I joined Burnley in the late 40s I had no idea I would be spending 27 years with the club; those years contained incredible happiness but also periods of great sadness, both as a player and manager. The downfall of this great club began with whoever made the decision to sell Jimmy McIlroy. There is no doubt in my mind that the disastrous decision was made by chairman Bob Lord, the club's megalomaniac dictator of the day. I do not want to say anything that sounds like sour grapes because the club has given me too much pleasure for that. But I think it is fair to say that Bob Lord helped to build up one of the finest club set-ups in British football; and then destroyed it.

'I joined the club before the Lord era just after the war when I was signed by Cliff Britton. He got the club on the road to success and was followed by the best manager the club has ever had in Alan Brown. He did more for the club as both a player and a manager than any other individual. He was the instigator of the Gawthorpe Hall training centre and was the inventive mind behind all the early coaching techniques which encouraged players to exploit their individual skills instead of stifling them.

'And then came Jimmy McIlroy. He was the finest player I have ever seen wearing a Burnley shirt. The whole club in those days was geared for success which eventually led us into the European Cup. The commercial side was under the guidance of Jack Butterfield with the scouting system under the eagle-eye of Dave Blakey. Young players started to come through the reserve side like Andy Lochhead and Willie Irvine.

'Whilst I was manager we had success in the early 70s, getting promotion to the First Division in 1973 built on a team of both ability and team spirit. A tragic injury to Frank Casper against Leeds United only a week before the FA Cup semi-final against Newcastle United could have been the reason why we didn't get all the way to Wembley. But the game itself when we thrashed Leeds United 4-1 at Elland Road whilst they were well clear at the top of Division One, I remember as a great victory with Collins, Nulty, Waldron and captain Martin Dobson all outstanding.

'I have had many wonderful experiences with Burnley Football Club. Looking back along the road I may have done a few things differently... but the trip itself... I wouldn't have missed it for the world.'

You wonder what he might have done differently. Hindsight is such a wonderful thing but you wonder if he ever regretted that 'Team of the Seventies' claim he made. Might he have regretted the sales of Brian O'Neil, Dave Thomas and Steve Kindon? Might he have handled Bob Lord differently? He must surely have rued the sale of Ralph Coates and was certainly distraught at the sale of Martin Dobson. Should he have opposed them more vigorously? Did he come to regret his eventual aloofness and indifference towards Harry Potts in the two years leading up to Harry's departure?

But the absence of any mention of Harry Potts in the article maybe answers that query. There is not one mention of him, the man acknowledged to have taken the club to the First Division title, to Wembley and into Europe – the latter not once but twice. The omission of his name and the praise heaped on Alan Brown is significant. Journalist Brian Glanville who had almost unlimited access to the team whenever they were in London is adamant that the success of Burnley Football Club was less to do with Potts, and much more to do with the foundations laid by Alan Brown, and then the outstanding presence of two players in particular – Jimmy McIlroy and Jimmy Adamson. Glanville in fact once wrote sketches for that early 1960s satire show, *That Was the Week That Was*, hosted by David Frost late on Saturday nights on BBC TV. The sketch he wrote about the tyrannical Bob Lord and the cap-doffing, subservient Harry Potts was never shown.

Twelve years after Lord had got rid of him, Adamson's bitterness was unabated. His reference to him as the megalomaniac dictator that destroyed the club is a testimony to that. It became a mutual dislike. Lord admitted to Margaret Potts while she was out walking one day, and he was driving by in his car, that he had made wrong choices. He stopped beside her and she always felt that he was about to say more, but then he stopped, bade her farewell and drove away. He commented to former player Les Latcham, when they met several years later, that Adamson was 'his problem'.

In 1963 Adamson still respected and admired his boss Potts, and even wrote that he did. He made it clear in a newspaper piece.

He suggested that the new England manager, Alf Ramsey, needed regional advisers to assist him (Ramsey probably thought 'that's the last thing I need'). He proposed Bill Nicholson in the south, Stan Cullis in the midlands, Alan Brown in the north-east, and Harry Potts in the north-west. 'Potts, Burnley's ex-player manages the club so well,' he wrote. 'To run a First Division club on a tight purse is a task in itself, but to do it and keep the club among the best in the land says a lot for his shrewdness and judgement.'

But as the years went by Adamson changed his opinions and had little time for Harry Potts. While Potts was manager with Adamson his chief coach, and presumably in Bob Lord's head manager-in-waiting, there was certainly an undercurrent that some players noticed. The more time that passed by, the more Adamson wanted full control. Potts was from the old era, tactically limited, and Adamson was from the new with a visionary mind. Potts was a manager who simply put out his best players week after week with never a thought of a change. If they could walk, they played. That was the game in the 1950s and even into the early 1960s.

Adamson, however, was from the new era, with an imaginative mind brimming with ideas and thoughts, many of them based on the Alan Brown training sessions and others on coaching courses at Lilleshall. Once Adamson became manager and Harry was pushed 'upstairs' into a vague general manager role, the rift was unconcealed.

If Jimmy Adamson was the subject of a four-part drama, you might have the playing career as part one, then the coaching career, part three the managerial time at Burnley, and then the final act of broken dreams and the sadness of failure at Leeds United. The drama of the final years at Leeds is clear. The personal and family heartbreaks border on tragedy.

Or, you could simplify his life into two distinct eras: pre-January 1976 and post-January 1976, for this was the date that was a real and life-changing watershed.

But, whichever way you look at it, one question dominates; just how did it all go wrong for Jimmy Adamson? One character undoubtedly involved in the answer is Bob Lord. There are always two sides to everything and although this book looks at Jimmy Adamson's story, the problem is that there was no one to turn to in order to investigate how Lord himself felt about Adamson and how he viewed the change in their relationship.

I met with his daughter Barbara many times in connection with other books and it was whenever Adamson's name was mentioned she bridled and it became evident that her opinions of him were none too complimentary. I do remember her saying of her father one day, 'He did so much for that man.' It was clear from the way she emphasised and pronounced '*that man*' that she had a poor opinion of Adamson. Barbara died some time ago.

His daughter Margaret, when I telephoned and who still lives in the Burnley area, straightaway answered that she had no wish to talk about him. That is not a criticism of her in any way and I immediately respected her response and pursued it no further. But, what it meant was that there was no one to speak on her father's behalf and maybe her response illustrated the depth of feeling that remains regarding these old wounds.

From previous conversations with her I do know that as Bob lay desperately ill in the final week of his life, Margaret spent a great deal of time by his bedside talking about the past and the club that meant so much to him. They talked about good times, great games, great players, celebrations and banquets, and tellingly 'the people who had stabbed him in the back'. Did he feel that Adamson was one of them?

Maybe Bob Lord's side of things lay in the letters and documents that he had kept at his home, but Barbara told me that on his instructions she spent a week burning them all. Despite his wonderful achievements at Burnley Football Club, in the final years things fell apart, so that it is now all too easy to be critical of him and the general perception of Bob Lord is that yes he was forthright, hard-working, visionary and proud, but he was also irascible, belligerent, cantankerous, bloody-minded, ill-mannered, dismissive and despotic. What tends to be remembered is his legendary rudeness along with the chaos and near bankruptcy at the club in the final years of his chairmanship. All of that is unfortunate for he was the man who created the greatness in the first place.

There is all of that, plus the question of interpretation and how easy it is to see Lord as the villain. Paul Fletcher told me a lovely story about him. Prior to one game Lord left gifts for one of his favourite referees in his changing room – various cuts of meat and succulent sausages. The referee however had a stinker of a game with a number of decisions going against Burnley leaving Lord none too pleased. When the referee returned to his changing room at half-time the meats and sausages had been removed. Perception: was this Bob Lord being vindictive, or was it Bob Lord displaying a sense of humour? Or was it even his wife Hilda?

If there was a frustration in the writing of this book it therefore came from the lack of first-hand source material showing Bob Lord's 'other side'. At the end of chapter eight, however, is one of his letters to Jimmy Adamson, the only one that surfaced, and from this a different picture emerges; a man of kindness, thoughtfulness and compassion, not to mention intense loyalty. One or two more that I was told existed couldn't be found, including the key letter from Lord to Adamson about the money Lord had borrowed.

I knew the whereabouts of another cache of Bob Lord documents. Again the person in whose house it lay, someone who knew him well, wanted nothing to do with this book, save for the comment, 'Jimmy Adamson – not my favourite person.' Again, there is no criticism on my part, only disappointment; that Lord's perspective would remain untold.

Nevertheless, this is primarily a Jimmy Adamson book and if things began to go wrong at Burnley for him in the year leading up to his dismissal, his decline accelerated after he left Sunderland and joined Leeds United. By October 1980, he had simply had enough of the whole football business; of malicious fans, working under the shadow of Don Revie, unsupportive directors, and the sheer, never-ending, day-to-day demands of running a football club.

It all ended with the ignominy and stress of a libel action he took against Leeds, a number of newspapers and the man who replaced him, Allan Clarke. He was only 51. He retreated into the shell of his family and the love of his wife May. The man who could have been England manager in 1962 reached a point in the mid-1970s when his reputation was still immense; he had the football world at his fingertips and might have become one of the most influential football thinkers and managers of the age. At the end of the decade he turned his back on all of that and retreated into privacy.

This book attempts to chart the ultimately unhappy story, one of failed hopes and broken dreams.

Chapter 2

Send me a winger

I THINK it must have been seeing that old picture of Jimmy with the Scottie in his garden that set me thinking I really had to do something about this Adamson book. It intrigued me. It made me feel a link with him because for several years I had a Scottie too. What little beggars they are, stubborn and independent; but they grow on you, make you smile, a big dog in a little body. These dogs have a heart the size of a bus.

Then it was while working with one of Jimmy Adamson's proteges, Paul Fletcher, that I learned that in addition to all the memorabilia in the club's glass cabinets, Jimmy's grandchildren had collections of his souvenirs and pictures. I had my own collection too that I had amassed over the years along with huge scrapbooks of the 1970s that someone gave me years ago. I had written books about Harry Potts and Jimmy McIlroy, and articles about Bob Lord so the 1960s was a familiar period. The library in Burnley I knew had newspapers going back years on microfilm.

The urge to do something grew. Paul gave me a phone number, Jennie Halstead, one of the grandchildren who lived in Chorley, and I got in touch. On the Claretsmad message board I came across the pen name 'Ashingtonclaret'. I had no idea who it was but put a request on that board that he might get in touch with me. A reply came quickly. His name was Alan Parker and yes it turned out he lived in Ashington. He even knew John Angus who played alongside Jimmy in the great team of 1959/60.

Alan, retired from the RAF, happily agreed to help and dig out what he could up in the north-east. With help assured from Alan including an invitation to stay with him should I ever head up to Ashington, and contact details for the local historian Mike Kirkup, the decision to press on with the book was confirmed. That first e-mail from Alan was a huge boost.

Mike runs an Ashington local history magazine called *A Creeful of Coals* and immediately agreed to put a short feature into it outlining the book and inviting anyone who had known Jimmy to get in touch. 'I have a copy of Jimmy's signing-on papers,' he added.

May 1947: Jimmy was just 17 and had joined Burnley in the previous October having been 'spotted' by Burnley scout Jackie Dryden at East Chevington Juniors. Yet here he was on the train to London with people like Harry Potts, Alan Brown, Harold Mather and manager Cliff Britton. Was he wide-eyed and filled with anticipation? Did he look at the players around him in awe or was he mature beyond his years and take it all in his stride?

Having already spent three years working down the mines he was already well on the way to being a man. Jimmy Strong was Burnley's goalkeeper and came from Morpeth near Ashington. Harry Potts was from the north-east. It is reasonable to think they put an arm round Jimmy's shoulder and helped him along and tried to make him feel at home. At least, hearing their voices he wouldn't feel too out of place.

There was a hotel bedroom the like of which he had never experienced before, three-course meals for the first time ever, the sights and sounds of the bustling city, and then the first sighting of the Twin Towers on an unseasonably hot day. It is reasonable to assume he might have pinched himself. Only months earlier, he had been just an ordinary lad working down the pit in Ashington and maybe thinking he would be there for the rest of his working days with the background of a home life that had never been easy.

There used to be this joke up in the north-east many years ago that you could shout down a pit for a footballer and a dozen would appear. In Ashington they refined that. You could shout down not just for any footballer but you could shout 'send me a winger' or 'send me an inside-forward'. Burnley Football club made full use of this and the stream of footballers from the north-east down to Lancashire seemed endless. There was a time in the 1950s and early 1960s when a Burnley first team could easily have been made up of Geordies.

Ashington was once labelled the biggest pit village in the world. It had five mines and a huge workforce; the Ashington Coal Company alone once employed 10,000 workers. In 1960 the total workforce in the town was 30,000 although by 1980 it was declining to under 20,000. By then only half of them were men and only a small proportion of that number was employed in mining. While a woman's role was once solely in the pitman's home, today the gender of employment has changed and employed women outnumber employed men. The world of Ashington that Jimmy Adamson entered no longer exists. It was a man's world and men's values dominated everything. They were pitmen – and in this there was a fierce, provincial pride.

Mike Kirkup, in his introduction to *Images of Ashington*, provides a snapshot view of the development of the town which was to shape the young Jimmy Adamson:

'The Industrial Revolution of the nineteenth century shaped both the landscape of Ashington and the lifestyle of its inhabitants. Prior to this, the few village residents had huddled together for warmth and security in their tied cottages next to one of the mere half dozen farms in the vicinity.

'Lying sixteen miles north of Newcastle upon Tyne, Ashington's strength was always destined to lie, not in historic buildings or scenic beauty, but in its people, the canny folk who worked long and hard in an effort to put Ashington on the map. Yet until the pits arrived, no cartographer even bothered to include the village on the map of Northumberland. However, that changed when the entrepreneurs moved in, howked great holes into the green fields, and decreed that Ashington should be the biggest mining village in the world.

'That village soon became a town with all the trappings of an urban district council. The Reverend J.E. Gordon Cartlidge, vicar of St John's, Seaton Hirst, highlighted the problems facing the first council in those early days: "It is difficult to realise the arduous task – poor roads, ash footpaths, little lighting, pools of water all over the place where ashes were worn down or washed away, open ash-pits, earth closets, no Picture Palaces, no public park, no buses – and yet there was an amazing friendliness wherever you went."

'The new community in Ashington was a rare mixture. Most counties in England were represented: tin miners from Cornwall, lead miners from Cumbria, coal miners from Durham whose own pits had closed. All were intent on making a new life for themselves and their families. Irish men and women, who had abandoned their native isle during the potato famine, discovered pots of gold, black gold, on every corner-end in Ashington. Italians found that the local children were ready-made customers for their particular brand of ice-cream and fish and chips. After the Second World War yet another ingredient was added to the Geordie pot when a large Polish community settled in town; little wonder that the broad Ashington accent reflects this heady concoction.

'With the influx of people came the mushrooming of houses; colliery rows, back-to-backs, built within spitting distance of the pit yard. Amenities were few and wages were kept pitifully low. But the miner accepted his lot, not knowing his true worth to the coalmine owners or the country. This was to come with the conflicts of two world wars. When the government of the day shouted out for coal to fuel its munitions factories, trains and ships, their plea did not fall on deaf ears. The Ashington miners responded to a man. But, when the time came to give the miners a lift, a helping hand, political backs were turned.

'With the growth in population came the need for more shops, more schools and more places of worship. Soon, Ashington spilled over to join Hirst, the division between the two being the railway line. The population grew to almost 30,000 between the two wars, almost 10,000 of whom worked in the coal trade.

'In the heyday of the town in the 1950s it was thought nothing could change the euphoric optimism that swept everyone along with it. Miners' wages crept to the top of the earnings ladder; a strong, well-led union saw to that. Much of the surplus cash was spent in the splendid shops that lined Station Road, the main street. The five-day week meant more leisure time and holidays could be spent either at home or abroad. How could the good times possibly end? Didn't the experts say that the town was sitting on enough rich seams of coal to last well past the year 2000? Perhaps they did.

'But time proved them wrong.' (*Reproduced courtesy of Mike Kirkup*)

The mining way of life vanished from the 1960s onwards as one by one the mines closed. All that is left today is a museum. It was this community way of life of comradeship, danger (there were 13 deaths in one incident in 1916), injuries, coal dust, and lines of terraced housing; domestic hardship, poor facilities, and limited leisure into which Jimmy Adamson was born. Some of the tunnels the men worked in were no more than three feet high. The associated illnesses were pneumoconiosis (a lung disease), and nystagmus (an eye problem). Day after day Jimmy saw his father come home covered in pit grime and coal dust, face blackened, limbs aching.

At the beginning of each shift his father had a metal disc with his number on. A second disc was given to the banksman on entering the cage at the top of the shaft. The banksman then signalled to the engineman that they were ready for the descent. The disc was then hung on a board at the pithead. At the end of the shift the disc that the miner had taken down with him was handed in to match the one hanging on the board. It was a kind of symbolic proof that another day had been survived underground. Just as his father did, Jimmy did the same until football provided his release. At home after his shift he washed in the tin bath in front of the fire, his mother no doubt washing his back, just as she washed his father's. Not until 1947 and nationalisation of the mines were showers gradually provided at the pitheads.

Jackie Milburn's father also worked down the mines and Milburn's words in later life might well have been echoed by Jimmy Adamson. Milburn would wave to his father as he crossed the back lane to the pit not that far away and said, 'I used to shiver as he disappeared into the deep shaft leading down to the coalface.' Bobby Charlton used to go with his father to collect the wages, waiting in the canteen with a pie and a bottle of milk.

While waiting he would watch the black-faced, weary-eyed miners returning to the surface, getting out of the cage, all of them relieved they had emerged into the natural world once more.

Adamson worked down the pits as soon as he left school and the background to his teenage working years was the Second World War. Air-raid warnings happened often with industrial targets in and around Newcastle. Ashington itself was hit just once by a bomb that landed on the ice rink according to one report, or on Woodhorn Colliery according to another. When the sirens went and bombs dropped on Newcastle, families would hide under the stairs until air-raid shelters were built across the streets.

Mining wasn't a vocation that you were born for; it was more a sentence to which you were condemned unless you found a way to escape. So Ashington produced its share of footballers who found a way out – the Charltons, Jackie Milburn, Billy Gray and Jimmy Adamson among them. The Jackie Milburn statue that Ashington boasts today is a tribute not just to Milburn himself but represents just how significant the area once was in providing the players who graced so many football teams.

Eight people lived in the Adamson home; three of them his sisters and two his brothers. Local historian Mike Kirkup says the Charltons and Jimmy were born in Laburnum Terrace. Cissie Charlton writes about the terrace in her book *Cissie*. It was only much later in life, in old age in fact, that Jimmy talked to his grandchildren about his boyhood. They had been difficult times with a father who (granddaughter Katie thinks) drank most of his wages away and then upped and left them. If that is the case, his mother must have had a hard and debilitating time raising the family. As a result Katie thinks Jimmy eventually disowned him and significantly he is certainly absent from any of Jimmy's wedding photographs. When his older brother left to join the RAF, it was left to Jimmy to help his mother bring up the remaining siblings.

The Charltons eventually moved to Beatrice Street. In one of his many books Mike Kirkup wrote about Laburnum Terrace:

'Laburnum is a street of about 25 red-brick houses built in 1897 by W. G. Gordon of Stakeford for the Ashington Coal Company, and costing £93 and 10 shillings. The back doors are really front doors, opening onto a concrete surfaced back lane which was both a thoroughfare and a communal backyard. The houses when first built were described as four-roomed cottages with two rooms downstairs and two up, designed for miners with larger families. During the Second World War each house had on average two sons, and because in Ashington boyhood and football were almost inseparable, this meant about 50 soccer fans and aspiring players were kicking a ball around the street from the moment they could walk.

'Among them were the two Charlton lads, Bobby and Jackie from number 18, and young Jimmy Adamson from number 31. Cissie Charlton often said that the greatest footballers were born not made. But the same streak of lightning which endows football players must have struck the same place, not twice, but three times. On Thursday, 14 May 1967, Jack Charlton, the Leeds United and England centre-half was to receive the title of "Footballer of the Year" from the Football Writers' Association. By doing so he was following in the footsteps of his younger brother, "Wor Kid", and of Jimmy Adamson, to form a neighbourly triple crown of winners making Laburnum Terrace the most famous soccer nursery street in Britain.'

In the daytime, boys spent most of their free time kicking a ball around Hirst Park and then when night fell continued in the streets or the back alleys in between the terraces if there was a lamp. Jackie Milburn kicked stones all the way from home to school, and then back again. It's what Jimmy and most lads did. Pitman Laurence Robinson told Mike Kirkup for his book that, 'Us fellas would often have a game in the backstreet and join in with the lads. The polis didn't like us playin' here though and there was always the fear of getting caught. Although ah have never heard of anyone bein' prosecuted. Just to be on the safe side though, like, we used to run when we heard him comin'.'

Jack Charlton remembers how it was impossible to get a football during the wartime years of blackout curtains and 'making do'. If someone had a ball they were the envy of the neighbourhood. So, they made do with tennis balls and played with them going to school, on the way home, in the schoolyard, against walls and in the games that often had 20 on each side. There were street competitions and the doors where the coal was delivered to each house were the goalposts as they played across the alleys.

The imagery of mining is still vivid; the underground heroism, grime, darkness, blackened faces, washing in the tin bath in front of the kitchen fire, long hours, back-breaking work; the descent in the cages down to the workplace, roof-falls, pit ponies, the galas and treasured days of leisure. The men were dominant while the women ran the little houses and brought up the kids virtually single-handed.

The men might have been employed, but there was real poverty and hardship. Life was a continual struggle to survive but this in fact provided the common bond of togetherness that held communities together. The miners' clubs and the pubs on the way home for a 'wet' and a 'broon' after a day down the pit were sacred places. Women were unwelcome unless it was to collect a jug of ale for their men. And if there were six kids to bring up as in the Adamson home, in their different ways the mother and father worked relentlessly to keep them fed and clothed; that is to say if the father was a fair man and gave his wife his wages. It didn't always happen that way. Luxuries were a rarity in any household.

There is this nostalgic image of the dignity of the miner, his sense of pride in his labours, the miners' picnics held every summer, the 'coal queen' atop the float in the procession, brass bands, bright colliery banners, for some an allotment, men's running races and occasional outings. But this belies the daily drudgery in a house that had no hot running water, no bathroom and meals were cooked on a fire-range; or what to do when injury and illness meant absence from work and the wages stopped. Becoming a footballer was one of few avenues of release. Such was the pride felt by the community when a local lad made good that when the Charlton brothers returned to Ashington for a reception at the Town Hall, they were feted in style and paraded in a Rolls-Royce. No one begrudged them that. 'They're one of us,' said the townsfolk, proud that they had brought such fame to Ashington.

Even then it is possible to surmise that these young lads who made the break never deliberately set out and said, 'I will be a footballer and get away from all this.' They might have had their dreams, as all of us do, and depending on where they lived in the north-east there were the two great cathedrals of football at St James' Park at Newcastle, and Roker Park at Sunderland. But the progression from pit to professional football came from playing in the local leagues for local clubs and by chance you might be spotted by the 'scouts' that came to watch. But, there were so many teams, and so many leagues with such huge numbers of players that to be 'spotted' and invited for trials at one of the leading clubs meant you had to be outstandingly good.

Jimmy Adamson was born in 1929. By the time he was 14 he was one of legions of lads who left school for the only world available to them – underground – and he worked down the pit for something like three years. Under-nourishment was widespread so the Ashington Coal Company gave all these lads, initially employed as trainees, a bottle of milk each day before they went down the mine. The fact that this was done is evidence of the poor diet of the day where the women did their best to make ends meet seven days a week. On some days the children were barely fed.

The Ashington in which he grew up, a place of row upon row of crowded, straight-lined, terraced houses was a busy, bustling place. There were 26 fish and chip shops and 19 working men's clubs. On Woodhorn Road alone there were five, almost all next door to each other. It was a strong man or a rare teetotaller who could walk past them all on the way home from work. Cheap beer slaked a working man's thirst and cleared away the shift's coal dust.

Improvements to living conditions had taken place through the preceding decade; lighting, roads were paved and earth closets were replaced with flush toilets, but these had never quite solved the problem of the palls of coal-fire smoke that hung over the town, covering the washing with flecks of coal and ash. For those who lived near the railway lines it was even worse as the engines that pulled the laden coal wagons belched out their thick black smoke.

Maybe his mother found some consolation from the Littlewoods catalogue that supplemented the shopping; or maybe she found it represented a distant unobtainable world with its glamorous models and pictures of washing machines and vacuum cleaners. The Provident, however, provided a way of buying on credit with weekly repayments – if you could keep them up. She shopped, no doubt at the Coop, known as the Arcade with its different departments and upstairs dance hall, or Doggart's department store, or corner shops like Rodways that sold everything you could possibly think of.

As Jimmy grew up in the 1930s and 1940s, Ashington thrived with places like Arrowsmith's Department Store, Hiller's Bazaar, Brough's the grocers, Bertha Lewis's corset shop, Russell Cook's Department Store, and Blacklock's Emporium where there was waitress service in the cafe and an open-air dance floor on the roof. Main's bike shop was actually close to the Adamsons on Laburnum Terrace. The Co-op in fact had shops all over the town and employed hundreds of people and the Co-op 'Divi' was a system whereby a tally was kept of everything spent and then once a year you could claim the 'dividend'. Everyone who shopped there had a number and was given a tiny coupon after every purchase. To this day I can still remember my own mother's coupon number was 6014 and collecting the 'divi' was one of the special days of the year when you walked away from the accounts department with cash in your hand. On the day I was entrusted with the job of collecting it, I felt ten feet tall. It was a small annual windfall that meant treats for many families.

If there were a few pence going spare then 'pop' wagons toured the streets selling lemonade, dandelion and burdock, and ginger beer. Bottles were returnable and re-usable so there was a 1p deposit on them. It was quite an industry for lads like Jimmy to collect them and retrieve the deposits, either to buy another bottle of 'pop' or an ice-cream from one of the ice-cream tricycles that rode round the town with their containers of ice-creams fastened to the front of the bike. Giovanni Rossi had an ice- cream and confectionery shop and was one of several Italians who settled in Ashington.

If ice-cream and 'pop' were rare extravagances in an otherwise tough, hard world, then an even greater treat was a holiday. The few who could afford it went to the Butlin's holiday camps at Ayr, Filey or Skegness for a week. But that was rare and it was more likely to be a day out at Newbiggin-by-the-Sea just a few miles away. Cissie Charlton wrote about her family outings there using their horse and cart. Or there was Whitley Bay and until Beeching devastated the railways there were trains to both of them. At

Newbiggin there were acres of fine sands, maybe an ice-cream from Bertorelli's cafe. There were slot machines in the penny arcade. Down below the wall of the quay were the swings called 'shuggy' boats; the boat being a wooden contraption in which you sat opposite a partner while you pulled the rope that made it swing back and forth, higher and higher.

At Ashington's Methodist Central Hall concerts drew world class musicians and singers. There were five cinemas; the Wallow, Regal, Pavilion, Hippodrome and Buffalo, their heyday being the years after the Second World War.

If Jimmy had visited home in May 1949 he could have seen Bob Hope and Jane Russell at the Regal in *The Paleface*, or Peter Lorre in *Casbah* at the Pavilion. Had May been with him he might have danced at the Arcade on 6 May for three shillings to J. Dalkin and his Rhythm Boys. The premier location for dancing was, however, the Princess Ballrooms. From the outside it was a drab building but inside it was a fantasy world of lights, fine fittings and a sprung floor. Alas Jimmy never had the chance to take May. It burned down in 1944 and was never replaced.

In Jimmy's schooldays a favourite game was 'Chucks' where five small stones were thrown and caught, first one, then two, then three and so on until the fifth. Schools were places then where desks faced the blackboard at the front of the room and you spoke in class at your peril. Children's gala days were just as important as the miners' day. Each school added its pupils to the parade one by one and they made their way to the park gates led by brass bands and banners. As many as five brass bands were part of the processions and in the park there were all kinds of events; races, exhibitions and a huge picnic. When he was just eight years old, just like hundreds of other children in the town, he would have enjoyed the street party in honour of the coronation of George VI.

Jimmy had been a centre-half at school but then later switched to inside-forward, football terms that are no longer part of football's vocabulary. His favourite team was Sunderland and his favourite player was Raich Carter, surprising perhaps when the nearest team was Newcastle United. Maybe Sunderland became 'his' team when he heard they won the FA Cup in 1937 by beating Preston North End 3-1. He would have been eight years old, that magical age when interest in football can first begin and when imagination takes hold and dreams begin. Maybe he had heard the men on street corners or outside the clubs talking about it or reading of it in their newspapers. Newcastle too had won it during his childhood, but that was in 1932 and he'd have been barely three years old with no concept of the magic of football.

When he left school for the mines, the war was raging in the world outside Ashington so League football stopped but local games and leagues continued as best they could. When he emerged from the gloom of the pit he played for Ashington YMCA in the Ashington Welfare League Junior Division and then East Chevington Juniors. In 1945 when he was 15 he played in trials for Northumberland Youth.

Inside-forwards were of two kinds, the schemer and the striker. Adamson belonged to the former group. Half-backs were the players who played in the midfield. In those far-off days teams had one centre-half as opposed to the two of today. There were two full-backs, three half-backs, and five forwards. Either the left-half or the right-half would be the second schemer who would link with the inside-forward schemer. The remaining half-back would be the more rugged and defensive of the two. The centre-half played in the middle of them and had one rigid job – to stop the opposing centre-forward. For years these positions and roles were firmly defined. It was something that years later Jimmy Adamson would question and change. You wonder just how soon in his football career he began to ask questions about these rigid formations.

Football and mining were the forces that shaped Ashington. The Ashington Colliery welfare ground had seven football pitches catering for three separate leagues and more than 20 local sides. To maintain them, a penny a week was deducted from the miners' pay. The working men's clubs had their own sides. It was no wonder that Ashington was able to supply a stream of footballers to league clubs.

But if the war played havoc with football, the scouts nevertheless still continued to watch these local games. Jackie Dryden, an ex-Claret, watched Adamson progress and noted his early skills and ability. The rangy Adamson must at this time have been all skin and bone, tall and thin, gawky arms and bony elbows, long-legged, with a slightly less than graceful, lanky running style, covering the ground in long almost slow strides. Dryden recommended him to Burnley.

Alan Parker spent hours in the local libraries searching for early references to Jimmy. They proved to be few and far between. During one long session in Blyth Library he went through the newspapers for 1945, 1946 and 1947. There was just one snippet from Thursday 7 November 1946. It didn't even get his name right. And he was certainly taller than 5ft 10in unless at that point he was still growing.

It said, 'James Anderson, a 17-year old inside-right of Ashington has signed amateur forms for Burnley. While on trial in the last fortnight he impressed Burnley's manager Cliff Britton, the former Everton and international half-back. He is 5' 10" in height and 11st in weight. Playing for East Chevington Juniors this season he has compiled a high total of goals.'

Burnley the place was no nirvana immediately after the war. Mills, chimneys, smoke and fog, it was a bleak industrial town even worse than Ashington. Geoffrey Green described the Burnley that Adamson found: 'Burnley the town is no beauty spot. It forms part of a backcloth of tall chimney stacks and slagheaps that scar the Lancashire countryside. On the surface it looks dingy and dirty, a cotton town that has known hard days. Yet beneath the surface a warm, friendly, dignified heart beats. And outside just out of sight, there are some fine, cold moors where even the sheep look drab. And, when the mist drifts in from the hills there is soot in it, hanging at times like a thick garland.'

Within two weeks he had returned to the north-east, possibly homesick according to some accounts. But, according to Adamson, he was at Burnley only for the two-week trial and returned as planned to continue to play for East Chevington Juniors.

His initial journey was horrendous enough; just 17 and Sunderland, having been to an occasional game there, probably the furthest he had ever been away from home. The journey to Burnley involved a change of train at Newcastle, then York, then Leeds, and then either two slow bus journeys from there to Burnley, or another train from Leeds to Todmorden and a bus ride from there to Burnley. If a player landed at Todmorden he was usually met by the club secretary. Some of these trialists somehow managed to get right to Burnley by train all the way.

John Angus, from Amble, another place north of Newcastle, was one of them and described to Tim Quelch his first sighting of Burnley in the 1950s and how this trip was so daunting: 'It took ages. I remember finally getting off the train at Manchester Road Station in Burnley. That's the station half-way up the hill above Burnley town centre. I looked down on this town with its mill chimneys and smoggy atmosphere and it was quite unlike anything I had ever seen before.'

Jimmy Robson was one more from the north-east who made the journey to East Lancashire in the early 1950s. He too was yet another who was initially dreadfully homesick. His words along with John Angus's could just as easily have been spoken by Jimmy Adamson: 'When I first came down to Burnley I was dreadfully homesick. Remember I came from a small mining village. I hadn't seen much life outside. A lot of us were like that. But those first three months here were hard. The digs were good but I knew the big test would come after I went home for the first time.'

Tommy Cummings was yet another who came from the north-east. He arrived the year after Adamson, getting off the train at Todmorden. If any of these young lads, who after one of these marathon train journeys, thought that Todmorden, another place of smoke, mills and chimneys, was Burnley and were shocked at what they saw, they would find an hour later that Burnley was even worse. Assistant secretary Albert Maddox recalled meeting these boys, usually bewildered, at Todmorden on several occasions and saw first-hand how disoriented they were; some of them utterly exhausted by the whole experience.

Tommy Cummings recalled, 'I arrived by train in a place called Todmorden and I hadn't been on many train journeys before. I was like a little boy looking out of the window and taking everything in. They had arranged for someone from the club to come and meet me and we caught the bus to Burnley where they had arranged digs for me.'

Tommy also recollected that many of them married local girls. Jimmy was no exception, meeting his wife May at a cinema not long after he became settled in Burnley. Once married, many of the players lived near each other.

Years later Jimmy Adamson remembered the lonely experiences he had on his first arrival, and they must surely have impacted on his attitudes and sympathy towards the young lads still arriving from the small villages of the north-east: 'As soon as a youngster arrives at Turf Moor he is made to feel part of Burnley Football Club. And, just as important he knows he is not going to be tossed out after just a short spell. Every young player arriving at Turf Moor is guaranteed four or five years on the staff. In that time he gets the chance to learn the game. He is not tossed out if he fails to live up to expectations in one season. If he wants, the lad can be apprenticed to a trade. Or he usually goes on the ground staff doing all the odd jobs around the ground.'

The manager was Cliff Britton but there were two characters at the club on the backroom staff who were the stalwarts and bedrock of most of what went on. Ray Bennion and Billy Dougall had been at Turf Moor since before the war. Dougall was a Scot who came to Burnley and played for them for eight years. Bennion, a Welshman, had played for Manchester United with distinction and then for Burnley for two years. They knew every nook and cranny of the club and had coached and trained just about every player that ever arrived there, one of them being the great Tommy Lawton in his teenage years.

It was Bennion who eventually made a recommendation that would change Jimmy's life. Dougall, who had also been a miner, was first-team coach until Alan Brown left, and then himself became manager until ill health ended that. On his recovery he was brought back as physio – too valuable not to be used in some way. What the two of them didn't know about football wasn't worth knowing.

Jimmy McIlroy acknowledges them as the most influential people he ever met. Harry Potts too was a Dougall disciple. They had a 'boot-room' at Turf Moor where they sat and talked about the game for hours, long before Bill Shankly ever thought of the idea at Liverpool. Even the great Matt Busby acknowledged their importance and football knowledge. Bob Lord described them as the finest servants a club could have, 'jewels' in their training and coaching roles.

Jimmy McIlroy said that many of the free kick routines came from Dougall's coaching; his mantra was always do what the opposing team don't expect you to do and he would have had the same influence on Jimmy Adamson as he had on Jimmy Mac. 'Always look for the perfect ball,' said Dougall.

Arriving in October 1946 as a junior trialist, it was not until January 1947 that Adamson signed his first professional contract.

Facing him was progression through the A, B and C teams, then the reserves. At its peak, the club at one time in the 1950s had 55 players on its books.

If indeed he was initially homesick, he was not the first and he was not the last. Perhaps he realised that he faced a hard slog to work his way through these teams. Perhaps he was just totally overawed and missed his family. Maybe the gloom and murk of Burnley was just too much. But, he was only 17 and for any 17-year-old the whole thing was a huge culture shock. From the intimacy and warmth of family life and familiarity with a street filled with neighbours to the impersonal world of living in digs in a strange new world; football is littered with dozens of stories of young players who took the first train back home. But like so many others, he also came back to Burnley.

He wrote about these early days in a football annual of 1960/61:

'When I first went to Turf Moor as a 17-year-old Northumberland Youth player from Ashington's East Chevington Club, Burnley had eagle-eyed scouts like former left-winger Jackie Dryden, the man who persuaded me to go to Turf Moor instead of my favourites Sunderland, and wonderful coaches like Ray Bennion and Billy Dougall. It was Ray Bennion's patient coaching that made the young Tommy Lawton into the player he became in pre-war days.

'October 1946 was the month I began my long career at Turf Moor after a two-week trial. Actually I went back to my amateur club, Chevington, to help them win several important trophies before I began in earnest at Burnley. At first I made little progress for in those days I was rated as an inside-forward. In fact, when Burnley reached the FA Cup Final in 1947 I was the club office boy and I was taken down to Wembley with the official party. I remember that when Charlton's Chris Duffy scored the only goal, I was so upset that I got up from my seat and left the stadium.

'Until my National Service call-up I was plodding along in Burnley's "A" team as an inside-forward. Then the club did not see me for the better part of two years for I was posted out to Aden. There, I got plenty of football, often as many as four games a week at the RAF Station.

'On my demob I returned to Burnley determined to make the grade or go bust at the attempt. For the next 12 months nothing much happened to advance me very far. But then dear old Ray Bennion had the idea of trying me out as a wing-half. Like many inside-forwards who can never quite make the grade in attack, I seemed cut out for the middle line and it was a turning point. After ten games with the Central League reserves side, I was promoted to the league side at Bolton.'

Ever-present in the background was what has come to be known as 'the austerity years'. The war might have ended in 1945 but rationing still dominated daily life. There were shortages of everything from basic foods to clothing. Burnley FC had to appeal for coupons to buy new boots for the players. Everything was governed by coupon books, the coupons being exchanged in the shops for whatever goods were needed. The appeal must have been successful when the directors announced their gratitude for the response.

When he returned he faced the horrendous winter of 1946/47. Not only had he to contend with learning to live in a new town but like the rest of the country it was locked in by ice and snow. The conditions lasted for months so that the league programme went on into May. It was at its worst in February and March so that grassy surfaces were seldom seen. These were the days though when the game went ahead in the most dangerous and ludicrous conditions. The pitches sometimes resembled skating rinks and after some games the players literally had to thaw out in the bath.

Even before the Siberian conditions gripped the whole country, abnormal November rainfall and gales created horrendous conditions. It was the end of anything resembling a normal pitch as they turned into mudbaths and became heavier and heavier. Reports described teams 'frolicking' in the mud. Players sank deeper and deeper into the quagmires; 'rugby scrums in the goalmouths' became commonplace. Burnley versus Leicester summed up the conditions everywhere. In appalling conditions and fast-fading light, continuous rain before the match turned the pitch into a series of miniature lakes. Some players were near to physical collapse when the game came to an end in near darkness.

By December the incessant rain was replaced by freezing fog. Travelling was a lottery with train journeys in unheated carriages taking hours as teams criss-crossed the country. Players talked about 'railway train cramp'. Then the snow began, yet somehow teams managed to train, play games and huge crowds were the norm. Fuel shortages added to the misery and eventually disrupted some fixtures and the authorities even began to advocate the cancellation of football games as they were interfering with coal and industrial production. The production of coal to keep the nation going became the new Battle of Britain.

February 1947 was the point at which all normal life stopped for over two months. The cold descended just before the FA Cup fourth round on 25 January. It was the beginning of weeks of misery and yet more shortages but somehow football kept going, though postponed matches were commonplace. Huge crowds still turned up wherever there was a game and the public came in and helped to clear the pitches. Sometimes frozen plumbing in the dressing rooms meant no bath after a game. The government despaired of midweek Cup replays when people took time off work and production stopped.

At Turf Moor over 26,000 people turned up on 28 January, on 18 February over 28,000 and four days later 26,000; on 22 March there were 28,000 and on 4 April a staggering 31,000 with 23,000 the very next day. This was Easter with three games in the space of four days. To catch up on the backlog of games Burnley then played six games in May and even one in June. By the end of this most dreadful season Burnley won promotion despite the herculean journeys and stamina-sapping privations.

The end of February marked the worst weather ever. The Labour Government could hardly cope and the Conservative slogan was 'Shiver with Shinwell'. And through all this, Burnley battled on through the FA Cup rounds one by one.

They hosted Middlesbrough on 'the worst-ever' Tuesday afternoon, 4 March. There were burst pipes in the dressing room and to get there in the first place players had to use all their determination to beat the snow. Referee Arthur Ellis said that 'conditions were so bad when I looked at the ground that it seemed hopeless to think about playing football at a snow-bound, windswept Turf Moor'. The application of brine and sand worked wonders not to mention men with picks and shovels levelling the jagged ice corners and ridges. The players floundered in the snow on top of the ice and their feet tripped and stumbled in the potholes that formed even as they played.

By this time there had been seven weeks of cold, 43 continuous days on which snow covered the ground everywhere, and 46 nights of temperatures below freezing. The pressure was now on to simply cancel the season. How fortunate that this decision was never made. Some 67,672 saw the game at Maine Road between Manchester City and Burnley in the game that decided the divisional winners. And then in April came one last sting in the tail. If Burnley v Leicester and Burnley v Middlesbrough had been endurance tests, then Burnley v Chesterfield on Easter Saturday, 5 April, was the absolute rock-bottom. Two Burnley players were carried off near-frozen, and three of Chesterfield's players went under as soon as they left the pitch. One was put into the hot bath complete with football kit, the other simply collapsed into it.

All of this was Jimmy Adamson's introduction to the world of professional football. He shivered and went hungry, he huddled round his landlady's meagre fire (when there was one), he played his first games in the junior teams on ice rinks. In faraway Ashington, Burnley's success was noted, especially the Cup Final appearance. Even though in 1947 he was nowhere near the reserves let alone the first team, he was a player at Burnley Football Club and Burnley Football Club was much respected (though not in Middlesbrough) so they were proud of young Jimmy Adamson. And he would never, in the following years, experience such appalling hardships again.

He must have felt proud to be part of a club where there was promotion to the First Division. The team was captained by the iron-man Alan Brown who became manager in the mid-1950s when Frank Hill left. Brown became a massive influence on Jimmy Adamson through his teaching, coaching and his standards of discipline. Harry Potts who would become manager later in the 50s was the golden boy of the team. Burnley lost to Charlton Athletic in the FA Cup Final but despite this, it had been a wonderful season. It is reasonable to assume that Adamson must have been thrilled to have been a part of it, even if he was still very much a junior and well down the playing ranks.

After his early struggles to establish himself, his first-team debut came at Bolton on 10 February 1951. He replaced Reg

Attwell at right-half and kept the place for the remainder of the season. This was no mean feat; Jimmy McIlroy rated Reg Attwell as one of the best footballers he had played with. These were the days of big crowds and over 35,000 spectators filled Burnden Park to see the 1-1 draw with Bill Holden scoring for Burnley.

Years later Adamson remembered the game vividly: 'I shall always remember one incident in that game. It was nothing really but it affected me personally and led to a perpetual "leg-pull" between goalkeeper Jimmy Strong and myself. At one stage of the game, Nat Lofthouse was right through and was just drawing back his lethal left foot to smash the ball past Strong. But, I cut in and booted the ball off his toe for a corner. As this was my first league game I felt I had done something wonderful in averting what seemed a certain goal. But all our goalkeeper could growl was, "Find a man can't you?" At first I took him seriously and felt very deflated. Afterwards I discovered that Jim had realised as much as anyone how I had saved Burnley a point, but he was going to make sure I didn't get too cocky about it.'

He made 14 appearances that season and in the next one kept his place permanently. The decision to move him to half-back had struck gold and from then on he developed into one of the finest players of his generation. With his long legs covering the ground, he could make telling passes, was a superb tackler, and read the game superbly so that interceptions won him the ball countless times. His deft touch and control were exceptional. On top of all this he could drive forward powerfully.

What was marvellous however was his partnership with the great Jimmy McIlroy. This was a partnership that grew to be one of the most influential in the game and this they maintained for over ten seasons. Mac had come into the team slightly ahead of Adamson but once they were together, a thing of beauty was created. They had an uncanny sense of where the other was positioned. If one was under pressure, the other was there to receive the pass. They were the thinkers in the team; they pulled the strings and made the others play. Most teams at this time might have had one 'general' who dictated the play, but Burnley had two, their thoughts and play perfectly in tune.

His first goal for Burnley was away at Fulham in a 2-1 win on 22 December 1951. For more than ten years he would be a permanent fixture although for a long spell over two seasons he reverted to centre-half, his old schoolboy position, when Tommy Cummings was out injured. Back he came to half-back in 1958 and there he would stay until retirement as a player.

Football in the 1940s, all through the 1950s and maybe even the whole of the 1960s was a working-class sport, watched by the working class and played by working-class footballers. It was no golden ticket to gated mansions and huge pay-cheques as it is today.

Jimmy McIlroy wryly remembers his greatest achievement at Burnley was not a First Division championship, but becoming a member of the exclusive tennis club. But while the tennis club might have been attainable, becoming a member of the even more prestigious golf club, rubbing shoulders with the bank manager or the mill owner – was definitely not. If Burnley had given Adamson his passport away from the world of pits and toiling underground, it was certainly not a passport away from his working-class origins.

Chapter 3

Alan, Bob and Harry too

THERE WAS absolutely no freedom at all for the footballer of the 1950s. Once a contract was signed the club owned that player and the registration was so binding that there was no way a player could leave without the club's permission. It was a feudal system. Even in mining a man was free to move from one pit to another, not that any mass migrations ever took place simply because a man felt like it. When Jimmy Adamson signed his contract in January 1947 he virtually signed his life to Burnley Football Club until George Eastham's campaign for freedom of movement was successful in 1964 when his case at last came to court.

It is a myth that despite the contractual problems, footballers were financially better off than other working men. Of course the top players on the maximum permissible wage were better paid, and some like Tommy Lawton, Tom Finney, Stanley Matthews and Denis Compton had incomes from advertising. In 1952 the average manual wage in the country was £8 13 shillings and footballers could certainly earn more than this with a £14 wage during the season and £10 in the summer, but that was only if they were actually on the maximum wage.

Many were not and Players' Union figures found that only a fifth of footballers were on the top wage at this time. Even in 1955 the union put the average wage for a footballer at only £8 and by this time factory workers were earning almost £11 a week. There was a vast difference between playing for lowly Darlington and mighty Tottenham Hotspur.

The minimum retaining wage in the early 1950s was only £6 a week and the word 'retaining' was simply a polite term for the way in which footballers were bound to their clubs. How unfair it was that while a footballer could be 'chained' to a club for the rest of his playing career, he only enjoyed a 12-month contract. He might well have a club house at a favourable rent, but he and his family could be turfed out of that house as soon as he was unwanted. For a jobbing footballer of average ability they were uncertain times.

At the end of a season a number of things could happen to a player. He might be kept on, in which case there would be a sigh of relief. He could be put up for sale at a fair price. He could be put up for sale at a ridiculous price that no other club would want to match. He could be retained but on reduced wages. He could be retained and paid no wages. He could ask for a pay rise and refuse to sign. In that case he would definitely be paid no wages. He could demand a transfer that might be ignored, or again a price was put on his head that was too high. He could simply walk out but if that happened the club still held his registration and could prevent him playing anywhere else. Even during the season a new manager might walk in and without consultation reduce the wages of every player. There was nothing those players could do except protest.

The majority of players who wanted a move or a pay rise simply gave in. Some left the game altogether. A small number who did not want to lose their independence had a full-time day job, trained a couple of times a week in the evenings and turned out for the team on Saturdays.

As the season neared its end the 'retained list' dominated a player's thoughts. At some clubs they were called into the manager's office one by one to be informed of the decision to offer another contract. At some clubs it was a small note in the final wage packet of the season; at other clubs the list was pinned up on a notice board in a prominent place for all to see. At a very small number it was a registered letter through the post box.

It was worst when there might be a huddle of players outside the manager's door all waiting together to be told the good or bad news. Crestfallen faces indicated the worst as one by one they walked out of the office. It might be they were simply no longer wanted. It might be that they were on the 'for sale' list. If that was the case they worried about what interim pay they might receive. If they were in a club house and it was bad news it was a case of wondering if you would be asked to vacate it. And even while you were living in a club house a new player might be brought to take a look at it.

Not until 1964 was this system changed. Prior to this, Bobby Seith at Burnley in the later 1950s stood up to this iniquitous system and the dictatorial Bob Lord. He insisted on his right to move and told the club if this was not allowed he would simply leave the game and find other employment. Seith was fortunate in that this was no idle threat; he was a fully qualified chiropodist. He was allowed to move and went to Dundee back in his native Scotland.

Prior to that, Burnley winger Brian Pilkington was sold to Bolton Wanderers simply because chairman Bob Lord insisted on it. Pilkington had no wish to leave at all, but a fee had been agreed and with no choice in the matter, off he went. It was one of dozens of similar stories up and down the land when a player had to uproot his family and home sometimes to move to the other end of the country. Conversely, earlier, when Pilkington had the opportunity to move to Manchester United after the Munich air disaster, Bob Lord would not allow it.

It was George Eastham though who freed footballers from these punitive restrictions and archaic conditions of service that dominated their lives. Eastham, a top player and member of the 1966 England World Cup squad, was in dispute with his employers at Newcastle United over the conditions of the club house he was supposed to live in and also the job outside of football the club had arranged in order to circumvent the maximum wage rule. On top of all that they attempted to stop him playing for the England Under-23 side.

Unable to leave, Eastham went on strike at the end of the 1959/60 season and said later, 'Our contract would bind us to a club for life. Most people called it the "slavery contract". We had virtually no rights at all and it was often the case that the guy on the terrace not only earned more than us, though there's nothing wrong with that, but he had more freedom of movement than us. People in business or teaching were able to hand in their notice and move on. We weren't and that was wrong.'

In October 1960, Newcastle relented when they realised that there was no possibility of Eastham moving back. He had moved south to work for Ernie Clay who later became chairman of Fulham. They sold him to Arsenal but Eastham continued the fight arguing that Newcastle owed him unpaid wages and bonuses, and that the whole system was an unfair restraint of trade.

Backed by the PFA, who provided £15,000 for the legal fees, the case went to the High Court in 1963. Mr Justice Wilberforce rejected the claim for unpaid wages, saying that as Eastham was on strike this was at Newcastle's discretion, but he did change football forever when he ruled that the retaining system was unreasonable. The 'retention' element was overhauled and transfer tribunals were introduced to settle disputes. It was a landmark decision and the maximum wage had already been abolished thanks to the work of Jimmy Hill.

While excellent for the footballers these two alterations to football employment and salaries were alas bad news for the town clubs who could no longer compete with the city clubs on equal terms. One by one the East Lancashire clubs, Blackpool, Blackburn, Bolton and Preston, were relegated. Burnley were the last, hanging on until 1971.

Once in the Burnley first team, Jimmy Adamson, subjected to all these employment shackles, was a fixture unless injuries intervened.

It is reasonable to say that three people hugely influenced him and his life. Alan Brown, who he met for the first time when Brown was captain of the first team in 1947 and who would then later become his manager. At this point he would have been a distant, lofty figure to the teenage Adamson. Harry Potts was in that team of 1947 until 1950 and as Adamson made his way into the reserve side, he would have played against Harry in practice games. And then there was the legendary Bob Lord; lord and chairman of all he surveyed for over two decades at Turf Moor.

Lord did not become chairman of the club until 1955 but was there before that in the background, unsuccessfully attempting to join the board in 1950, following the players and making a great favourite of Harry Potts. In 1951 he did join the board and once he was chairman dominated every aspect of the club.

Alan Brown was from Corbridge, Northumberland, and his father was a painter and decorator. He attended grammar school, was an outstanding athlete and wanted to be a schoolteacher as well as a professional footballer. But, being one of four children in a far from affluent family ruled out a university education during the depression. However, through good fortune he was able to join Huddersfield Town because his cousin was captain there. It was his experiences as a youth there that soured his interest in football so that in fact he left the game and joined the police force, returning to the game later. Because of the player-retention system he could only return to Huddersfield.

He once confessed that he disliked the 'Iron Man' name that was bestowed on him. It followed him everywhere. The defence in which he had played at Burnley was known as 'the iron curtain'. His first post as manager, after a coaching post at Sheffield Wednesday, was at Burnley where he had played centre-half with such distinction. He later related that the first thing he heard on the grapevine after his Burnley appointment was that four of the leading players who enjoyed a drink and a cigarette, had muttered and grumbled about him saying that 'if yon so and so comes here I'm in for a transfer'. Quite how they would have worked a transfer in those feudal days is a debatable point.

His creed was simple: 'I tell all my lads under 21 that they must never let me see them with a cigarette. With those over 21, I advise against it; I advise against a drink as well. When we're in public as a club you'll never see a drink. Suppose a man's sitting in a railway carriage with a glass of beer in front of him. Little boys may see it and think it's the right thing to do. If adults see it they may put two and two together to make five. I make sure I never have to send for a man for boozing. I ask, no demand, the highest code of conduct.'

On arrival as manager his problem was that he was seen as such an aloof, cold man with all his values so set in their ways as to make him totally unyielding and lacking in any form of compromise. He was totally committed to truth and frankness, to what was morally demanded and legally right. When he left the game and became a policeman for two years it affirmed his beliefs even more. All that might have been just about tolerable with the four grumblers, but it produced an unbendable disciplinarian, 'a tower of moral rectitude', totally the opposite of his predecessor, the more liberal Frank Hill. There is no way of knowing who 'the four' were, or what happened to them.

His passion for the game was such that he described it as 'one of the biggest things that happened in Creation'. Virtues such as integrity and hard work were compulsory in his world where there were no shades of grey, only black and white. Rules were sacrosanct. Bribes to young players were abhorrent. The sale of cup tickets was banned in contrast to previous manager Frank Hill who once bought himself a fine pair of shoes courtesy of tickets he himself had sold.

No manager was regarded as being straighter or harder and the legacy he left at Burnley was most of the team that flourished under Harry Potts and then went on to win the title. His toughness however did not prevent him from being one of the most innovative and inventive coaches of the time. He was fascinated by coaching and strategy and devised free kick routines and short corners which all came to be copied elsewhere. It was claimed that Northern Ireland invented the short corner routine in the 1958 World Cup, but if they did, they did so courtesy of Jimmy McIlroy who had trained under Alan Brown.

For any non-thinking footballer who enjoyed a drink, Brown must have been a nightmare, on top of which he was in a tracksuit more than a lounge suit, continually on top of the players on the training pitch. For Jimmy Adamson he became a role model and a great teacher of the game. Brown's lessons stayed with him and formed the basis of his own coaching skills.

He arrived as manager in August 1954 and stayed until July 1957. Established players like Jimmy McIlroy and Jimmy Adamson hung on his every word and realised his value. As well as nurturing young talents such as John Angus, Brian Miller, Ray Pointer, Jimmy Robson and John Connelly, he was the instigator of the Gawthorpe training area which was unique at the time.

If it was Bob Lord who oversaw the purchase, it was Brown's vision and hard work that turned it into reality. He led the gang of labourers himself digging the ditches and laying the bricks. One or two of the players, Jimmy McIlroy among them, were in fact skilled brickies. Several of them spent a summer literally digging it out of the ground.

'The players got down to it, famous ones like McIlroy and Adamson, and dug ditches with me,' he said.

A central feature of his approach was that no one should be treated differently. First-teamers would act as ball boys for the youths; his senior players were told to brew the tea for everybody else after training, a habit Brian Clough later copied when he adopted very much a 'Brown persona' in his managerial style.

Clough spoke about his time at Sunderland and an early meeting with Brown. 'Browny was there with his shorts on; he had the body of a 20-year-old, muscles all over. If he got into you after a match, short and sweet, you never answered back. He was a stickler for discipline, a right bugger. That was the side I got from him. He detested shabby clothing and he insisted all his players had a regular trim.

'I don't scare easily and never did. But I remember times when I was frightened of Alan Brown. A bollocking from him was like ten from anybody else. Alan Brown was not simply my manager – he was my mentor. I can remember looking at him at Sunderland and thinking this is the way I'll do the job if the opportunity ever comes.'

Jimmy Adamson might have said much the same.

'You lived in fear of him but there was no need, because he was a really genuine nice guy,' said another player of him in later years.

That 'fear' was well illustrated by John Connelly's recollections of when he signed for Brown. A blank contract appeared and Brown instructed him, 'Just put your name on that and we'll do the rest.' It would be filled in later. Connelly did as he was told.

After pictures had been taken by the photographer, Brown said, 'Now get your clothes on and come with me.' Off they went down to the railway station and on arrival Brown disappeared into the left luggage office and emerged with a battered old suitcase. It was the shabbiest Connelly had ever seen he said years later. Then he handed him the grubbiest possible raincoat. 'Put that on,' he was told. Connelly obeyed. The photographer was there again to take pictures of him in the raincoat with the ancient suitcase standing by a steam train.

Connelly thought that the caption was, 'John Connelly arrives to sign for Burnley.'

'And my mother was mad as hell when she saw it because she thought I looked like a refugee,' he said.

Margaret Potts recalled that when she married Harry it was Alan Brown and Bob Lord who took them to the station, but it was Alan Brown who found them a compartment of their own by 'persuading' the solitary occupant who was already there to leave, so they could have it to themselves. She remembered that the occupant looked at the impressive Brown and didn't argue.

He got just as much satisfaction from seeing players he had taught, themselves going on into coaching. He wanted to instil a desire in them to do that. Jimmy Adamson was one of his success stories.

In his first season the club finished in mid-table; in his two remaining seasons they finished seventh each time. He left quite simply because he and Bob Lord, who by 1957 was well in control, were two such strong-willed characters, that the longer they were in the same building, the less they could get on with each other. The frequency of the differences of opinions they had, or the number of occasions that Brown did or organised something that irritated Lord, increased. Lord later said they had not spoken for 12 months and that 'Brown had got too big-headed for his own good'. That was in fact rubbish. Brown simply had a mind of his own, something you were not allowed to possess if you worked for Bob Lord. Brown decided to leave and Jimmy McIlroy still remembers his cryptic remark to him on leaving: 'One day you'll understand why I had to leave.'

Alan Brown was one of a legion of people affected by Bob Lord in one way or another. The very name Bob Lord even after all these years invokes so many opinions and memories in Burnley and at Burnley Football Club. He was the classic 'muck and brass' arrogant patriarch running his extensive butcher's business. Born in 1908, the son of a barber, he was the archetypal, self-made businessman who was blunt, rude, dismissive, domineering and opinionated, but determined that his beloved Burnley would be the best club in the land, and his players the best looked-after. It is significant that player after player will praise him and say how well he treated them. Jimmy Adamson might have said the same but for the events of 1976.

Now living in Tasmania where I met him while on holiday, Burnley fan Terry Ridout once worked for Bob Lord in his butcher's business. When we were all seated at dinner in Terry's rural bungalow, up in the north of the island with the sound of cockatoos screeching away outside in the trees, he almost casually announced, 'I used to work for Bob Lord.'

There I was 12,000 miles away from home on the other side of the world and nearly fell off the chair in surprise at the surreal unexpectedness of it. He remembers that in 'the model meat factory' as Lord liked to call his premises, Lord frequently worked from a glass-fronted office from which he could survey all that went on, keeping a close eye on his staff and what they were doing. Out he would come to berate someone who wasn't doing the job right.

'He didn't so much speak to you but bark at you,' said Terry. '"Terry do this, do that, there's too much meat left on them bones," he'd tell me and anyone else not doing the job to his liking. He smoked Passing Cloud cigarettes and pride of place on one wall of the office went to a portrait of Winston Churchill.'

Ridout recalled that Lord spent much of his time on the telephone, frequently looking agitated, balling out 'OW MUCH' with his face getting redder and redder, as he argued about the costs of his meat contracts. 'Monday was pig-day; they came from a farm in Norfolk,' said Terry. 'Another day would be lamb from New Zealand or beef from Argentina. Another day he'd be sacking someone.'

No matter what criticisms were levelled at Bob Lord by the time he passed away in 1981 leaving the club in administrative and financial turmoil, no one can take away the fact that he was besotted with the club, and years earlier he had built it into a force to be reckoned with. It was as a young lad that he stood in the crowd to welcome home the Cup-winners in 1914. He was only six years old but it fired his imagination as he saw Tommy Boyle lift the trophy for the crowds to see in an era when the FA Cup Final and the eventual victory was something to bring such huge pride and sense of achievement to the town of Burnley.

Later at the end of 1920/21 another inspirational moment for him came when the club were champions. Two years before that he had managed to get into Turf Moor to see a game. Bob Kelly was his favourite player as Lord saved his money and eventually bought a season ticket. He was heartbroken when Kelly left

Burnley and Lord wrote that because of that he understood how people felt when years later Jimmy McIlroy left Burnley.

Over the years he worked and worked, his butcher's business grew so that eventually he owned a chain of 14 shops as well as building up the number of contracts for his factory to supply meat to hotels and schools. His success, the result of ruthlessness as much as business acumen, inspired Jimmy Adamson to say that it had never changed him. Danny Blanchflower replied, 'Yes, he was always insufferable.'

If there was no end of people who found him 'insufferable' then perhaps the classic examples were the Cobbold brothers who presided over Ipswich Town when they won the First Division title in 1962, pipping Burnley at the post. At the grand celebratory dinner at the Savoy Hotel, London, Lord had upset them all by making derogatory remarks about the achievement, suggesting they had only won it because Burnley had let them. They made fun of Lord at every opportunity deriding his pronouncements such as, 'I believe in calling a spade a bloody spade.'

They thought the fancy seats in the directors' area of Turf Moor were the height of pomposity, joking that they looked like they were covered with elephant skin. John Cobbold refused to sit in them. They regarded him as humourless and unsociable and on the occasion they were ignored and not offered a drink in the Burnley boardroom they simply helped themselves which infuriated Lord even more.

Lord's football obsession never abated. Somehow he made himself known to manager Cliff Britton in the 40s, visiting the dressing room and befriending the players, particularly Harry Potts. It was reported that when there was a rift between Harry Potts and the club in the late 1940s it was Lord who acted as peacemaker. It was a friendship that continued after Harry left the club and moved to Everton. By 1948 he had bought his first three shares in the club. He joined the board in 1951 and joked that they let him on by accident while the team was in Turkey.

Once Jimmy Adamson had achieved his regular first-team place, he became better known to Bob Lord and they too became early friends. Adamson was a 'footballer' in the proper sense of the word, and Lord was knowledgeable enough about football to recognise a good player with skill when he saw one.

In 1951 he had acquired a seat on the board but other directors viewed him with trepidation and disdain. A working-class director – what was that? The gulf and social distinction between players and directors had always been vast but at Burnley Lord bridged it, and in 1955 steamrollered his way to becoming chairman, having in the meantime seen to the purchase of Gawthorpe.

By the time the club had won the title in May 1960 his influence and control was total, so his remaining ambition became membership of the Football League Management Committee. This he achieved in 1967 but his rudeness reached the point where the committee had to censure him: 'It was decided unanimously that the committee would not tolerate the irresponsible comments of Mr Lord.'

This was ironic for neither would Lord tolerate what he deemed irresponsible reports or comments in the press about Burnley. Eventually he banned three daily newspapers and six individual reporters from Turf Moor. To be banned became almost a badge of honour among press circles.

The presidency of the Football League eluded him, always losing out to Lord Westwood, until in March 1981 he became the acting president for just a short three-month spell before illness forced him to relinquish the position. He died in December 1981.

In 1962 Kenneth Wolstenholme described him as being recognisable as any soccer star or pop singer, one of the few real characters in football and a Lancashire man through and through. To his enemies he was just a loud tub-thumper, but to his friends a brilliant chairman and a fair man. 'I'm the chairman of Burnley Football Club, the best club in't world, working the sort of day that would make younger men wince,' he boasted.

Arthur Hopcraft described him as 'the Khrushchev of Burnley', which was not the most complimentary of tributes. He described himself as just someone who expected something back for his money and that anyone who wanted him out of the chair at Burnley would have a fight on their hands.

Steve Kindon described him as the greatest of all the greats at the club. One of his abiding memories was Lord standing in the players' tunnel after an FA Youth Cup game when Kindon was just 16. 'Well done Stephen,' the chairman said to him. Kindon still remembers those three little words today. If as a player you were summoned to see him you automatically worried you had done something wrong but when he summoned the young Frank Casper who had just played his fifth game for the club it was only to tell him that he'd had sleepless nights having spent £30,000 on him, but now felt it was money well spent.

For his players he wanted nothing but the best, whether it was hotels, travel and transport, or the treats he provided like the Christmas turkey for each player; or on tours abroad remembers Paul Fletcher, some spending money under their pillow. Fletcher still thinks that the bigger the turkey the more he liked you. Those who received the smallest turkeys feared they were the next to be sold.

Dinners and end-of-season club trips to exotic places and the Mediterranean, or on the QE2, were the norm. Fletcher laughingly remembers that good as the hotels were, Lord always stayed in a better one nearby. He supported the abolition of the maximum wage though he opposed the changes to the retain-and-transfer system. Very few players of his era at the club ever say a bad word about him although some felt his discipline and a reprimand if they stepped out of line or misbehaved – including on the pitch.

He kept Burnley Football Club in the top flight by selling players to pay the wages and the First Division place was safeguarded far longer than any of the other 'smaller' East Lancashire clubs. In the mid-1960s when he realised that Jimmy Adamson was being courted by other clubs he made him first-team coach under Harry Potts. Exactly when he formed his plan to make him manager one day will never be known; possibly it was as early as 1962 when Adamson turned down the England job. But what is certain is that Lord was astute enough to realise that Adamson with his 'modern' approach was the man needed to take over one day.

Above all else Lord was a visionary and predicted the things that would happen in football on a regular basis.

The most telling was perhaps, 'Burnley has no future as a club with status or influence. Ipswich and many other teams will be also-rans within the next five to ten years. Their main functions will be to groom players and sell to bigger and more powerful clubs. Just like Burnley have been doing for years. You won't recognise the Football League. An economic blast will blow through the League and many of our clubs, lots of them with proud traditions, will be driven on the road to ruin.

'Our big city clubs will band together and outstrip the rest of us so the rest of us will be on the outside looking in. We'll have to content ourselves discovering kids and then flogging them, just to stay alive. The day may dawn when we get back in the First Division but the future remains bleak for clubs such as ourselves.'

These were astonishingly prophetic words.

'Discovering kids and flogging them' became the norm at Burnley and in the 70s led to Adamson making his remark to Paul Fletcher, 'I want to build a team, but the chairman wants to build a stadium.'

Lord, in fact, might have argued with that. The old Brunshaw Road Stand was in a poor state and needed replacing on safety grounds alone. His daughter Barbara Lord once told me that Lord had sleepless nights about it with its twisted girders and ageing facilities.

The structural report commissioned, that he kept to himself so that few people knew about it, condemned it as unsafe. It is reasonable to think that had it become public knowledge at the time there would have been an outcry.

He would certainly have argued that players were sold, first and foremost, to pay the generous wages. That might well have been the reason why winger Brian Pilkington was sold in 1960 even though he was at the top of his form and had even scored the winning goal at Maine Road that sealed the title win. To this day Pilkington wonders what would have happened if he had dug his heels in and refused to move.

Every pre-season Lord visited the Gawthorpe training ground to welcome the players back. In an old *Burnley Express* there is a wonderful picture of him and the players. The players are lined up facing him as if they are behind an invisible white line and have been instructed to cross that line at their peril. There he stands, hands clasped behind his back, besuited and with his trademark pork pie hat, addressing the troops looking rather like Captain Mainwaring from *Dad's Army*, except he is dressed in civvies. You can well imagine the instruction, 'Do not interrupt the chairman, do not answer back, speak only if you are spoken to; doff your caps when he has finished.'

Peter Higgs, the *Burnley Express* sportswriter for several years from 1972 onwards, was well aware of just how difficult a person Bob Lord could be and tells the story about the week he arrived at

Burnley to start his new job just as Harry Potts resigned. This was a massive story.

'The club issued a terse statement on his resignation which did not do justice to his service to the club. So, as a result, I did what any journalist would do in the circumstances and contacted, or attempted to contact the club, for elaboration and tributes. After the article appeared, I received a telephone call telling me I was to report to Bob Lord's meat factory in Lowerhouse on the Wednesday morning. I duly turned up, was ushered into Lord's office and was told by the "great man" that in future when the club issued a statement I was to take it at face value and not start delving into matters that did not concern me.

'The message was that I was new to the area and this is the way we do things in Burnley. In other words you report what we tell you to report. It was an extraordinary dressing down and over the coming years I did my best to ignore it. Lord was uncouth and rude and was, remarkably, allowed to get away with it.

'I went to a dinner once at a posh place in the Simonstone area of Burnley where my wife was appalled by his behaviour. When the waiters brought the food, Lord had to be served first and promptly began eating straightaway, while everyone else waited to be served. Nobody complained because he was Bob Lord, and he could do what he wanted.'

You crossed or angered Bob Lord at your peril. Derek Gill remembers the letter that was written to Lord being deeply critical after Adamson was sacked in 1976. Not only that, but the letter accused him of being a pie-maker. Lord must have gone apoplectic and his lengthy reply was acerbic and threatening, with comments such as, 'How blind and inexperienced you are... how poisonous is your mind regarding myself... I warn you that if any statements reach my ears which can be classed as being made by you and are of a defamatory nature I shall not hesitate to take steps to prevent you uttering irresponsible and untrue statements. I hope you take note of this warning; remember I have two letters from you which are damaging to myself.'

And more amusingly, 'Regarding your remark about meat pies, I take this opportunity of indicating to you that never in my life have I made or sold a meat pie.'

Stuart Hall summed him up: 'Turf Moor was his personal temple. Gruff, uncultured, maybe uncouth, his manner was a cross of rottweiler with Margaret Thatcher, a total despot, a ruthless manipulator, yet a benefactor. He typified the local dignitary who rules the town. Built like a pampas bull, deaf as a post – unless you uttered something derogatory. Then you were banned. Yet he, and his like, built football teams par excellence...'

His daughter Margaret sat with him every night as his life faded away. They talked into the night of past glories, people, places and the good times. They remembered banquets and celebrations, people they had met and laughed with and all the happier days. They talked too of the hurt he felt, betrayed by people who stabbed him in the back, particularly the press who had once hung on his every word and now portrayed him as insufferable. Margaret always maintained that there was a softer, gentler side to him that few people saw and that he could be just as hurt as the next person, but that he thought it was a weakness to show it.

John Connelly certainly remembered the good side to him and recalled that he did more for people than he ever let on. John had arranged to hire a car for his honeymoon but the car hire firm later said it was unavailable. Harry Potts was away on holiday so Connelly went to see Lord at his meat factory. If you set Lord a challenge he would usually respond helpfully so Connelly told him he was the only man who could help him at such short notice, that he needed a car and could Lord help. Lord told him to report back the day before the wedding. Connelly duly did and to his astonishment there waiting for him was a huge Wolseley for him to use.

Jimmy McIlroy too explained that it was no good making demands on Bob Lord. Provincial star players found it difficult to generate extra football-related income, but one way was by writing columns for newspapers. McIlroy discussed the situation with Lord suggesting to him that it was impossible for players such as him to get a column. Lord took up the challenge and within days he had a column in a Sunday newspaper.

The poignant interview that Bob Lord did with Radio Lancashire at the end of his life remains plaintive and difficult to listen to. It comes across as almost a deathbed confession as he answers questions about his life, his achievements, and the final years of decline and unpaid Turf Moor bills. The report on the state of the club that was undertaken by new director Derek Gill after Lord died was a damning indictment of a shambolic Turf Moor.

On the radio tape the voice is strained and sometimes faltering as he searches for answers. Towards the end he explained that the demise of the 'Team of the Seventies' was purely due to economics. No one person was to blame. The sale of players was to do with paying wages, not building new stands; the latter of which he was accused and it always hurt him.

'And how would you like to be remembered?' he was asked finally.

'To have been a man that can take stick,' was the gist of his reply. 'And as a man who when he set out his stall to do something, did it to the best of his ability.'

Yes he could take criticism, as long as those who accused him of being responsible for the club's decline would also be prepared to acknowledge it was he who had made it special in the first place.

Lord's influence and spirit lived on within the walls of Turf Moor even after his death in the most unusual way. Brian Miller used to tell the story that he truly thought the place was haunted. On several occasions during his time as manager, to his consternation he heard Bob Lord's voice drifting down the corridors. Eventually he discovered it wasn't anything spectral. He voiced his fears one day to the secretary Albert Maddox. Albert looked a tad embarrassed and explained that no, the place wasn't haunted; it was only him listening to tape recordings of old Bob.

All in all, Bob Lord was a very difficult man to work for and work with. Alan Brown eventually found it impossible. For 12 months they hadn't spoken. Harry Potts, however, seemed to absorb the stresses of working with him like a sponge. Jimmy Adamson, too, coped and largely accepted Lord for what he was, until eventually it became too much for him. Was it the stress of working for him that led Jimmy to begin drinking more than was good for him?

Of all the stories surrounding Bob Lord, the people he upset, the accusation that Manchester United were a bunch of Teddy

Boys (that he denied), the choice of words in referring to 'the Jews that run television', his banning of reporters, the taking out of his hearing aid if he didn't want to listen to criticism, his alleged involvement in the demise of Accrington Stanley – there is one story that makes me smile.

Jack Cochrane was a man who came to know Lord through their involvement at Lowerhouse Cricket Club and after Lord's death and funeral, used to visit Lord's grave. A friend asked him if he went there to pay his respects. 'No,' he replied. 'I just want to see if he is still there.'

Lord and Harry Potts, with supreme irony, are buried near each other in the same churchyard. It is reasonable to think that the good-natured and affable Harry Potts would never have given one minute's thought, as the 1960s went by, to the notion that Jimmy Adamson actually wanted his job or ever felt like standing up to the domineering Bob Lord. It was always Margaret Potts's biggest contention that Harry just never suspected it, never saw it coming, or knew how to deal with it.

Harry and Bob Lord were close friends in the late 1940s when Harry was a player. If Harry wanted advice it was to Bob he turned. Lord helped him furnish his first house.

Nearly eight years later he was the obvious man (to Bob Lord) for the Burnley managerial post when Billy Dougall had to relinquish the position on health grounds. Harry was manager of Shrewsbury when Lord contacted him and when he arrived he found a team that was established, was consistent if not brilliant, and there were young players coming through to join the regulars like Jimmy Adamson.

Adamson's regular position at this time was centre-half. The later re-shuffle came in the title season when Bobby Seith dropped out, Tommy Cummings came back into the middle, and Adamson moved to wing-half where he stayed until retirement as a player in 1964.

As skipper of the side manager Potts relied and leaned on him. In training Adamson was already providing ideas. Potts was never the greatest coach or tactician; his skills were to do with man-management; the fatherly arm-round-the-shoulder kind of bloke who could smooth the ruffled feathers and calm the angry waters. He was also incredibly loyal to his players, leaping up at any perceived injustice or bad decision.

But although Potts certainly had his FA coaching qualifications he was not a 'football thinker' of the new 'breed' whereas Adamson saw changes in the game taking place and new approaches. What developed over time was the classic 'new man' versus the 'old' situation. Not that there were overt confrontations or arguments; it was simply a slow steady realisation on Adamson's part that as the 1960s passed by, something different was needed other than week after week simply sticking with the same 11 players with the same simple instruction; basically play with a chuckle in your boots and pass to a Claret shirt.

Bob Lord too must have realised this and you do wonder when and how the dialogue between Lord and Adamson began with regard to Adamson becoming coach, effectively assistant manager, and the beginning of the grooming process in readiness for him taking over fully. More than once in the press he was referred to as Potts's protege. Lord was no football fool; he knew that one day he had to change things and he also had to make sure he tied Adamson to Burnley especially when other clubs like Sunderland were showing interest in him.

But what is clear, from talking to Margaret Potts, is that if there was a quiet agreement between Lord and Adamson that one day the job would be his, Harry Potts knew absolutely nothing about it until Lord informed him in 1970 of the changes to be made, and that this in fact was a measure of Harry's naivety and innocent vulnerability. Margaret maintained in her book that she received warnings about what was going on, but that Harry simply brushed them aside.

Peter Higgs had the impression that Adamson disliked Harry Potts, whom he eventually regarded as a bit of a bumbling fool, because he had been given too much credit for Burnley's past successes. Higgs over the years has not been alone in that view. But Higgs was one of a legion of people who thought that Potts, in turn, was a genuinely good man who never had a bad word to say about anybody.

'But,' thought Higgs, 'as far as the press were concerned, Potts was not averse to avoiding the truth so that he would not have to face up to it.'

That is not to suggest for one minute that Potts was untruthful; he was as honest as the day was long. But avoiding the truth was perhaps his way of dealing with things that he couldn't cope with, or did not want to cope with; one of them being Margaret's suspicions that Lord and Adamson were planning to replace him as manager.

Does wanting Harry Potts's job make Jimmy Adamson duplicitous? Probably not. Harry's football era was over and Jimmy had seen a much wider football world developing through the decade. The younger man with ideas and visions wanted to make better use of them; on top of that no doubt it seemed a reasonable supposition by Adamson that he and Bob Lord would form a great partnership.

Alas, it would only have a six-year lifespan, and Harry would tolerate just two years of his new 1970 position as a sort of managing director. The notion of the three of them being the inseparables was ended in 1970 when Adamson as good as stopped speaking to Potts. When Harry left in 1972 it was an event that in earlier years no one would have thought possible and just four years after that, Adamson too would be discarded to the amazement of everyone.

Chapter 4

Through the 1950s

J ENNIE HALSTEAD is one of Jimmy and May Adamson's five grandchildren; when I phoned she was immediately smitten with the idea of a book about her grandfather. She lives in Chorley and put me in touch with Burnley-based granddaughter Katie Bolton who had all the boxes of papers and photographs.

What was even better was her clear excitement at the prospect of finding out more about Jimmy.

Of course as grandchildren they had known him well although Katie described him as a very private man. But it was clear that in later years he had shared with them some of the memories of his family and life up in the north-east. Even in the first phone call, as Katie was walking the dog, she offered tantalising titbits of news that in the boxes there were items relating to his time at Sunderland and then at Leeds; that he had told them about growing up with the Charlton brothers from the same street though they were younger than Jimmy; that she had never been to Ashington and would love to visit. She had assumed the street where he lived would have been demolished years ago, but was delighted to hear that it was still there.

Better still, after Jimmy died, someone who had known him in Ashington had written to Katie; someone up there who knew him as a boy over 70 years ago; someone to contact and write to and see what we could unearth about not just Jimmy, but presumably his family, daily life, school maybe, and for sure his early football.

Sometimes you get such feelings of excitement writing a book, finding leads and making contacts.

A February 1956 *Football Monthly* magazine appeared on eBay with a piece written by Jimmy. I snapped it up for a few pounds to add to the collection of memorabilia. The excitement and buzz reminded me of a time in my other life as head of a little village school when a wartime evacuee who had stayed in the village wrote to the school 50 years later, on the off-chance that someone in the village might remember him. That single letter sparked one of the biggest school projects I ever undertook.

I was brought up in the 1950s, the era to which Jimmy Adamson belonged as a player. He inhabited a different world than the one we know now until it all changed so quickly in the 1960s. I started the decade as a five-year-old and ended it as a fifth-former at the local grammar school. Every home game in the 1959/60 season I went to Turf Moor to watch Jimmy Adamson and the team that would win the title.

Jimmy always struck me as being such an odd-looking physical specimen; there seemed nothing athletic about his build or his loping running style but it also struck me he never seemed to lose the ball once he had it in his possession. It was as if he seemed able to wrap his long legs around any opposition player and retrieve the ball. Great player though he was, in our school playground games, none of us pretended to be Jimmy Adamson. Mainstay of the team he might have been, but he didn't have the appeal of the rampaging Alex Elder, or the film-star looks of Jimmy Mac, Ray Pointer and John Connelly.

Today, for those who were born after the 1950s, like Jimmy's grandchildren, and did not experience them, that decade is distant history.

How many people have knowledge of the times back then; the social background, the political events, the slow progress that was made in living standards, the great divide between those who 'had' and those who had little, not to mention the death of King George in 1952 and the first British atom bomb test, the coronation of 1953, Ian Fleming's first James Bond novel, the first ascent of Everest, the death of Stalin, the Korean war, Winston Churchill, the Rillington Place murders, the Lynmouth flood disaster. Astonishingly hundreds of orphans were still being sent to Australia. And we still hanged people.

How soon we forget, or never knew in the first place. In 1952 and 1953 came the birth of new sorts of music. Charlie Chaplin was driven out of the USA, the Comet jet airliner began to make commercial flights, the *Goon Show* began on radio, children watched *Bill and Ben the Flowerpot Men* if they had a TV, and adults watched *The Quatermass Experiment*. The big films were *High Noon* with Gary Cooper and *The Greatest Show on Earth* with Charlton Heston, or *Shane* with Alan Ladd. Rocky Marciano won the world heavyweight boxing title. Russian tanks rolled into the streets of Berlin and quelled a workers' uprising. The Piltdown Man was revealed as a hoax.

The early years in which Jimmy played were the years of shortages, of polio, rickets, malnutrition, and drabness; there was real poverty for many and for the majority the absence of anything resembling indulgence. And yet, as with all things to do with the past, we who were brought up in the 1950s, despite the authoritarianism, restraint and uniformity look back on them as an era of trust, and law-abiding neighbourliness. We view them through rose-tinted spectacles perhaps, and think of them as 'better times' even though few people had washing machines, fridges, televisions or telephones.

But, there were proper town centres for shopping and 'corner shops' at the end of many streets. There were no supermarkets and you bought food as you needed it. In northern towns the Co-op was all-important.

I never wore long trousers until I was 14 and education was formal and regimented, strict and disciplined. The 11+ ruled our school-life and determined our secondary education. By the time I was seven I could already chant most times-tables. At home there were coal fires not central heating. In winter my bedroom had ice inside the windows. There were no ready-made meals, freezers, ranges of designer clothing or instant entertainment except the cinema or radio. For thousands of people there was an outside toilet, gas lamps not electricity and still no running water or baths. Money was in short supply, the war years still had their effects and the nation until the second half of the decade was still recovering. Few people had cars, there were no motorways. We travelled by steam train and holidays abroad were unheard of.

Decades later those of us who were there still have a nostalgic, probably distorted view, of a 'simpler' happier life, of children behaving themselves, attitudes of make do and mend, getting on with things, improvising and being content with one's lot. What we remember is the absence of hooliganism, violence, stabbings or drunkenness in town centres every Saturday night.

My own memories involve walking to school every day and playing out every night in the streets and the fields. We played outdoors in all weathers; there were no computers or TVs in our bedrooms. We climbed trees, played conkers, got a clip round the ear if we were naughty and sometimes from the local bobby if we fired catapults at the Post Office van. It was an innocent time, gone forever without the curse of political correctness so that we could play Cowboys and Indians, or WW2 English against Germans.

If you lived next door to a footballer you could actually talk to them. They went to the game on the bus or walked just like the rest of us. At Burnley some of them walked down Brunshaw Hill and Jimmy McIlroy was in digs somewhere up Todmorden Road. Brian Pilkington remembers getting the bus and talking football with the supporters but if he was tired after a training session he would bury his head in a newspaper and try to remain hidden. As the decade speeded up we read *Football Monthly* with its hand-coloured pictures and articles about our Burnley heroes in brown boots that seemed to come up to their shins. One in particular, Billy Gray, is a vivid reminder of the time.

On the downside, meat, cheese and sugar and sweets were still rationed. Cities blitzed in the war were still half derelict. Respectability was all-important, being deferential to your 'betters', the doctor, the bank manager, the teacher, was the norm. What we remember too are the endless fogs closing in, at their worst when it was dense smog making life intolerable and a walk down the street hazardous and even life-threatening if a bus suddenly loomed out of the mist.

Smog was what happened when hundreds of homes churned out smoke and it mixed with the fog. Sometimes it was so dangerous it was unsafe to step out of the house. It got in your eyes and down your throat; you could smell and taste it. On the worst of these days we wore makeshift masks.

In the 1949/50 season Jimmy was still in the Burnley A team. It was a team that won the West Lancashire League and the Richardson Cup and was runner-up in the West Lancashire

Cup. When he played his first game in 1951 for the first team, the official Burnley Corporation handbook made fine reading despite Burnley being a place of noisy mills, towering chimneys, smoky back-to-back terraced houses, and for many absolute poverty.

It was a place of small shops, a busy town centre, and street traders, delivery men selling bread, meat, fish and groceries. Rag and bone men went round with their horses and carts. In the town centre there was the bustling market, the railway station; men in heavy overcoats and caps were the norm, along with street-corner pubs and by and large it was a place (described by Margaret Potts) where a woman's place was to be seen and not heard.

In 1950 it was a thriving place with an official population of 84,590. Cotton might still have been king but soon the decline would start and workers would be sent home. By 1952 there were thousands unemployed because of the numbers of 'temporary' stoppages in the cotton industry.

Two years later in 1954 unemployment did not prevent over 52,000 people attending one of the greatest ever Burnley FA Cup games against Manchester United with Adamson, by now, well established in the side. After only five minutes the score was an astonishing 2-2. It was a game played at a furious pace for the whole 90 minutes with United containing the nucleus of the great Busby Babes side that would soon sweep all before them.

Burnley scored a third but United equalised again. Goals from the electric McIlroy and then Billy Gray sealed the game for Burnley but even so, with almost 20 minutes remaining, United continued to pour forward in a truly wonderful game. Matt Busby always had a soft spot for Burnley and said after the game that if he had to lose, he would rather be beaten by Burnley than anyone else. After victories like this it was just wonderful to be a footballer in a small town where people looked up to you.

In addition to the town's cotton mills there were the attendant engineering firms, loom makers, bleachers, dyers and sizers. But, it wasn't all mills and acres of terraced housing with their white-chalked doorsteps. There were the coal mines, leather tanners, rope-works, clothing firms, bottle makers, paper works, sheet metal works; there were manufacturers of steel springs, washing machines, weighing scales, raincoats, kettles and kitchen tools, uniforms, toys and furniture manufacturers. There was electrical engineering, breweries and brickworks. There were two theatres and several cinemas; at the Empress Hall there was dancing and roller skating; Thompson Park and the boating lake covered 480 acres. Once a year those who had work and could afford it decamped to Blackpool for Wakes Week.

But what the Burnley handbook did not mention were the industrial injuries; that Burnley had one of the highest suicide rates in the country and a depressing procession of child neglect cases in the courts. Nor did it mention the low wages and the exploitation, the palls of coal-fire smoke and for those who were unemployed the helplessness of poverty and despair. Burnley had some of the worst slums in the north.

On a Saturday the men wanted their football team to do well and to provide some respite from the drudgery of factory work. They streamed in from the surrounding areas, clambering aboard the special buses, then to alight and surge like a human tide beneath the canal bridge and up Yorkshire Street to Turf Moor. A 1952 *Football Monthly* had Burnley down as the most improved side in the First Division. By then they were a comfortable mid-table side.

Football was the topic of conversation for much of the week at a time when there were exciting forwards and dribbling wingers beating full-backs, unless they were kicked first into the stands. There were physical confrontations and bone-jarring tackling the like of which has now totally disappeared in today's sanitised game.

Opposing fans mixed happily on the terraces. At Easter there were three games in the space of four days. Matches were played on Christmas Day right up until 1957. It seems inconceivable today that mum would cook and prepare Christmas dinner while her husband went off to the match. There was hardly a foreign player to be seen.

My father would come home after a game and talk of players like Harold Mather, Billy Elliot, Tommy Cummings and a wonder goal he scored one Boxing Day against Newcastle, a rare event for a centre-half when he went the whole length of the field, beating player after player and then scored with a thumping shot. And, he talked of Jimmy McIlroy and Jimmy Adamson who he said could cover 50 yards in about ten long strides. He talked too of a series of games against Chelsea in the FA Cup when there were a staggering four replays. In later years Jimmy, like many of the team who played in those games, remembered them well.

'I played in four of the games and ended up with a broken jaw in the third replay at Arsenal,' he said. 'Mind you, it was a complete accident. I went up to clear a corner with Roy Bentley and got an elbow in the jaw. That put me out of the fifth game of the series and we lost it 2-0. The first one ended in a draw at Turf Moor. Then came a 0-0 draw at Stamford Bridge on a bone-hard, freezing day that was the coldest I've ever remembered. We should have won the next replay at Birmingham. We were 2-1 up and playing really well. But Roy Bentley snatched a late equaliser. Then came the game when he broke my jaw.'

By the mid-1950s, a decade after the end of the Second World War, the country was beginning to emerge from these years of austerity and greyness. Burnley might still have been typified by terraced rows, mines, mills and chimneys, fogs and the beginnings of industrial decline in its local industries, but the world outside was changing.

Bill Haley and the Comets had been around for a while already but suddenly Elvis Presley burst onto the scene. There is probably no exact moment that rock and roll was born but the mid-1950s is often quoted. Its impact changed the way young people behaved. 'Culture' had a new chapter and the idea of the 'teenager' was invented at this time as a result and they in turn populated the coffee bars with their jukeboxes that sprang up. Burnley teenagers went just as wild as their US counterparts when they heard 'Heartbreak Hotel' and 'Hound Dog' for the first time. Carl Perkins was blasting out 'Blue Suede Shoes'. People listened to Little Richard, Gene Vincent, Chuck Berry, and Jerry Lee Lewis. Slightly more refined were Dean Martin, Frank Sinatra and 'Que Sera Sera' by Doris Day. It was still an age when people listened to the radio more than they watched TV.

Jimmy Adamson could choose from over a dozen cinemas in Burnley and they showed *High Society*, *Guys and Dolls*, *The King and I*, *Around the World in 80 Days*, *Forbidden Planet*, *The Ten Commandments* and John Wayne's *The Searchers*. The space race inspired such classics as *Invasion of the Body Snatchers* and *Menace from Outer Space*. The heart-throbs were Tab Hunter, Stewart Granger, Robert Taylor and Rock Hudson. For those who had flickering black and white TV sets there was *Lassie*, *The Lone Ranger*, *Sgt Bilko*, *The Perry Como Show*, *Hancock's Half Hour*, *Armchair Theatre*, *Opportunity Knocks*, *I Love Lucy*, *Dixon of Dock Green*, and *Come Dancing* which amazingly first began in 1949.

Footballers in Burnley went dancing at the Empress Ballroom and once upon a time it was unseemly to be a girl hanging round the footballers there. Nevertheless it was where several footballers met their future wives.

The 1956 *Football Monthly* magazine I acquired gave an insight into his thoughts. A captain's role was far more than just winning the toss. He was the intermediary between team and manager, making suggestions and trying to bring harmony to the club. Three of the best captains he knew were Joe Mercer, Johnny Carey and Alan Brown. He paid tribute to Stan Matthews who taught him the virtue of letting the ball do the work. He confessed that Len Shackleton, the supreme entertainer, had him running all over the place.

An FA official was once asked why Shackleton had so few England caps. 'Because we play at Wembley not the London Palladium,' replied the bigwig. Adamson recalled that he was the first youngster of the new post-war signings by manager Cliff Britton. And then a telling comment, 'Burnley didn't need to do much shouting to sign me. I hated mining and the idea of being paid to play football was heaven.'

In 1957, the year the Sputnik 1 satellite was launched, Manchester United won the First Division title, Aston Villa won the FA Cup, Stanley Matthews made his last England appearance, Bobby Locke won the British Open golf tournament, Britain beat the USA in the Ryder Cup, Juan Fangio was the Formula One world champion, and Lew Hoad and Althea Gibson were the Wimbledon tennis champions. England beat the West Indies in the Test cricket series.

Burnley were by now solid and well-established, and Adamson believed that they were good enough to get to Wembley, but it was Aston Villa that ended their hopes. They fancied their chances later in the decade and in 1959/60 they had a 3-0 lead in the sixth round against Blackburn, but the game ended 3-3 and Burnley lost the replay at Blackburn. Jimmy, like the rest of the team, was devastated, and those in the team alive today still wonder how it happened and remember the controversial penalty given against the young Alex Elder that began the Blackburn comeback.

Jimmy, by now, had been married to May Ormerod for a number of years. The wedding had been at Holy Trinity Church, Burnley on 7 June 1952. His father was not present, noticeably absent from the wedding pictures. Photographs of his mother show a dark-eyed, tired woman who looked as though she had the cares of the world on her shoulders; the life and vitality drained from her by the demands of six children and a never-ending harsh domestic life in her cramped little house.

If his mother's marriage had been far from ideal, then Jimmy's to May remained lasting and incredibly strong until the very end, with each of them devoted to the other. It was a devotion that gave them the strength to survive the trials of football management and later family tragedies. Photograph after photograph through the decades picture them hand in hand with a closeness that is almost palpable.

One of the reasons for the togetherness of the teams and players through the 1950s was that so many players married local girls. Players were encouraged to marry and it was one of Hilda Lord's functions to 'vet' prospective brides. When Harry Potts was manager Margaret Potts saw it as her duty to 'mother' the other wives. Alex Elder remembers how fortunate he was to come into such a great family club where the younger players and the reserves baby-sat for the senior players.

'We all went out together and had meals together, we all lived in and around the town,' he said. 'We all knew each other so well and socialised. Our wives went shopping together and all this camaraderie meant that once on the pitch you were so close that you never wanted to let your team-mates down.'

Bobby Charlton commented on this togetherness in his Manchester United autobiography; that at any England get-together the Burnley boys would always stick together as if they were from some sort of 'Republic of Burnley'.

Jimmy Robson remembers much the same about the famed 'closeness' and described it to Tim Quelch. Jimmy was yet another lad from the north-east:

'Tommy Cummings was from the north-east too, and he and Jimmy Adamson were already in the first team when I arrived. In my first year I played for the Colts and we would kick off at 1.15 and then get over as quickly as we could for the second half to see the first team. We all felt so at home. Jimmy was the hub of the team with Jimmy McIlroy, in the middle of the field. They had such a good relationship on the field and were friends off it which helped. But the key was the togetherness of everybody. As a player Adamson had everything; he could pass it, carry the ball from back to front and he could tackle. He had a telescopic leg and could hook the ball and then start an attack again. There were a lot of young players in the side and we all needed help. He gave us that guidance and support; he was that type of bloke. He always passed information and always helped you; he was always talking to you in the game and putting you right. His knowledge of the game was first class and we all looked up to him. We all hit it off and we had a good spirit in the team at the time, a mixture of experience and youth. Everybody appreciated what everyone else could do.'

In a moving tribute to her father-in-law in October 2012, Dany Robson wrote about John Connelly after he had just died of cancer. It was another illustration of the closeness that existed between the players of the time. The Robsons and Connellys had family holidays together; they went out every Saturday night without fail. Dany, when they were growing up, used to look at what the eldest Connelly daughter was wearing, as it would be passed over and Dany would be the one wearing it the next summer.

Jimmy Adamson's first team playing career lasted from 1951 to 1964, making the 1956/57 season just about the halfway point. It was a season when Wembley seemed so close and in the early rounds there were wins by 9-0 and 7-0. Then Aston Villa did for them in the sixth round replay. The 1952/53 season had so far been the closest he had been to any success when it was only in the last few weeks of the season that a real chance of the title faded away. Other seasons had passed by with Burnley well established as an average First Division side, with manager Frank Hill being replaced by Alan Brown in 1954 coinciding with the year that rationing finally ended.

Shortly before joining, Brown wrote a four-page feature in a football album of the time. In it he emphasised his view that intensive coaching was essential to the progress and improvement of any footballer. England had recently been humiliated by the magical Hungarians at Wembley resulting in the realisation (at least by some) that English football was outdated and under-coached.

Brown wrote, 'I myself am absolutely convinced that naturally athletic boys can be made into good footballers through coaching; that any young footballer can have his performance bettered by intensive training and coaching.'

The prevalent view was that in England footballers were 'born', never 'made'. Brown's view was simple: the weakness was that professional footballers in England just did not practise system-atically enough, or weren't coached enough, especially with the ball at their feet. Astonishingly some of the leading players including Stanley Matthews thought that coaching was unnec-essary and that players should be able to develop their own game.

One of the senior players at Burnley, Bobby Seith, was adamant that it was Brown who laid all the foundations at the club for the successes that would come later, describing him as the architect and the first real coach: 'He was a tremendous innovator and brought in many things that had not been brought in before. He devised "shadow" training where the whole team would attack against just a goalkeeper and maybe a couple of defenders. This would create momentum, positional sense and rhythm. This was done for half an hour or so regularly every week.'

Playing to feet was the norm, with winger Brian Pilkington relating that they had such a small forward line that keeping the ball on the floor made more sense than launching long, high balls to players who would never reach them.

It was in 1954 that Adamson was called up to play for Young England against an England XI at Highbury. On his side was his team-mate Brian Pilkington, Duncan Edwards, Albert Quixall and Dennis Viollet. But on the opposing side were names such as Stan Matthews, Wilf Mannion, Tommy Lawton and Len Shackleton. These were illustrious names and today would be in the £30m bracket.

It was Brown who changed the whole style of the club in the mid-1950s. Adamson outlined this in one of his newspaper pieces written in 1962:

'My own club was renowned for their cast-iron defence in the 1946/47 season when they only gave away 29 goals in 42 games and I'm told there were lengthy inquests on how some of those were let in. Strange as it may seem it was the king-pin of that defence, Alan Brown, who started the transformation on his appointment as manager in 1954. Burnley were soon to be known as an attacking side. Studious Brown gave us confidence in our own ability; then he started to draw up the first plans for the 'new' attacking methods. He asked us to give them plenty of thought and to try and improve on them. Finally, he gave us a fluid defensive set-up which could quickly turn a defender into an attacker. Harry Potts carried on with these ideas when Brown left for Sunderland.'

All those ideas formed the basis of the title-winning team of 1959/60. 'We do not believe in sticking to the numbers on our backs,' he continued. 'If a full-back or even a centre-half finds himself in a position to attack then he goes forward.' That philosophy was one of the foundations of his managerial style. Today this might sound basic, but in the middle and late 1950s it was quite radical. 'Our methods gained us quite a measure of success – the unexpected often does,' said Adamson. If Adamson preached the virtues of doing the unexpected, it was a mantra taught to him by trainer Billy Dougall.

Brown's request that the players go away and think about his ideas fell on fertile ground. There were several 'thinking' footballers at the club at this time – Adamson and McIlroy being the best remembered, but Tommy Cummings, Brian Miller and Bobby Seith all eventually went into management with Ray Pointer and Jimmy Robson going into coaching.

Brown was physically tough and hard and instilled that into Adamson as well. There was no way in the 1950s that you could be a centre-half unless you could look after yourself and give as good as you got. Elegant and slim though Jimmy may have been and never a 'dirty' player, he was no wallflower and years later commented that with the greater protection given to players by referees he would have been booked or even sent off in many games.

Brown could certainly 'encourage' his players to intimidate the opposition and some years later the Leeds United winger Albert Johanneson was on the receiving end of some torrid treatment from the Sunderland players when Brown was manager at Sunderland. The game was only in its second minute when Johanneson was punched and stamped on. The game was continually marred by Sunderland's treatment of him and his knee swelled up like a balloon. No other player, he said, was targeted like he was.

After the game Alan Brown (ever the gentleman) apologised to Johanneson for the kicking he had received and told him he didn't think he would have stood up to it. In other words, it was clear to Johanneson that this was a deliberate tactic designed to intimidate him. Morally upright and honest as the day is long, Brown might have been, but it didn't prevent him from encouraging players to rough up the opposition when necessary.

The 1956/57 season was a significant one for a number of reasons. Alan Brown decided to leave, but not before he had blooded a number of young players who would go on to form the great team of 1959 to 1962. John Angus, Jimmy Robson, Adam Blacklaw and John Connelly made their debuts. Ray Pointer would emerge a little later. It also marked the end of Peter McKay's career at Burnley. McKay's name might not appear too readily on people's lips but he was in fact one of the most prolific scorers in Burnley's history. Jimmy McIlroy rated him as the finest and most naturally instinctive goalscorer he had ever played alongside. Then there were the astonishing scoring feats of 17-year-old Ian Lawson in the FA Cup.

Adamson's position at this time was still at centre-half, direct opponents including Nat Lofthouse, Dave Hickson, Bobby Smith, Derek Kevan and the fearsome Welshman Trevor Ford. Centre-forwards at this time were basically of the battering ram variety. It is a tribute to Adamson's toughness and bravery that he stood up to them week after week at a time when there was little protection from referees. Adamson might have been tall but he was hardly muscular or 'meaty' yet he gave as good as he got. It was a recognised tactic that as soon as possible any centre-forward would clatter firstly the goalkeeper to test him out, and then the centre-half to put the fear of God into him.

An exception to the rule was the legendary Jackie Milburn of Newcastle United whose skill and speed more than compensated for his smaller than average size for a centre-forward. Other regular opponents were Danny Blanchflower, Tom Finney,

Stanley Matthews, Len Shackleton, Wilf Mannion, Jackie Mudie and Stan Mortensen. Jimmy Greaves scored over 100 goals for the Chelsea youth team that season; his path and Adamson's would cross later.

Bobby Charlton made his debut for Manchester United in 1956. Jimmy had once played football on Ashington's Hirst Park or in the street behind Laburnum Terrace where the Charltons did just the same; plus they had a common bond knowing all about the terrible hardships of mining. Many years later Bobby provided poignant reminders in his autobiography. He wrote that the houses belonged to the mining company... footballs like square meals were not readily available... getting hold of a ball was one of two priorities... the other was satisfying the hunger that was ever present... there was a street cooperative that had allotments and fattened pigs for slaughter... poaching was commonplace even though it was illegal and rabbit stew was a highlight... there were trips to Newbiggin by the Sea... coal washed up on the shore could be collected... and a mining company concession was the coal they would leave outside the houses.

You just wonder what went through their minds on the first occasion they played against each other, the one for Burnley and the others for Leeds United and Manchester United. Ashington provided an invisible bond that lasted through the years so that Bobby was there to pay his respects at Jimmy Adamson's funeral.

The 1956/57 league programme began on 18 August with a 2-0 win over Chelsea. The players might well have groaned when they saw the opening fixture having played them seven times the previous season because of the protracted cup game that went to four replays. Burnley lost the last of them but then with that wonderful irony that occurs so often in football, promptly beat them 5-0 in the league game that came immediately afterwards.

The Everton game was the sixth of the season and four of them had been wins. Peter McKay, by the seventh game, had already scored seven goals and then two more followed in a 4-1 win against Sheffield Wednesday. It was then that Alan Brown astonishingly decided that McKay was no longer needed. The history books say that Brown wanted a greater work-rate from him but in fact McKay's taste for a drink or two was a more likely reason.

Another possibility was that he had upset the chairman, Bob Lord, when in a pre-season voyage to the Isle of Man where rough seas made just about everyone seasick, McKay collared Lord on the boat up on deck and gave him a piece of his mind. No one, just no one, could do that to Lord and get away with it. Football works in funny ways. Another departure was Roy Stephenson who later played for Ipswich Town and was in the side that snatched the title from Burnley in 1962.

Despite the good start to the season, progress and results were below average between September and November with only two wins. Another lad made his debut, this one being Adam Blacklaw when regular keeper Colin McDonald was injured. It was a good game to make a start in football when Burnley thrashed Cardiff City 6-2.

If the 1956/57 season is remembered for anything it will surely be the debut of Ian Lawson when he scored four times in the 7-0 FA Cup win over Chesterfield. To follow that up he then scored three more in the 9-0 win in the Cup against New Brighton. It was as if a new star had been born and even then he hadn't finished and scored another in the next Cup win away at Huddersfield. In seven league appearances he scored twice but then, sadly, that was it for Lawson as he spent most of the remainder of his career in the reserves.

Yet another young lad made his debut. This time it was John Connelly who would go on to have a superb career including England appearances in the 1966 World Cup ten years later. His goal away at Reims in the European Cup, when he set off from the halfway line, is arguably one of the greatest ever Burnley goals. He was only 18 on his debut and had only been signed that season from St Helens. Scouts had gone to watch another player at St Helens but it was Connelly they came back with.

Years later Connelly recalled that one of the biggest problems back in the 1950s was wearing in a new pair of boots. They were like concrete, he said, and so stiff that you had to break them in gradually in training to soften them up, before you dared wear them for 90 minutes in a game. Nor were they replaced every couple of weeks or so; they were repaired at Cockers, a sports shop that is still there in Burnley, over and again until they fell apart.

Even though the season ended with four defeats from five games, Burnley finished in a creditable seventh place, but it was a poor away record that hindered better progress. Adamson made 36 league appearances and four in the FA Cup. It was a season that provided debut games for a string of young players with the club's youth scheme and the Gawthorpe set-up, clearly set to provide over a decade of exciting talent. The credit for that has to go to Alan Brown for having the vision and Bob Lord for enabling the purchase of the training area. For senior players such as Adamson it was a marvellous place to be coached and to learn to coach.

The 1956/57 season ended with one of the games that Adamson always rated as one of the best he had played in, with Burnley giving one of their finest ever performances. It was Bilbao 1 Burnley 5 in an end-of-season May tour. Such was the brilliance of the display that Burnley were then invited to play Real Madrid, but having played seven games already the invitation was politely turned down. It was a superb tour all round with manager Brown delighted. The *Burnley Express*, however, chose to concentrate on weightier matters – local cricket and the Lancashire League, especially the local derby game between Burnley CC and Lowerhouse.

The 'factory-floor' for Adamson was the training area at Gawthorpe. Harry Potts always said it was better than being in Switzerland. It could be blowing a blizzard but Harry would come in beaming from ear to ear and rubbing his hands announcing, 'What a grand day for football.' There were full-sized training pitches and the old barn was converted into a very basic gym with two changing rooms.

Jimmy McIlroy, in his 1960 book, wrote about it being the sort of spot to make even the most reluctant footballer feel good to be alive with possibly the first ever all-weather pitch in the league. Not that it was a palace or a picnic area. Early photographs show it to be spartan in its changing facilities where players simply picked up the nearest grubby training kit from a heap on the floor, and it was a mudbath in winter.

Bobby Seith recalled that before Gawthorpe the 'gym' was at Turf Moor under the stand where they would train and have their five-a-side games surrounded by turnstiles, toilets, pillars and a sandpit. These natural hazards caused frequent injuries especially broken noses if someone crashed into a turnstile or a pillar. In the very early 1950s it was where players Harold Mather and Arthur Woodruff kept their greyhound and where Adamson and all the rest fed it on tit-bits. This was a greyhound that was so slow that on the training runs they took it along the canal, the two full-backs tried to run away from it and lose it. It is hard to picture Rooney and Van Persie doing the same thing today; training under the stand at Old Trafford and then trying to escape from a useless greyhound along the canal.

With Alan Brown in charge, Burnley were the pioneers and Gawthorpe was the envy of most of the football world. It became Adamson's 'home' for 20 years and the classroom in which he would make average players into good players, and good players into very good players. What Brown laid down was a comprehensive scouting system, impressive coaching, the most up-to-date training area of the time, and a strong youth policy. His value and lasting influence was enormous.

The early relationship between Adamson and Harry Potts was based on trust and respect. It was later that Adamson came to see him simply as 'the highest paid five-a-side player in football', a comment shared with Jimmy McIlroy. Potts was sensible enough to obey that old maxim, 'if it ain't broke don't fix it'. The players during his tenure were guided by him and his traditional principles based on the simple idea that you put out the best 11, and let them get on with it.

Not until the 4-1 defeat at Hamburg in the European Cup in 1961 did anyone at Burnley publicly admit that perhaps different games and different situations need different approaches. They went to Hamburg with a 3-1 lead and a semi-final place at stake but with Harry they knew only one way to play; the idea of playing defensively was alien. It was clear to Jimmy McIlroy that they should have adopted a more cautious approach. It is more than reasonable to assume that the lesson of this defeat stayed with Adamson, who, when he became coach in 1965, certainly adopted different tactics for different games.

But through 1959/60, the go-out-and-play approach was fine and there were cavalier wins of 5-2 over Everton, 4-1 over Wolves, 8-0 over Nottingham Forest, 4-0 over Bolton, 4-2 away at Arsenal, 5-2 away at West Ham, and at last the championship was sealed in the very last game of the season at Maine Road in May 1960, one of the greatest nights of Jimmy Adamson's life and one when fingernails were chewed right off as the final minutes ticked away.

As City ferociously swarmed all over Burnley towards the end it was Adamson at the back along with Cummings who held firm. One of the great stories is that the players celebrated afterwards in the dressing room with sherry out of old stained tea mugs. In a 42-game season you can argue that every win has been vital to ultimate success but one stood out in this season of seasons and the images of that tumultuous night are as clear to me now as they were just a day or so after.

On 1 March 1960, Spurs arrived at Turf Moor as league leaders with a five-point lead. By the end of the game it had been whittled down to just three and the race for the title was wide open again. It was Adamson who was involved in the move that released Connelly to whip over a bullet cross that Pointer headed home. Until then Spurs had opened Burnley up time and again but this goal changed the game and Connelly wrapped it up with a classic, trademark, 20-yard strike that was simply unstoppable.

Although it was a defeat, another memorable night in the following season was in France when Burnley knocked Reims out of the European Cup. It was a frenetic, firework-filled night in front of a baying crowd, even more incensed when Harry Potts ran on to the pitch to place a French free kick in the correct place. Burnley won on aggregate but lost the game in France 3-2. Connelly scored his wonder goal, running with the ball from the halfway line, but it was Adamson, despite being injured, along with goalkeeper Blacklaw who was the rock. Time and again he broke up French attacks; time and again he made great headers, over and again he won the ball and broke the French resolve. Afterwards he could barely walk.

As well as lasting glory as Burnley legends after the title win, it also earned them the dubious 'treat' of a trip to New York to play in an international tournament. Such things were rare in those days; they were almost guinea pigs and it was a month that was not without its problems, including the sweltering summer heat, a second-rate hotel; a resultant change of hotel, slanging matches with Kilmarnock (one of the other teams), and accusations that they were a difficult club dissatisfied with everything. Bob Lord was in his apoplectic element complaining about the sub-standard facilities in hotel number one, so bad that they demanded to be moved. The whole thing left an indelible memory in Jimmy's head especially the novel approach to soccer that the organisers adopted. He later wrote:

'Some strange and funny things happened when Burnley were out there. I remember one game being held up as a goal-kick was about to be taken because the referee had received a signal that the game was being televised and it was time for the commercials. Another time the American referee and his linesman had a discussion in midfield and held up the game for minutes about what decision he should take following an unusual foul. One match resulted in both teams playing in white shirts. Neither side had an alternative strip. While we were there, training facilities were confined to the big Polo Grounds, scene of some of the greatest boxing matches. With six teams needing facilities, training was only arranged on a rota basis. It took 40 minutes by subway to get there from our hotel.

'The commentator at the games was a real character. I recall that both teams lined up on opposite touchlines before a game and when the commentator called out the player's name, he jogged out onto the field and the commentator gave a run-down on his career. This generally ended with him saying, "Let's give this boy a big hand." Comments during the game were made in order to educate the crowd in the rules of the game. It was not unusual to hear him say "THE BALL IS IN THE CAGE" after a goal had been scored. A corner was known as a "corner shot". Whenever a foul was committed the announcer would attempt to give reasons for the free kick. Quite often it was something like, "Hey, the guy just took a kick at him."'

Jimmy found it vastly amusing. Only a couple of years ago Burnley played a game somewhere in the USA and the game was shown on the internet. A shot whistled narrowly wide. 'Close but no ceegar,' announced the commentator. Some things never change.

Norman Giller's fine book, *50 Seasons of Footballer of the Year*, naturally included Jimmy Adamson who received the award in 1962. It was an award that had been earned for everything he had done, and the way he had played in the preceding years, just as much as anything in particular he had done in 1962. What 1962 did do was to bring him to the forefront of attention via the Cup Final and the fact that Burnley came so close to achieving the double. Giller summarised him as, 'The thinking man's wing-half', always a composed and authoritative figure as a defensive anchor-man. His job was to win the ball and then pass it to playmaker Jimmy McIlroy who would in turn feed it to the strike force that included England internationals Ray Pointer, John Connelly and Gordon Harris.'

Jimmy himself wrote of 1962:

'Three things made the 1961/62 season memorable for me. There was the honour of skippering Burnley in the FA Cup Final, the Footballer of the Year award, and then my appointment as coach to the England team for the World Cup finals in Chile. It then all fell a bit flat because we were beaten at Wembley, and failed to perform as well as we might have done in the World Cup. But nobody could take away from me the Footballer of the Year statuette, nor the fact that we had made it to the Cup Final. Mind you, we had some scares along the way. We beat Queens Park Rangers 6-1, and then needed a replay before beating Leyton Orient. Our finest performance was beating an excellent Everton team in the fifth round. We then accounted for Sheffield United in the quarter-finals and then had a close call with Fulham, winning 2-1 in another replay.

'We were fighting an uphill battle against a magnificent Tottenham team in the final after the ace of goal-scorers Jimmy Greaves had scored in the third minute. But I have to say, the 3-1 scoreline at the end of the match flattered them a little. It was a season of near misses for Burnley. Our success was built on teamwork with individual stars like Jimmy McIlroy, Ray Pointer and Gordon Harris functioning within a well-constructed formation. We were essentially a footballing team and concentrated on skill ahead of brute force. They were wonderful years at Turf Moor and I was content to spend all my playing days there.'

In his 'dream team' Jimmy stuck with players he had played with or against. He chose: Gordon Banks; Johnny Carey; John Charles;

Duncan Edwards; Roger Byrne; Danny Blanchflower; Jimmy McIlroy; Stanley Matthews; Jimmy Greaves; Denis Law; Bobby Charlton.

When he looked back over the decade he wrote about the 'ball-players', John White, Tommy Harmer, Johnny Haynes, Danny Blanchflower, George Eastham, Alex Young, Len Shackleton, Wilf Mannion, Stan Matthews, Bobby Charlton and Tom Finney, and how essential they were in the game. The 1950s was a time when every team had one to make the others play and pull all the strings. He, in fact, would have said that he himself did not fall into this bracket.

He wrote, 'The classic example is Jimmy McIlroy; the artistic flick, superb control, clever trapping, split-second timing, accurate passing and confident composure, are all factors that brighten the game of soccer. Such a player will always rank number one in my book and the complete ball-player is; someone who, when running with the ball at speed has instant control; is able to control the ball played at him without it running away; possesses a body swerve; has superb timing in evading a tackle or in meeting the ball; can accurately distribute the ball including swerve passing; has great ball manipulation skills; can always do the unusual and the unexpected; and finally, has an air of composure and confidence.'

He wrote these thoughts at a time when there seemed fewer of these maestros like McIlroy and White in the game and they were becoming a disappearing species.

If those thoughts developed through the 1950s, it was 1962 when he penned them and in them was the basis of what he looked for in a player when he became coach at Burnley FC and then manager. If he was lucky a boy would arrive possessing maybe some of them but the aim was always to develop every player who arrived and teach them in the basic skills that were the foundation of his football philosophy.

When he singled out Jimmy McIlroy in the article he might have already suspected that McIlroy's days at Burnley were numbered. It was Adamson who warned Jimmy that his friendship with the Cook family was in danger of infuriating Bob Lord to the extent that Lord would eventually react to it. Jimmy was particularly good friends with John Cook whose father had once been a Burnley director in Lord's early days on the board. In truth, the friendship with a family that Lord disliked was probably only one of the reasons why McIlroy was sold. But on the night in February 1963 when McIlroy departed from Anfield after a defeat in the FA Cup, not on the team coach, but in Cook's car, it was the last straw for Lord, bitterly disappointed at the defeat and the loss of FA Cup revenue.

Lord never forgot the supporters' reaction to the McIlroy sale. Twelve years later he would be asking Adamson if there would be the same storm if he sold Leighton James.

Adamson's peak year as a player was 1962. From then on, 12 years of playing football at the very top in an era of bruising confrontations and bone-jarring tackles would take its toll on his body, fitness and recovery periods. His back by now was wrecked, and his wish to continue playing was optimistic. His time as one half of the fulcrum of the side would soon be over and his appearances on the playing field more and more intermittent.

Chapter 5

Peak season 1961/62 and a World Cup

I DUG out the old *Radio Times* I had dated Saturday 5 May 1962, and on the front was a picture of Adamson and Danny Blanchflower shaking hands before a game at Turf Moor. Inside, it described the game as the match of the century. I was still at school in the sixth form and went down to London with a pal by train on the Friday. The FA Cup meant something far more then than it seems to do today when the kick-off between Chelsea and Liverpool in 2012 was at the ridiculous time of 5.15pm, and in the week running up to it the coverage was minimal. The quarter-final replay at Blackburn with a semi-final at Wembley in prospect could only generate a paltry 8,635 in 2013.

The build-up 50 years ago was intense; the coverage on the day began in the morning and clubs didn't field reserve teams. Thousands of us queued at Turf Moor in a line that snaked its way round two sides of the stadium to get tickets. We hung on every word that our heroes said in the press interviews. I had a bulging scrapbook as well but that disappeared years ago when we moved house.

The old *Radio Times* cost five pence, although it was in old shillings and pence back then, and coverage started at 11.15am.

From then it was continuous until 5pm. If you were one of the few to stay at home in Burnley, afterwards you could watch *Circus Boy* at 5pm, then *Mr Pastry*. *Juke Box Jury* was at 6pm and through the evening there was Andy Stewart, *Perry Mason*, the Saturday film, and then Harry Worth. There was 30 minutes of the Cup Final at 11.05pm until closedown.

As Ed and I changed trains at Manchester, a small, frail, elderly figure joined us in our carriage. He wore a suit and waistcoat and eventually spoke. He told us he too was going to the Cup Final. 'Up fer't Cup' as they said up north in those days. Being young and consequently disinterested we merely nodded and smiled when he said he had played in a Cup Final. Pulling back his jacket he revealed a medal hanging from his waistcoat. It just didn't dawn on us that he was referring to a Burnley Cup Final in 1914 when Liverpool were beaten 1-0. It didn't dawn on us that he was in fact a Burnley hero and legend who had played in that Cup Final. Years later I have worked out that it must have been little Billy Nesbit, who was only seven stones dripping wet, and kicked myself ever since that we hadn't the wit to talk so much more to him and ask him what he thought about Jimmy Adamson's chances of lifting the trophy.

For those of us who were there, the community singing, led by Arthur Caiger and accompanied by the Band of the Coldstream Guards, was a well-established part of the day. At half-time it was the Massed Bands of the Brigade of Guards. In all honesty without the *Radio Times*, I would have forgotten all that.

Her Majesty the Queen presented the medals, for Jimmy Adamson a loser's medal. Jimmy McIlroy went up those steps with him to the Royal Box. Life works in funny ways. Both of them remained residents of Burnley all their lives but while one eventually received the MBE and became the town's ambassador, the other retreated into obscurity.

In 2011 McIlroy was made president of Burnley Football Club and almost 50 years to the day since he and Adamson went up those Wembley steps, McIlroy sat down to have lunch with the Queen at the club when she visited Burnley as part of her Jubilee Tour. The meal took place in the Jimmy Adamson Suite in the Jimmy McIlroy Stand, the two players' names still inextricably and permanently linked. But while Jimmy Mac still embraced the club, Adamson shunned it.

The beginning of a new decade is always significant in the hope that it brings that things will become better. It is possible to say that most people might have been glad to see the back of the 1950s but the 1960s certainly saw huge changes in attitudes towards the way we lived. The satirical TV programme *That Was the Week That Was* would have been unthinkable in the 1950s. The age of the cheap car had just arrived in late 1959 with the new Mini. The Austin 7 and the Morris Mini-Minor were 'the people's cars' and you could fill the tank with petrol for under £1 and then drive along the newly opened stretch of motorway between London and Birmingham.

The 1950s drew to a close to the sounds of Cliff Richard and Buddy Holly. Italian coffee bars became the vogue. At the cinema Joe Lampton made his way to the *Room at the Top*. People were buying stereo record players for the first time. The consumer society was emerging.

If the 1960s had their downside, the decade more than any other claimed its very own distinctive character, becoming synonymous with Kennedy, the Beatles, the mini-skirt, Carnaby Street, flower power, student protests and 'Swinging London'. When the prosecution failed to have *Lady Chatterley's Lover* banned on the grounds of obscenity in 1960, it was the signal that a censorial era was over. Morality became blurred at the edges and permissiveness became the byword although if it all began in the capital, it maybe took two or three years to arrive in provincial Burnley.

Jimmy Adamson and his colleagues at the football club couldn't quite afford the new lifestyle until their maximum wage had been abolished. If Tottenham Hotspur became the first of the new-style glamour teams in the early 1960s, homely Burnley still had a long way to go before Adamson produced his 'special' team briefly ten years later and even then they were only nibbling at the edges. Some of the Tottenham stars wondered that anyone could actually live in grimy Burnley with dolly-birds still hard to find in the town. Bob Lord's wife Hilda still reigned supreme over the players' wives at Turf Moor on a Saturday afternoon and May Adamson had to mind what she said and the way she dressed. When Margaret Potts arrived in a trouser suit, there was hell to pay.

A First Division winner's medal in 1959/60, Footballer of the Year in 1962, FA Cup finalist, assistant England manager of the side in Chile at the World Cup, and on his return offered the post of England manager to replace Walter Winterbottom. The early 1960s was a staggering time for Jimmy Adamson.

The league triumph of 1959/60 is well covered in a number of books already: *Harry Potts – Margaret's Story*; *Jimmy McIlroy – Prince Of Inside Forwards* and *You've Never Had It So Good*. Amazingly Burnley only reached top spot in the very last game of the season at Manchester City. In *The Sixties Revisited*, Jimmy Greaves positively drooled over the midfield pairing and performances of Jimmy Adamson and Jimmy McIlroy. 'The two of them purring with power and precision like a Rolls-Royce engine,' said Greaves. 'This was where Adamson, the greatest player never to be capped by England, and McIlroy reigned supreme. Adamson, tall and stately, won the ball with determined tackles and then drove them forward with purposeful passes, conducting and orchestrating the attack.'

Ironically, it wasn't really a season when Burnley played their best football; that came the season after and in the first 30 games of 1961/62. In 1960/61, it was playing in four competitions that was the problem. They performed well in the league, were semi-finalists in the FA Cup and the League Cup, and quarter-finalists in the European Cup. But it was all too much in the end and these were not the days when clubs carried a huge squad and practised player rotation. The same handful of players played week in and week out in a gruelling season. Exhaustion and burn-out was the result and they had not one trophy to show by the end.

Harry Potts maintained that they actually won the title a season early. At this stage the partnership between him as manager and Adamson as skipper was firm and seemingly unbreakable. Wolves might argue that it was they who threw the title away rather than Burnley winning it in May 1960. In the Maine Road dressing room after the final triumphant game Adamson sat back and contemplated what they had achieved. That a small-town provincial club should win the title was astonishing.

Until the final ten games of 1962, Burnley simply crushed any opposition, not by brute force but with football of a skill and quality that was in some games quite breathtaking. The moves and passing were a joy to watch and huge scores were frequent. Jimmy McIlroy was runner-up in the Footballer of the Year awards. It was a season when Burnley Football Club might have achieved the double but it was not to be. Adamson was featured in the *Daily Express* (a broadsheet then) on the morning of the Cup Final.

'When I have whiskers I hope somebody will come to me and say: "I remember Wembley way back in '62. What a wonderful game that was,"' he said.

'That is what this game means to me – more than money, victory or anything else. I want Burnley to win. Don't have any doubt about that. After all, I've been at Turf Moor since I was 17, which is nearly half my life. But, we hope it won't be a dull game as many other finals have turned out to be and we hope there won't be any injuries.

'Both teams can put on a great show and I hope that the circumstances permit both sides to play the attacking, entertaining game that they are capable of. Spurs are a fine side. They have been worthy representatives of England in the European Cup. They have a lot of power and skill. We respect them but we do not fear them. In fact I think they are inferior only to Burnley.

'Much is said about the great spirit in the Burnley club. We at Burnley don't talk about it. It is taken for granted. Skill comes first. All the other factors count and club spirit as much as any. But you must get them in their correct order.

'Why have we slumped? Why did we lose our grip on the championship? I refuse to make any excuses. Every club has a bad spell. We hit one. Where we were taking half chances earlier, we did not take better ones later. It is rubbish to suggest we have gone over to a defensive game.

'Today's is a different game altogether. We know we are at Wembley. We will be more relaxed and confident. We are determined to put on a good show. But make a forecast – no sir.'

These were stirring words but looking back it's easy to suggest that they masked a deflated side and someone as shrewd as Danny Blanchflower might well have seen through the bluster. Some of the players in later years referred to the occasion as being flat. It was almost as if it was enough of an achievement to have been finalists. And, on the next page of the *Daily Express*, it was Blanchflower advertising Peter England Stylesetter shirts in a lucrative deal, not Adamson. It was Spurs bringing an early kind of glamour to the game in 1962, not the team from the grey, industrial north.

In truth the Burnley performance at the Cup Final was limp and listless. The spark had gone with Jimmy McIlroy below par, less than 100 per cent fit, and the whole team suffering from an end of season when the final ten games had seen them win just once and Ipswich snatch the title away from them. Until March they had been magnificent, playing some of the finest football of any season so far. And then it all went wrong.

It was no coincidence that Jimmy Mac missed several of those final games. In his most recent biography, *Prince Of Inside Forwards*, he tells the story that on the actual morning of the Cup Final he met people from Italian club Sampdoria and was offered a fortune to play in Italy. If his mind wasn't on the game, was it any wonder? But the man of the match on the Burnley side was Jimmy Adamson and his dignity afterwards was immense.

The late Ralph Coates remembered the Cup Final banquet in the evening, saying, 'I was on the ground-staff at Burnley when I watched the Cup Final. We were all taken to Wembley for the game. Jimmy Adamson was captain of Burnley and was just making his speech after the meal. What sticks in my head is Bill Nicholson and Danny Blanchflower came in while Jimmy was speaking. They stood at the edge of the dining area. Jimmy noticed them and at the time Danny was advertising Weetabix and Jimmy saw them and said, "And yes Danny, we all had Weetabix for our first course tonight." It was a nice moment. Jimmy then stopped his speech and welcomed Bill and Danny and everyone stood up and clapped, congratulating each other. I don't think that would happen in today's game.'

For Jimmy Adamson though, Cup Final disappointment aside, the significance of 1962 was the invitation to accompany Walter Winterbottom to the World Cup finals in Chile as assistant manager. Not only did he have his coaching qualifications and had been a staff coach at Lilleshall with Winterbottom, but he also had a persona that was statesmanlike and he gave an aura of being earnest, dedicated, ultra-professional and supremely knowledgeable. He spoke in his slow, measured way, and people listened. He was seen as the fulcrum of the ideas and the elegance that had oozed from the Burnley side at its peak and it was known that under Harry Potts he had been responsible for many of the training routines at Gawthorpe.

In November 2008 former player Colin Waldron was contacted by a historian at the National Football Museum. He was keen to learn why Jimmy was never selected to play for his country. They had been trying to contact Jimmy for some time but had received no response. The historian, having discovered that Waldron visited Jimmy every Christmas, asked Colin if he would visit Jimmy again and ask him the question. Both Colin Waldron and Paul Fletcher made the visit early in December with the intention of dropping the question into their usual topics – Bob Lord, Harry Potts, the Team of the Seventies and Burnley in general.

'Boss, how come you never got selected for England?' they remembered asking him along with pretty much most of his answer.

'I was a bit mystified myself,' he began. 'The manager, Walter Winterbottom, always wanted me to take the training sessions and work on all the free kicks and set pieces, which was odd as I was only in my late 20s. For a match he wanted me sat next to him in the dugout and he would discuss the game with me as it progressed. On a number of occasions at the pre-match meetings when he announced the team, I sat there waiting for my name to appear but it never did. In those days nobody ever questioned the manager. When he left the position he recommended me as England manager, but I turned it down. I've often wondered why he didn't pick me in his team.'

Adamson's appointment as assistant met with general approval and although he was registered with FIFA as a potential player, the FA explained that he was going to Chile principally as a coach. His team-mate John Connelly, a winger who could play on either flank, was also in the party. His room-mate at the training camp was Bobby Robson who after injuring an ankle in a knockabout game in Peru was unfit for the whole tournament.

Everyone departed on 17 May for Lima where the team was due to play Peru. It was a 17-hour journey via New York and then Kingston, Jamaica. The big surprise was the inclusion of a young Bobby Moore instead of Bobby Robson in the team to face Peru.

After a reasonably easy win, Winterbottom and Adamson had reasons to feel pleased with the performance as they left for Chile the next morning.

In 1958 for the World Cup England had chosen to stay in a large and busy hotel where there was minimal peace and quiet between matches. This time the FA chose a camp that was totally the opposite. At the invitation of the Braden Copper Company they based themselves at Coya, a small settlement 2,500 feet up in the Andes and an hour's ride away from Rancagua where England were due to play the first group games. Coya, located amid the trees on either side of a river, was the home of the company's executives and their families. It was quite the opposite of the capital Santiago and all its frantic clamour.

The players occupied three large bungalow-type buildings that were normally used as a rest centre for the executives from the company's various settlements. Two players shared a twin-bedded room with its own bathroom. The meals were served in a large dining room with the cooking done by an Englishwoman, Mrs Bertha Lewis, who fussed over them all like a mother. The training pitch was just a few yards away along with a golf course, a cinema of sorts where most films had Spanish soundtracks, a 'sort-of' ten-pin bowling alley and several tennis courts. None of this cost the FA a penny. Apart from food the copper company provided everything free of charge and even the golf clubs were provided, courtesy of the employees who loaned them to the players.

Jimmy Armfield remembers one round of golf with Ray Wilson when a young local lad offered to caddy. As the lad became exhausted Armfield carried the caddy and Wilson carried the two bags of clubs. It all sounds idyllic but in fact it was so basic that today's pampered players would not tolerate it. None of the squad was presented with complimentary shoulder bags brimming with computer games, iPods and touchpads. The England squad of 1962 had a few packs of cards and an occasional sing-song. The giant spiders they found in the bedrooms looked like the sort you could buy in a joke shop. Trouble was; they were real.

Armfield remembered a club where they could play billiards, snooker and table tennis. The cinema occasionally showed an American film. When a Brigitte Bardot film was shown one night, alas it was in French with Spanish subtitles but it was the only time there was a full attendance of all the England party. Armfield recalls they sat glued to it.

'How Walter found the place I'll never know,' he summarised.

'Spartan,' said Bobby Robson.

But one thing was remembered by everyone who went and that was the friendship and hospitality of the Grant family from the USA. Grant was the copper company manager and his home was an open house to all the England party. On the final night he entertained the whole party to a farewell dinner that Armfield described as fit for a king.

Even though it was only an hour from Rancagua, nevertheless it was remote and isolated with few if any distractions or intruders. The ride into Rancagua was time-consuming and bumpy over an old bullock track by bus or, the alternative and usual route down and to the stadium and then back up again was the single railway track and carriage that resembled a converted bus that wound its way round the mountainside. On their arrival the train had been festooned with flags for their first ride up into the hills. A little band played and greeted them when they arrived.

Even the stadium was owned by the company and they had built a new stand and dressing rooms. It was set in the Valley of the Flowers with the Andes towering in the background. Surrounding the running track were hundreds of geraniums and the entrance to the ground was through a series of flower beds. Even though it hadn't rained for weeks the pitch was fresh and green. Rancagua was a typical Chilean town with pockets of affluence but a lot of poverty.

If the training camp sounded idyllic to the bosses of the England team, or to the stressed and harassed employees of the Braden Copper Company who went there to recharge their batteries, it was far less so to the England players. No different than easily bored footballers of today, the players of 1962 craved a bit of life and action.

Jimmy Greaves recalled, 'A five-star holiday resort, this was not. One of my clearest memories is of Adamson's Burnley team-mate, John Connelly, sitting on a cornerstone on the training pitch, simply staring into space for hours on end. It was also, as a working mine, completely dry of alcohol. One evening the boss tried to alleviate our crushing boredom by allowing us all out to the only bar within a ten-mile radius.

'As we got on the bus, thirsty for a taste of freedom, Jimmy Adamson told us that, while we were free to have a couple of jars, we were at a World Cup, we were representing our country and we had to act like ambassadors. Anyway, a few hours later, as we clambered back onto the bus, Jimmy was standing at the front by the driver, this time leading the singing of salty songs on account of him being more inebriated than any of us.'

Bobby Charlton also remembers the boredom that some players experienced. There was a story that as soon as he arrived, Bryan Douglas said he felt homesick already. For players who didn't get a game out there there was real monotony and feelings of 'what am I doing here?' Charlton recalled one player who didn't actually play imploring his team-mates not to score so that they could get home sooner. Even if he wasn't serious, it was a joke that was symptomatic of the mood of several of the squad. It was something that Jimmy Adamson was well aware of and spoke to Charlton about it on the journey home.

Adamson knew that a different approach, a new psychology, was required when a squad of players was far away from home for up to three weeks or more. He knew as a player himself that most players had domestic and personal anxieties and worries that they could transport with them to any overseas tournament, and that homesickness was a real stress for some of them. If Winterbottom was the 'schoolmaster' it was Adamson straight from the shop floor in tune with the needs of footballers.

A player's problems might be real or imagined, but that didn't matter, what mattered was how they were recognised and addressed. Not that this made him a soft touch, anyone who ever played for him will refute that; he was indeed hard-headed about the demands that had to be made, and indeed should be made playing for England. What he also realised up in the mountaintop retreat was that if not all players felt fully involved then this was the fault of management, not the player.

Winterbottom and Adamson had two concerns. Firstly the organising committee had decided that there would be no play-offs or replays in any round but the final. Goal average would count in the preliminary games and if teams were still level then the result would be settled with the toss of a coin. Along with other managers, Winterbottom and Adamson pointed out that it was ludicrous that teams should travel all this way and then face elimination simply on the toss of a coin. They argued that they would rather lose in a play-off through exhaustion. Their second concern was the use of the lighter Chilean ball, something that European teams were simply not used to in 1962. The Brazilians retorted that using the heavier European ball in 1958 hadn't stopped them winning that particular tournament.

The 1962 World Cup finals were not the finest. This was the tournament that came to be characterised by, and remembered for, violence on the pitch, some terrible physical confrontations and frequent injuries, many of them deliberately inflicted. Game after game was marred by ill-temper with one of the leading Santiago newspapers describing the whole thing as 'World War'. At one stage the organising committee called all 16 managers together to warn them that the dirty football and strong-arm tactics would not be tolerated and that teams faced the risk of being sent home. The worst of these war-games were in the preliminary rounds when teams were unashamedly intent on not losing and were determined to stay in the competition at all costs. Time and again the topics of conversation were the tough tactics and the intent of some sides to maim the other, with demonstrations of skill and good football at a premium.

England's first game was against Hungary and fortunately it was a football match rather than a bad-tempered battle. It was on a difficult pitch, the ball often skidding away causing errors. The grass was longer than the England players were used to. The 2-1 defeat was disappointing with England on the defensive for most of the 90 minutes. Only Armfield was impressive and would eventually be voted the outstanding full-back of the tournament. In front of just 5,000 spectators Flowers scored the England goal from a penalty.

The journey back up to the training camp was subdued; for Winterbottom and Adamson it was back to the drawing board and the next game was just 48 hours away against Argentina. Whatever Adamson did or said in the training sessions breathed new life into the jaded England players so that when they met Argentina they were in the right frame of mind to win 3-1.

A decent referee put a stop to the early rough stuff, the Argentinians having been involved in an earlier nasty game against Bulgaria. Once Flowers had put England ahead with another penalty, the nerves were settled and England comfortably mastered the team that had been tipped to win the tournament. Charlton scored the second, Argentinian heads dropped, and Greaves scored a third so that England with the right result against Bulgaria in the next game would be in the quarter-finals. The Argentinian consolation goal ten minutes from the end had no dampening effect on the cheerful return to the copper camp. There were smiles again.

Yet still the violence continued. It reached its climax in the Chile versus Italy game, one that brought shame to football. For anyone who ever saw it, the images are still clear of the outright thuggery that took place. Within four minutes referee Ken Aston ordered an Italian off the pitch but Ferrini refused to leave so the game was held up for ten minutes. It took armed police to protect him as he eventually left. The pitch quickly became a battlefield as players only wanted to kick each other and launch into flying tackles. Another Italian was sent off after a savage attack on a Chilean and at last, down to nine men, the Italians succumbed to two Chilean goals.

On the eve of the final round of preliminary matches, Sir Stanley Rous, president of FIFA, made a plea to all 16 nations that sportsmanship should return. Even taking into account the violence that had preceded it, the Chile Italy game had shocked everyone. The Rous plea must have had some effect; no more players were sent off and there were no more broken legs.

Delightful though the Rancagua setting might have been, the rows of empty seats in the stadium at every game robbed them of any real atmosphere. Hungary led the group with Argentina and England joint second but England had the better goal average. In their next game against the Bulgarians England faced the weakest team. It was the third game in eight days for England and defensive tactics prevailed. There is suspicion that Bulgaria were quite happy for England to proceed at the expense of the Argentinians and that they deliberately sat back.

Kostov headed a perfect cross wide from a perfect position when it would have been easier to score, cementing the suspicion. Even with Bulgaria having no interest in winning, England remained nervy and weary, yet played out the game for a forgettable 0-0 draw and progression to the quarter-final stage, with the crowd and press making their feelings clear at the boredom they had endured. Bobby Charlton described it as the worst game he ever played in.

The game between England and world champions Brazil, however, produced possibly the best football and contest of the tournament so far. The problem for Adamson and Winterbottom was whether to change the team and bring in players with fresh minds and legs. They chose not to for the game that would lead one team to the semi-finals. England missed good chances with Armfield having a superb game. Then Garrincha had a shot cleared off the line. The game ebbed and flowed, Garrincha getting more and more influential and eventually scoring the opening goal. It might have been thought that the floodgates would open but England equalised and proceeded to play so well that even the hardened press reporters began to think an England win was possible.

Alas Garrincha had other ideas, creating the goal for Vava to put Brazil two up. Not much later he scored his second goal with a 25-yard shot that dipped, swerved, curled and moved all over the place before landing in the net. The remaining England attacks were easily snuffed out but at least they had gone down fighting, so much so that some of them were broken-hearted at the end.

The likes of Armfield, Flowers and Charlton, however, knew they had put on a good show in front of hundreds of Brazilian fans who had made the journey. Jimmy Armfield was distinctly unimpressed by the incessant samba rhythms, saying, 'the only instruments are tin cans of every variety on which a hideous clattering tattoo is beaten interminably'. But what did impress him was the way in which it seemed on occasions the Brazilian football matched the tin-can rhythm when they were seeing out the game and showboating.

Armfield's words, written just a year later, about coaching a team could as easily have been said by Adamson. 'It is not sufficient to field 11 men fit as men can be. They must be a team. Good coaching alone can ensure that each has a perfect understanding with the others, so that each knows, almost by instinct in the end, where to move for a pass or to close a gap, how to play not only with the ball, but off the ball.'

Those words would become the foundation ten years later of Adamson's 'Team of the Seventies'.

Perhaps it was Bobby Charlton, in the second of his autobiographies, who gave the best insight into Adamson's role in Chile and the impact of his football philosophies. Today the name of Jimmy Adamson is often prefaced by the word 'great'. History and many football writers have frequently bestowed this distinction upon him.

Bobby Charlton devoted a complete chapter to him in his autobiography *My England Years*. Chapter 11, titled 'Jimmy Adamson Talks', is almost reverential.

Appointed in 1946, Walter Winterbottom had been England manager for 16 years. Recognition for a new kind of leadership was growing. Adamson had certainly impressed Charlton during the tournament who regarded him as a fine and intelligent professional with a body of opinion favouring him as a replacement for Winterbottom. The surprising thing is to read that not only did they sit and talk football for the whole of the journey home, but Charlton also visited Jimmy in Burnley. Jimmy lived then near Scott Park in Burnley at Western Avenue and Burnley supporter David Binns, a young lad then, remembers being fascinated when they spotted Charlton and other people from the world of football visiting Jimmy.

Charlton realised that here was a man capable of achieving major improvements in the way England were selected, trained and psychologically prepared. The more he talked to Adamson, the more he realised that a stronger form of leadership was required. Winterbottom was 'donnish' and immersed in theory, a teacher rather than a former player. Adamson knew the reality of playing and all the ups and downs of the professional game. He argued that any player had to raise his game a level to play for England, that more was expected and that character was as important as ability. Levels of exertion and responsibility were greater; actual performance was more important than potential.

He was appalled by the levels of homesickness he saw out in Chile and recognised that more attention had to be given to the overall mood of the squad. He said, 'Everyone has to feel that they have a part to play. If so-and-so plays well, it may be that he's relaxed in the company of those around him – and that he understands that this is a tough but relatively brief period in a player's career but one that could easily define the rest of it. Some degree of homesickness is inevitable, but if it gets out of control, it's a symptom of other problems.'

Charlton saw in that long journey home how different Winterbottom and Adamson were, the former trained to be a teacher who had come to the England job via a post with the RAF Association, while Adamson's basic training in life had come from being down a pit. He had never played for England, yet still had the standing and charisma to impress his fellow pros out on the England training pitch, his vital role being reminding the players of their basic strengths and the need to display them in a game. Charlton referred to his great authority.

His philosophy became apparent, one that he had formed as a player; that as a captain if he played badly, the rest of the team might play badly. A good pro was responsible to his team-mates especially those not so gifted. Adamson was specific about his requirements of individual players, and his requests were made in the language of a professional footballer.

Charlton wondered over the years what Adamson might have made of the England job if he hadn't been so immersed in the challenge of keeping Burnley in the company of the most powerful football cities in the land. And then he finally added something significant which echoes the basic theme of this book, 'The promise remained unfulfilled.'

The invitation to become England manager was duly made but was turned down. In truth, there is no great mystery why. Adamson never ever said a great deal about it but there were suggestions later that he was quite disillusioned with the 'pessimistic, griping attitudes of several of England's internationals'.

Another reference to the decision came in *The Times of Malta*. Quite how he came to write a series of columns for a Maltese newspaper is a mystery but he wrote 40 in all. In his column of 9 October 1962 he wrote:

'I went to Chile with the England squad in the summer as assistant to Mr Winterbottom. When he relinquished the post as from January the next year it was only natural for some to assume that I would be among the many applicants for the job. I want to make it clear that I did not apply. It is my belief that I have a couple of seasons or so still in me as a footballer, and taking part in the game still means very much to me. Every footballer reaching maturity in playing years knows how hard it is to hang up his boots. The first official indication that I was being considered came via my own chairman, Mr Bob Lord who was asked by the Football Association to sound me out as to whether I wished them to consider me for the job. It was a great honour to know that they wanted me but I felt that perhaps I was not yet equipped for such an exacting role and I politely declined.'

A month later he wrote again how he had still had time left in him as a player. There was speculation about who would replace Alf Ramsey at Ipswich with Ramsey due to take over the England job. Adamson was strongly linked with the post but again he confirmed that he had, as yet, no interest in management. Tellingly, he wrote that his future was at Burnley and that he wanted to finish his career there. He liked the locality and had a fine circle of friends. If Lord had discussed the England job with him it adds to the feeling that Bob Lord as early as 1962 was assuring him that he had a job for life there with Lord already seeing Jimmy as coach and then as manager one day.

In a magazine article shortly after the 1968 FA Youth Cup Final success he looked back on the decision and the reasons why he had turned it down, 'It sounds corny perhaps but I'm in love with Burnley just as much as I was in 1947 when I joined them as a junior player. My heart is with the club and with the town. I have had plenty of chances to leave and I can't deny it, but I'm glad I stayed. Put it this way, when you sow some seeds you like to watch and see them grow into something good. That's how I feel at Turf Moor now.'

His reasons therefore seemed on the surface quite uncomplicated. Or was there an unspoken reason? Was it something he could not possibly say publicly; that he saw the job as a poisoned chalice?

The FA was notorious for its team selection procedure. The days were gone when every position was debated with each committee member trumpeting their own particular favourites from goalkeeper through to the outside-left; when at its worst one of the selectors had been a Grimsby fish merchant. By skilled diplomacy and tact, at least Winterbottom had got it to the stage where he nominated his chosen team and then it was debated and finally agreed. By not insisting on all of his choices some of his nominations were more readily accepted. But it was still no way to select an England team.

Winterbottom had once described the process. When he first took the job each selector would arrive at the meeting with his personal list of who should play. Discussions would go on for each position until there were just two names for each position. So it went on all the way through the team until there was a final list of names. Winterbottom would then be asked to leave the room while the votes were cast for each position whereupon he was called back and informed of the final team selection.

He said, 'At least in later years I was able to present my team and then let them try to argue me out of it. The trick was to stick to the men who were most important and to make concessions to the committee in positions where it didn't matter so much.'

Adamson might also have looked at the organisational set-up. The players weren't quite treated as the lackeys and second-class citizens they had been in the days when Stanley Rous once remonstrated with Jimmy Greaves for having a slice of cake at the station cafeteria while waiting for the train. But nevertheless it was still an 'us and them' situation with the officials enjoying the first-class tickets and privileges and referring to the players by their surnames. In Chile there wasn't even a team doctor with the group. It was trainer Harold Shepherdson who distributed medication such as the diarrhoea and dysentery tablets every day. Peter Swan fell seriously ill with stomach problems and ended up in hospital.

If Adamson was wary of all this, who can blame him? One can possibly speculate that he might not have been as utterly single-minded as Alf Ramsey. Or, when he said he did not, as yet, have the necessary management experience, he might well have had in the back of his mind the lack of experience in dealing with the FA and imposing his own will and demands. Ramsey made it a condition that he would have sole responsibility for all team matters. Did Adamson have this same bloody-minded resolve or would he have acquiesced and continued with the same inadequate system? When he wrote that he was 'not yet equipped for such an exacting role', did he mean that he was not ready to face the FA mandarins and beat them down?

Nor will we ever know what part Bob Lord played in Adamson's decision. He knew full well the kind of FA people that he would have to deal with. It is certainly within the bounds of possibility that Lord might have done all he could to dissuade him from taking the job. How easy it would have been to talk in public of the great honour for Adamson and the club, but privately to make promises to him that there would be a role for him at Burnley for as long as he wanted it, if he stayed. On the other hand, there is also the possibility that his appointment as England manager would have appealed to Lord's ego and vanity. 'His' player and protege the England manager; how grand that would have sounded, especially as at this point Potts was still doing a fine job with yet more superb young players to come from the Gawthorpe production line.

Years later, Florence Angus, who used to babysit with her husband John for the Adamsons, said that May had told Jimmy she would not move to London with him; that she wanted to stay in Burnley. In the press, Adamson spoke about his reluctance to leave his home in Burnley and his wish to continue playing, telling another of his former players, Martin Dobson, in a much later interview, 'It was tied in but it would have meant the family moving to London. May and I decided it would be too much of an obstacle especially with a young family.'

His family was of the utmost importance to him and Burnley supporter John Lingard remembers bumping into Jimmy and his family one August:

'My recollection is seeing him at Hollingworth Lake in the 1960s with his wife and two daughters, driving a basic A35 Baby Austin car. His lifestyle was modest and the affluence of current footballers was not shared by the championship-winning side of 1959/60. Jimmy was unmistakeable to us Burnley supporting Littleborough kids, with his long neck, angular features and telescopic legs. He was slightly embarrassed by our recognition of him. Notwithstanding, he quietly acknowledged our presence, looked gently pleased with this "recognition" and then got on with life as a proud family man taking them for a local day out in the summer. No Mediterranean sunset for the Adamson family but just a view of the lake, the pleasure boats and the Pennine Hills faraway over Blackstone Edge.'

I could identify with all that. Hollingworth Lake was like a bit of the seaside inland, and in the austerity years with its boats, the bit of sandy shoreline, and some tea rooms with pots of tea and ham salads on the other side of the road, it was a day out for any family. Many were the times my father and mother took me there for a Sunday afternoon in the days when a 'Sunday drive' on uncongested roads was a weekend treat. You can almost picture Jimmy and May in the front of the tiny car, the two young girls in the back, setting out from Burnley for their Sunday excursion driving through the Cliviger Valley, then through Todmorden and at Littleborough heading off to the lake.

But then, there was a telling comment, just six words long, in the Martin Dobson conversation: 'In hindsight, we regretted that decision.' The regret at not taking the England job may well have been to do with the way things went sour for him at Burnley as the team he built in the 1970s was sold one by one, and his eventual departure was ignominious and thoroughly unpleasant.

The one certainty, however, is that Adamson, by turning down the England job, unwittingly did English football a huge service. Whereas Adamson 'might' have won the World Cup in 1966, Alf Ramsey actually did win it. The England win was Ramsey's win. They were his team selections and they were his tactics. Perhaps it was only Ramsey who could have tamed the FA hierarchy at that time. The players were 'his' players and today those that remain are still devoted to him.

Ironically, after England's failure to qualify for the 1974 World Cup, while Ramsey's star had waned and the FA knives were being sharpened in readiness for his dismissal, that of Jimmy Adamson was rising spectacularly at club level. His prediction that Burnley would be the 'Team of the Seventies' was almost succeeding with a style of football that was a delight to watch.

Sadly, what Adamson would discover in 1976 was that his dream was unravelling; he did not have the job for life that Bob Lord talked about, and Lord had become a nightmare to work for. No doubt he did think at that point about what might have been and the glory that could have come his way as England's manager.

Chapter 6

From player to coach

IT HAPPENS to all footballers. Age, aching bones, bad backs, knocks and bruises take their toll. Recovery rates lengthen and the day comes when much as they would love to continue, common sense and weary limbs suggest the time has come to call it a day. It happened to Jimmy Adamson in 1964.

It was a time of transition said manager Harry Potts and chairman Bob Lord. Just over a year earlier the incomparable Jimmy Mac had been sold and 1963/64 was the first full season for many years without him. It was debateable as to what was talked about most in Burnley, the sale of McIlroy or the Great Train Robbery that same year.

Most of the great title team were still at the club and other than Jimmy Adamson were still only in their late 20s; Blacklaw, Angus, Elder, Miller, Adamson, Connelly, Pointer, Robson and Harris. But appearances by Robson and Pointer were intermittent and Elder was absent for the first half of the season. Adamson was almost totally absent and in came Brian O'Neil. Andy Lochhead was by now in the team and Willie Morgan would emerge in the second half of the season.

But not all was well; the team was inconsistent, players were asking for transfers, the season was plagued by injuries, gates were falling, and there was restlessness and uncertainty about the future. The city clubs were pulling ahead and swathes of fans could not relate to a Burnley without Jimmy McIlroy. The team was likened to an orchestra without a conductor. The end-of-season summary in the local press was, 'A grand season of mediocrity.'

Nor were Adamson and team-mate Gordon Harris the best of friends. You messed with Gordon Harris at your peril as more than a few opponents found out in their time. There was certainly a serious incident in training when Harris had flared up and retaliated when Adamson appeared to be goading him. It happened during an indoor training session and Potts ordered all players to say nothing about it. It was, after all, no less than the Footballer of the Year, and former assistant England manager, who had been laid out.

It was described as a scuffle but was serious enough to warrant a meeting of the directors. But somehow, it appeared in the papers and goalkeeper Adam Blacklaw could only suggest that one of the players must have leaked the story. Potts denied that he himself had seen it, saying there was no incident in his presence. What he did though, was take Harris to Adamson's house where for 30 minutes they discussed the matter. When they came out Harris was furious that it had become public but Harry Potts persisted in saying to a *Daily Mail* reporter that there had been no incident.

'There has been a lot of fuss about nothing,' he said. 'I was told there had been a fight between Gordon and Jimmy. I had been with the players all morning and hadn't seen anything. Nevertheless I decided to investigate. Gordon came to see me and together we came to sort this business out. Nothing at all took place as far as I can gather. Gordon and Jimmy are the best of pals and deny there was any argument or fight.'

Willie Irvine, who was to make his debut not long after the incident, remembered it, saying, 'What happened is still crystal clear in my mind. For a start the two of them weren't getting on very well. In the game in which some of us ground-staff lads were playing at the end of training, matters came to a head. Adamson body-checked Harris. They had words. Jimmy Adamson laughed. Adamson again body-checked him and this time brought him down. Nobody could say that Jimmy wasn't brave but you could sense that Gordon was not best pleased and wanted retribution.

'He kicked the ball hard against the gym wall and in the same movement kicked Adamson up into the air. As Jimmy came down

Gordon caught him with a solid punch and Jimmy landed with the blood running from his nose into his mouth. I stared wide-eyed at him lying at my feet with the blood in his mouth and him making funny little gurgling noises. Gordon turned and walked straight out of the gym without a word. The newspapers said that Harry took him to Jimmy's house so that he could apologise but to my knowledge he never did.'

The 1963/64 season began with great optimism. Jimmy Adamson announced that he wanted to carry on playing for another two or three seasons but by now recurring back problems bedevilled him. Nevertheless, he and other senior players believed that another position in the top six was achievable even though there was no Jimmy McIlroy and the bigger city clubs were beginning to dominate the game. As it turned out it was a poor season compounded by the controversial defeat in the FA Cup at West Ham. Bob Lord described West Ham's third goal as one that should have been disallowed for an obvious foul. Gordon Harris was in the news again for knocking out West Ham's John Bond.

As the season went on it was clear that Adamson's playing career was drawing to an end, and speculation grew about his future. Bob Lord was certainly thinking about what to do and there was conjecture that someone would move aside to make room for Adamson to take a coaching role. There were already rumours in one newspaper that this would happen but Lord and Adamson denied any such move.

Lord announced that he did have something in mind but it hadn't been implemented yet. But he emphasised, 'Jimmy Adamson goes with the wallpaper at Turf Moor. One day Potts and Adamson might well form a team at the head of the dressing room.' Indeed, it would not be long before Adamson officially became coach.

Only the FA Cup provided any joy. The further they got, the more hope grew that the club was heading for Wembley again as one by one Rotherham, Newport County and Huddersfield were taken care of with Adamson making rare appearances. In the quarter-final they were drawn against West Ham United.

They were expected to win but the game ended in a controversial defeat with Bob Lord furious in the newspapers. Adamson would not return to Wembley. Not that he was guaranteed a place anyway in a season of injury and only occasional fitness.

The FA Cup game against Huddersfield was one of his rare games; his first in four months but he was outstanding. One report read:

> 'A re-organised, re-vitalised Burnley had little difficulty in reaching the Sixth Round of the FA Cup when they beat Huddersfield Town 3-0 before a crowd of 39,307, their biggest of the season. The game was a triumph for Burnley boss Harry Potts who had shaken Turf Moor fans by bringing back Adamson, Pointer and Harris to his Cup side. How they justified his confidence in them in a display which had a vintage Claret look about it.
>
> 'Adamson, the midfield master, strolled through the game with a confidence that was a tremendous inspiration to his colleagues. He hardly broke into a sweat as he relied on his vast experience to make Burnley tick. In his own inimitable style he calmed down his defence and prompted his forwards to a less hurried and more accurate display than they have given previously this year.
>
> 'Master tactician Adamson provided a fine steadying influence on his thoroughbred forwards and his ability to dictate the pace and pattern of the game was something that Huddersfield could not match with a top-class display of generalship... Feeding the sleek machine Burnley with rich measured doses was the delightful Adamson, gracing the team with his cool elegance for the first time since early October.'

It was the kind of superb display he had been producing for the last decade and he kept his place for the game at Blackpool but back trouble struck again. He said afterwards he didn't want to make excuses for what had been for him a poor performance, 'But I felt my back go after about ten minutes and it troubled me for the rest of the match. My back is very sore indeed at the moment.'

Three days before the start of the season he had already strained his back in training and missed the first 11 games. On his return in October he outlined that he had always had back trouble and thought that this time the pre-season injury had put him out of the game for good. After the Blackpool game it would do exactly that. It had almost ended his career two years earlier. In later years he always maintained that it was ironic that he ended his playing career at Blackpool, and then his Burnley managerial career as well.

It was 1964/65 when Bob Lord put his plan into action. Not until the ninth game of the season did Burnley win for the first time. Maybe it was during this period, that included a 5-1 defeat at Sheffield Wednesday, when Bob Lord began to feel that he needed to give Adamson more of a say in team matters and that new ideas were needed. Speculation ended when an official announcement was made a week after Sunderland were refused permission to speak to him about their managerial vacancy. It is reasonable to assume that the Sunderland approach made Bob Lord's mind up for him and he now felt he had to tie Adamson down to the club before any other club moved in and tempted him away.

This was not a man he wanted to lose to any other club. It was a player-coach position that he was offered since Adamson hadn't quite accepted his playing career was over. The announcement caught everyone by surprise and even Keith McNee, the *Burnley Express* man, described it as 'coming out of the blue'.

Harry Potts was given a new five-year contract as manager. Lord clearly still had confidence in him, or, saw him as the figurehead while Adamson would pull the strings on the field. Adamson was given a five-year contract as first team coach. It is speculation, but Bob Lord must surely have been thinking already that he would change the manager at the end of the five-year period? In theory it was the dream partnership; in practice it was doomed to failure as Adamson more and more wanted to impose his own ideas and tactics on the team and became more and more frustrated.

Some who played in the potentially great team of 1965/66, when they finished third in the table at the end of the season and were good enough to have won the title, pointed to Adamson as being the reason why they didn't go on to the ultimate success because of his growing influence and tactical meddling and restrictions. This was the team of Ralph Coates, Willie Morgan, Brian O'Neil, Gordon Harris, Willie Irvine and Andy Lochhead. Gone were the days of the simple instruction to go out and enjoy yourselves, take a man on and beat him, and just make sure you pass to a claret shirt. As the season progressed the tactical alterations began.

Arthur Bellamy, who was making his mark in the team, noted the changes, saying, 'When Jimmy Adamson became coach things changed a bit. Harry Potts was never a great tactician but Jimmy introduced new routines, moves and free kicks. Harry's championship side had one way of playing and that was to go forward and attack and the number of goals they scored shows that. But as the 1960s went on, the next game was planned more carefully. Gradually Jimmy became more and more responsible for the training; things became more tactical and planned. The man from the next era was slowly replacing the man from the old.'

These changes did not go unnoticed by supporters and while a year later reports linked Adamson with vacant managerships at Aston Villa and West Bromwich, there were muttered mumblings on the terraces about his 'tinkering'. Regarding the rumours of moving to another club and the criticisms of supporters he said, 'I've heard nothing official but you can say that I have no wish to leave Burnley. I still have three years of a five-year contract to serve. I am happy at Turf Moor, and I believe Burnley are happy with me. If I didn't think the board had confidence, I wouldn't be here.'

More tellingly he added, 'You can also say that I feel some Burnley supporters would like to see me go to another club. They have been critical of our tactics and I must take a share of the blame. In fact I deserve to be criticised.'

The criticism was aimed at the lack of pace, stopping the ball before using it, the sideways square passing, the slow build-ups and the concentration on taking no risks and keeping possession. Players who had what might be described as a 'free spirit' and a sense of adventure were shackled by the new mantra, and all of this put the brakes on the superb team that was heading towards the title in 1965/66. It is absolutely true to say that Adamson's first years as coach were far from successful. In fact it took him until the back end of 1971/72 to find the formula that brought success.

Nevertheless, having won third place in the league at the end of 1965/66, Burnley qualified for the Inter-Cities Fairs Cup the following season. The new campaign began with three straight wins and just one defeat in the first 12 games. Football writers in raptures over the performances descended on Turf Moor and Gawthorpe to analyse the secrets of their success. The firm forecast was of a top six position and it was not Harry Potts taking the credit but Jimmy Adamson. He was the man described as grooming this next batch of players that had come off the production line.

The most significant article came in the highly prestigious American publication of the time, *LIFE*. This was a large-format, glossy periodical with a worldwide circulation. It was astonishing to find a feature about small-town Burnley Football Club in such a glamorous magazine, and in it the pictures included a magnificent full-page action shot of Brian O'Neil. The text, however, focused on Adamson:

> 'Football is a living as well as a passion for the team, for Jimmy Adamson, 37, the lithe, greying head coach who fills somewhat the same role as a film's director, and for portly, short-fused manager Harry Potts, whose job is like that of a producer.'

It is reasonable to assume that Potts's wife, the feisty Margaret Potts, would have bridled at this short and almost cartoon description, 'portly and short-fused' of her amiable and agreeable husband Harry. It was the only mention for Potts while Adamson took centre stage:

> 'Adamson holds a light rein but they say his players would charge smack into a brick wall if he told them to. On Saturday, Adamson moves among the nervous players as they dress; quietly telling them each what performance he expects that day.'

An almost full-page black and white picture shows him sitting with Willie Morgan giving him his instructions. 'When wingers are hot, Burnley usually scores well,' says the caption.

By this time, Burnley had comfortably disposed of Lausanne in the Fairs Cup, then Naples although not without a vicious game at Turf Moor and then the most appallingly violent scenes in the away leg. After a 0-0 draw there they came back absolutely shell-shocked. There was a good, well-earned 1-1 draw away at Eintracht Frankfurt. 'What a glorious night,' said the headlines as the semi-finals beckoned. 'A great tactical triumph,' said Ronald Crowther in the *Daily Mail*.

Meanwhile, league form was decidedly average and that was the form that Burnley showed in the home leg against Eintracht. The home defeat had the critics out in force and the supporters were vehement in their clear criticism of Adamson.

'All we got was fiddling on the wings and the usual square passes'; 'This is the time for a shake-up'; 'Eintracht played football like we used to see at Burnley but since Adamson was appointed chief coach we have seen negative football'; 'When the job was left to Potts, Burnley were noted for their attacking football and the sooner he takes charge again the better'; 'This was the biggest flop of the lot'; 'The season is over'; 'A confused ragbag offering'; 'A baffling team selection'; 'Irritating tactics'.

The season also saw the emerging confusion developing as to exactly who was in charge, Potts or Adamson? Willie Irvine was dropped for the away leg at Naples and he silently fumed. He related in his book that it was Harry Potts who told him that he wasn't playing but Harry also told him the decision was nothing to do with him.

'But he was the bloody manager,' recalls Irvine. 'What did he mean it was nothing to do with him? Who was picking the team, him or Adamson?'

One game in particular was symptomatic of the problems. Comfortably winning 3-1 at Sunderland, the game was thrown away and Sunderland won 4-3. Potts was not at the game; he was in Zurich for the Fairs Cup draw so Adamson was in sole charge at Sunderland. After the game, Harry in his next programme notes did something that was rare for him and publicly criticised the display.

He wrote, 'Instead of building up our lead we proceeded to put the brake on our commanding enterprise ... In the light of what we had done earlier and could so easily have continued, the result from our point of view was ridiculous ... It was a punishing reminder of our folly ... The remedy is in our own hands and must not be ignored in future.'

In these words lay Harry's simple philosophy; if you have scored three then go and score four; don't sit back and settle for what you have. Whether intentional or not, it was a public rebuke for Jimmy Adamson.

Clashes and differences of opinion that took place between them, for now, were kept well quiet.

The season ended with a 7-0 humiliation away at Sheffield Wednesday and then a 4-1 thrashing at Turf Moor by Arsenal. A tame 1-1 draw with Everton closed the curtain. The spotlight that shone on Adamson in the *LIFE* article was well and truly dimmed.

The developing situation at Burnley was unhealthy and unsettling. Alex Elder was sold to Stoke City having requested a transfer. He pointed the finger at Jimmy Adamson as the reason. 'I left Burnley in August 1967 to go to Stoke City but not because I wanted to. I felt that my face didn't fit with the new coach of the side, one of my old team-mates, Jimmy Adamson. For whatever reason, we just didn't seem to hit it off when Jimmy took control, and I felt it was best that I leave.'

Elder was too used to the Potts philosophy of just go out and play your own natural game, but now there was a new man in control of coaching who made more demands on them, imposed restrictions on them, had 'game plans' and expected specific things of specific players.

Potts, he referred to as one of the last true gentlemen of football and his attitude towards the players was, 'I'll treat you as men and you'll respect it. And we did. He didn't lay down any laws such as, you will not drink after Wednesday, and we didn't as a matter of course. So we had a good time at the weekends and come Monday morning were back in slogging our guts out for the next game.'

That willingness to slog his guts out on a Monday morning changed as Adamson imposed his own philosophy. It didn't make the Adamson philosophy wrong, it simply meant that there were players who found it hard to adjust. And on one occasion when Willie Irvine called in at a club for what he described as just a couple of shandies, he was reported to Adamson and dropped for the next game.

It was becoming more and more clear that the partnership between Potts and Adamson was not working. There were similarities to that between Joe Mercer and Malcolm Allison at Manchester City. Adamson increasingly wanted sole control but as coach he still remained answerable to Harry Potts.

Ralph Coates remembered that following his debut it was Adamson who told him he would keep his place for the next game and that he should let his family know so they could come down and watch him make his home debut. Accordingly, a whole coach-load of friends and family made the journey from Hetton. But Coates did not keep his place and it was Harry who had decided that he would not be playing thereby overruling Adamson.

He recalls, 'Friday came and I bump into Jimmy Adamson in the corridor and he says he has nearly lost his job and the boss wants to see me. So I see Harry and he tells me I am not playing and Gordon Harris is back in the side. It was pretty clear that they'd had a row and Harry had told Jimmy he had no business telling me I would keep the place.'

It all added up to a growing confusion as to exactly who was in charge and whose instructions should be followed. If there is one thing that footballers want it is clarity but this was becoming blurred at Turf Moor and loyalties were becoming split.

The problem of split loyalties began to increase. Burnley became a 'buying' club. For years they had produced their own players but in the late 1960s there were gaps to fill in the playing staff.

Frank Casper from Rotherham was the first to be bought, then Colin Waldron from Chelsea, Jim Thomson also from Chelsea and Doug Collins from Grimsby. Martin Dobson was picked up as a 'free' discard from Bolton.

Years later, after a distinguished career as a player and then a successful spell in management at Bury, Dobson wrote about his early time at Burnley with Potts as manager and Adamson as coach and the relationship between Potts and Adamson still interests him. He found them to be a good combination although at the same time well aware that behind the scenes there might well have been differences. Adamson might well have been in control of coaching, organisation and tactics, but he did not control the one thing that mattered – team selection:

'When Jimmy Adamson retired from an illustrious playing career he was destined to become involved in coaching and then management. Why? Because of his knowledge, experience and love of the game. He was an innovator, always looking to move the game forward. But the basic beliefs always had to be adhered to and one of them was discipline.

'We were told that we must abide by the laws of the game and show neither dissent nor retaliation. We were told we were ambassadors for Burnley Football Club and, as such, we had a responsibility to future generations. Even after being given offside away from home we would be encouraged to bring the ball back and place it for the free kick. Both Jimmy and Harry knew what they were doing. It was explained that these little things would help us. The away fans would respond and applaud us. If you like someone you don't shout obscenities.

'In my first year at the club I was sub on a number of occasions. There was only one sub in those days so I sat with Harry in the dugout. Jimmy tended to watch the game from the stand. Harry changed on match-days. He became all consuming, shouting instructions and demanding more from each player. He was 'hyper', totally committed and sent the message to every player that he demanded the same passion and commitment. Then at half-time he was composed and informative.

'During the week they were a perfect combination. Harry the enthusiast, the smiling face always telling us even in the depths of winter when we came out to train at Gawthorpe with snow and freezing conditions how lucky we were to be involved in such a great game. "People are in factories and you boys are outside in the fresh air doing something you like, wonderful, just like Mont Blanc." And you know what, he was absolutely right.

'Jimmy would take the training and his coaching sessions were brilliant. Every day you'd learn something new; how to be a better player; how to win games; how to be a team; how to look after each other and how to be smart. So we had the best of both worlds; the enthusiasm, warmth and excitement of Harry and the brilliance of the master tactician that was Jimmy Adamson. To me, the relationship between Jimmy and Harry was perfect in the late 60s. Everyone can speculate about what happened between them and certainly their relationship did change over the years.'

Up until this point many of the players felt themselves to be a 'Potts man'. He had been the manager who had signed them, nurtured them as young lads, visited their families and taken them under his wing. It was a rare player that questioned his approach and philosophies. The great thing about Burnley up to this point was the 'family' spirit and the unity. The downside was the insularity. This was now about to change. 'Outsiders' were joining the club and two of them had worked with Tommy Docherty, bringing with them a different outlook and attitudes. One of them in particular, Colin Waldron, found Harry Potts hard to take.

Waldron became one of a rare breed, a player who eventually came to deeply dislike the avuncular Harry. There were confrontations between them. This was unheard of. Despite their differences Potts made Waldron captain and one wonders if this was at Adamson's behest. As captain, however, Waldron never felt any rapport with Potts, whom, as far as he can remember, never talked to him or asked him a question.

Some players noticed that Adamson had a distinct attitude towards Potts and even went as far as to say they sensed that he was 'after' the manager's job. But Waldron refutes this, saying that there was never any sense that Adamson was manoeuvring Potts out of the job because 'all of us were totally surprised by the announcement that Adamson would be the new manager so it couldn't have been something we suspected'.

The latter scenario of Adamson being made manager was still two years away and in the meantime the sense of discomfort and uneasiness grew. Bob Lord, shrewd man that he was, was increasingly aware that things were 'not right' in the dressing room.

Stan Ternent was another player to wonder who was in charge and in his book cites something quite curious. Ternent left Burnley in 1968, sold by Potts, but he recalls that a week before he was due to leave he was contacted by Adamson who urged him to stay. Adamson told him that Potts would be moved upstairs and he would soon be manager. Potts's and Adamson's five-year contracts were due to expire in 1970 so it is fair to think that Adamson clearly knew that he would be given the manager's job that year.

This fits in with Frank Casper's recollection that there was a major row between Potts and Adamson resulting in Adamson going to see Bob Lord to demand changes. Lord promised him that he would make the changes and there was an agreement between them that would enable Adamson to go ahead with his plans to play the team his way and Potts would be left to do the paperwork. According to Margaret Potts, Harry certainly had no knowledge of this meeting or what was going on.

Supporters too continued to be unhappy. A 2-2 draw at Manchester United prompted grumbles. Burnley had taken a 2-0 lead but threw it away. Letters in the papers blamed the Adamson tactics and formations for the ordinary season. Several demanded that the team went back to the old Harry Potts way, attack and be damned; if the opposition score two then never mind, we'll score three. Nostalgia grew for the good years that hadn't seemed all that long ago. The club finished 14th at the end of 1967/68 with Burnley struggling more and more to compete financially with the big city clubs. A procession of names left or were about to leave; Irvine, Elder, Blacklaw, Lochhead and Morgan.

John Connelly had been gone for some time but when he became dissatisfied at Manchester United there were moves to get him back to Burnley, initiated by Bob Lord. Significantly, he chose Blackburn, years later citing that he didn't want to return to a club where it was unclear who was in charge. It was a telling comment and indicative of the state of affairs that existed.

By now Adamson was clearly the dominant figure but it was Potts who was still manager. There were two opposing philosophies at work on the training field, one being the freestyle approach of Harry Potts and the other the far more technical and tactical approach of the coach. Supporters could see it too and made criticisms that defensive tactics were being stamped on the players. But it was Potts who fielded the criticisms of the faults that were being laid at Adamson's door.

In 1968, however, with little publicity, the youth team was making its way to the prestigious FA Youth Cup Final. Another batch of young kids had been unearthed and gathered largely by the persuasive powers of Harry Potts. Parents of young lads could identify with him and his homespun, fatherly approach. If Don Revie offered holdalls of cash, which he certainly did to Dave Thomas and his father in their parlour, Potts offered the prospect of good coaching and a fair chance to make the first team. Parents and the boys themselves knew they would be in good hands.

The best of Potts's managerial career was over but he would have one last triumph with the youth team. The victory in the

Youth Cup Final brought a measure of pride and a sense of achievement back to Burnley. On a dreadful and sodden night and a mudbath pitch Burnley overcame Coventry 2-0. Dave Thomas remembers the extra coaching that Adamson gave to them. Five of the team went on to have good careers in football; Dave Thomas, Steve Kindon, Mick Docherty, Alan West and Eric Probert. Dave Thomas would become a full England international. Without the Youth Cup triumph perhaps there would have been more angry letters to the local press than there actually were but the season ended with huge optimism.

It prompted Clement Freud to write a piece in *The Sun* lauding Potts and his relationship with Bob Lord. It read, 'Come wind or water on the field of play, his chairman gives him a weekly smile of reassurance and says; never mind lad, at least your job is safe. Go home and have a good night's sleep.' In the interview that took place to prepare the article, Potts naively told Freud he was probably the safest manager in football. He left the coaching to Adamson while he himself concentrated on policy and plans.

At this stage Potts still had two years of his manager's contract left but this may well have been the season that clarified Bob Lord's thinking, leading him to realise that at the end of the contract he had to let Adamson take over. There had been an 8-1 defeat at West Brom which hurt and embarrassed Lord, but he might well have thought that the future of the club was assured with this new batch of youth team players – especially with Adamson in charge of them.

England's win in the 1966 World Cup had changed football thinking and tactics and Adamson was one of the new breed of coaches changing the way the game was played. But while Bill Nicholson at Spurs had been able to adapt, Harry Potts had not and Bob Lord was sharp enough to have seen this. He could see Adamson knocking on the managerial door and knew by now that he wanted the job. Behind the scenes it had reached the stage when according to one player of the time, Adamson demanded of Lord that he kept Harry away from the training ground even though Harry was still manager.

Labelled as a 'soccer tactician' schooling his band of dazzling young footballers, Adamson was seen as producing a football revolution. He spoke of time and talent being on his side and how the game had changed since he had been a player:

'Since I stopped playing four years ago the game has changed tremendously. Our effort has been to put more emphasis on the attacking side of the game. These days, of course, a man of genius, a George Best, is simply beyond price. It is these players who hold the key to success, who can break out of the straitjacket. And at Burnley we believe that we have young players with the basic skill and flair to stamp themselves across a game which is becoming increasingly tighter.

'On the plus side there is the tremendous rise in the standard and volume of young players. This means that right across the game there will be more evenly distributed skill and proficiency. This is a direct result of the new high pressure coaching schemes which mean that the serious development of young players now begins at 15. But against this there has been the great increase in the more physical side. There was a time when a team realised that any honours were probably beyond them and settled on being simply a good football side.

'But that is a thing of the past. The result is a far more ruthless game than I had to play in. Quite frankly, I think I would find it a great strain keeping my temper, if I was playing today.'

For various reasons – illness, injury, loss of form – wholesale changes were made to the line-up in season 1968/69. The kids were brought in alongside players like Martin Dobson and Frank Casper and these 'Burnley Babes' had a run of six consecutive wins with an exhilarating brand of football. The highlight was a 5-1 victory at Turf Moor over the all-conquering Leeds United. It was a result that put the spotlight on Burnley; Revie was stunned and the media flocked to Gawthorpe to see how 'the Turf Moor boffins were once again having success in their laboratories'.

Prior to the game some supporters had questioned Adamson for playing so many young boys but Keith McNee, the local reporter, put them in their place afterwards and wrote, 'How weak their arguments look now. Their rifles still point towards Turf Moor, but what a shame; they appear to be clean out of ammunition.'

Revie was filled with praise and admiration. Steve Kindon had run Paul Reaney ragged the whole game but it was the young Dave Thomas who Revie described as the best prospect in Europe.

Yet, at this point it was very much Harry Potts in the national headlines not Jimmy Adamson; the latter possibly feeling more and more aggrieved and resentful.

In an article in *Northern Soccer Annual*, Adamson himself had the chance to explain all that was going on at the club:

'There is no magic formula to explain why our youth policy at Burnley is such a success and the envy of all the clubs around us in every division. The secret is that here we are thorough. Starting with our scouting system we have two full-time scouts and 12 part-time who operate on Saturdays and at evening games during the week. We pay particular attention to Scotland and are no longer drawing purely from the northeast of England where so many of our players have come from in the past. We are finding that this area is well covered so we have to cast our net further afield.

'It is becoming increasingly difficult to get the right standard of player. It used to be possible, years ago, to pick up talent quite easily but now the standard is getting higher and you've got to get in and capture budding players when they are quite young, even looking at 12- and 13-year-olds. Even at a county trial match nowadays you'll find that out of the 40 or 50 boys, as many as a dozen or twenty are already signed up to professional clubs.

'We used to be predominantly a Geordie club and in a team we'd have as many as seven players from the northeast. In last year's successful youth team, we had only one.

'Gawthorpe Hall our training centre is just four miles from the club. This provides excellent training facilities with three grass pitches and one floodlit and two smaller five-a-side pitches. We have no less than six shooting boards where many clubs make do with just one. We try to go to Gawthorpe every day but if it is pelting with rain then we concentrate on work in the gym.

'Our indoor gymnasium, opposite the main stand at the ground, is also used by members of the public. This is a large gym, 145 by 90 feet. We've called the group who use the gym The Young Clarets. At the moment there are some 500 members. We're developing Burnley along the lines of a family recreation centre rather along the lines of Continental football clubs. We are planning to develop along the same lines and are going to spend up to half a million pounds on the social side. How this will develop we're not exactly sure but we have in mind things like a swimming pool, sauna baths and training and recreation facilities for every sport. Without the extra activities and the sale of players to the larger clubs, we find it difficult to survive.

'I have been at Burnley some 22 years now. Thus, I have seen a lot of changes and we have weathered problems in the past. I am sure we will in the future. We had a youth policy as far back as 1936/37 but it wasn't until the influence of Cliff Britton showed itself that we really started to develop. In 1947 we reached the FA Cup Final at Wembley and lost to Charlton Athletic. And, of course, in 1968 for the first time, we reached the final of the FA Youth Cup competition.

'At Burnley we field four teams under four coaches. All are qualified FA coaches and most of them are ex-Burnley players. Every morning we meet about nine o'clock to decide on the day's programme. This, of course, depends on several things – the weather, whether we have a midweek game, injuries and the availability of facilities. We only stay in the gym as a last resort and normally, we travel in coaches to Gawthorpe Hall. With a total staff of some 38, including juniors and ten apprentices, we find it best to split up into squads. So we generally work with four of these making team groups.

'We generally train mornings and afternoons, five days a week. This is mainly for the youngsters between 15 and 20 as we feel that it is at this stage of their development they must train hard on the basic skills of the game; skills like heading, shooting, passing and tackling. It is only practice that will produce a better player. There is no secret formula. We try to introduce as much variety as we possibly can into our training schedules. This we do by having good coaches and good facilities. We can go for as long as a fortnight doing something new every day without repetition. Divided into team groups we only mix in altogether on Tuesdays on what we call our "fitness day". On Tuesdays no teamwork is done at all and we concentrate purely on getting fit. This includes gym work, PE, running and so on.

'We are not a club that lets its players have Monday off. Sometimes we get together on Monday morning and discuss Saturday's game while it is still fresh in our minds. Then the afternoon is devoted to normal training. If we have a midweek game tactics are practised and discussed in the morning and the team get together just to loosen up. Then they go to bed for the afternoon and report about quarter to seven in the evening for the game. They will have the next day off completely. If it is an away game at the weekend they will report on Friday morning just to loosen up and for travelling in the afternoon. During the Youth Cup run in 1968 we often trained on Sunday afternoons.

'Of course, a youth policy takes time to develop and it is something you've got to stick at unceasingly. Our present success where we are fielding one of the youngest teams in the league is due to the efforts started four or five years ago, as the youngsters we took on then are just starting to show now. Of course we've had to go into the transfer market as well when we've needed quick replacements to fit a particular situation. But in the last three years we're one of the few First Division clubs that spent less than £100,000 on three players – and these three were all bought to fill particular gaps. In the same period we've sold six or seven, these being internal products that we brought up ourselves through our youth scheme. Over the period we are showing a profit.

'We had some reshuffles in our first team at the beginning of the 1968 season and this was the time we started introducing a lot of youngsters into our first-team squad. This was following the 3-1 victory over West Ham and since then we have had a run of wins.'

It was the 3-1 win that was the first of the six, the run that brought the temporary rave reviews. Adamson's article in the last two paragraphs went on to praise Bob Lord handsomely. Maybe that was significant, keeping old Bob sweet perhaps. But what was notable the more one thinks about it, is that there was not one single mention of Harry Potts, the manager.

The run of wins could not last however and mediocrity returned. A supporter who saw the game at Newcastle wrote, 'Watching Burnley move out of defence at Newcastle was like seeing my grandfather getting out of the bath.' There were more references to sideways passing, the lack of pace and the laborious build-ups.

At Turf Moor, 1969/70 was just more of the same; during the season 27 players were used. There were continued allegations of an unhappy camp and rumours of several transfer requests. Years later, Brian O'Neil told me that behind the scenes players grumbled, didn't know who was in charge, and were bewildered by some of the tactics. Other players were unhappy at Jimmy Adamson's sometimes sarcastic remarks about Harry when Harry wasn't around.

Local reporters Granville Shackleton and Keith McNee pointed to players such as Dave Thomas, Brian O'Neil and Steve Kindon, players with immense natural talents, having the brakes put on them and being subjected to the rule of the blackboard rather than what they did best spontaneously on the field. Taking a man on, and beating him, getting past him, was now taboo under the law of keeping possession. If Potts's game was all about the talent of the individual being given licence to express itself, then Adamson's was the new ethic of teamwork and 'the team player'.

There was just one win during the first 12 games. There were boos, whistles, abuse and a continued barrage of angry letters to the local press. There was no way it could continue. Bob Lord had to do something about it. But, what he did was totally unexpected when he granted Jimmy Adamson his wish. In February 1970, Lord rocked everyone by announcing that Jimmy Adamson would replace Harry Potts as manager and Harry would move into a new role as general manager.

It was doubly surprising in view of Harry's run of four wins in five games (the other was a draw) and the final game of that run saw a 5-0 win for Harry over Nottingham Forest. The switch to Adamson produced no immediate miracles with just three more wins during the remainder of the season. In fits and starts somehow Burnley reached a position of 14th by the end of the season.

Adamson had his wish, the 'top man' role. He was no longer answerable to Potts and he could do something else; he could as good as banish Potts from the training area. As Bob Lord and Jimmy Adamson became closer, the gap between Adamson and Potts widened.

Their relationship had entered a stage of terminal decline. Bob Lord's bloody-mindedness and refusal to listen to supporters' criticisms protected Adamson from the calls for his head. After five years of no great success since his appointment as coach, other than keeping the ship afloat in the top division, another chairman might well have had grave doubts about appointing him as manager. Therein lay the irony of his appointment.

And worse was to come.

Chapter 7

1970 takeover and a prediction

I WELL remember the hours I spent talking to Margaret Potts when we wrote *Harry Potts – Margaret's Story*. I used to travel over from Leeds to Burnley every week for something over six months to talk, listen to her stories, make notes and look through the boxes of pictures, letters and documents she had. Her memory was phenomenal and the collection of memorabilia was a treasure trove. I have a ring binder filled with the hand-written letters that she sent me between the meetings. Many of them are several pages long. Given the opportunity, she would have expressed her aversion to her mother-in-law on just about every page of the book. But someone else she was deeply offended by was Jimmy Adamson. Whether it was justified will always be debateable.

Margaret was protective of Harry and could see what was coming while Harry could not. What happened in 1970, the appointment of Adamson as manager and Potts's move to general manager, then continued until Harry's departure in 1972 and was deeply upsetting for her. In fact, by the end, her resentment turned to antagonism and never left her. Just as Adamson was later aggrieved by Lord, Margaret was equally angered by Adamson. Where once there was so much closeness, so much friendship, between people who were the bricks and mortar of the club, now there was just a cold distance.

More and more as the 1960s went by she liked less and less the way in which even though it was still Harry who was manager, it was Jimmy who was becoming the face of the club in interviews, the press and football magazines. Forty years later she still bristled at the memory of the *LIFE* magazine feature that as good as ignored Harry. On one of their first holidays abroad it turned out that the Adamsons were there as well and it particularly galled her that a doctor they befriended automatically assumed it was Adamson who was the manager. Margaret firmly put him right.

Whether she was right or not in her dislike of Jimmy, I suspect we shall never know. I remember I gently tried to tell her that what happened was that the new man with new ideas was replacing the old. It was a natural progression; it was the way football worked and still does. I talked with her and said that no one knows exactly what went on between Lord and Adamson, what conversations they had, what promises were made and when. No one knows for sure if it was Adamson, frustrated by the out-of-date Potts, who initiated things and persuaded Lord to give him the managership, or whether it came from Lord himself. We can only surmise. But both Lord and Adamson were members of a Masonic Lodge. Harry was not.

Martin Dobson summarised things succinctly, 'As the saying goes, "nothing stays the same".'

Another meeting in Burnley with Jimmy's two granddaughters, Katie and Sarah, went well. The box of old photographs was ready along with a delightful album of Jimmy as a young 17-year-old sitting with the ground staff on the pitch at Turf Moor, Jimmy in the RAF, Jimmy visiting family back in Ashington, Jimmy and May together, and there was the Scottie puppy as well, just a small ball of fluff and hair looking impishly at the camera.

One picture made me feel quite nostalgic and reminded me of my own childhood. It was a picture of the impressive bandstand in Centre Vale Park in Todmorden, my home town. It was June 1950 and there was a concert by the Syd Lewis Band. I would have been six years old and my father was a 'big-band' enthusiast. I have no recollection of being there but who is to say that we weren't there watching and listening; me, my mother and father, along with Jimmy and May somewhere close by?

Most of the pictures are tiny but from them you can glean the feeling of what Ashington was all about, families posing in front of doorways, the closeness of the community, the terraced houses, even a horse and cart in one picture. An occasional yellowing newspaper clipping fills a space; Jimmy was best man at team-mate Jock Aird's wedding in July 1950. And then a bit of a surprise: a clipping about Jimmy's debut game against Bolton and the reason behind it. There was to be a 'toning-up' trip to Southport due to last eight or nine days and two players had refused to go, goalkeeper Strong and right-half Attwell. They were therefore omitted from the team to play at Bolton. As it happened Strong resolved his differences and was selected. Attwell then developed tonsillitis and would probably have missed the game anyway. But that's how Jimmy got his chance and never looked back, thus beginning the partnership of Adamson and Jimmy McIlroy which was to bring so much success and glory by the end of the decade.

'He was a private man,' said Katie, 'and stubborn, but we had some lovely times with him as grandchildren. And so devoted to May; they were inseparable. He didn't really know what was happening to him at the end with the dementia and we were so glad about that. He and May were together even in the care home until she was taken away to a hospital in Blackburn. I'm not sure he was aware that she had gone. If by some chance he had known she was no longer with him, it would have broken his heart I think. They called us all to say that he was about to pass away but we got there just ten minutes too late. Just one person was with him, one of the carers, and the irony was – it was one of Bob Lord's relatives.'

I brought a few things home with me; a bundle of papers relating to a claim in 1981 for libel Jimmy made against the man who followed him at Leeds United, Allan Clarke, along with the club itself, various newspapers and Yorkshire Television. There was no indication of the result. The correspondence seemed to come to a sudden stop without any indication of a conclusion. Anyway there would be that to find out from interviews. Eventually I did find out what happened.

Something else I brought back was the letter of condolence that Katie had received from an old pal, Bill Ogilvie, who knew Jimmy as a schoolboy back in Ashington. It was a gem, mentioning how they had both played football and cricket for their school and done all the things that young lads do, collecting cigarette cards of footballers and cricketers and playing in the streets. There were no cars to disturb them, only the horses and carts that delivered groceries or fish or milk.

'Unquestionably he was the most accomplished player in schools football in East Northumberland ... Your granddad was one of the most respected professional players in England,' it finished.

And then there was something that had me wide-eyed. It was a small Basildon Bond writing pad that Katie showed me. Jimmy had made lists on ten of the 40 sheets. The lists were headed 'Good', 'Bad' and 'Evil'. It was reasonable to think they had been compiled in 1976 after his 'resignation-sack' as he called it at the foot of the first list headed 'Good'. In this he included the title win of 1960; next to it in neat print was '42 games'. The list continued with just one caution in 500 league and FA Cup games, the Cup Final of 1962, the championship of the Second Division in 1973, his relationship with players, singing in the coach, the Cat's Whiskers club presentation, first class travel, accommodation, tours to Majorca and on the *QE2*.

Next were the names of Winterbottom, Greenwood and Brown. Winterbottom was the England manager of course out in Chile. Greenwood would have been Ron Greenwood, who went on to become West Ham's manager, born in Worsthorne, a village just a couple of miles outside of Burnley. Like Jimmy he was a football thinker and tactician. The name Brown was less straightforward. Was it Alan Brown his former manager, or Joe Brown, Adamson's coach at Burnley?

Alan Brown seems the more likely. He revered Alan Brown in the 1950s but by 1976 when he was dismissed by Lord, there were reports that Jimmy was not exactly on best terms with Joe Brown. If that was the case he must surely have resented Brown's appointment by Lord as his replacement.

Towards the end of the list was being coach in Chile in 1962, Player of the Year in 1962, club outings to York Races and then a reference to the players' sympathy after his 'resignation-sack'. Finally he included Bob Lord's support for him following the relegation season. I couldn't help feeling that here was a magnanimous acknowledgement bearing in mind that these pages had probably been written after the same man had just sacked him.

Were the pages the musings of a man preparing for the scathing article about Lord that was never published? Were they the early notes for a possible book? If the latter was the case, how ironic that here they were and could now contribute to this book. Sometimes, a chance find opens up a surprise window and provides unexpected insights into a man's thoughts and feelings. Not only that, here was something to show to people that knew him well, the people I planned to meet and talk to; Colin Waldron, Paul Fletcher, Jimmy Robson, Stan Ternent, and Brian Flynn. On these pages were over 100 different headings, some of them cryptic but some of them immediately recognisable as referring to incidents and people during his time at Burnley. I held that writing pad in my hand for some time thinking that here I was seeing into Jimmy's mind and all of his concerns.

The final page was headed by the title 'Amusing'. It was the shortest of the lists. I found that sad.

* * *

Coach Adamson was bullish and believed that with a team made up mainly of members of the 1968 Youth Cup-winning side, along with players like Martin Dobson, Frank Casper, Colin Waldron and Ralph Coates, Burnley would win the league title not once but several times. 'Our potential,' he said, 'is better than that of all other clubs, and I do mean all. Some First Division managers would give their right arms for our teenagers.'

If there had been a game during which Adamson saw a vision of the future it must surely have been the 5-1 win over Leeds United on 19 October 1968. This was the Leeds of Giles, Hunter, Reaney, Bremner, Charlton, Gray and Madeley. Ten years later he would be managing some of them. This was a Burnley side containing names no one had heard of outside of the town – goalkeeper Harry Thomson who sadly died as this book was being completed, Blant, Latcham, Murray and Smith along with some who would eventually become better known, Thomas, Kindon, Coates, Dobson, Casper and Waldron. There was already bad blood between the two clubs because Harry Potts had criticised Leeds United and Don Revie in earlier seasons for all that their rough-house and win-at-all-costs style stood for. Harry had even challenged Revie to a TV debate but Revie refused.

It was a game in which the press oozed praise:

'The Burnley unknowns were truly inspired as they impudently toyed with the opposition. Time and again United's defenders were drawn out of position by the bewildering mobility of the Burnley forwards who all responded sharply to the inspiration and subtle guidance of Coates. The way in which Burnley find unknown young players and fashion them for stardom is their own enviable brand of magic. They are rich in promise and if their heads are not turned by fulsome adulation they should all make their mark in the game ... their capacity for producing the goods just when they seem about to join the other Lancashire clubs in the Second Division is enough to send rich clubs flocking to see what the Turf Moor boffins do in their mysterious laboratories.

'The best defence in England was thrown into confusion by players who have not yet achieved the status of household names in Burnley, never mind the country ... they buzzed around Leeds United like a swarm of angry bees, got into their hair and stung them well and truly five times. Their enthusiasm was extraordinary, their speed and stamina remarkable and their individual talent considerable ... Ralph Coates was Raich Carter class ... Thomas is as tricky as a football cat ... and Kindon runs like a horse.'

Even Don Revie was impressed and judged Dave Thomas as being one of the finest talents in Europe. It was a display that stayed in Adamson's memory for a long time. If his boys could play like this against Leeds United, surely there was no limit to what they could achieve when they matured. In 13 previous games Leeds had conceded just ten goals and they would go on to win the title while losing just two games. What Adamson's boys did to them was remarkable.

In the 1969/70 season Burnley were putting a team out with an average age of just 21. No fewer than eight members of the youth side had seen first team duty. Dave Thomas, Steve Kindon and Mick Docherty were regulars with what the press, as well as Adamson, judged as having brilliant futures in the game. No matter what features you came across in the press, most if not all of them referred to Adamson as one of the top coaches, 'a brilliant mentor and strategist' in the English game, with his reputation increasing by the day.

'Rated as one of England's finest coaches' became a frequently used description of him, even though results were patchy and inconsistent. What was clear, however, was that it was a minor miracle that Burnley were still competing in the top division, and Adamson, 'much admired', along with the youngsters he was nurturing was seen as one of the major reasons.

The question was asked several times why Adamson preferred to stay at Burnley. 'Why is it that this tall, greying son of Northumberland continues as a number two in such a quiet corner of East Lancashire when he could without doubt have been manager of a top glamour club?'

What journalist James Lawton said shortly before Adamson took over as manager was typical:

'Jimmy Adamson dresses formally, talks in the precisely clipped tones of a rising executive, and only if hounded into a corner will admit that his grand ambition is to work a revolution. Like most revolutions, the one at Burnley, where Adamson schools his band of dazzling young footballers, has had its reverses. But Adamson and much of English soccer believe that a bright banner has been raised across what has become a mostly sterile battleground, where the instinct is to survive rather than succeed.

'He believes too, that on his side is both time and talent and he says, "Burnley have been tagged a blackboard team but I simply do not understand how this has come about. Our policy is to concentrate on our own skills rather than the opposition. Of course modern football insists that you have to study the technique of opponents, but I disagree with the trend of the last few years which has been trying to organise the other team out of the game. What we have attempted to do is inflict our own ability on the opposition, make them counter our own ideas."

'You will have gathered that Adamson, like his contemporary, Jimmy McIlroy, views the advance of modern soccer with serious misgivings. But in terms of black and white he can see one massive gain, and a reverse of the same dimension.'

'ADAMSON IS NEW CLARETS MANAGER' said the shock headline.

The feisty Margaret Potts, never short of an opinion in an age, and certainly at a club, where a woman's place was to be seen and not heard, was furious at the events that saw her husband replaced. Her account of the events that took place is clear and unambiguous:

'It was totally unexpected and when he came home he was devastated. "Jimmy ... Bob ...", he kept saying over and again. Jimmy and Bob were Masons and I think they played snooker together on a Saturday night after a game. I certainly knew one person who said to Harry that he needed to watch out for what was going on there. I knew as soon as he came in that something was wrong; never before had I seen him as inconsolable as he was that day. I'd heard rumours that something like this was going to happen; I'd had phone calls, heard whispers, even a visit to the door by someone to warn me. Burnley is a small town and people talk. Harry shrugged it off.

'This was before the public announcement came in the local paper and he'd had a chance to come round and gather his thoughts. I have the old newspaper somewhere. "ADAMSON IS CLARETS NEW MANAGER" it said in great high letters and there was a picture alongside it with Harry shaking hands with Jimmy and Bob. It hurt him enormously to look at it but nobody but me saw the hurt although maybe Bob Lord did when he told him his plans. I can't imagine Harry would have looked anything but shocked unless he had seen the writing was on the wall. But Harry was so innocent in many ways. There wasn't a devious bone in his body and it made him vulnerable and unsuspecting.

'After it was announced in February, the club had one of their dinners at Mitton Hall. This was the one for staff and management and directors and their wives and they were always lovely occasions. There had been so many of these dinners over the years and for this one I expected to be treated as we had always been treated – for Harry if not myself. We had always been on the top table with Bob and Hilda Lord and the "management". But this time we were not, we were on a table near the door.

'I was rather taken aback and then noticed that on the menu I was to make the ladies' response when it came for the speeches. During the speeches they talked about the changes that had been made with Jimmy Adamson becoming manager and Harry becoming general manager. Then it was my turn to respond. I got up and thanked them for the flowers, fruit and cards I had received in hospital. But as for the latest news, I did not agree it was in the best interests of the club. Harry, however, had accepted it so I would support him and stand by him. Then I sat down. The silence was ominous; you could have heard a pin drop. Well before the dinner finished, we left quite early.'

My jaw still drops when I re-read the line that describes that after the changes were made Harry's place at the dinner was not even near the top table but a table by the door. It almost defies belief after all he had achieved at the club. At Turf Moor his new place was not in the dugout but in the directors' box. He lost all his close contact with the players both at Gawthorpe and in the changing rooms before and after a game. He was as good as banished from the places that mattered.

Quite soon he stopped going to the home games but chose to go to other grounds scouting the opposition or looking for new players. But, his general manager role was little more than cosmetic. There is no doubt that Jimmy Adamson did not want him anywhere near the players.

Margaret Potts added another indignant grumble, 'One thing that irked me was an announcement by Jimmy Adamson that he planned to give Burnley some style. Style! How could anyone think that Harry's teams did not already play with a great deal of style?'

Burnley Football Club made their official announcement on Monday 23 February 1970. Adamson and Potts signed new five-year contracts. It had been a closely guarded secret and the news came right out of the blue, astonishing everyone. Even local reporter Keith McNee, the man who always knew what was happening, was taken aback.

The players assembled at Gawthorpe to be addressed and given the news by Bob Lord. Player Arthur Bellamy remembers how Potts stood at the back of the group and the players could tell how unhappy he was now that he was no longer manager. Bellamy says he could clearly see the hurt in his face. Lord told them all he had an important announcement to make; that Harry was relinquishing the managership of the team and they would all want to thank him for what he had done over the years, and that Jimmy would take over. The players were told that they should now take all their problems to the new manager Jimmy Adamson. The ground was cut from under Potts's feet with the team and everything connected was now Adamson's responsibility.

As Lord continued his speech, Potts smiled and put on a cheerful show to mask the hurt, making a dignified response, expressing his gratitude for his 12 memorable seasons and all the support he had received. He went out of his way to thank Adamson for his support as club captain while he was a player. 'I could not hand over to a better fellow,' he concluded, adding that he would continue to be at the club helping and looking.

Jimmy Adamson made his response, adding later that Harry would be able to concentrate on matters away from the team. What those matters were 'away from the team' were vague and never made clear. He had been 'sent upstairs' to what in effect was a desk job with his days in the dugout over. He was as good as banished from the training ground and ironically all this happened after the run of five unbeaten games, the last of them being the 5-0 win over Nottingham Forest when big Steve Kindon scored a hat-trick. At any other club it might have been enough to earn the manager a reprieve but in this case it seems reasonable to assume that Lord had made his unalterable decision to promote Adamson, and had negotiated the change with him, well before the announcement. It was no spur of the moment decision.

Potts still provided the programme notes for Adamson's first home game. He was an excellent writer and in them he outlined the changes. As he wrote them he must have been deeply saddened. He wrote that the changes were in the best interests of the club (echoes of what Bob Lord had probably said to him), and that he wished to congratulate Jimmy Adamson on his richly deserved promotion. He was honoured to be the new general manager and assured everyone that he and Jimmy would continue to work happily together. They could not have a better man than Adamson; a man worthy of the sky-high reputation he had in the football world, an outstanding player and a much admired chief coach. Now, he was destined to become one of the game's most prominent managers.

You can see the dignity and eloquence in the notes and they give no trace of the devastation he surely felt and had shown privately to his wife Margaret. The discussions between Lord and Adamson had taken place without Harry knowing; that much is clear from his wife's account. Even if he had been fully aware of the manoeuvrings taking place and the plans being made, it is arguable that he was too non-confrontational a man to know how to counter them and fight for his job. Potts, in the testimony of so many people who knew him, was a man without one shred of deviousness. It was, therefore, something he was unable to see in others, or did not want to see. Margaret described him as vulnerable and unsuspecting, so innocent in many ways.

What she said at the dinner at Mitton Hall was unplanned. It was entirely unpremeditated but sitting in the lowly position by the door of all places, had incensed her. She had seen what the changes had done to him; the table by the door was the last straw. Eventually there was a sprinkling of applause. Lord looked thunderous and his wife Hilda was wide-eyed with astonishment. Margaret had always said her piece about this and that at the club. Everyone who was due to stand up and say something at the dinner had a little witticism under their name. Under Margaret's it said, 'She knows most who says the least.' This too she took as a deliberate snub and the sense of injustice grew even more, prompting her indignant speech. She and Harry left the dinner early for the first time ever.

Harry was yesterday's man; the team and everything connected with it was now Jimmy's duty. Any ambiguity about who was in charge was gone. It was this very ambiguity that had made former player and England international John Connelly think twice about returning to Burnley when he decided to leave Manchester United. Bob Lord would have had him back and sent trainer Ray Bennion to sound him out, but Connelly had no wish to be in the middle of the uneasy Adamson–Potts relationship at a club where Stan Ternent remembers that by then Harry would give one instruction and Jimmy Adamson another.

Potts's assurances in the programme notes that he and Jimmy would continue to work happily together were well meant and genuine. The problem was, at that point he had no idea how hollow they were. It was a thoroughly unhappy relationship that was now in prospect. They would not work together successfully. As far as Jimmy was concerned Harry was a nuisance, an anachronism, and no longer of value. But the problem was, many of the players were still loyal to him. Some of them had perceived that Jimmy had been 'after' the job for some time.

Les Latcham, a key player at Burnley until he was moved on by Adamson, had a feeling that change was imminent: 'Towards the end of Harry's time as manager you could sense that something was going on. Jimmy Adamson was slowly taking over all the team talks and the older players could see that he was going for the job. You couldn't put a finger on what the signs were but they were there, maybe a comment or a remark, a dig or a little niggle, when Harry wasn't around.'

Martin Dobson's view remains that this was not manoeuvring but simple change and progression and that Bob Lord must have pondered over what was for him a real dilemma. If he didn't make Adamson manager he would surely lose him, and the outstanding coach was now the one wanting to make all the decisions. But Lord was also conscious of all the loyal service that Potts had given to the club so to dispense with him was unthinkable. What Dobson saw as a perfect team might have had some chance of success if better thought had been given to Harry's role as general manager. Did the three of them sit down and talk things through? Clearly not Dobson surmises, so the whole thing floundered on Potts having no clear job description and thereby becoming more and more frustrated. Once those major changes had been made, thinks Dobson, then the relationships would have changed.

The majority of the players, Latcham among them, were still 'Harry's boys' but Adamson had the job of forging a new team that would live up to his claims that this would be, indeed, the team of the 1970s.

He had declared, 'Burnley will be the team of the 1970s. We are building one of the finest stadiums in the country and we have a great young team to go with it. In the next few years we will win the championship not once but several times.' If ever a man said words that would come back to haunt him time and again, they were these.

Meanwhile the lack of any cordiality between Potts and Adamson became obvious to everyone. There was clearly no partnership between them. Potts became more and more marginalised and unhappy, using the word 'lonely' to a good friend, Alan Reid. Alan was a local vicar who had become a trusted and close friend of the family. He became a prop to him and more than once went down to Harry's office at the ground to console him and offer a shoulder when Harry had telephoned to say how miserable he felt. The once bright and permanently optimistic Harry was now anything but. One of the things that Harry said to Alan was that other than Albert Maddox, the secretary, he now felt there was no one at the club he could trust. This was the man who once had been overjoyed to go to work every morning of the week and had proclaimed so many times that there was no finer job than football, or place to be than Gawthorpe.

The kingpins now were Adamson and Lord; theirs was the relationship that once existed between Potts and Lord. With huge irony none of them could have forecast that relegation was but months away. Confidence was high; Adamson had genuine belief in his young team but perhaps his confidence was slowly becoming closer to something almost resembling arrogance. It was a claim that years later star player Dave Thomas would level at him.

The 1970/71 season began with a home game against Liverpool and Adamson's programme notes continued to be buoyant. He wrote that he thought it would be a wonderful season; that the talent and determination was there. He felt as the season went on they would surprise a few people; that they were at the beginning of something good. 'Burnley Football Club is on the threshold of a most exciting period in its history. The players are convinced, and so am I, that we will emerge as the team of the seventies.'

'But oh dear,' wrote Keith McNee, the local and much respected reporter as Burnley lost the first game at home to Liverpool. 'What an unhappy way to launch a new season. What a wretched start after all that talk about "The Team of the Seventies" and getting into the honours list. This was a sad and sorry show and left the Turf Moor fans heavily dejected and plunged manager Jimmy Adamson in to a pit of deep disappointment.'

James Mossop featured Adamson on 23 August 1970, by which time Adamson had been manager for almost six months. Burnley had drawn the next two games following the Liverpool opening game of the 1970/71 season, making everyone feel a little better. One of them, against Everton, had seen some pretty robust challenges from the Burnley lads. But Burnley, their youth system and training area were all the rage with Adamson seen as the inspiration:

'In the long, harsh turmoil of the English football season, when Saturday is so often a battle-day, Burnley are the brave boy soldiers in the fight; the front line drummer boys. They are the youngest team in the First Division, a squad of stupendous potential, brave yet inexperienced, their talent promises to make them the team of the seventies. Yet their unknowing bravery which showed in a display of particularly hairy tackling against Everton last week drew this rasping comment from a leading coach, "Team of the 70s, more like 1870s."

'Jimmy Adamson, their brilliant mentor and strategist, fully knows his task of uniting talent with courage and keeping it in check. We sat in the stands at Turf Moor with the ground to ourselves the other day. Adamson, the tall and sallow Geordie, squinted into the sunshine and talked with passion about his young charges.

'He told me: "At Everton they were defending something. They had taken an early lead and they meant to keep it. There was anxiety in their play. They were going in hard to win the ball as we expect them to. But no one was trying to maim anybody. They are great competitors and we are lucky that they are this way. When I say they can be the team of the seventies I really believe it. But for a year or two people may need to forgive us a few things. I would like them to be a little more arrogant and cocky with it. I want them to stride onto the field knowing they are as good as the household names they are playing against. Burnley too often seem to sneak on to the pitch while no one is looking."

'Adamson has one massive advantage as he gives his lads the big build-up. He was a brilliant Burnley-reared youngster himself once upon a time.

'"I tell them I was hard AND good," he jokes. "In fact our chairman, Bob Lord, always says I was the luckiest man ever not to be sent off. If I was playing now I would be sent off five times a season. I like to think I was a good competitor and that by leadership and talking I can give these youngsters a similar outlook. The spirit here is unbelievable. Three of last year's regulars, Peter Mellor, Martin Dobson and Frank Casper have not played this season. The first two will be out a long time. They cannot train but they all turn up just wanting to be there, watching, and feeling that they are involved. When I signed Tony Waiters, young Mellor who kept goal all last season was entitled to feel put out. But he just said: "Great, I should be able to learn a lot from him." That's what I call club spirit.

'Burnley's unique star-finding is legendary. They have sold almost a million pounds-worth of talent in post-war years and spent a mere fraction on recruits. And still the players emerge. Adamson's words become a rhapsody when you mention another north-easterner, 19-year-old David Thomas. He played for Burnley as a 16-year-old and Adamson says: "He teases opponents, he slips through a defence."

'It is a marvellous, heart-warming course that Adamson, appointed team manager after five years as chief coach only this summer, is taking. As he guides the destiny of a club notoriously bad in its public relations, he is ready to bang the big drum. The game's the thing, but it will be a bigger and better thing up Burnley way with Thomas, Kindon and company stealing the back page fame from the Bests and Balls.

'To capture the whole panorama of the new Burnley I walked up to the ridge above this town of chimneys and terraces. Amid it all is Turf Moor. A new stand soars behind one goal. Another side of the ground lies flattened. From that will rise a fine new cantilever stand and the most extraordinary entertainments project undertaken by any football club. Jack Butterfield, a 47-year-old full-back who broke his leg playing for Burnley reserves, is behind this £450,000 venture. He talks of bringing Shirley Bassey and Frank Sinatra to entertain in a cabaret room to seat 1,450 people. In the same building – a banqueting hall for 750, a dance hall, a cinema, a nursery, a pensioners' parlour and bars; he produces architects' plans to prove this is no pipe-dream.

'Butterfield runs the club's development organisation and carries the slogan "Our Object Your Comfort" to incredible extremes. "In four years we have given the club £200,000," he says. Which seems to answer Jimmy Adamson's fear as he surveyed the rubble and confessed: "I am not the businessman round here but I sometimes wonder how we are going to pay for this lot. It is a fact that we could not, at the moment, exist on what we take through the gates."

'Adamson and Butterfield are working together and Burnley Football Club is bristling with pride and determination. Big-time football's most amazing club is on the march again.'

The admiration for Burnley Football Club and Jimmy Adamson was based not so much on the results they were getting, which were patchy to say the least, but on the gallant fight they were making to continue to compete with the bigger clubs. Their emphasis was on youth, on honing the skills of the young lads they found in an increasingly competitive market. There was no longer a level playing field, that was long gone, but Burnley were doing everything they could to hang on to their place in the top division.

The plans for the vast entertainments centre was way ahead of its time, further proof of Bob Lord's visionary football mind. In later years none other than Ken Bates commented that had Lord possessed the entrepreneurial skills to match his ideas there is no saying how far Burnley might have progressed. Had he possessed a winning personality and smooth interpersonal skills he might have raised the money needed to finance the venture. Alas he did not. The plans were shelved. But what he envisaged all those years ago is now standard practice in the building of any new stadium.

Nevertheless the Burnley David was still in there fighting the Goliaths of Manchester, Liverpool and London, and the media admired the sheer pluckiness of it. There was a romance about the Cinderella club clinging on to the midnight carriage that was in danger of disappearing. There was something appealing and brave about these young kids taking on the older professionals. It was raw talent against experience.

'Ability of this calibre has just got to break through,' said Adamson, convinced perhaps more than he ought to have been, that their sheer youthful energy and bravado would see them through.

Unfortunately, he was wrong.

Chapter 8

A time of struggle

'NOBODY KNEW him better than me,' said Stan Ternent over the phone when I rang to ask could I call and talk to him. Stan started his playing career at Burnley in 1962 so he knew Jimmy as both player and coach until leaving in 1968 for Carlisle. Then they were together again at Sunderland and Leeds United (a living nightmare, says Stan in his own book about the time at Leeds). Living only a mile or so apart, in later years Stan would call in and see him regularly to talk.

It was only a preliminary meeting we had to establish that Stan was able to help and outline the insights he could give. We had met before several times in connection with other things I had written and Stan's knowledge of the game and people in it are exemplary. He has a fund of memories and droll little details such as this one about his old boss Alan Ashman: 'He was a gentleman. Whenever he dropped a player, he would hand over a polo mint to sweeten the blow.'

It was one of those pleasant warm days when we could sit outside. Stan lives in a beautiful old farmhouse on the outskirts of Burnley and the lane to it took me through buttercup-filled meadows that you don't see too often these days. Now, working at Hull City, he spends the rest of his time in his extensive and immaculate garden.

His opinions of Harry Potts are mixed, made up of part-amusement at seeing him as a curious, balding man who resembled a dapper middle-aged geography teacher more than a top soccer boss. In the main however, never given any real chance in the Burnley first team, Stan's views echoed those of several others; that any of Harry's success was largely due to other people, one of them of course being Jimmy Adamson.

While Adamson was a supremely gifted coach Stan simply described Harry as 'useless'. Harry was always fit as a fiddle, always first at the head of any cross-country run, always doing push-ups for fun, he remembered. 'But his coaching methods took some beating. During coaching sessions on the Turf Moor pitch, he pulled wingers to one side, pointed at advertising billboards and would shout that they were crossing it too early, telling them to wait until they got to Woolworths.'

As soon as the conversation moved to Adamson's coaching ('He was a genius' said Stan), I was treated to a tutorial in the art of defending from free kicks and blocking the runners. He might have regarded Jimmy as a football mastermind but he certainly didn't view him through rose-coloured spectacles, confirming opinions already expressed that Jimmy could be aloof, dismissive and terse. 'He could walk straight past you on some days.'

But Stan accepted that this was just the way Jimmy was and that this is the way of people who don't suffer fools gladly. But he questioned suggestions that Jimmy was 'arrogant'.

There is huge satisfaction when things begin to come together. Alan Parker had been busy up in Ashington and let me know that the letter asking for anyone in Ashington who could remember Jimmy to get in touch had been in the local paper. Not only that, but I was astonished to read that he actually knew Bill Ogilvie, the guy who had written to Katie with memories of his younger days with Jimmy.

I had given Bill's address to Alan in a nearby village and suggested if he just happened to be driving by one day he might just knock on the door. I would imagine Alan was as surprised as me to read the name. I couldn't resist asking Alan if they all knew each other up in the north-east and did they still all leave their front doors unlocked and borrow cups of sugar?

* * *

Alas, the march that James Mossop envisaged for Jimmy and his team would not get very far; in fact the club was about to start a different journey – downhill. At the beginning of the 1970/71 season there were injuries to three key players; Martin Dobson, Peter Mellor and Frank Casper. The first two were long-term and it was a catastrophic beginning to the season. On top of that the club sold the outstanding Brian O'Neil and he would be badly missed.

O'Neil was a powerhouse player, dynamic and utterly fearless and Bob Lord described him as one of his favourite players of all time. But to this day no one knows if he was sold because he had blotted his copybook at Turf Moor in some way, or his free spirit did not fit the Adamson teamwork ethic, or it was simply the need to raise more money to pay the wages. Adamson's official explanation that came later was that he couldn't guarantee him a first-team place. It didn't quite ring true with supporters who suspected there were other reasons.

Bob Lord had once said that players were only sold when they were past their best, but this was a policy that was changing. Players were now being sold who were at their peak or whose best was yet to come; Willie Morgan to Manchester United was a perfect example or Andy Lochhead to Leicester City. Brian O'Neil was at his peak when he was sold, in fact it could be argued that he was even better at Southampton with manager Ted Bates urging that he be picked for England. Lochhead, in 1968, was another example of a player that Adamson did not want to be sold, seeing him as a centre-half as well as a centre-forward, more evidence that Adamson could see things in players that others could not. Stan Ternent was another player that Adamson wanted to keep but was in no position, as coach, to affect the decision.

Les Latcham recalled something that Jimmy Adamson did do when he became manager, something that would have long-term effects. The scouting system in the north-east had worked like a dream but Adamson informed all the scouts, including the legendary north-east scout Jack Hixon, that they would now be answerable to Dave Blakey. Hixon, who for years had sent a string of players to Burnley, thought that he might have been offered the post. He wasn't and disgruntled, he left Burnley, taking his network of scouts with him. It was a disastrous decision. Talented teenage players still came to Burnley but in nothing like the numbers that they once had. Now, even fewer would arrive. The bigger city clubs could entice them far more easily.

After just seven games of the new season Adamson was calming the anguish of the bottom-of-the-table position and 533 minutes without a goal. He insisted there were no plans to buy their way out of trouble and insisted it was not a huge problem.

'It's a cause for concern – but not a crisis,' he said. 'The patient is poorly perhaps but not on the critically ill list. It's no good saying we are in a false position, we are bottom of the First Division for the first time in many years and that is a cause for concern. The problem is we have an extremely young side and they are showing a lot of anxiety.

'I don't intend to make excuses but we have to be fair to ourselves. We have several key men unfit and have had our stiffest ever start. Perhaps we could do with an older head. Certainly at present we may look over-youthful but would that criticism apply if we had won a couple of matches? I know the fans are saying we should buy a striker but where do we find one who would be better than the ones we have, and would cost what we could afford?'

He went on to acknowledge that they were on the look out for players but emphasised that they were not thinking of buying in the immediate future. He urged supporters to be extra patient. For the moment they were.

After 11 games, Malcolm Allison of Manchester City gave his verdict. He knew Adamson well from their days at Lilleshall together. Their personalities may have been poles apart but they were both similarly innovative, imaginative coaches, bringing so much that was new to the game. Allison described Adamson's position as dark and desperate, said he was a top-class man, and reminded everyone that he had once been offered the England job. He supposed that Adamson would be having sleepless nights, a not unreasonable suggestion. He had seen Adamson at work on the coaching fields, and he said, 'He knows the game, he knows players.'

What he urged was that £100,000 be made available to Adamson to strengthen the team and that without it there was the firm possibility that a plunge into the Second Division awaited. He listed over 30 players sold by Burnley since 1960 and the income they had brought. Now was the time to spend some of it. He looked at Burnley as one of the most amazing operations in English football, thereby reinforcing the view that they were so much admired within the game.

And then he said something compelling, 'The great irony to me is that Jimmy Adamson after all his years as coach at Turf Moor as a man with ideas and style should find things going so disastrously as a manager. It is the sort of bad luck that always lurks in football, ready to strike at any man, however gifted, however strong.'

By the time of the Crystal Palace game on Saturday 31 October, Burnley were in dire straits. This was supposed to be the 'Team of the Seventies' but after 14 games there had been just four draws and ten defeats. Keith McNee, in his reports, was using words like 'dismal' and was urging that strengthening was needed. Manager Adamson talked about anxiety and nerves and there had been more injuries. Occasionally Ralphie Coates or Dave Thomas lit up the gloom but there seemed no end to the poor results.

As they lost 2-0 at Liverpool, McNee wrote, 'Burnley's star of hope hangs lower than ever after a weak as water, almost amateurish exhibition at Anfield, which led to a definitely deserved defeat number nine. In all my travels with the Turf Moor club I have never felt more dejection and the only crumb of consolation on the pensive journey home was that the standard can't possibly drop any further. This, truly, was a rock-bottom display. Burnley just don't look like a team anymore.'

After the next away defeat at Southampton, Burnley even missed their train connection home, at which point Adamson must have felt that every football god in the heavens was conspiring against him. But at last came the Palace game and a win, a precious 2-1 victory to bring relief not just to the football club but the whole town. The Sunday sports pages emblazoned the news all over their pages and after the weekend came a huge spread in Monday's *Daily Express*.

A massive picture filled two-thirds of one page. It showed the laughter in the directors' box on a unique occasion. For the first time in the season they had actually won a match. The smiles filled the stands after all the crashing defeats, the disasters, the criticisms and the humiliations. Jimmy Adamson sat, arms folded, in his dark coat, not with a huge smile but a look of clear satisfaction. Next to him was Bob Lord in his characteristic pork-pie hat, leaning forward grinning and looking directly at the camera. In front of Jimmy was Hilda Lord in the hat that Stuart Hall always described as resembling an upturned flower pot. Elsewhere spectators stood and clapped. Burnley folk could still laugh even though the win-record and the league table still looked more like an obituary.

Eric Probert scored the two goals but Palace pulled one back with 15 minutes to go. They were 15 minutes of purgatory. Adamson then walked into the press room after the game and talked about the longest 15 minutes of his life:

'Those 15 minutes were the worst I have ever known. I thought the final whistle would never come. The only thing I can compare with the situation was back in 1960 when we won the league title. We were playing Manchester City and were leading. I died a thousand deaths before the final whistle came and that's how I felt against Palace. My heart went out to those youngsters. They were so anxious to win a game for Burnley that they were doing everything too quickly. This was the time I wished that we had got a couple of old heads in the side to calm things down. If Jimmy McIlroy and I had been playing we would have been fighting one another for the ball.

'To have a two-goal lead was luxury, sheer luxury. Those two goals could be the turning point for the team. It's only the second time this season that we have been in front. Six of the team played in the 1968 Youth Cup-winning team. The youngsters give everything and chase everything. All they wanted was some reward for their enthusiasm. I have never seen such delight on the faces of players. You'd have thought they'd won the Cup.'

Adamson was tactful enough not to mention the penalty missed by Dave Thomas. The players danced and jigged on the pitch like schoolboys. Despair had changed to hope and supporters gave them a standing ovation. Ralph Coates was generally acknowledged as the man of the match with his performances through the season seen as the one thing worth paying to see. But already there were predictions that he would be sold with Manchester United, Arsenal and Nottingham Forest all willing to pay hugely for him. Coates was happy at Burnley but at the end of the season would be on his way. It was the Burnley way – sell to survive.

The euphoria did not last long with a 4-0 thumping in the next game away at Spurs. Burnley managed to score twice against Huddersfield, but Huddersfield scored three.

But then, another ray of hope as Burnley beat Nottingham Forest 2-1 on a mudbath of a pitch made worse by a second-half hailstorm. The win lifted them off the bottom of the table. Adamson was upbeat, saying that a point a game from now on would keep them up. Coates was the fulcrum again, involved in everything but receiving a battering from the Forest side.

Adamson had made a big decision before the game and gave 17-year-old Leighton James his debut. Only the fans who had watched the reserve games knew how good he was and what his potential would be. He was to become an outstanding player.

After the game Adamson was infuriated by two things, the rough play by Forest and the lenient performance of the referee. 'It was downright vicious at times but the man in the middle was completely reluctant to blow his whistle,' he said. 'What sort of an example was this for our young team? I'd give the last 20 minutes of this match an X-certificate. Our players were repeatedly hacked down.'

Behind the closed doors of the dressing room he told them that if he thought this was the only way to escape relegation, he would pack in with the game. He was utterly incensed, demanding that more managers should speak out against rough-house tactics.

His comments regarding rough-house play were ironic. Jimmy always had his fair share of players in the side who knew how to intimidate the opposition and who could look after themselves. No club could ever succeed or survive without a core of 'hard men' in the team. Any team consisting of 11 'gentlemen' would have sunk without trace.

At Leeds United, Albert Johanneson remembers a game against Burnley as being his last. It was the same game in which Eddie Gray scored his 'wonder goal' when he dribbled round seven Burnley players in the box and then scored. But Albert remembered the game because, 'It didn't help that Burnley kicked lumps out of me and were on my case from the kick-off. No matter what I did I seemed to end up being hacked to the floor or knocked off the ball. In the end I could take no more and gave up.'

Ironically he was dumped on the floor as Gray weaved his way in and out the Burnley team as if they weren't there, and then slotted the ball home.

Still at the bottom of the table and struggling, nevertheless, the media was still sympathetic referring to the young lions, the Burnley Babes, the young team, the brave battle and the disruptions caused by injuries. No one was pointing any finger of blame at Jimmy Adamson, 'one of football's most respected professionals', and Bob Lord backed him totally. Coates, alas, would miss the next five weeks, his ankle made black and blue by Forest's flailing boots.

At Newcastle in the next game, the defeats began again with Adamson bemoaning, 'When things go wrong you are hit by everything.' Martin Dobson, now recovered from his broken leg, and Dave Merrington collided and left the field with blood streaming from head wounds.

Bullish as ever, in December, Bob Lord announced his 'manifesto' and Jimmy Adamson announced he wanted a new-look soccer. Lord was defiant and vehemently insisted that Burnley would crash through their biggest post-war crisis. With a point taken from West Brom, they were still not quite the bottom team with Blackpool below them. Lord was emphatic on five points.

He insisted that the growing reality of Burnley's relegation fears would not bring an inch of change from the club's commitment to build a revolutionary football set-up on the Lancashire moors. By this he was most certainly referring to the plans to build a huge new stand along with a money-making community and leisure centre. Secondly, the Burnley board still had absolute faith in the abilities of their backroom staff led by Jimmy Adamson, whom he named specifically and pointedly. Thirdly, players' welfare and wages would be maintained at one of the highest levels in the First Division – despite the fact that the most recent gate of 12,437 was a new low for the season. Fourthly, the scouting system, considered by many to be the most elaborate in the country would continue at full throttle (Lord failed to mention that the north-east network had gone). And finally, he announced that the showpiece Gawthorpe training area would continue to be developed.

'We are justly proud of what has been achieved at Burnley,' he stated. 'I'm as certain as ever that Jimmy Adamson is still going to take Burnley Football Club right up to the stars. I'm surprised that people should be tempted to write us off as a First Division organisation. Without making excuses it is true we have had shattering injury problems this season and it is also true that we lack some maturity on the pitch. But what sort of people would pack things in just because the going got tough for a while? Of course I believe we can beat the drop.'

Lord, sitting in Adamson's office because the manager was off with a streaming cold, added that he had held a series of 'morale-building' talks with the backroom staff.

'I know that as the chairman of the football club it is important for me to set a tone of confidence,' he said. 'If I showed that I had lost my nerve the mood would sweep through the club. Football can be like a vice – squeezing the life out of you. This is one reason why I believe no manager should be expected to do more than 15 years in absolute control of the team. It is also one reason why it is so important not to let things get on top of you. And this is why we are fighting now.'

His comment about a manager having a 15-year life span was a curious one. Did it mean that come what may he would have replaced Potts? For how long had he held this opinion? Did Potts ever know that this was his belief? Potts, almost the invisible man, continued with his peripheral role in his lonely office.

Meanwhile, Adamson had suggested that as part of his new-look soccer, two things should be done. His reputation unsullied by the lowly league position, respect for him still high, greatly admired for his attempt to make men out of boys every Saturday afternoon, and 'highly regarded as one of the country's top soccer brains', he put forward the controversial suggestion that the offside law should be abolished and that the goals should be widened.

His programme notes explained:

'Abolish the offside law and seriously consider enlarging the goals. That is what I honestly believe football should do before negative play strangles the excitement and entertainment out of the game even more than it does at present. Let me emphasise very strongly indeed that my suggestion is not made because we are having an unsuccessful season. I have weighed this up for at least four years and I think it would be beneficial.

'Soccer today is surely not as open or attractive as it should be with the talent that exists. There is plainly a shortage of goals. In the First Division last Saturday there were two goalless draws, one game produced only one goal, and another four games produced only two goals in each game. Is that enough to satisfy the fans? I say no, even if things in Italy are worse.

'I feel the trouble is that forwards, attackers, strikers, call them what you will, are tied up in chains. Defenders have too many advantages working for them for the good of the football game in general. For a kick-off, they always outnumber the forwards they are watching and with the offside law as an extra weapon, life for the attacking players is so difficult that it really is unfair. Of course I can see snags to throwing the offside law out of the window, but they would be overcome. This, and widening the goals a little, would help bring the spectacle back to soccer.

'There are those who are against change. But football brought in substitutes which was a big alteration to tradition. Why not introduce more of a new look? At least if we abolished offside there would be fewer controversial decisions for referees. And spectators would not have to tolerate long periods of matches in 30-yard player-packed corridors across the middle of the field. The space between goalkeepers and the back line is too often dead land. And that is bad.'

His notes mentioned the injury to Coates. He would be badly missed and when the final reckoning took place at the end of the season and relegation was a certainty, his absence might well have been the difference between an extra three or four points.

Mr R. Redmond, in a letter to the *Burnley Express*, was caustic in his response to the new suggestions, writing, 'After watching the West Brom match I am sure that if he makes the goals as wide as the River Mersey his forwards still won't score.'

Again Burnley were referred to 'as one of the great traditions of English football' as more wins remained elusive and performances were punchless. Even the manager of lowly Oxford United of the Second Division said he expected to beat Burnley in the FA Cup. And yes they did win, 3-0. Mind you, mighty Leeds United were also knocked out by lowly Colchester United although that was scant consolation. Not until 27 February was there a third league win. In the meantime Adamson had to fight hard to keep Ralph Coates at Turf Moor, insisting that he was staying at Burnley and there was no chance of him moving. Coates by now had played for England.

Six draws in seven league games kept Adamson's side in touch with teams above them and Newcastle's manager Joe Harvey said he was amazed that Burnley were in such a lowly position. Then, at long last there was the third win away at Crystal Palace, 2-0. If ever a game demonstrated the value of confidence, this was it, wrote Keith McNee. Scottish team manager Bobby Brown summed up the feeling of many spectators, 'How is it possible for Burnley with their talent to be in relegation trouble? What a fine young team they are.' Palace players said that Burnley were easily the best team to have played them that season.

Jimmy Adamson was delighted, visibly happier than he had been for weeks, saying, 'I am pleased for the boys. They have worked so hard and now they have at last won an away match. It should do us the world of good and we are really determined to follow this win with a few more.' Keith McNee predicted that the end of the season would be one of the most exciting since they had won the title in 1960. Ralph Coates was back on form, so were Steve Kindon and Martin Dobson. Optimism was back in the air. It was, alas, short-lived.

Having been linked with a move to bring Derek Dougan to Burnley, and having been urged to buy reinforcements, at last Burnley did move into the transfer market. Adamson turned to Bolton Wanderers and centre-forward Paul Fletcher. He was a local boy schooled by Nat Lofthouse and had once practised his heading by leaping up at his mother's washing line in the back garden. Bob Lord parted company with £60,000 for the player who would have no immediate impact but within 12 months would be a key part of the group that almost did become the 'Team of the Seventies'. The new man made his debut in the home game against Southampton but it was a 1-0 defeat and for good measure he had his nose rearranged by legendary Southampton centre-half John McGrath.

But still, the slim thread that tied Burnley to their precarious First Division status held up as there was another win away at Huddersfield. It was a display that had the hacks insisting that Adamson's position at the foot of the table was more to do with rank bad luck than lack of ability. It was a game that Burnley totally dominated as they swarmed about like bees and again Ralph Coates was superb. Fletcher won virtually everything in the air which is why he had been bought. They were only three points away from safety. Huddersfield manager Ian Greaves commented, 'No matter where they are in the league Jimmy Adamson could still be right in saying they will become the "Team of the Seventies". These Burnley youngsters have so much talent.'

Six weeks remained until the end of the season and while Burnley hearts saw hope, bookies' heads saw relegation as manager Adamson admitted that time was running out. Notes in the Leeds programme paid tribute to Burnley and mentioned the constant injuries but the Leeds players were less sympathetic and gave them a 4-0 drubbing. It was described as men against boys and that this was a contest that should have been stopped at half-time. West Ham were now six points above Burnley but Adamson refused to give in and accept that relegation was now certain. 'We fight on. We will continue to fight on until survival is no longer possible. That day has not yet arrived.'

Astonishingly there were two consecutive wins, the first against bottom club Blackpool, and then the second was the one that was craved against West Ham. Against Blackpool, Paul Fletcher scored the winner and was overjoyed at scoring his first goal since joining. It was a poor game but nobody cared one jot about that. The West Ham win again put Burnley within touching distance of safety but cruelly, it was undone in the next round of games when West Ham won and Burnley lost at Coventry. They were now four points adrift but with a game in hand.

'We are not down yet,' said Adamson, adding that the boys in the dressing room were saying the same and had a game in hand.

'What a fight,' said Bob Lord.

A despairing Harry Potts, sitting helplessly in the job created for him, watched from the sidelines without any input, presumably feeling totally impotent. Within the club he was the forgotten man; outside it there were many who wanted him back at the helm.

The 'fight' was to no avail. Arsenal beat them 1-0, Derby beat them 2-1 and it was all over. The battle was lost. The inevitable had happened and Burnley were dumped back into the Second

Division. As they lost at Arsenal, Ralph Coates was helping England win 3-0 against the Greeks. Loyal though he was to Burnley he now wanted to get away and would get his wish even though Adamson was saying that ALL his players would re-sign for the next season. Such words were but a smokescreen; he knew full well that Lord would select a player to be sold to pay the bills and it would surely be Coates. Their fate assured, Burnley then beat Chelsea 1-0 at Chelsea and in the very last game fittingly lost at Wolves 1-0.

The pundits saw it all as a gallant fight, the club hit hard by injuries all season and trying their hardest with a bunch of kids, something that was brave, bold and almost romantic. But supporters were less impressed and a letter from Mr R. Kippax was typical of many that swamped the local press. 'Firstly, Mr Lord's statement when admission prices were raised, "If they don't like it they can lump it". We have certainly lumped it Mr Lord, but the lumps are in our throats now.'

Referring to Lord's claim that the average footballer couldn't run a fish and chip shop, another letter stated, 'Most footballers couldn't manage a fish and chip shop. I wonder if he would like to add as an afterthought, that not many can manage a football club. Mr Lord's frequent references to 'our backroom boys' has come home with a vengeance. They could only have led us one place further back.'

There were several others:

'On TV, the statement that O'Neil couldn't command a first team place was true. Neither could any other player. Since Mr Adamson took over one could only surmise that the team had been chosen by means of drawing names out of a hat.'

'Then there was Mr Adamson's statement about widening the goals. In most of this season's games we wouldn't have scored if the goal posts had been where the corner flags are.'

'When Mr Adamson said he had sent Dave Thomas home because he was jaded, he didn't mention there were 15,000 other people at Turf Moor feeling the same way. These people were recently thanked by him for their loyalty. They are gluttons for punishment.'

'Mr Adamson should go on the terraces and hear the comments made about his management. He would discover there is not much praise for him. Burnley have not been relegated. They have been sacrificed. To me, a supporter for 60 years, it is a tragedy.'

More letters continued in the same vein. Some demanded that Harry Potts be brought back. Of that, there was no possibility – until later in the decade.

After the Derby game Adamson's words had a plaintive ring to them. 'I'm afraid our boys are mentally shattered after the events of the season. It was an ordeal for them to have to go out with the relegation business all wrapped up. They just want to get the season over and concentrate on getting us back up next time.'

Down and out, dejected and dismayed, but the final blow for club and supporters was still to come. Managers are not supposed to have favourite players – but they do. Match-winner Ralphie Coates, supremely gifted and skilful, hard-working, a fellow Geordie, quiet and modest, was Adamson's. Burnley were now demoted to the Second Division and to rub salt in the wound, Coates was about to be sold.

Bob Lord sent a deeply moving handwritten letter to Jimmy Adamson at the end of the season:

'Dear Jimmy,
'I had intended to have a private minute or so with you this morning but I realise you were somewhat pressed for time when we finished. However, I want to say to you, please enjoy your holiday with your family and if you can YOU MUST relax and put behind you all the cares, anxieties and worries of the last twelve months.

'Our maker only knows what you have gone through. I want you to know that I have a fair idea and I also wish you to feel that I am 101% behind you as I have always endeavoured to be. You deserve a break, now you can take one with the knowledge that those that matter understand you, and in spite of the terrible results they are more endeared to you now than ever before.

'Look forward to the future Jimmy, carry on doing things the straightforward and honest way, and before long the breaks will come your way. When they bring the results you are entitled to expect, you will bear them in a similar manner as you have borne disaster, which as you know you have carried like a gentleman.

'I have written this letter to indicate to you that in all my life I have never before been privileged to work with such an honest, hard-working and loyal partner. Please accept from Mrs Lord and myself our best wishes to you and your charming wife May, who we hope will enjoy her holiday with you better than any other you have spent together.

'Our love to May and also our sincere and kindest regards to you both.

'As ever, R Lord'

If ever a letter contains genuine love and affection then it is this. This is a Bob Lord who clearly doted on Adamson at this time. But one line perhaps gives an unwitting insight into the man that Adamson was: namely the reference to 'those that matter understand you'.

It suggests that the deeply private and perhaps enigmatic Adamson was not the easiest man to know, comprehend, or relate to, and Lord felt that he was one of the few people that did really know him. But not too many years later when their relationship was falling apart, who knows if Lord might have felt a sense of wounded injustice, and that his loyalty to Adamson deserved better acknowledgement. Alas, there is no way of knowing.

Chapter 9

Goodbye Ralphie and a test of endurance

THE ACCENT was unmistakeably from the north-east when Jim Nichol phoned from Ashington. He had seen the piece in the local paper and had spoken to Alan Parker. He didn't actually know Jimmy but was proud of the fact that Ashington had produced three footballers of the calibre of Jimmy and the Charlton brothers, all Footballers of the Year.

When I talked to Jim about how interested I was in Ashington and life there in the 1930s and 1940s, and the kind of things that Jimmy would have done as a boy growing up, Jim was quick to answer, 'Why that's easy. It was football, football, and football. That's all that we lads did.'

Now 75, Jim still does scouting work and in his time has scouted for Leicester City, Coventry City, Notts County, Newcastle United; everybody it seemed but Burnley. But he did know Dave Blakey the Burnley scout under Adamson and in 1974 Jim had taken an under-14s team to play games in Burnley and Blackburn.

It turned out he also knew a well-known north-east journalist, John Gibson, whose name was already familiar as a result of contact we had regarding other books he had done about north-east players. In short, what John didn't know about the north-east clubs wasn't worth knowing. I called him the next day; his number was already in my book.

The first thing I always say on the phone is, 'I'm Dave Thomas, but not the famous one.' It always works a treat and I've never had anyone put the phone down thinking I'm selling double glazing or solar panels.

Just the once I varied it when I phoned Jimmy Greaves and the first thing I said was, 'Jimmy McIlroy sends his best wishes.' Jimmy was hooked. 'Ah my wife's favourite player,' he answered. He and Jimmy Mac once formed a sort of mutual admiration society and there had been one game when with fisticuffs flying in another part of the pitch at White Hart Lane, and play temporarily stopped, the two of them sat on the grass in the centre circle and passed the time away deep in conversation about this and that.

John Gibson was immediately delighted to help. I told him that all I was doing for now was establishing contacts and sources of help. Now retired, he works from home (still as busy as ever) in the northern end of Newcastle. Yes, he had covered the two years Jimmy was at Sunderland, and yes, he had met him several times. He mentioned that Jimmy had a tough time there and that he had scrapbooks that related to the time. He agreed that the Adamson story really was one of broken dreams, not of failure, but certainly of unfulfilled ambitions. His enthusiasm was evident.

Bill Ogilvie wrote back:

'Jimmy was in my class starting aged five, at Hirst South School, Infants and Junior. Aged 11 we both went to Hirst Park Senior School. In those days pupils left at age 14. He started to play for East Chevington Juniors; they were the crack team then, about 6 or 7 miles away from Ashington. When we played together at school, he was my vice-captain. Jimmy lived about 200 yards away. His house then was in Pont Street. Another local lad was Billy Gray who also lived in Pont Street. He was a gymnast and boxer and a brilliant winger.

'He started his pro football career at Leyton Orient and then moved to Chelsea, to Burnley where he was in the same side as Jimmy, and finally Nottingham Forest. Jimmy and me lost touch on leaving school but I remember

Jim at East Chevington. They were so successful that it led to a ruling on the signing of players within a certain radius. I heard his name again when I was returning from National Service on a troopship from Ceylon. Three of us were chatting away leaning against the rail overlooking the ocean on what seemed a never-ending journey and a Geordie voice called out to me. "You're a Geordie then?"

'When I said yes, he said he was looking forward to seeing another Geordie he knew, Jimmy Adamson, and seeing him play again. Sometimes it's a very small world.

'Our paths crossed again sometime when Burnley were playing at Newcastle and were staying overnight on the Friday. I was involved in local football and Jimmy Adamson with Jimmy McIlroy had permission to present the prizes at a football function in Cramlington in connection with the Northumberland Miners Welfare League. It was then that McIlroy told me that Jimmy's mother had committed suicide. It was a terrible thing to happen.'

From this letter it was clear that the Adamson family had eventually moved from the two-bedroomed Laburnum Terrace to Pont Street where there was the luxury of a third bedroom.

Sydney Carr in *The Fourth Lad* lived at Pont Street two years after Jimmy left for Burnley in 1947. It was a winter when the snows were deep enough to just about bury the back doors of the cottages along the street and families huddled round the black-leaded, cast-iron ranges where the fire burned all day and all night for warmth. These were three-up, two-down dwellings with the best room reserved for special occasions; a street consisting of 'a long dreary row of red-bricked, grey-slated colliery houses, one of many such rows'.

Carr describes it as the toughest street in one of the toughest towns in the north-east; a place where women were perpetually pregnant. 'You didn't live in Pont Street, you survived it,' in houses where as a general rule two double beds would be squeezed into the biggest bedroom to accommodate the children. 'There was almost a stigma attached to living there,' added Carr. It was a street where the roughest, toughest families lived, arguing, fighting and playing rough and ready games.

* * *

The football world was saddened by Burnley's demotion. For years since 1947 they had been a shining example of how to run a football club, and how a small club could survive and compete. Football journalists had long admired them and there is no question that while once Harry Potts had been the figurehead, now it was Jimmy Adamson, and despite the relegation, Adamson was still much respected.

Burnley's relegation was seen as something inevitable, almost romantic perhaps, with Adamson heroically trying to stop the tide coming in. While Burnley supporters might have been critical of him, the media certainly wasn't. In fairness, it had indeed been a season of constant injuries and disruptions. If there was a shining light it was Bob Lord's loyalty to him and insistence that Adamson was still the man for the job. It was exactly this that Adamson later referred to in the Basildon Bond notebook. It was, eventually, just about the only good thing he could ever find to say of Lord.

But the loss of Coates was a hammer blow. You could argue that it was the first of the 'big deals' that would prevent Burnley from ever fulfilling Jimmy's dream of being the 'Team of the Seventies'. To follow, one by one, would be Dave Thomas, Steve Kindon, Martin Dobson, Geoff Nulty and finally Leighton James. No club, let alone a small-town club like Burnley, would have been able to succeed with losses like these.

Adamson made a dramatic 'please understand our position' plea only a few hours after the completion of the Coates deal in a Staffordshire car park. It was a record £190,000 that took him to Spurs. Because he hadn't asked for a move Coates received £9,500 but said that if Burnley hadn't agreed to let him go then he would have indeed asked for a transfer and refused the new contract that was offered to him.

Keith McNee sympathetically mentioned how tired and jaded Adamson looked after all the problems he had endured during his first full season as manager. He urged that the soccer world should look urgently at the system by which, currently, the rich clubs got stronger and the poorer clubs ever weaker, and it needed to be done without delay to save us as a competitive soccer nation. There was something almost forlorn and plaintive about his plea.

Adamson was aware that he, and the club, had constantly told supporters that Coates would not be sold, so they now felt misled, even deliberately deceived: 'Look, I know what they are going to say. They are going to ask about all the denials and the statements from the club from us that Coates was not for sale. This was done calculatedly to put us in a stronger selling position and I do not deny this.'

He said that offers had been received in Lord's office and because of the economic position at the club they had to find money and sell a player. It was his duty to get the best possible price and the denials had been made to mask that need for money. If clubs had realised how desperate they were, it would put those clubs in a far stronger bargaining position. He stressed that they did not want to sell him but HAD to sell him if the club was to remain competitive with players on first-class contracts. Without them they wouldn't re-sign.

He went on to emphasise that the money that came through the turnstiles was simply not enough to pay the wages that were required. That was an interesting observation about inadequate turnstile money. The story, which may be apocryphal, according to one Burnley director, was that sometimes Bob 'used to have his own turnstile'.

'What has happened to us has happened to a lot of town clubs,' said Adamson. 'Look at Bolton Wanderers. They did not want to sell Paul Fletcher. They did not want to let their public down. They were reluctant to sell, but like us had no realistic alternative. We had to find some quick money.'

Adamson went on to say he didn't like the five per cent that was paid to players who did not ask for a transfer and saw it as something else that gave the city clubs an advantage when they could pay a big fee knowing that the five per cent would entice the player even more. He could not emphasise strongly enough that he was concerned about the supporters' reaction. He did not want fans to think they had sold them down the river but it was a very difficult world they lived in. His team of scouts had constantly been looking for new players but had found none of interest. Now they were likely to find it even harder if they identified someone, since other clubs suspected they had £190,000 nestling in the bank.

The sheer speed of the deal had taken supporters by surprise and reporter Keith McNee contemplated that Coates would not be the last to be sold at Burnley in the rat race that was now football.

The deal was completed in top secret with Coates and his wife travelling to a hotel just off the M6 in Staffordshire. According to the local press the signing took place in the back of a car of all places, the hotel being far too crowded for anything to be done in private. McNee asked Coates how he felt and got the reply, 'I am in a bit of a whirl but I must be honest and say that if this had not happened there is a good chance I would have refused to sign my new contract later this week. Not because of the money, which has been excellent at Burnley, but because I don't like the idea of playing in Division Two.'

McNee asked Adamson how he felt, and was told, 'I feel sad, very sad. Ralph is a good boy. He has never been any trouble to us. I feel as sad as any supporter.

His sadness was genuine. Years later Ralph Coates told me that both he and Adamson had shed tears.

Many years later he also told the whole story of the transfer and the day of the move. The subterfuge was as good as any blockbuster spy movie. Coates explained:

'On the last Wednesday of the season the manager rang me at home and asked where I was training. I was still keeping fit in the local park for the England game. He said why didn't I come on down to the ground to train. He said he'd put a bath on and was really insistent. I was quite happy to run in the park but I agreed to go down to the ground. However, after lunch I didn't feel like it and at that point had no idea there had been an offer for me. They were still denying that they were selling me.

'So, I went shopping instead, came home and was just about to start cutting the grass when I heard this voice in a sort of hushed whisper over the garden wall. It was Dave, our chief scout. He told me to get into the house and he'd talk to me there because the papers had spies everywhere. In the house he was still whispering and told me that there had been a secret meeting somewhere on the M6 because Tottenham had made a bid.

'Naturally I wanted to phone Sandra but as soon as I picked up the phone he stopped me and said you never knew who was listening. Next, Dave made a phone call to his own wife and told her to pass on a message that he had made contact and he'd be there, but he'd be three-quarters of an hour late for the rendezvous. I said that the whole thing was ridiculous. He said it all had to be dead secret.

'In the meantime Sandra was back at home and Dave put us both in his car, except that it wasn't his car. He'd been to a garage and driven in, in his own car, but driven out in a showroom car so he wouldn't be recognised or followed. It was just like a James Bond film. We drove down the M6, got in the back of Bill Nicholson's car in the Post Horn car park, chatted for half an hour, heard him say my five per cent would be £9,500 and I signed the forms there and then.'

Coates was in such a state he probably didn't know whose car he was in. In another version of the story he was in the back of Adamson's car. You can only surmise that Adamson drove back to Burnley feeling quite numbed by the whole thing. His star player had just been sold. His team had been relegated. Not many months earlier he had said this would be the 'Team of the Seventies'. He returned to the sanctuary of his home and the sympathy of his wife May, the rock of his life. The one consolation was the continued faith of Bob Lord.

But there, still in the background at the club, was Harry Potts, an unwanted, marginal presence. Astonishingly there is no real record of what Harry actually did in his two years 'upstairs'. He still attended the board meetings; he scouted and prepared reports. Presumably he handed those reports to Adamson but might even have done that via the secretary, Albert Maddox. No player I have spoken to can actually remember any cordiality between them. This poor relationship was eating away at harmony and was divisive as long as there were still players there who admired, in fact loved, Harry.

It is reasonable to suppose that chairman Lord recognised that Harry's continued presence, painful though it might have been to say after all they had achieved together, was not in the best interests of the club.

The immediate impact of relegation was the postponement of the project to improve Turf Moor with the huge new entertainments centre being planned by Lord. His priority was a return to the First Division, so anything requiring capital outlay was shelved. At the AGM in August of 1971 he told shareholders that the previous season was 'just disastrous, starting with a trio of broken limbs before a ball had been kicked in a league match', and added, 'We did try with all energy to find appropriate players who would have probably helped us overcome our serious predicament but in our wildest dreams we cannot afford to pay six figures on our modest income for one player.'

Manager Adamson also presented his report: 'The catastrophe of relegation has been a personal nightmare but going into the Second Division was not the end of the world. It was something that had to be accepted and taken on the chin. No stone would be left unturned in the bid to get back to Division One.

'Last season's lack of goal power was under official scrutiny. I have in my drawer a list of 34 experienced forwards we have looked at but I was not willing to pay the price asked for some of them. One player who we were willing to pay for refused to have anything to do with Burnley because it was not a city club.'

Lord referred specifically to Jimmy Adamson. During the last 12 months he had undoubtedly experienced torture. He had not deserved what happened. Some managers had faced the sack having experienced similar circumstances but time and again during the last season the directors at Burnley had told him he could bank on their full support. The past season must have given him terrific experience which would give him and his colleagues the confidence to carry on. But, he added, the accounts showed that they had lost £27,137 during the year and £46,000 the year before that. Also, £88,000 had been spent on extending the Bee Hole end of the ground behind the goals.

It remained unspoken that supporters could deduce for themselves that the Coates money would not be splashed by Jimmy Adamson on new players. At least there was some more young talent in the pipeline, they thought, but in truth they were far below the standard of players who had once arrived at the club in the 1950s and early 1960s.

The first home game of the new season was at home against Luton Town and followed pre-season friendlies that had hardly been inspiring or successful although the opening league match, away at Cardiff, was a creditable 2-2 draw. Malcolm Macdonald had left Luton for Newcastle. It was a name that would return to haunt them three years later.

In his programme notes for the game Adamson was forthright and referred again to the events of the previous season:

'There will not be any excuses for relegation from me. A manager should try to legislate for injuries and for a bad run of the ball. We shall fight our problem with just one aim in mind – promotion. These catastrophic last 12 months have been a personal nightmare for me but I look not backwards but forwards. I would like to point out that no matter what anyone outside the club might care to say to the opposite effect, tremendous efforts were made behind the scenes to find new players during 1970/71.

'One way and another it was an experience my staff and I could have done without but we realise what we are up against in this game and the system is not exactly geared up to clubs like ours. But last season was not all loss. I learned a lot about people and in Mr Bob Lord I had the biggest ally that any manager could wish for. The Board as a whole assured me that money was available for players – and that was before the inevitable transfer of Ralph Coates – but I was not going to go out and buy for the sake of it.'

He went on to praise the supporters and said that in the opinion of his players as well, no praise could be too high. There was never any slow hand-clapping; there were no jeers, because the supporters knew that they were giving their best. It was true enough. Supporters had in the main been fair and tolerant. Most could see the problems although when the end of the season came, some letters to the local papers did express dissatisfaction.

It would, in fact, be in the coming season that the jeers and the abuse would begin in earnest. But Adamson had no crystal ball, and had no idea of the calls for his head and the demonstrations that were in store later in the season. He had been coach or manager for six years and in terms of tangible successes, there was little to show for it. In his first full season as manager he had won just seven of 42 games.

There was a new incentive system in place to encourage the players to get the club back to the First Division as soon as possible. Adamson suggested that though they might not be favourites for promotion at the first attempt, they must surely have a good chance and the early signs were reasonably good with only one defeat in the first seven games. As the season progressed, however, it was clear that promotion was a pipe-dream as mediocrity became the norm. They were knocked out of the FA Cup as early as the third round at home to Huddersfield. It was February of 1972 when things reached a head and supporters' patience was finally exhausted. In the middle third of the season, wins were infrequent and there was increasing gloom and dissatisfaction with things in general, and Jimmy Adamson in particular. The home game against Hull City on 12 February brought a new low.

Against a background of Edward Heath, the miners' strikes, blockaded power stations (the one at Padiham near Burnley had been closed for two weeks), electricity cut-offs and black-outs, reduced factory production and newspaper headlines such as 'We Can Take It', with pictures in the local press of barmaids pulling pints by candlelight, Jimmy Adamson was given short shrift by those supporters who still bothered to go to games at Turf Moor. He had splashed £50,000 on goalkeeper Alan Stevenson bought from Chesterfield. If supporters had known just what a superb buy Stevenson would turn out to be, perhaps they would have been a little more tolerant of Adamson. He didn't often go into the transfer market, but when he did they were shrewd purchases.

Hull weren't pulling up any trees when they arrived at a muddy Turf Moor and had already lost at home 2-1 to Burnley earlier in the season. While Burnley were in a respectable eighth place, but not respectable enough for fans, Hull were down near the bottom on a dull, damp, classic February day. Goals had been hard to come by and this performance continued the trend with Burnley seemingly incapable of anything worthwhile.

Other than Leighton James you could have taken just about any Burnley player off the pitch. Hull took the lead, could have added more, and duly did when an individual run from inside the Burnley half ended with the ball in the net. The shouts of 'ADAMSON OUT, ADAMSON OUT' rang round the ground. The inept Burnley performance was somehow even more galling when the player skated his way through the complete defence and planted the ball in the net. It was embarrassingly easy.

It was an abject performance and Adamson made no excuses, 'It was a poor game and one we shouldn't have lost.' He talked about anxiety, players being below their best, explaining, 'We are entertainers and we must do a heck of a lot better than this. All I can say is this has happened to better managers than me and will again. This is part of the hazards of being a manager.'

The press suggested that what Burnley lacked was a player of the style and calibre of Adamson himself, someone who could take stock, point the way and calm the players down. One hack wrote, 'Burnley's prodigies always look hurt and surprised if their dazzling footwork fails to bring goals. Lesser players smack their lips when they see that.'

The supporters' protests were loud and long but Bob Lord defended his manager, saying, 'This is not Jimmy's fault. The players are not getting the results. Our team didn't play well. Jimmy Adamson has done a lot for Burnley and will do a lot more in future.'

It cut no ice with the critics who had noted by now that in all his games in charge as manager, Adamson had amassed just 24 wins, 23 draws and 41 defeats. It was not far short of a 50 per cent defeat record. By anyone's standards this was poor and there in the background remained Harry Potts with a section of support calling for his return. In today's football climate it is a certainty that Adamson would have been asked to step down. Lord stood by him. It is not unreasonable to suppose that Margaret Potts was privately delighted at Adamson's discomfort and the 'Team of the Seventies' claim once again was thrown back at him in derisory fashion.

The next game was away to an in-form side, Birmingham City. Keith McNee provided an in-depth analysis of the situation as Burnley tried to steady themselves for the next ordeal while the angry fans continued with their inquests and grumbles. He pointed out that the sympathy that was evident in the relegation season had now dissipated and that this was apparent in the strength of the demonstrations both during and after the Hull game.

To his credit, said McNee, Adamson was still 'available' for comment even when he would probably rather be in hiding. There was no question of his resignation, or that it would be asked for in the boardroom.

Adamson himself was defiant, even if rather flippant, 'It's the first time my name has been on their lips for a time. I've had other bad moments and the worst of all was the day we lost to Tottenham in the FA Cup semi-final.'

That was the occasion they had dominated the game in 1961, had a perfectly good goal disallowed, and had then gone on to lose 3-0. Bob Lord repeated to McNee his earlier comments, that it wasn't Jimmy's fault, and those fans who had been chanting for his head would not get their way.

McNee revealed that Adamson had mentioned that there were 'problems that the public don't know about'. Is it possible that they were to do with the continued presence of Harry Potts at the club and that this was splitting the camp? Whatever they were, they were never revealed, assuming they existed in the first place. The letters to the local paper poured in.

'The booing of Jimmy Adamson has been on the cards for some time, distasteful though it was. Surely it is time for a change away from the youth policy which is a dead loss. There is no drive; passes go astray and it is seen as just one of those things. The tactics are way out; it was a mistake to say this would be the team of the seventies. Let's do something and then start bragging ... I am honestly worried we will finish in the Third Division.

'What a disappointment this team is at home. They have me baffled and all those I know who support the club. It is even more depressing now than it was last season ... players who might bring a total of £500,000 in the transfer market give Central League performances.

'I left Turf Moor in disgust on Saturday ... in my opinion Mr Adamson could bring a team of internationals to Turf Moor and within a month under Burnley's style of play they would be unrecognisable... At the present rate of progress we shall be applying for re-election to the Fourth Division in 1975... What a disaster for the "Team of the Seventies".'

McNee gave his own view, 'Last Saturday was Burnley's worst day for years, taking all into account. The manager and the team must expect to share a bitter reaction. There are severe problems even for a club paying out huge wages and they are terribly difficult to sort out. Where the Clarets go from here, especially in their strained relationship with the supporters remains to be seen, but the mood at the moment is black indeed.'

Burnley had lost at Birmingham but somehow in the very next game Adamson managed to inspire them to a 5-3 win over Sheffield Wednesday and then days later another home victory, this time 1-0 against Carlisle. If Adamson and his players perhaps thought the crisis was over, how wrong they were; away at Blackpool there were unprecedented scenes after the game and a 4-2 defeat that for supporters who were there was the last straw. They were fed up of Adamson turning on them just as much as losing. After the previous game, a 1-1 draw at home to Fulham, Adamson had savagely criticised the supporters and accused them of singling out his players. He referred to them disparagingly as 'these people' and wondered if they ever thought about what they were doing.

He said, 'They can shout for my resignation as much as they want. It doesn't bother me in the slightest. But when they start roasting a kid who has only just started in the game it makes me sick.'

Supporters hit back and said they weren't singling out young Harry Wilson. They retaliated and said they no longer had faith in Adamson, that Fulham was the worst display in 40 years.

Supporter Tony Scholes, who attended the Blackpool game, remembers, 'Outside the ground after the game the scenes were as bad as anything I've ever seen as Burnley fans waited for the manager. He remained inside the ground for some considerable time before emerging and was protected by several police officers. The level of abuse was staggering. One fan shouted at Bob Lord and asked him was he going to sack Adamson. Lord laughed in his face and told him the club didn't need fans like him, as he pointed to the hundreds who were there baying for him.'

Surely Bob Lord would review his defence of the manager, thought fans, especially just days later when Burnley lost again at Sunderland. A 3-1 lead became a 4-3 defeat leaving Adamson beside himself with frustration. Watching was his old manager Alan Brown and they met after the game with Brown commiserating and advising his former player to stick to his principles. The demonstrators were there again although not in the same numbers but still Lord defended Adamson. 'It is not the fault of the manager,' he announced and a couple of days later he was the front page headline in the *Burnley Express*. Normally, he explained, he would keep what he was saying until the AGM of the football club but now was the time to say something.

The board was still 100 per cent behind manager Adamson. Club policy was unchanged – Burnley could only be run with a youth system. Manager Adamson was not to blame for player-recruitment failures over the last five years. The current situation could mean a stay in the Second Division for a few more seasons. And, regarding the position of Jimmy Adamson, he appreciated that the large majority of supporters were still behind him. The unrest was understandable but fans should not get vicious about it.

Again he said it was not Jimmy Adamson's fault that the youth policy had not produced the players it should have done. Burnley FC had begun to slip up in the mid and late 1960s by not recruiting enough youths of the right calibre. There were other people to blame for this, he added, not Jimmy Adamson. They might therefore need time to recover from these failures of the 1960s. Who were these 'other people' fans wondered?

His final comment was blunt, 'In my opinion, however, it is the players who are to blame. And no matter how much chanting there is, it will make no difference in the boardroom. I back Jimmy Adamson to the hilt and so do my directors. I hope our fans will be patient and try to understand the problems and give us the time. They have made their point and we have received the message.'

His remark that other people were to blame for the recruitment failures of the 1960s was cryptic. Was he pointing a finger at Harry Potts? Was he the unnamed scapegoat? It must indeed have been a clear reference to Harry Potts and his staff. Who else was there? One thing was certain, and it was that Harry Potts was now on borrowed time at the club.

More letters poured in from fans:

'The Burnley crowd have been over-patient with Mr Adamson ... Jimmy Adamson should not be manager of Burnley Football Club ... People who pay every week are entitled to better than the fare that was served up on

Saturday ... The blame lies at the feet of the manager ... Since Mr Adamson took over, the fortunes of Burnley Football Club have declined ... Our manager has contrived to put forward every conceivable reason for the last two disastrous seasons; off-form players, injuries, bad luck, poor referees, even would you believe – the press ... Mr Adamson needs to look closer to home, I suggest a mirror ... Does he expect the paying supporters to put up with the rubbish being served up at Turf Moor ... The fans stood by him last year but now I must echo the cry from Turf Moor of ADAMSON OUT ... The time is right for a new approach, one of flair and first-time passing ... 10,000 fans are not all wrong ... Everything has been lashed by Mr Adamson's tongue, even members of the joinery profession who do not make the goals wide enough.'

One of football's great heroes and entertainers, Len Shackleton, now a reporter, pinpointed the very reasons for supporters' dissatisfaction – the lack of pace, the continuous backwards and sideways passing, any way but forwards. It had been a complaint for more than just the last two seasons.

Years later, while this book was being written, Jimmy Adamson and the events at Blackpool were still provoking discussion and memories on the Claretsmad internet website:

'I remember a home match towards the end of the next season when one fan was allowed to make a public apology from the centre of the pitch. Some of the vitriol aimed towards Adamson was ridiculous ... Adamson was a strange bloke and didn't help himself by having a go at the fans at every opportunity. But the Blackpool demo was as bad as anything I've seen. Incredibly it all changed to what is still one of my favourite all-time seasons – one thing with Adamson, we played football that was good to watch ... I think a lot of us were disillusioned with Adamson because of the "Team of the Seventies" statement ... You have to give huge credit to Bob Lord for believing in Adamson and keeping him despite the protests ... I always got the impression that Adamson was a peerless tactician but a bloody awful man-manager.

'The Blackpool demo was nasty. It was something new for most of us at that time. These things just didn't happen at Burnley ... You also need to look at the context of the time. Burnley were still perceived as a big club so if struggling in the top tier was uncomfortable, then relegation was unthinkable. Only ten years earlier they had been champions. At the same time, Bob Lord had been carving out for himself his niche as the old-fashioned, eccentric, "out of touch", loud mouth with a kind of "muck is brass" hard-faced persona.

'It started to look seriously incongruous as the 1960s disappeared and the 1970s emerged with a collective working-class consciousness and powerful trade unions. To all intents and purposes Lord was the antithesis of progress. It was fans against the crude dogmatist and his urbane, side-kick manager making statements against the fans. The chairman and the manager represented just about everything the fans hated at the time.'

The last analysis there is a crucial one. The times were changing. Autocratic domination by Bob Lord was by now greatly resented. It was fine while it was bringing success but now it was seen as condescending patronage. Alongside it was Adamson's aloofness from the fans and his hitherto ineffective football. It was a recipe for protest.

And then something almost miraculous happened on 4 April; out of the previous debacles, upsets and protests, a 3-1 win over Charlton Athletic was the precursor to a three-year spell of football that would have fans, pundits and other teams drooling with admiration. The remaining five games of the season were all won and Burnley finished in a creditable seventh position.

Adamson could look back over the season and say if only we hadn't had this bad spell, or that bad spell. If only – the biggest words in football. Success comes from having the right collection of players who will then play as a team rather than 11 individuals. Adamson had endured a hard and rocky road since he had taken over as manager but somehow the right blend was found and the team that ended the season was very much the team and players that would go on to provide so many lovely memories for those supporters who grew up with them.

No one could say that this was the team that Adamson had inherited, or that someone before him had done all the hard work. It was his team, and his alone. He was about to enjoy the rewards of all his labours and all that he had suffered, but the tragedy would be that it would be so very brief and would all end in despair and heartache.

Thought to be Jimmy's father William Adamson on the left.

1948 Jimmy's brother Bill with sisters, left to right, Dorothy, Florence and Jean. Mother Mary seated. All pictures from family collection.

1947: Jimmy aged just 14 would have had milk and pies in the canteen just like these lads.

The grandchildren think he worked with the pit ponies. Both pictures courtesy of Mike Kirkup.

Adamson middle row end right and Dave Blakey back row end left at East Chevington Juniors. Picture courtesy of Alan Parker.

In Aden with the RAF station team, Adamson middle row second left. Courtesy of Adamson family collection.

S. H. Q.
WINNERS OF
ADEN COMMAND
FOOTBALL LEAGUE
48-49

1950 flying to Germany, Jimmy third from left and Harry Potts kneeling second from right.

1951/52 back row second left. Top picture family collection. Bottom picture courtesy of G Bradley.

1952 proud wearer of the Burnley club blazer, courtesy of family collection.

Burnley in 1952 courtesy of Gerard Bradley.

Hirst Park football team, 1952. It was very much a Sunderland v Newcastle presentation at the Park School in 1952. They had asked Jackie Milburn to present the trophies, but that fell through. Then someone suggested Jimmy Adamson, Burnley's stylish half-back. And so it was that Jimmy, who later managed Sunderland, handed out awards to a future Newcastle United player, Bobby Whitehead, and a future Sunderland goalkeeper, Ronnie Routledge. From left: teacher Sam Hart, Jimmy Adamson,

Bobby Whitehead, Ken Millican, Les Barron, Ron Routledge, Brian Bennett, Walter Lavery, Micky Cummings. In front: Jim Bartholomew, Torn Herron, Bob Mavin, Alan Smith and Harry Dodd. Courtesy of Mike Kirkup.

The big day, June 7th 1952, Jimmy's mother left, mother in law right, from the family collection.

1953, training at Turf Moor with Billy Dougal 'always do the unexpected'.

The Scottie that inspired this book. From the family collection.

In the Turf Moor dressing room 1955, the great Jimmy McIlroy front row first left.

Bottom picture 1955 and daughter Julie, both pictures from family collection.

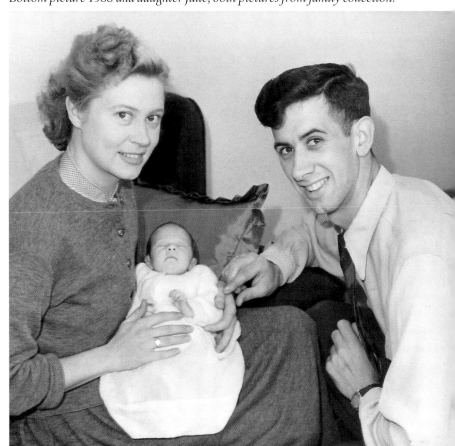

1955 Alan Brown end right, Ray Bennion and Billy Dougal end left standing, family collection.

1956 in the mud at Gawthorpe with Alan Brown and Billy Dougal, family collection.

1956 Friendly against Flamengo at the Nou Camp, family collection.

1956 larking about, Albert Cheesebrough about to get wet, family collection.

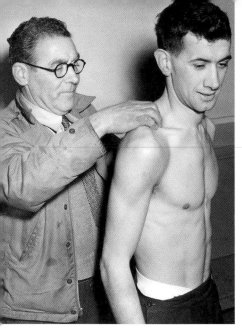

All from the family collection: top left 1956 treatment from Billy Dougal.

1957 versus Aston Villa.

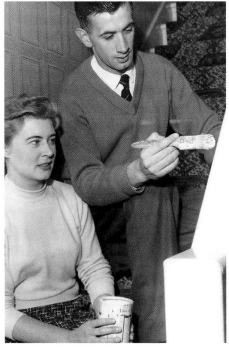

Domestic bliss, an expert cook.

How to paint in a shirt, tie and best jumper.

1957 jokes in the ancient bath with left to right Jimmy McIlroy, Doug Newlands and Jock Winton.

1957 knee injury and tender care from George Bray and Ray Bennion, both pictures from the family collection.

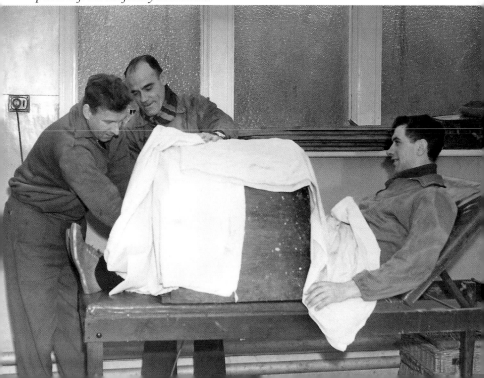

1957 pots of tea and muddy legs at Gawthorpe with left to right, Ray Bennion, Bobby Seith, Jimmy Mac, and Ian Lawson.

Action 1958 against Villa.

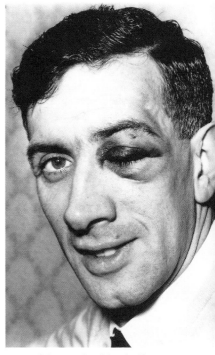

One of the perils of football. Top and bottom left pictures from the family collection, bottom right courtesy of Howard Talbot.

Talking tactics with Bobby Seith and Tommy Cummings.

Harry Potts, Billy Dougal and Ray Bennion, both pictures from the family collection.

Here is a hair dressing with a new approach—a style all its own. **Silvikrin Lotion with Oil** controls your hair the whole day through, yet leaves it looking perfectly natural (that's the secret of hairdressing in good taste!). It gives your hair the brilliance and gloss that come from vigorous hair health. **Silvikrin Lotion with Oil** is the hair dressing of today!

Silvikrin
LOTION WITH OIL
The Right-style
HAIR DRESSING

1958 with manbag and shampoo.

1959 Christmas party with Bob Lord. Family collection.

1960 at Lilleshall, Walter Winterbottom front middle, Jimmy fifth left, family collection.

1960 The League Champions, back row left to right, Alex Elder, Jimmy Robson, Tommy Cummings, Adam Blacklaw, Brian Miller, John Angus and Trevor Meredith. Front row, left to right, John Connelly, Jimmy McIlroy, Adamson, Ray Pointer and Brian Pilkington. Courtesy of Burnley Express.

May 1960 toasting the trophy courtesy of Burnley Express.

1960 in the bootroom, Angus, Cummings, Jimmy, Pointer, Robson, courtesy of Howard Talbot.

Commemorative
programme cover,
courtesy of Burnley
Football Club.

1960 welcome home with the trophy, courtesy of Gerard Bradley.

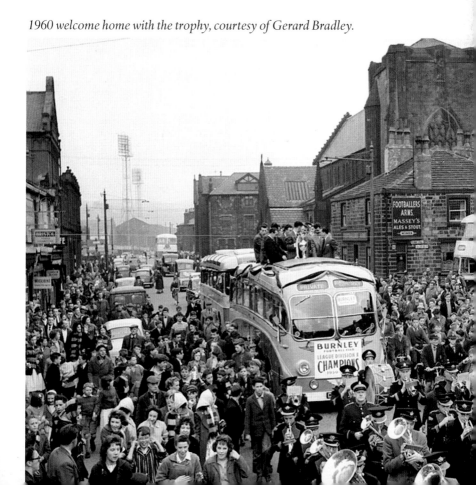

1960 the title is won, top two photographs at Maine Road. From the display in the Jimmy Adamson Suite, courtesy of Burnley Football Club.

1962 Wembley, a 3-1 defeat. Jimmy was man of the match, courtesy Gerard Bradley.

1962 Cup Final wives, May Adamson in the middle, family collection.

1962 leading out the team, a proud man. Courtesy Gerard Bradley.

1962. Courtesy of Howard Talbot.

Footballer of the Year trophy, courtesy Burnley Football Club.

The Cup Final banquet, talking to Brian Glanville with May left of picture. Courtesy Gerard Bradley.

1962 in Chile as England assistant manager, top the training camp, front row left to right, Walter Winterbottom, Bobby Charlton, goalkeeper Springett, Johnny Haynes and Jimmy Armfield. Jimmy number 22 and next to him Bobby Moore.

At high altitude not the warmest place, family collection.

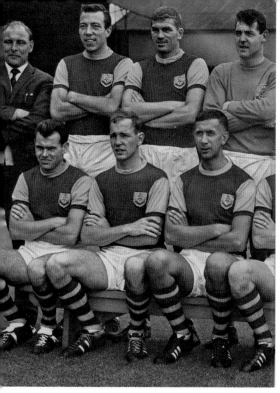

1964 *and final year as a player,
back row Harry Potts, John
Talbut, Brian Miller and Adam
Blacklaw. Front row John
Connelly, Andy Lochhead and
Jimmy.*
Football Monthly Archives.

1968, *Potts manager and
Adamson first team coach.
Next to him, Martin Dobson
and then Dave Merrington
who would follow him to
Sunderland and Leeds. Front
row second from right, Ralph
Coates. Front row end left,
Dave Thomas and behind him
Willie Morgan.*
Author's collection.

1973. *His pride and joy, so nearly the 'Team of the Seventies'. Courtesy Howard Talbot.*

1975 *Turf Moor office. Family collection.*

1976, *putting on a cheerful face after his dismissal. Courtesy of Burnley Express.*

Left, 1976 in Rotterdam.

Back home with daughters Julie on the left and Jayne, both pictures from the family collection.

Courtesy of Sunderland Football Club.

1977 with Kenneth Wolstenholme, Dave Merrington on right.

1978, Stan Ternent end right, both pictures courtesy of Sunderland Football Club.

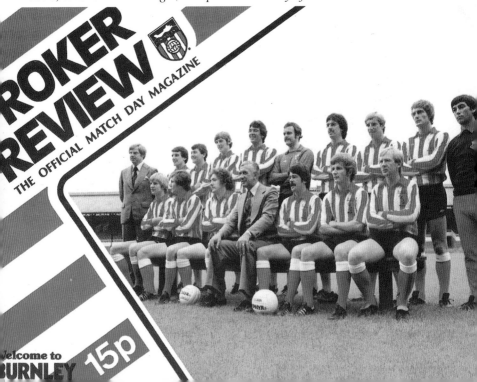

Top 1979 Leeds United on the European trail, family collection.

Below 1980/81 Neville Chadwick.

Welcome to Alan Curtis, courtesy Leeds United.

1981, Bob Lord's last ever speech, he died in 1981, author's collection.

1980, weary, drained and dispirited; the resignation of Jimmy Adamson. Andrew Varley.

A couple of years later, finished with football, happiness with his beloved May beneath the blue skies of Spain. From the family album.

From the Jimmy Adamson Suite Turf Moor, opened 2011, courtesy Burnley Football Club.

2011, Jimmy and Burnley Football Club Chairman Barry Kilby and the grandchildren from left to right, James, Katie, Jennie, Sam and Sarah, open the Jimmy Adamson Suite at Turf Moor.

The final wave and closure, after many years of estrangement, both pictures courtesy of Burnley FC.

Chapter 10

1973 triumph

I AM one of the people who were there and can still vividly remember what a beautiful team Jimmy Adamson eventually produced at Burnley during the 1970s. It was just such a good time to be around and those of us who saw it perform were privileged. It never won any honours, unless you count the Charity Shield, but it came so close. Maybe it's because those players were pretty much the same age as me that I can identify with them. I can still hear The Carpenters over the tannoy before the games; still feel the sense of anticipation as we drove to the game, and still appreciate the entertainment that we enjoyed – for entertainment is what it was. It was such a good time to be at Turf Moor. You could imagine that all was well with the world.

It was a time of flares, curly hairstyles, tank-top jumpers and kipper ties – especially on the front of a couple of Burnley programmes of the time as the players began to look like fashion models, even in Burnley. Concorde flew regularly, Neil Armstrong stepped on to the moon; *Monty Python's Flying Circus* had us in stitches, the first jumbo jet landed at Heathrow. Decimal coinage arrived and old people swore they would never get the hang of it. Mark Spitz won seven gold medals at the Munich Olympic Games.

We had moved to Leeds at the close of the 1960s and travelled to Burnley for every home game, unburdened, as yet, by children. My parents still lived in Todmorden so after the game there would be a crusty potato pie, mashed carrots and pickled cabbage with the jar plonked in the middle of the table. My mother had the habit of cooking with a fag in her mouth so sometimes you found a bit of cigarette ash in the pie as well. It was a lovely way to spend a Saturday, seeing your team win (usually), winning promotion and eating well, if you didn't mind the ash.

In recent years I've come to know Frank Casper, Colin Waldron, Paul Fletcher, Martin Dobson, Steve Kindon and Dave Thomas through the books I've written. They are far removed from today's distant and unapproachable superstars but are twice the players that many of today's very average internationals will ever be.

I am in regular contact with Paul Fletcher in connection with his own book, *Magical*, that I helped him with. But Dave Thomas; I hadn't spoken to Dave for at least a couple of years and knew full well what his feelings about Adamson were so I gave him a call on the grounds that he might be interested to hear what the latest project was. Plus I had read in a newspaper clipping that he had been suspended by Burnley for a two-week period in the early 1970s and wanted to check if this was correct. It was something that I had not come across before. He had no recollection of such a thing happening.

An e-mail from Alan Parker was waiting for me when I got back at the end of June 2012 from Greece. He had been busy. If this book wins any prizes (that would be nice) Alan will merit huge thanks. A chap called Ken Dixon had phoned him to say that there might have been photographs that had previously been in the old Ashington FC clubhouse. It was now the site of an Asda supermarket and there was uncertainty as to what happened to all the old pictures. Maybe Jimmy was on one or two of them, but Alan who had been in the old clubhouse many times could not recall seeing any of him.

Ken Brown contacted Alan and remembered being at school with Jimmy. He said they were in a class of 46 pupils and Jimmy was the top lad in maths. He was always cheerful, a natural sportsman and in whatever sport he played he excelled, and in fact was at that age a better cricketer than footballer. Sportsmen are often so multi-talented; Harry Potts was the same, as good at cricket as he was at football in his younger days.

Alan had also spoken to Alf Martin who had played with Jimmy at East Chevington Juniors; Alf remembered that it was not Jimmy's father who used to take Jimmy to matches but an uncle. It begged the question, did his father not have any interest in Jimmy's sporting abilities? Alf recalled that East Chevington were so successful and won everything they entered, that a rule had to be introduced that imposed a ten-mile radius on the catchment area. Crowds of up to 400 used to watch these games. A crowd of 3,000 watched a representative game that Jimmy played in, when the best of the North-East Minor FA played the Scottish Minor FA at Portland Park in Ashington.

The north-east lads won 5-4 and Jimmy scored the fifth goal. On the team sheet Adamson was listed as a Burnley player so this must have been a game he came back for. It was significant that the name Dave Blakey was listed in connection with East Chevington. From this it was instantly clear that their relationship went right back to boyhood and Blakey, who played hundreds of games for Chesterfield, teamed up again years later at Burnley with Adamson to become chief scout and then followed Jimmy to Sunderland and Leeds.

The network of people involved up in Ashington now totalled seven – Mike Kirkup, Alan Parker, Bill Ogilvie, Ken Dixon, Ken Brown, Jim Nichol and Alf Martin. Kirkup, another huge source of help, expressed the feelings of perhaps all of them when he referred to Jimmy as 'our working class hero whose name is spoken with pride and reverence in his native Ashington'.

* * *

In the summer of 1972 two much-loved people left Burnley Football Club. On 30 June Harry Potts was dismissed. Secreted away in his small, windowless office under the Cricket Field Stand, having nothing to do at all with first team matters, shunned by Adamson, he must surely have been astute enough to realise his position was intolerable and his time at the club was coming to an inevitable end. Totally marginalised, his position within the club was almost completely irrelevant. He could possibly have sat tight and banked his generous salary but there had been a reported fall-out between him and Bob Lord.

There is no record of what it was about; it's guesswork but possibly it was in connection with Lord's accusation in the press that the standard of player recruitment had been insufficient during the 1960s. That would have stung Harry badly if he had felt it was aimed at him, even unwittingly. But as things stood, in June 1972 Harry was no longer kicking a ball on the fields at Gawthorpe but was just kicking his heels in a cheerless office. Margaret Potts told the story in *Harry Potts – Margaret's Story*:

'There were times when Harry felt a real sense of loneliness and no-one knew that better than his great friend, the Reverend Alan Reid, who remembers the dull, drab Friday morning when Harry asked him to come down to chat to him and to provide some welcome company. Reid recalls how Potts confided in him that he was fed up, and that he felt there was no-one now he could talk to or trust other than the secretary, Albert Maddox.

'People in this position know full well when it is time to leave with quiet dignity, when other people around them simply want rid of them. His dismissal was ratified at a board meeting and the circumstances were brief but illuminating. Under normal circumstances both Potts and Adamson attended meetings, Potts as general manager, and Adamson as manager. This was one meeting, however, that Adamson did not attend.

'The meeting proceeded, various matters were discussed and then not until normal business had been concluded did Potts and his legal representative enter the room. The minutes reported that "it was resolved that in the best interests of Burnley Football and Athletic Co. Ltd. that the services of Mr Harry Potts as general manager be dispensed with. It was further agreed that Mr Potts be offered the sum of £28,125 in full settlement".

'In blunt terms he was sacked. There were no sweetening words, nothing to acknowledge or thank him for his successes at the club and the glory he had helped achieve; there were no words such as amicable, reluctant or mutual. We can only suppose what was meant by "in the best interests of Burnley Football and Athletic Co. Ltd". It was a bittersweet and humiliating way to end his time at Turf Moor.'

In truth it was in the best interests of Jimmy Adamson and Bob Lord that Potts should leave. It must have been uncomfortable for them to encounter him in a corridor or on a matchday. Just how do you conduct yourself with someone you no longer want around the place? More disconcertingly for them, there were still players there who looked up to Harry, older players like John Angus, Arthur Bellamy and Les Latcham, along with younger ones like Dave Thomas and Steve Kindon.

By this time there was no love lost between Thomas and Adamson. At the same time as the Potts/Adamson 'partnership' was finally expiring, so it was at Manchester City with Malcolm Allison and Joe Mercer. The parallels were striking; the younger man wanting to usurp the older and the older being moved 'upstairs'. Harry Potts never walked by anyone without some kind of cheery greeting or health enquiry or brief conversation. Jimmy Adamson could walk right by a person on some days without even an acknowledgement. He could be moody and unpredictable.

'HARRY POTTS GOES' said the headline on Tuesday 4 July. Hundreds of Burnley folk were going as well – except they were going to Blackpool for the annual holidays. You wonder if the timing of the announcement was deliberate as Burnley became almost a ghost town. The railway and bus stations were filled with them clutching suitcases and bags. Potts and Lord issued a joint statement to say that he had relinquished his duties as general manager.

Lord added that the matter was settled and several weeks later at the AGM confirmed that Potts had been treated handsomely. He had received a £28,000 pay-off. The arrangement had not worked out, he added, omitting to mention that Adamson just did not get on with Potts and could barely tolerate him. While Harry Potts and Margaret must have felt deflation and sadness, Adamson must surely have felt a sense of achievement and satisfaction.

Years later, Paul Fletcher thought of another possible reason why both Lord and Adamson might have wanted Potts out of the club. Harry's wife Margaret was feisty, independent and had no hesitation in saying what she thought and this in an age and a town where a woman's place was to be seen not heard.

Fletcher e-mailed, 'Running up to the 1970s, women played no part in football. Burnley, like all clubs, had a directors' room for the men and a ladies' room quite separate where the wives could meet whilst they waited for their husbands. It was very much a man's world both on and off the field. So, I can imagine Margaret wanting to say her two-penn'orth at a time when her comments would not be welcome. I wouldn't rule it out that her views unwittingly helped Harry get the sack.'

Hilda Lord was a stickler for certain traditions at the club and on match days. Margaret questioned most of them.

The summer also saw the sale of the hugely popular Steve Kindon to Wolves just four years after he had burst on to the scene as part of the victorious Youth Cup team of 1968. As ever, someone had to go in order to fund the generous wages. With Leighton James coming through, Kindon was superfluous. But years later, Kindon still bridles at Adamson and the way things were done:

> 'Jimmy Adamson was a better tactician than Harry. He was like Bill McGarry [at Wolves], much more of a tactician than a man-manager. But Jimmy Adamson was as far as I'm concerned a two-faced so-and-so. One day towards the end of the 1971/72 season, Jimmy sought me out. He put his arm round my shoulders and he told me that next season I'm going to build a team round you. It surprised me a bit because I never thought I was really his sort of player. I was the knock and run type whereas Adamson wanted the tippy-tappy team sort.
>
> 'Dave Thomas didn't fit in either because he was too individualistic. My fiance and I had decided to marry on 3 June and we were thinking about buying a house locally. I asked Adamson whether I should buy or rent as I didn't want to commit myself to a mortgage if I was about to move on. He told me emphatically I should buy. Assured by this, we went ahead and bought a place just off the Manchester Road. I spent most of the summer doing it up. Then just eight days after our wedding, I was transferred to Wolves. Apparently, the deal had been stitched up for some time before.'

Dave Thomas and Jimmy Adamson did not see eye to eye. 'He wasn't my cup of tea as a person,' said Thomas years later but he simultaneously acknowledged what a good coach he was and mentioned the hours he spent with the youth team prior to the final in 1968. Perhaps Thomas made his affection for Potts and his dislike of Adamson too obvious; he would play only a handful of games in the early parts of the promotion season before being sold.

'Burnley are the tops,' wrote Bill Mallinson, who then went on to point out that Jimmy Adamson might well have the last laugh over those who mocked his claim that Burnley would be the 'Team of the Seventies'. Rather than talk about that, Adamson preferred to talk about the emergence of Geoff Nulty. Dave Thomas was still at the club but a transfer seemed inevitable. He was supremely talented, two-footed, could whip over a cross with pinpoint accuracy, and possessed pace and acceleration. They had yet another confrontation when Adamson accused him of lacking mental toughness. Adamson constantly referred to 'mental toughness'. Thomas was furious and to this day regards it as an absurd claim. If Thomas possessed flair, then Nulty fulfilled the 'worker' ethic. In Leighton James Burnley already possessed one wing wizard. Two was a luxury. Thomas was therefore dispensable.

'I just couldn't get on with Jimmy Adamson; he was totally different to me,' Thomas said. 'There was no future at Burnley for me. I said to Jimmy Adamson that I wasn't happy and that I wanted to leave. The biggest problem at Burnley was the policy of bringing up the players and then selling them, but the supply dried up. Putting kids in the team was a big gamble by Jimmy Adamson; he was thinking we're getting beaten with all the first-teamers, so we might as well get beat with all the young lads who are going to give him more of a response.

'We beat Leeds 5-1 but it all caught up with us; it worked well for a while but then it went pear-shaped. Adamson had to go back to the first-team regulars that he'd ditched and ask them to come back and I feel certain it did more harm than good in the long run. He wasn't the best man-manager, Adamson; he had a funny way of dealing with people. I always remember Steve Kindon getting changed thinking he was playing, and Adamson asked him what he was doing. He'd dropped him but not told him; he'd left it right until the last minute. Adamson wasn't open and up front. He played games with you.'

Bearing in mind that Adamson only added one more player to the squad, had sold Steve Kindon, and within weeks sold the unhappy and stubborn Dave Thomas, plus much of the season previously had been mediocre to say the least; it makes the promotion of 1972/73, and the elegant style of that promotion, all the more remarkable. Full-back Keith Newton was the one person to be brought in. An experienced England international stagnating somewhat at Everton, he readily joined Adamson's Burnley and went on to have two of the best seasons of his career.

'I think we'll be among the promotion contenders,' announced Adamson, forgetting perhaps that his previous 'Team of the Seventies' prediction had been so inaccurate. In his favour were the six consecutive wins at the end of the previous season although Burnley folk were unimpressed by his confidence with gates down to less than 9,000. Neither Kindon nor Thomas had featured in those six games. Adamson's new team was planned not around them, but without them. Only 17 players were used during the season and three of those hardly featured meaning that it was just 14 players that played week in and week out.

It resulted in stability and consistency, two things that were missing previously. It was the key to the season, plus goalkeeper Alan Stephenson and Keith Newton, the two most recent acquisitions who shored up the once suspect defence. This might have been a team that played slick, attacking football, but it was also the most parsimonious team in the division, conceding just 35 goals.

Adamson said that he now knew what to expect in the division and felt better equipped this time. He didn't expect to give away soft goals as they had done previously. He was absolutely right. Something else he said was at the club's Annual General Meeting at the town's Keirby Hotel, just prior to the start of the season. Not many months earlier he had informed the supporters he felt they were too critical but now at the AGM he told them they were needed to work for the good of the club. Adamson, whose public relations skills would never be his strong point, added, 'Sometimes the criticism is beyond a joke. I know that I am not a popular figure in Burnley. I would like to be, but that is not so.' It was a remarkable thing to say.

A shareholder responded by saying that he did used to be. 'That was in my playing days when things were easier,' Adamson responded.

Sometimes a group of players that gel come together. Some had been there three or four seasons already but came good in this particular season. Only Fletcher, Stevenson and Newton had been brought in during Adamson's managerial time. If a successful team needs to fit like a jigsaw puzzle, this one had all the right pieces in the right places. Adamson could truly say it was his creation. Sadly it was Lord's to break up and this he eventually did, breaking Adamson's heart when Dobson went.

The pre-season games were disappointing but also misleading. Against a background in the town of strike actions at the Lucas factory and on several building sites, Adamson opened the season with an impressively long unbeaten run but football, as ever, produced a real upset when it was Orient who ended it.

Maybe in the long run early cup exits helped. Burnley lost in the first round of the League Cup and in their first contest of the FA Cup against Liverpool but only in the replay at Anfield after a 0-0 draw at Burnley when they outplayed Liverpool for long spells. The 14 players who formed the backbone of the season were then free to concentrate on the league. One of them was Leighton James and as Thomas's star waned, James's rose spectacularly. When Thomas went to rivals QPR for £165,000, plus the £80,000 for Steve Kindon, Bob Lord had swelled the coffers considerably.

Perhaps it was when Aston Villa came to Burnley and were beaten 4-1 that optimism increased. It was only early days but Villa were top of the table already. It was a game and a result that as good as made a statement. Take us seriously; we mean business. The unbeaten run began and went on and on and on.

Burnley topped the table after 21 games with a four-point lead. By that time they had lost just the one game after one of those daft results when a bottom team comes and unexpectedly wins; one of the goals being of the variety that will either hit the nearest church spire, or rocket into the net. This one did the latter.

I can still remember being astonished and so was Stevenson, the Burnley goalkeeper. Colin Waldron is still embarrassed by the circumstances. The Orient centre-half had the ball with Waldron mockingly urging him to have a shot at goal assuming it would head high over the bar to safety. To Waldron's amusement he shot from 30 yards but the smile left his face as the ball flew like an arrow into the net.

In the *Burnley Express*, Peter Higgs gave his half-term report as supporters, players, Lord and Adamson all patted themselves on the back, happy but by no means certain yet of promotion:

'If this was a school report Burnley's grades for the first half of the season would go something like this: Conduct A-minus, Diligence A and Progress A-plus. For in every sense the opening to the 1972/73 season has been tremendously encouraging for Burnley FC. In the first half of the season, the Clarets have emerged as the outstanding team in the Second Division. So strong is their position that even though they were without a match on Saturday Burnley could not have been toppled from the leading place.

'Before the season began, manager Jimmy Adamson said, "We can win promotion."

He added, "A good start is important. If we get this, it will give us the confidence to go out and play football."

'At the same time, no-one could have foreseen that the Clarets' start would be better than just good. It was fantastic. After 20 games they have lost just once. This was made more surprising by the pre-season form which hardly indicated such instant success. Defeats against Bristol Rovers and Blackpool followed by a home draw against Carlisle seemed to suggest that Burnley were still seeking the right formula and the fans might have to be patient. But after two indifferent draws the Clarets hammered high-riding Aston Villa 4-1 at Turf Moor and scored four wonderful goals in the process. Suddenly they were on their way.

'The confidence that comes with success saw the team grow in stature. The obvious skill and natural ability, combined with understanding and faith in each other, put them in a different class than almost every other team they have met. Even when they have not won, the Clarets invariably have been the better team. Only Queens Park Rangers and Middlesbrough have looked promotion threats. There was of course that sad defeat against lowly Orient. But any team is allowed one slip-up, and the three victories that followed have surely made up for it.

'When searching for the reasons for Burnley's rise to the top, one need not look any further than the 11 men who currently make up the team. Strength and consistency throughout have been its driving forces. But, it has been interesting to note how some members of the side have developed over the first half of the season. Stevenson, Waldron, Thomson, Dobson and Casper have all played an important part in Burnley's progress. But none, one would suggest respectfully, have surprised anyone. We all knew they could play as well as they have.

'When Keith Newton arrived no-one really knew what to expect. At the age of 31, and following a season languishing in Everton's reserves, was he over the hill? Any doubts were quickly dispelled when Keith showed that all the ability of an England international was still there. He has tightened up the left side and brought a steadying influence not only to the defence but the whole team. On the other flank Mick Docherty has made the right-back spot his own with many excellent displays. Can you remember a winger getting the better of him all season?

'Jimmy Adamson recently hinted that more Burnley players deserved U-23 recognition. Two names I would put forward are those of Docherty and Paul Fletcher. To his known assets of aerial skill and non-stop effort, Fletcher has added a scoring flair which has made him one of the division's top marksmen. If he can continue to knock in the goals at his present rate the ex-Bolton striker will soon make a big name for himself. One player who has done that already this season is, of course, Leighton James. A match-winner in Burnley's early season games, he was lifted into the superstar class by the press and television. Now, every full-back in the country is waiting for him.

'In midfield two players have emerged from the shadows to become vital cogs in the Burnley machine. The heading and tackling qualities of Geoff Nulty have done a lot to strengthen the defence. Doug Collins could justifiably claim to be the greatest success of all. He has become the 'general' of the Burnley team, and in the words of Adamson, makes the others play.

'One player who has not been mentioned is David Thomas. He was a key figure in Burnley's early-season run, hitting four goals in 10 matches, as many as he had scored in a complete season before. Fans who doubted the wisdom of his £165,000 departure to QPR might be interested in the following facts. In the first seven matches since he left, Burnley picked up 10 points and Rangers secured seven.

'In general, it has been a wonderful first half of the season. People in football seem unanimously agreed that Burnley are the best side in the division and you will have to search hard to find someone who thinks that they won't go up. But, the one place where promotion is not being taken for granted is at Burnley Football Club.

'With 29 points from 20 games the Clarets are well on course. If they double that total in the second half of the season they will almost certainly go up. I've heard it said that 56 points will be enough and with the level of competition in the Second Division this year that could well be true. Next month is likely to be crucial. After travelling to Blackpool on Boxing Day, Burnley face tough away fixtures at Villa and QPR, plus a third-round FA Cup tie at Liverpool. If they emerge from these encounters with their morale still held high, I can see little to halt a happy return to Division One.

'But one word of warning – as the school report says, "A very promising start. Now they must not slip back into old habits."'

Higgs's optimism was justified. This was now a highly cohesive, talented and determined bunch of dedicated players. Their closeness and camaraderie was obvious. They enjoyed each other's company when staying overnight on away trips with their games of bedroom golf and continuous pranks. On their return to Burnley Fletcher would take out his ukulele for an impromptu sing-song the nearer they got to home and then down the long slope of Manchester Road into the town. Jimmy Adamson always remembered these final moments of the return trips fondly. This was a real band of brothers and there was something special about them. Such a group doesn't come along too often.

If the early 4-1 win over Aston Villa made a statement, it was the 1-0 win away at Sheffield Wednesday that brought national attention when it was featured on *Match of the Day*. 'Did you see Burnley this weekend?' asked Frank Nicklin, sports editor at *The Sun*. 'How the hell do they manage it?'

He waxed lyrical about all things Burnley, the discovery of new talent, the production line at the Gawthorpe training ground and the stubborn pride of this club that had to sell to survive. This was a club that was dedicated to getting back to the First Division and the story of Burnley was a lesson to all the over-rich clubs who waved a chequebook in the pursuit of success.

Geoff Nulty was a Jimmy Adamson success story. Discarded by Stoke City, it was Adamson who took him under his wing as a full-back, but via a stint at centre-forward he returned him to the back four, and then finally to midfield.

The position became his own for the next three years until he too would be sold. Not that Nulty was treated with kid gloves by Adamson who had the infuriating habit in training, or during practice games, of stopping what was going on and beckoning with his finger, rather like a haughty headmaster would beckon a recalcitrant schoolboy, to an individual player to come to him to be given instructions, a dressing down or advice. It was something that seemed to happen to Nulty frequently and he eventually became incensed by it. It was something that infuriated Dave Thomas as well.

'I swear if he does that again I'm walking off,' said a fuming Nulty, or words to that effect to his team-mates one day. A small deputation went to see Adamson. 'Just ask him why he's the first name on the team sheet,' Adamson responded, employing a little bit of psychology.

Two of the three league games that Higgs referred to saw victories – at Blackpool and Villa and after them I can still remember all those years ago thinking that this must surely be a promotion season. Blackpool and Villa were up there at the top, clear rivals to Burnley and desperate to win themselves. At Blackpool there was the added spice of their manager being Harry Potts. It wasn't his day.

The night before, Christmas, Burnley stayed overnight in a motel to 'get away from it all'. Adamson wrote in the following programme that Waldron had distinguished himself as a bingo caller as they all had a great night. It paid off as two Casper goals and two Blackpool players sent off gave Burnley the points.

These chapters are not intended to be simply a procession of game reports and results, but of all the games in 1972/73 it was the 3-0 away win at Aston Villa that convinced us all this was it; this was the return to the big time, promotion was truly possible. It was an utterly brilliant display and the press were in raptures. 'WHO CAN STOP BURNLEY NOW' headlined the *Burnley Express*. The newspaper wrote:

> 'This was billed as Villa's big chance to prove that they are promotion material. They may still make it but only as very dim figures in the shadows of all-conquering Burnley who have now notched up five away wins on the trot. On this fascinating, fiery form, nothing is going to stop Jimmy Adamson's lads rolling right back into the big time. Yet even now, after thrashing Villa out of sight, manager Adamson will not admit he has promotion in his pocket.
>
> '"I remember some years ago Burnley were more than half a dozen points clear at the top of the First Division at this stage of the season, but Ipswich came through to win the Championship. I hope that sort of thing does not happen to us now, but from experience I know it is always possible. I will be satisfied if my team go on giving me the effort and skill they have shown so far. You could not get a better bunch of players. I am proud of them."
>
> 'Make no mistake; Adamson is entitled to walk tall with pride. This Burnley brigade bristles with enthusiasm and team spirit. Villa were overwhelmed by the crisp moves started by Dobson and fluently carried out by the slick skills of Casper, Fletcher and James. Whenever Villa managed to string together a couple of passes, the attack was snuffed out by defenders who always had a team-mate in support to allow the first tackle to be made with confidence. Burnley's aggressive attitude enabled them to make any ball a 50-50 chance, no matter how high the odds were stacked against them.
>
> 'Villa's long ball game aimed at the old Burnley striker Andy Lochhead was a complete waste of time, so certain was Waldron in his aerial supremacy. As if to rub salt in

the wound, Villa were shattered when full-back Newton opened the scoring. It was only his eleventh goal in a career of nearly 400 games and his first for Burnley. Remembering that the old England full-back was a no-fee cast-off from Everton must have hurt Villa even more deeply. A slick, free kick, set-piece involving Ingham and Casper allowed Newton to knock in the goal that put the skids under Villa.

'Two smart saves by Stevenson, from a speculative long-range shot by Evans, and a curling corner from Graydon, were the only moments of Burnley peril in a first half they controlled from first to last. Though James might have emphasised Burnley's domination by snatching a couple of goals, it was left to Nulty to send Villa off to a half-time dressing down from manager Vic Crowe. Casper's cross made scoring easy for Nulty.

'Proving that you can make your own luck by putting every effort into your game, Ingham strode on to his first league goal early in the second half when James miskicked a shot that turned into a glorious pass. Stevenson again showed his Young England class with superb saves from Graydon and Rioch, but these were hit-and-hope shots with no controlled build-up to the openings. Villa must sort themselves out quickly to keep in touch with the promotion battle. But Burnley were simply outstanding.'

Supporters, meanwhile, learned that the FA Cup game against Liverpool would not be televised when Bob Lord denied the BBC permission to bring their cameras, saying that in his view there was too much football on television and the financial recompense did not make it worthwhile. He wondered if other clubs would support him and follow his example. None did. He added that no club could give money away and still be run properly as he argued that the attendance would be drastically reduced by TV coverage. Supporters were not best pleased but this, as ever, was something that didn't trouble Lord too much.

Meanwhile Jimmy Adamson fumed again at Don Revie when Revie announced, 'Leighton James is the best prospect I've seen.' Adamson was already incensed at the way in which he felt that Revie was responsible for unsettling Dave Thomas and there was no love lost between the two managers. Hearing that Adamson was angry, Revie hit back, saying, 'I am happy to see that Jimmy Adamson has gone on record as saying that his brilliant 19-year-old Welshman, Leighton James, is the most exciting prospect he has seen for many years. I have seen the lad play twice and I'd like Jimmy to know that I agree with him.'

Adamson had earlier claimed after he sold Dave Thomas to QPR, 'Thomas has been unhappy for a while. I blame the system and the one or two managers who have made comments that have unsettled him.'

Revie countered with, 'Jimmy is a friend of mine but I think he is being childish.' The spat would continue the following season.

Promotion was clinched in a Monday evening game with a 2-0 win over Sunderland where Paul Fletcher scored both goals. 'Jimmy Adamson has brought my finest hour' headlined the Bob Lord article in the Thursday 19 April edition of the *Burnley Express*. He could afford to be bullish. His decisions to back Adamson and support him through the torrid previous seasons had been thoroughly vindicated. Both he and Adamson had endured abuse and criticism that had been relentless and personal. Now, Lord could defiantly say, 'I told you so.' He said:

> 'When Burnley clinched promotion to the First Division at ten past nine on Monday evening, it gave me more satisfaction than anything else I have experienced in football. We have had some great moments during the time I have been chairman at Burnley, but this was the best of all. When we won the championship in 1960 the maximum wage was still in force; there were not the huge amounts of money about, nor was football the rat-race that it is today. That is why I think it is wonderful that despite the very heavy odds against us, we have brought success to a town of this size.
>
> 'We have not only put Burnley back on the football map, we've put them on the world map. And this is something the town should be grateful for. When we were relegated from the First Division two years ago, I did not expect to get us back so soon. I would not have been disappointed if we had failed to get promotion this season.

'What has given me most pleasure is that everyone who criticised the policy of the club, and the policy of the manager, has now been proved wrong. In the past 12 months we have made many friends and reduced the number of doubters. I do not wish to deny the bouquets to anyone, but one man must take the lion's share of the credit – manager Jimmy Adamson. This is HIS victory!

'He proved himself 12 months ago when there was a section of people who literally wanted his scalp. But never in the three years since he has been manager have I myself, or the board lost faith in Jimmy Adamson. He has always had our 100 per cent support, and this must have helped him in his difficult task.

'I had faith in Jimmy the first time I met him in 1947; that faith grew by the time he made his first-team debut in 1951 and, by the late 1950s we had become very attached to one another because his views on life are very much on the same pattern as mine. I realised that here was a man of principle who was dedicated to carrying out those principles. He was not prepared to accept half measures.

'I have never lost faith in him, and have been prepared to wait for his policies to come right. So many clubs make the mistake of being impatient because of the importance of their supporters. We value the support of our fans, but we have our own methods and we stand by them.

'When the club was relegated I called a meeting of all the players and backroom staff and told them that the directors had decided to continue to run the club on First Division lines. We were not to consider ourselves a second-class outfit. I indicated that this was not a day of mourning, but a day of reckoning. We had been knocked down but there was nothing to stop us getting up again.

'To the undying credit of everyone at Turf Moor, we have managed it in two years. The players are a wonderful set of lads for whom I have every regard, and they have been aided by the loyalty and dedication of Jimmy Adamson's hard-working staff.'

Lord went on to spend another couple of hundred words praising Martin Dobson in particular. But, less than two years on he would be sold and it would mark the end of any future hopes that Adamson had for success.

The championship was secured at Preston North End. A draw would have been the perfect result for both clubs as it would have ensured Second Division survival for Preston. Not unsurprisingly it was a 1-1 draw and once Burnley had equalised with a Colin Waldron pile-driver the remaining minutes were played out in a gentlemanly, unthreatening fashion with each side seemingly desperate not to score again. Burnley fans crammed in like sardines could hardly breathe.

If there is one sentence in the Lord article that sums up his feeling of triumph and supremacy, it is surely, 'What has given me most pleasure is that everyone who criticised the policy of the club, and the policy of the manager, has been proved wrong.'

The close relationship between Lord and Adamson was now at its optimum level and would stay so for another season. His praise for him was fulsome. For now, it was a mutual admiration society and neither was there any Harry Potts around the place to make either of them feel uncomfortable.

Those supporters who had grumbled not many months earlier were silenced. Plaudits were showered on both the manager and chairman. The Sunday dinners at the Lord house were filled with conversation and smiles. Life was good.

Chapter 11

Back at the top

I T IS funny that the favourite period I have of football at Burnley dates back to a time when the team came so close to being triumphant, but eventually failed, and they won nothing – except legions of admirers. It was a period that began at the start of the Adamson promotion season of 1972/73 and ended in March 1975 when by then the effects of player sales ended all real ambition. But in between it was a magical time. There was a group of players that came so tantalisingly close to perfection and it was just such a good time to be around Turf Moor. Those players were of my own generation and I could dream and muse that it might have been me out there.

'The Team of the Seventies' ... I felt like I was one of them. I can still see the most perfect display of passing football in a game in what seemed like 90 degrees at a sweltering Molineux and a 2-0 win. I was there at Elland Road for the 4-1 victory over Leeds United and a Christmas 2-1 home win over Liverpool. I remember bumping into a group of college friends I hadn't seen for years behind the goals at Burnley (I now see them regularly, and we're all growing old together). There were still the meat and tatie pies at my mother's house and by now, as a bonus, she had stopped dropping the cigarette ash into them.

If I had to choose a decade to re-live I'm pretty sure it would be the 1970s. We were free of children; they hadn't arrived yet. My career was taking off and I was a deputy headmaster. We had money in our pockets and went out for a meal every Friday night – ah, the height of decadence – a schooner of sherry, steak and chips and a bottle of Mateus Rose at a Berni Inn (only those of a certain age will remember them) and we thought it was the peak of sophistication. Every day was a gift and the sun seemed to shine every day – or at least it seems so now. Nostalgia I suppose at its most blinkered. Colin Waldron was voted the best-looking player in football and we thought 'wow' when it transpired his favourite meal, in a magazine article, was steak au poivre, at a time when most footballers would have said egg and chips. His best pal Paul Fletcher still rags him that he had no idea what au poivre really was.

In truth it was a turbulent decade, both at Turf Moor and in the outside world. The Watergate scandal was Nixon's downfall in the USA, the IRA began their blitz on the UK, the USA failed miserably in Vietnam, by 1975 there was a severe economic crisis in the UK, Prime Minister Wilson resigned in 1976, almost amusingly there was the Cod War crisis in 1976, Elvis and Charlie Chaplin died in 1977 and in 1979 Earl Mountbatten was killed in Ireland by the IRA.

At the close of the decade early in 1979, discontented public sector workers made life almost intolerable as rubbish went uncollected, food and petrol supplies were disrupted and there were pickets at hospitals. Margaret Thatcher entered Number 10 as Prime Minister in May.

At Turf Moor the decade began with failure, then came Adamson's three-year period of beauty, the 'crash' of January 1976 with relegation by the end of the season and then a slow decline that saw Burnley in the Third Division by May 1980. By then, Adamson at Leeds United was on the brink of the end of his life in football, and endured car park demonstrations and the cruel taunts in pubs and clubs around Leeds that he was totally unwanted at the club.

If this chapter dwells on two games in particular, it is not without reason. Football is all about opinions, and personal opinions at that. The games and results at Elland Road and then at Hillsborough in March 1974, in my opinion shaped Adamson's remaining career at Burnley, and then the history of Burnley FC after that, since both games had such massive consequences for the club. Everyone who saw them, or who participated as a player, has never forgotten them.

One of them was against Leeds United and after that game, on the following Sunday morning, I was in the local newspaper shop just across the road from my home in Leeds and in came one of the cast of *Emmerdale*. A few of them lived locally in flats and apartments. This one came in, and I've forgotten his name, and announced to all and sundry, 'I've just seen the Cup-winners.' He had seen Burnley tear Leeds apart and forecast that they would do the same to Newcastle. How I wish that he had been right.

At the beginning of the new season, 1973/74, the only addition to the squad was Peter Noble from Swindon Town and the introduction to the season was the Charity Shield game against Manchester City at Maine Road. It was notable because Burnley won and secondly it was won with a goal scored from a classic Adamson free kick scam. If the word 'genius' was used to describe Adamson's coaching skills and his football thinking, this free kick routine was the finest possible example of that genius. He used it at Sunderland as well – and it worked beautifully. Those of us who saw it still talk about it and smile at the memory. You wonder too why no other Burnley manager since has ever used it. Unfortunately there were TV cameras to record the game and show it later nationally so that managers everywhere were alerted to the slick ploy.

One of the chief deceptions was that it appeared to have floundered before it was even taken as players seemingly argued. Then Doug Collins, the usual taker of free kicks, ran over the ball, leaving an apparently disinterested Frank Casper to delicately chip it over to an unmarked Waldron who had ghosted in from nowhere as the opposition seemed hypnotised by the whole thing, further confused by various other dummy runs from Burnley players. Waldron scored with ease. We simply purred at its precision and imagination.

The win made a statement and gave a warning that Burnley would be no pushovers in the coming season. Chelsea, all smooth and sophisticated from the trendy Kings Road, filled with swagger and charisma and no doubt wondering what on earth they were doing in small-town Burnley out in the sticks with its funny accent, were sent packing after a 1-0 defeat at Turf Moor. Football writers like James Mossop thought the whole tale was heart-warming as Burnley showed the millionaire clubs how to do things on a shoestring. The gate money was nowhere near enough to support the wages yet here they were entertaining Chelsea with a new stand going up along one side of the ground and in the youth ranks were young lads like Brian Flynn, Ray Hankin and Ian Brennan almost ready for first team duty.

The Chelsea game was on a night to remember with the brass band playing in the fading light before kick-off, hot pies with their special flavour and men straight from work in overalls and flat caps (perhaps James Mossop was being a bit over-nostalgic regarding the latter). Nevertheless it was Burnley's first night back in the First Division and a real test. In 2009 the opening home game against Manchester United was similarly significant and the result was the same, a 1-0 win for Burnley. The roars nearly brought the stands down at both games.

Before the game Adamson was apprehensive about stepping up a division and knew full well that Burnley had a lot to learn, saying, 'The Second Division is a slightly lower class of football and you can generally tell what a player will do with the ball. The First is different. The players are cunning and they will outwit you so I had to instil in the lads, don't buy anything. If a player shapes to shoot or pass, don't always believe him. Don't let him sell you anything.'

So far the players had shown signs of mastering this but Peter Osgood played for Chelsea, a player who had bundles of skill and class and could always fool the opposition.

After the game Adamson waxed lyrical about how the Burnley players had shown their own cunning. Casper did something that Chelsea were not expecting with the way he took his goal, taking the ball on his chest, swivelling and before it hit the ground, thundering it home with his left foot. The only thing the Chelsea players saw was a blur. It was described as the goal of a lifetime.

Adamson had done something equally original with new man Peter Noble. With Mick Docherty out injured, in an unexpected move that had fans scratching their heads, Adamson pushed midfielder Noble back to full-back. It was an inspired move and Noble played there for most of the season with a level of play that was a revelation.

By now Adamson's assistant was Joe Brown, who had played a few games for Burnley in the early 1950s. 'Just because he was never a great player does not mean he is not a very fine coach,' said Adamson. 'We even pull his leg here. We ask him if they had proper nets in the class of football he played in. The lads list his career as 42 appearances for Bournemouth reserves and 320 appearances for Aldershot "A" Team. In 1960 when Burnley were looking for a coach I was still a player but was helping with the FA courses at Lilleshall. I met Joe there and recommended him to Burnley. He has been with us ever since.'

Jimmy Robson, a former player and member of the 1960 championship team, was also back as youth development officer and played for the reserves prompting and guiding the youngsters coming through.

Week by week, the wins mounted up. Not until 22 September and game eight, did Burnley lose for the first time away at Ipswich. That was then followed by three consecutive wins and the weekly praise was lavish: 'Back where they belong'; 'Burnley flair a winner'; 'Exciting and adventurous talent'; 'back with a bang'; 'Slick Burnley look at home in Division One'; 'Burnley go storming on'; 'brave Burnley'; 'Burnley turn on the heat'; 'Burnley blitz'; 'Bubbling Burnley won't burst'.

And all this was before the near faultless performance at Wolves, resulting in a 2-0 win and second place just one point behind Leeds United in the table. If Adamson was quoted as looking for perfection it was almost here with possession football, passing moves, inventiveness, industry and a style that was a joy to watch. Even the home fans applauded the crisp moves that kept the ball constantly buzzing round the Wolves penalty area.

Adamson praised players like Leighton James, Frank Casper and Martin Dobson, men who had easily raised their game to the new level. 'It's just like Ajax,' said one report with Adamson quoted as saying he never expected to be as high in the table as this and playing so well: 'I am sure we now have a team who are a credit to the First Division.'

Leeds United were totally outplayed at Turf Moor but it ended 0-0. Star-studded glamour club Arsenal were defeated 2-1. Of course there were defeats but on Boxing Day there was a superb win over Liverpool. It was a defining game that announced that Adamson's Burnley could beat anybody. 'What a game, what a team,' headlined Peter Higgs in the local press.

With the aroma of brandy from flasks, cigar smoke pervading the air and a crowd of 24,000, there was no Christmas spirit extended to Liverpool and no repeats of the previous Liverpool wins at Turf Moor. This was the star-studded Liverpool of Kevin Keegan, Emlyn Hughes, Tommy Smith, Ray Clemence and Steve Heighway. Bill Shankly, who had once described Burnley as just a little village team, said if he had to lose it was no shame to lose to a fine team like Burnley and better them than anyone else.

The winner came just five minutes from time so Shankly could have been forgiven for any grumpiness but he displayed genuine magnanimity. Burnley's slick passing controlled much of the game, Leighton James tormenting Liverpool incessantly. The first goal was a classic Adamson-designed corner routine with the elegant Dobson flicking the corner on by the near post and Fletcher was in there to head home. Such was Burnley's dominance that the home fans were chanting 'easy, easy, easy'. Cormack equalised but it was Ray Hankin, the 'boy-giant', who hit the winner. Fletcher ceaselessly tormented Emlyn Hughes to reduce him to histrionics. It was a game to savour and remember in a pulsating atmosphere.

If Burnley had a fault it was inconsistency and eventually by the end of the season it would cost them a place in Europe. But for now, the good times were back and Bob Lord sat in his seat with his trademark hat beaming and accepting the accolades. It is not hard to imagine the roast beef and Yorkshire pudding Sunday dinners at Lord's house that Jimmy and May Adamson attended were extremely convivial and enjoyable. There would be no sign then of the way in which Adamson and his wife would come to resent their expected attendance so much at Lord's table.

But those who were realistic knew full well that the old problem still remained; finding the money to pay the very generous wages and maintaining the five-star standard of hotel accommodation and travel. Plus, there was a new stand to pay for. Behind the smiles from Lord and Adamson there was no complacency; both knew that at some stage someone would have to be sold. Maybe that scenario would have been avoided if Burnley had progressed to Wembley but it was not to be.

If the Liverpool game was a triumph, there was an even greater one to come at Elland Road later in the season. That, plus the following game, the FA Cup semi-final against Newcastle United, it could be argued decided the next 30 years of Burnley history. They were defining games with huge consequences. One was a great victory but as good as ended the career of the superb striker Frank Casper. The second was an unmerited defeat that in my opinion definitely affected the course of the Burnley and Adamson story.

If he had reached Wembley it might well have delayed player sales for at least another year. That might well have enabled Burnley to win the title in the following season especially if Casper had not been crippled in the Leeds game. Football is all about one small word, 'if'. Two players would be sold, both of them integral to the team. One of them ranked with the sale of Jimmy McIlroy, years earlier, in its effect and significance. 'If' they had not been sold; 'if' Frank Casper's career had not been ended – maybe there might have been a 'Team of the Seventies' and Adamson's dream would have come true.

Games between Leeds United and Burnley had become tasty affairs. There was no love lost between the two clubs; between Lord and the Leeds directors; between Revie and Adamson. Colin Waldron remembers the game well:

'Prior to the 4-1 win at Leeds they'd been to Turf Moor and it was 0-0. Whenever we played them it was always a battle and I don't know the origin of why it was like that. At Burnley there were several yellow cards I think and we also had this little player called Dougie Collins and he had a real mouth on him and irritated a lot of the Leeds players. After the game as we are coming off, he walks off with me for protection but as we do so, Revie in his sheepskin coat comes over and says to us quite seriously that when we come to Leeds, Collins will have his leg broken. This sort of threat does go on in football, but it is unusual to come from a manager.

'So, in April we go to Leeds and the referee asks both managers into his room to talk about the game and what he expects and when he asks Jimmy for any comments, he tells him, "Mr Revie has offered to break my number ten's leg." Revie goes ballistic and storms out and Jimmy tells us all this afterwards. After the game there was one player who was unmarked and spotlessly clean, and that was Dougie Collins.

'At full time when we came in the dressing room it looked like a battleground. There were cut heads, bruised legs, stitches going in and blood everywhere. We had been hammered. But Dougie – there wasn't a mark, he hadn't been touched. Obviously Revie had told his players to leave Dougie alone, but to thump the rest of us.'

The truth is, the physical side of the game was par for the course in the 1970s and Burnley forward Paul Fletcher will always say that nothing was ever a foul until the referee decided otherwise. In other words you did what you could get away with and Burnley too had their hard men who could certainly put their foot in as and when required, one of whom was Colin Waldron.

Leeds' Johnny Giles elaborated. 'Like a lot of teams we believed that gamesmanship was part of the game.' But, he asked, remembering games at Turf Moor in the 60s, 'Do you think that Leeds bullied everybody? How do you bully Gordon Harris, Brian O'Neil, Andy Lochhead [all of Burnley]? It was tough and it wasn't right.'

On a radio show in 2012 Giles cited Burnley (the only team he referred to by name) as being a 'hard' team. The physical rivalry between the two clubs was nothing new so even in 1974 it remained and there was a mindset that was simply a continuation of a decade of 'let's-get-into-this-lot' confrontations.

This was the season that would end with Leeds as champions, suffering only four defeats. One of them was this one as Burnley, despite all the provocation, methodically put four goals past them. One press piece reported it as 'The Invincibles' against 'shoe-string Burnley'. It was an accurate analogy.

I lived in Leeds then, still do, and was at the game. We stood in the Leeds end behind the goal close to the touchline very near the front. Fletcher's wonderful overhead goal was at the end far away from us and we didn't realise it had gone in until every Burnley fan's arms were raised high in the air and the roars rang down the ground. But we certainly saw Doug Collins's delicate chip from the corner of the box dink over goalkeeper Harvey's head for the third, and then Geoff Nulty bundle the ball home on his knees inside the six-yard box for the fourth.

Nulty remembers the goal well and that it was the result of the repertoire of free kick routines that Adamson had taught them. He recalls, 'We had some really sharp dead-ball routines in our repertoire. We reckoned that if we were awarded a free kick within 35 yards of our opponents' goal we had a decent chance of scoring. At Elland Road we were awarded a free kick about 30-35 yards from the Leeds goal on our right. Dougie Collins took the kick but instead of knocking it towards the far post, as the Leeds defenders were expecting him to do, he chipped it towards the near post. Colin Waldron anticipated Doug's intentions perfectly and made a run towards the near post. Here he headed the ball across the face of the goal, where I nodded it in, on all fours, at David Harvey's feet. At 4-1 up we were out of sight.'

Alas we also saw the tackle by Hunter that put Casper out of the game from our positions just feet away. Casper had crossed the ball but with the ball gone Hunter came clattering in and down went Casper. I can still see the snarling look on Hunter's face as he looked down on the fallen Casper.

None of the Leeds players were happy that afternoon. Their intimidatory tactics had failed. Fletcher still remembers the spitting and the threats against them in the tunnel as they came out for the game. Bremner asked Fletcher how he would feel to have two broken legs. Fletcher responded by telling him how surprised he was to hear him speak in a sentence.

Casper hadn't been back in the team for long. In a game against Spurs some months earlier he had been carried off after a tackle; it took him five months to get back in the side with a bit of Adamson psychology keeping his spirits up as he kept telling him he would be back in just a few weeks. Paul Fletcher, too, was 'kidded' into playing at Leeds. He had suffered a bad dose of flu and was still not recovered.

On informing Adamson he was told that if he didn't play at Leeds he would not play in the semi-final. He played and scored twice. To this day Fletcher says they would have traded the result for an uninjured Casper.

Colin Waldron commented, 'The tackle that took him out of the game has never been forgotten by the players or the supporters who were there.'

The Burnley players fumed after the game, incensed at the injury. Peter Higgs was there as well: 'Casper brought the ball down Burnley's left wing. He centred into the goalmouth and the ball must have been ten to 15 yards away when Hunter's kick from behind took both Casper's legs away and left him dumped on the edge of the pitch.'

Adamson refused to say much about the incident, save to say he didn't think they allowed tackles on the running track. His comments after the game regarding the result were down-to-earth. He was realistic enough to know that this stunning win guaranteed nothing the next Saturday in the semi against Newcastle.

He did say, 'We are concerned about the injury but hope it is not as bad as at first feared. But it puts us in a bad frame of mind for the cup-tie. We have got to get our feet back on the ground. A result like this helps bring confidence and that is alright as long as the players do not get too confident. We can't live next week off this week's result.'

Bob Lord had stayed away from the game having boycotted the Leeds directors' box but afterwards praised the players for showing their rivals how to play football. The week before, Manny Cussins of Leeds, still angry about remarks made by Lord about the role of Jews controlling television and thus getting football on the cheap on TV, had threatened to snub Lord if he turned up. Of course Lord was branded a racist and anti-Semitic but in truth he had good friends who were Jewish and to accuse someone of 'jewing' was still part of the vocabulary of the age. Had Lord witnessed the tackle by Hunter it is hard to imagine him not commenting about it in the strongest terms.

Paul Fletcher certainly hit out about the Leeds tactics, 'It was going on throughout the match. The Leeds players were spitting at us and elbowing us in the stomach and treading on us every time we went down. But we had the satisfaction of knowing we'd paralysed them.'

On the Sunday after the game the players left for some peace and quiet at a Scottish training camp. Not that they got much; the press followed them and even played golf with them. Casper went with them but when it became clear that the injury was a bad one he was rushed back to Turf Moor for special treatment. Miraculously the swelling was reduced and the fluid was drained. He had a chance of playing.

The players were quietly confident and Colin Waldron saw the game as a chance to show the football world that this team was up there with the glamour boys of Manchester, London and Liverpool, and that Newcastle's Malcolm Macdonald could be smothered. Macdonald, alas, had other ideas, and was equally confident that his pace and strength was more than enough to win the game.

James Mossop seemed to have a private line to Jimmy Adamson and wondered if Burnley would stay cool enough to triumph. With his hands behind his head and leaning back in his chair in his office under the stand, Adamson answered his question; could Burnley retain their assurance against a background of the Newcastle hordes and their songs?

'I don't know,' he answered. 'You can't tell with semi-finals. On a semi-final day nerves twang and muscles tighten. The slightest mistake chases after a player.' It had happened to him in the 1960s in two semi-finals, one lost and one won. He continued, 'It all depends on the team on the day. I remember the semi-final we lost against Tottenham 3-0 at Aston Villa. We didn't want to play at Villa in the first place. It wasn't a happy hunting ground. Maybe it affected our temperament. Today's team isn't too keen on Villa Park either. That is why we are glad to go to Sheffield. Skill will not count for a lot. There is so much at stake. Getting to Wembley is the goal; after a semi-final, Wembley is a day out for everybody.'

The 3-0 defeat against Spurs in the 1961 semi-final had stayed in his mind. 'Atmospheres affect people differently. Some semi-final mistakes have gone down in history, exaggerated beyond all reason.'

In the Villa Park semi-final Adamson had made a mistake failing to clear a ball that 99 times out of 100 he would have dealt with easily. The resultant goal put Spurs in the lead. Burnley were denied a clear penalty; goalkeeper Bill Brown later slipped and appeared to carry the ball over the line. And yet Burnley lost 3-0. Adamson had not forgotten how cruel football can be.

His comments about how some players respond to big games was prophetic, 'Some players perform tremendously in front of a big crowd. That is how one must explain Bobby Moore's consistently brilliant performances in an England shirt. A manager's job before a semi-final is to get the right degree of motivation into his players. Psychology plays such a tremendous part. Bill Shankly must have psychology as his strongest point. He lifts his teams to the perfect pitch and they go on and on winning things. I don't want to over-motivate my players; just bring them to the right pitch so that they go out sharp as razors.'

He spoke about the genius of Leighton James, Burnley's match-winner, explosive, brilliant but also infuriating: 'Leighton has tremendous fighting qualities and this is something a manager is always anxious not to destroy. We know that when he is on song the only way people can stop him is by hacking and clogging as was the case with George Best. Leighton feels he should have more protection and we try to tell him to keep his cool. Often his reply is to take on the whole of the opposition. This can be all right sometimes but it can also affect our general performance.'

The latter was a fascinating comment. More than one Burnley player today agrees with this and he was not entirely popular with his team-mates.

Mossop went on to praise Burnley and Adamson; their success a wonderful reward for all Adamson's work. He reminded readers of the earlier seasons when attendances had slumped, supporters had clamoured for Adamson's dismissal, the unfortunate claim that this would be the 'Team of the Seventies', and the constant sales of the best players. And yet Adamson had never shifted from his blueprint, the team's style was so attractive and Mossop revealed an interesting philosophy of Adamson's; that if you sent out ten inside-forwards and a goalkeeper and added a little organisation you would have a fascinating team that would require little coaching.

And then he said something rather plaintive about Wembley, 'I have been there only once in 1962. Every time I look back I wish I could play the game again, putting things right. It would be nice to be there and not having to stand at the bottom of the steps watching the winners receive their medals when all you want to do is crawl away and hide.'

Alas, after the semi-final against Newcastle, that is all that the Burnley players wanted to do. Adamson's remarks about atmosphere producing big players who respond to the bigness of the occasion could have been specially written for Malcolm Macdonald. Burnley played superbly well but got none of the breaks. Macdonald got two. Both his goals came from clearances that he latched on to round about the halfway line, and then went hell for leather for goal like a bull at a gate. He was unstoppable.

Adamson's comment about teams having the luck on the day was apposite. Burnley had none. They hit the woodwork twice.

McFaul, the Newcastle goalkeeper, was easily the man of the match, something that tells its own story. A patched-up Casper brought out one of the saves of the game. Eventually he was replaced by the burly Hankin. But nothing would run for Burnley and Macdonald himself said later that Newcastle looked like losing the game as for much of the time they simply could not get the ball off Burnley.

'Burnley wiped the floor with us,' he said. 'They were brilliant. Their football just flowed down the right and left, and our keeper Willie McFaul was on overtime. Burnley did everything except put the ball in the net. The second half started in exactly the same vein too, with them camped round our penalty area. But then ...'

But then, Macdonald took over and scored his two breakaway goals. The Newcastle hordes roared. The Burnley end was silenced, their heads bowed and downcast.

'Burnley didn't have a single scrap of luck,' wrote Keith McNee.

'All those who said that Malcolm Macdonald would be too much for the Burnley defence predicted correctly,' wrote Peter Higgs.

'We are sick,' said Jimmy Adamson. 'We are entitled to be upset because we were not beaten by a team who are better at the game than we are. The difference between the teams was that we had no luck and Newcastle had every bit that was going in the penalty area.

Malcolm Macdonald is the kind of centre-forward that no defender can hold when he is in the mood. When Macdonald got a lucky break for the first goal and this lifted them, it put a 10lb weight on our players' legs. They gave me everything.

'When Don Revie, Bill Shankly and Joe Harvey claim they have the best team in the land, they are wrong. I've got it. There isn't a better or more honest bunch of lads in the game. They are the greatest. Right now, my thoughts are for my players. They cried after the game. They gave me everything out there. No manager could ask for more. I'm proud of the way we played in a very sporting game.

'As for me, I'll cry my heart out later tonight but let me say I'll be at Wembley on Cup Final day, shouting for Newcastle and wearing a black and white shirt. We showed our temperament and particularly during the first half. But we needed luck and we didn't get it. Newcastle did. I didn't think Newcastle played very much football and for a lot of the match we murdered them. We're very sad about the result, and we would have loved to have gone to Wembley. But it was not to be.'

Forward Doug Collins was totally dejected and said of the game later, 'It's history now, how Malcolm Macdonald did a one-man demolition job on Burnley to send us out of the FA Cup. But if a survey had been done at 3.30pm last Saturday among the Newcastle players they wouldn't have given a brass farthing for their chances. At that stage several of the Newcastle players believed they were going to lose. It's difficult to tell on the terraces but we knew out on the pitch that a lot of their players had "gone".'

Waldron many years later talked about how and why they had lost. 'Casper's injury was the difference; that, plus not defending. We could dominate games and still lose. Training was geared to going forward and even in the semi-final defenders were encouraged to go forward and make runs. If it were me, I'd have defended with ten. But, says Adamson, go on some runs in the second half. He was always saying get forward. So, in the second half I go on a forward run, I get caught out, ten yards the wrong side of Malcolm Macdonald and up he goes and scores.'

Ironically Newcastle were demolished by Liverpool in one of the most one-sided Cup Finals ever seen. Newcastle were abject. It could be argued they should have been evicted from the competition anyway after disgraceful crowd scenes at Newcastle in the first game with Nottingham Forest in an early round. With Nottingham Forest winning with just minutes to go there was a crowd invasion that stopped the game. When it was re-started after the players had returned to the field several minutes later Newcastle saved the game with the Forest players clearly shaken and nervous. The FA should have had the courage to award the game to Forest but didn't and after a series of replays Newcastle eventually triumphed.

Newcastle beat Burnley again in the final of the Texaco Cup after extra time. It was a competition involving Scottish clubs and during it Burnley had slammed a record number of goals past the Scots, and then Norwich. Who did they come up against in the final? Newcastle of course, and they lost. In April, Burnley played a staggering nine league games. It was all too much and they won just three of them. One of them was away at Newcastle with a

2-1 scoreline. The tenth game that month was the Texaco game against Newcastle. The very last game of the season brought a tame end to proceedings with a 1-1 draw against – Newcastle. By then the players were probably sick of seeing each other.

'After all the drama, excitement and passion of the last eight months, Burnley's best league season for eight years, ended not with a bang but a whimper,' wrote Peter Higgs. The finale was an anti-climax with an angry Adamson complaining that the referee had given Newcastle far too much over-protection knowing that they had a Cup Final the following Saturday. Macdonald scored yet again in a game that Newcastle seemed to treat as a practice match.

Nevertheless it had been an amazing season with results and a position in the table that was unexpected and so close to a place in Europe. But if Adamson was pleased and looking forward to the next season this might well have been the time he wondered if it was all worthwhile. There is no record of when or how Lord informed him that someone would have to be sold. Lord knew the financial position regarding the new stand that was nearly completed. There were some players on several thousand pounds a year, some of them allegedly earning a five-figure sum. The conversation might have been in a quiet one-to-one in Lord's office. Maybe it was at one of the Sunday dinners at Lord's house.

It is not hard to imagine that Adamson, being realistic, half expected the news. It is also not hard to imagine that prepared though he might have been, the news was still unwelcome, hugely frustrating and enormously disappointing. There is no record of how they decided that it should be Martin Dobson, or even that Adamson himself was involved in the decision as to who it should be. But one thing is quite possible, and that is that Lord was a planner and could think ahead, and that as soon as the season ended, or even before, he had identified Dobson as being the most valuable and saleable member of the squad.

Adamson must surely have known that the writing was on the wall. In the oft-quoted conversation with Paul Fletcher that took place during the end-of-season club trip to the races, he was asked how he thought they would fare the following season. 'I don't know,' Adamson told Fletcher. 'I want to build a team, but the chairman wants to build a stadium.' Maybe he knew then that

Dobson would be on his way, maybe even before the new season began, but certainly not long after it got underway.

Adamson certainly knew how domineering Bob Lord could be and must also have been well aware of how deeply unpleasant he could be; after all he had worked with him for long enough. But a new aspect of their relationship emerged from the Peter Higgs e-mail. We can make a fair guess that Lord had the previous manager Harry Potts totally in his pocket. But did he completely dominate Jimmy Adamson in the same way? Higgs had dealt with Lord for 12 years and Adamson for four. His e-mail clearly inferred that Adamson too, for many years did as he was told and was possibly even afraid of Lord. It is an astonishing thought.

Whether he was afraid of him or just wary would, however, soon become irrelevant as the chemistry between the two men began to take on a new and different turn.

Chapter 12

Almost the 'Team of the Seventies'

ALAN UP in Ashington was meeting brick walls. He e-mailed to say he had just returned from another fruitless trip to Morpeth library to search for information, this time from the *Ashington Advertiser* and *Blyth News*. Then he had seen, according to City Council websites, there were copies held on microfilm for both papers at Ashington Library. He went there. Yes they had copies but only from 1940 to 1948 and sod's law being what it is, 1946 and 1947, the years when Jimmy might have had a mention for joining Burnley, were missing.

In the meantime I had looked at my long list of people to see and started with Paul Fletcher. It was a 40-mile drive from Leeds to Rawtenstall to see him but his wife had bacon sandwiches and coffee ready. Research is not always drudgery. Next up was Colin Waldron a week later. Colin's wife also had bacon sandwiches and coffee ready. Thoughts of losing a bit of weight seemed forlorn.

I knew from the lists that Jimmy had made on the Basildon pad that they were two of his favourite players. Paul bases all his opinions of Jimmy on the simple premise that Adamson changed his life for the better and as a consequence Paul had ten years at the top end of the football tree. He wouldn't trade his memories for anything. Colin Waldron was skipper of the Burnley side and had been taken into Adamson's confidence on occasions. Alan had been sent a list of questions to go through with John Angus.

Of course I was aware that John's memory might no longer stretch back to the mid-1950s when he first met Jimmy. Alpa Patel, labelled as an 'Events and Experiential Executive' at Old Trafford, had agreed to pass on my questions that I had e-mailed to Sir Bobby Charlton. Another e-mail went to Sparta Rotterdam where Jimmy had four weeks as manager, or was it just a fact-finding visit? The site had an English section so I explained in English what I needed to know. The reply came back in Dutch.

Other than the fact that Adamson had just four weeks there, little is known at all on this side of the Channel about his time in Rotterdam – except for a little notebook I had come across in his possessions in which Jimmy had jotted the dozens of things he had to do.

The bombshell in August 1974 was the sale of Martin Dobson. Not even local reporter Peter Higgs knew what Adamson's real feelings were. What could Adamson do about it anyway? If Lord said he had to go, then he had to go. Dobson had no suspicion until he was called to the office.

He described the fateful moment of discovery:

'At the start of season 1974/75 we'd played the opening games in August and I got a phone call on the Monday morning to report to Turf Moor instead of Gawthorpe. It came from Joe Brown, Jimmy's assistant. "What's it about Joe?" I remember asking but he didn't tell me. On my arrival I was told to go to the chairman's office. "Where's that?" I asked. I'd been at the club seven years and never once been there. I walked in and there was Billy Bingham and Chris Hassall, manager and secretary of Everton.

'I sat down and quickly realised it was already a done deal. Nobody at Burnley had informed me. There were no agents around at that time; I was a little confused to say the least but I signed within the hour. Everton were a big club and they wanted me. The revolving door in the Burnley dressing room had finally come round to me; it was my turn to move on.

'Subsequently I heard that Jimmy didn't want me to go and I would like to have heard that from the man himself.

> Burnley had a new stand to pay for and needed the money
> so that's when my involvement at Burnley Football Club
> came to an end. Jimmy was the manager, Harry Potts had
> left the club, Bob Lord was still chairman. Looking back
> three very strong characters and all so very influential in
> the history of the club.'

Here was a potentially great team at Turf Moor. It had shown during the previous season that it was capable of stunning wins. The football was a delight to watch. The FA took youth teams to watch it in action. Adamson's stock was high and the outward appearance at the club was one of harmony and cooperation, of a settled and happy team, of a club at peace with itself, a club that provided an object lesson in how to survive and compete with the city outfits. Behind the scenes, however, the reality at the top was different with the developing rift between Adamson and Lord possibly now in its embryonic stages as Adamson saw his team suffer the hammer-blow of Dobson's departure, with Adamson becoming more and more disenchanted with Lord's boorishness and increasing presence and interference at Turf Moor.

Before the season had started Everton had received a call to say that Dobson was available. Spurs and Leeds were also keen to land him but for £300,000 he went to Everton. Manager Billy Bingham chewed a big cigar and told the press that Dobson had been offered to him before the season had started and that he immediately made his offer. It was straight cash and Lord must have salivated at such a deal, cash in hand. It took two weeks to do all the necessary paperwork and Dobson was taken out of the team to play Chelsea as soon as the deal was tied up. To this day he says he had no idea until the moment he was sold that Burnley were prepared to let him go.

Adamson's football brain had to improvise. The departed Dobson left a gap that could be filled by moving Peter Noble to midfield and indeed he performed there superbly through the season. But it was a stopgap measure and stopgap measures in the long run fail. The reliance on young players coming through continued with Flynn, Hankin, Rodaway and Brennan to fall back on. But there were no others. The squad was threadbare and the production line was fast drying up.

The opening programme notes were cheerful. 'Exciting, entertaining times ahead,' was the header. There had been a ten-day tour to Norway and they had played games in Stavanger, Oslo and Bergen. He praised the preparations for the new season and claimed there were some of the best players in England in the ranks. There was a great team spirit. That was true enough and every member of that team will today readily talk about it. What he did not write about was the intention to sell Dobson and that negotiations were already under way with Everton. Supporters would have hit the roof had they known. You wonder what he thought as he wrote the notes and submitted them to the programme editor. He could hardly write 'we are about to embark on a great season, but by the way we shall be selling Martin Dobson'.

In the offing was the visit by Edward Heath to open the new Bob Lord Stand on the day of the Leeds United game. What a game to choose bearing in mind these were always tasty games at the very least, and spiteful and vengeful at worst. This one would be no different with a sending-off for Gordon McQueen of Leeds and Ray Hankin of Burnley. Heath had visited Burnley the previous season as part of a tour of Lancashire and seen the lads in training. Lord had grabbed the chance to invite him to do the honours opening the stand.

In Jimmy's memorabilia there is a large, torn, creased picture of them all laughing and joking at Turf Moor. Bob Lord was never more in his element than when hosting dignitaries such as this. Second World War hero Montgomery of El Alamein had once attended a match as his special guest. How ironic that this game too was against Leeds United and had been another horror show with the media suspecting that Montgomery must have thought he was back in the Second World War.

There was no win in the first four games and the fourth of them, a home game against Chelsea, saw the absence of Dobson. Burnley lost and his non-appearance was likened to the absence of McIlroy in the Burnley team in their first game after his sale to Stoke City in 1963. Fans were stunned. It had come out of the blue. There was disgruntlement and real anger at both sales. But when Dobson went there was also supporters' resignation that this was the end of any hope that Burnley could continue to compete. It was a watershed decision and we all knew it.

When McIlroy left they were likened to an orchestra without a conductor. Bill Elliott in the *Daily Express* said that without Dobson Burnley looked like they were all dressed up but had nowhere to go. They took the lead but lost 2-1. Adamson at that point must have wondered exactly where they were heading that season.

He broke his silence in an interview with Elliott, 'I did not want to sell Dobson. Chairman Bob Lord did not want to sell Dobson either. I have built my team around this boy and he is a marvellous player. But football is a cruel, hard, ruthless game and the only way we can survive as a small-town club is to sell our assets. We have no intention of going bust so we have to sell our players. Martin is like my own son and I am sorrier to see him go than anyone can possibly understand. I have sold more than £1million of players but it is the only way we can keep our heads above water.'

It was the party line he was churning out. But within the interview was the inference that this sale above all others had caused him the deepest hurt. Lord was booed as he took his place before the Chelsea game but with typical bombast he said that the same people who were now booing him would be hanging round his shoulders if they did well. March of the following year would be the last time he actually enjoyed anyone hanging round his shoulders.

In an interview with Eric Todd, Lord stuck out his chest and challenged the critics. No doubt he said just the same things to Jimmy Adamson in private. He explained, 'We buy and sell when we think it is necessary in the interests of the club. Criticism, I'm used to it. I am thick-skinned; I've got to be. They can call me all the names under the sun when I go to my seat but I can take it. I've got only the club's interests at heart and me and the directors only do what we honestly believe is best for Burnley. Me a dictator, never in a million years.

'I will tell you something else. About 50 years ago there was just as big a fuss in Burnley when they sold Bob Kelly to Sunderland as there was when we sold Martin Dobson. I died a thousand deaths when I read it in the paper. And I have died a few deaths since then. But I still believe in Burnley. And remember this. In spite of new stands, a magnificent training ground, wages and the like, we do not owe a penny piece to anyone. Don't take my word for it. There's the phone. Ring the bank and they will tell you.'

Adamson was now finding the relationship with him increasingly difficult; his wife May less than keen to attend the Saturday games and the Sunday dinners. If Jimmy had Bob Lord to bear, then his wife May had to endure the demands of his wife Hilda who ruled the ladies' room at the club with a firm hand. Margaret Potts had once felt her wrath when she attended a game in a trouser suit. You could well imagine Hilda in a Lady Bracknell voice looking askance and uttering, 'A trouser suit ... a trouser suit ...'

The players, according to Paul Fletcher, knew little or nothing of the growing irritation Adamson felt towards Lord. If there was acrimony, it was kept hidden. Fletcher says Adamson was the buffer and kept Lord away from them, absorbing the pressure, taking all the strain and shielding them from any interference. The only brief contact with him was on the summer trips at the end of season.

After the Chelsea defeat, fans and Adamson might have been forgiven for thinking the only way was downwards, but there were three immediate wins. Other good players still remained in the side. Four times in 1974/75 there were runs of three wins. Astonishingly against all the odds by the beginning of March they were second in the table and supporters wondered if they could achieve the impossible and actually become the 'Team of the Seventies'. At this point, Lord could still smile and take the pats on the back.

Colin Waldron, as soon as Dobson was sold, announced that great player though he was they were not reliant on him and could cope without him. But perhaps significantly, he said boss Jimmy Adamson was not normally a demonstrative man, but this was a rare occasion when he was very emotional as he told the squad that Dobson was being sold.

He continued: they were not a one-man team. Had they sold goalkeeper Stevenson there was no cover. Had they sold Leighton James there was no cover. But for Dobson they had cover in the form of Noble, Nulty, Billy Ingham, Doug Collins and Brian Flynn. It was a logical argument and who knows if Adamson and Lord had not discussed all the options.

But his point that Adamson was unusually emotional was perhaps indicative of a change in the Adamson mindset. If he had so far accepted Lord's dictates and moods, and possibly even been afraid of Lord as Peter Higgs suspected, then maybe this was the moment he became exasperated and determined that no more would Lord dominate him and get his own way.

Maybe this was the defining moment, the turning point in the relationship when Adamson became afraid of him no more, but determined to fight his corner. It is conjecture but maybe now he began to count up all his grievances and store them away; the same ones that sometime after his dismissal, he would list in the Basildon Bond writing pad.

'This team is going to be a good one,' wrote Peter Higgs after the Arsenal game at Highbury.

'What should not be forgotten was the quality of Burnley's football; much of it was brilliant,' he wrote after the 2-1 win over Leeds United. The football was as good as anything they had played over the last two seasons. And then came the Liverpool game on 24 September at Anfield.

It looked like Waldron's pronouncement that they could cope without Dobson was accurate. Shortly after victories over Arsenal and Leeds there was another win; this one a tremendous 1-0 success at Anfield when they ram-raided Liverpool and came away with the points.

At dinner engagements Paul Fletcher retells the story over and again likening it to the siege of the Alamo. It was settled by a 30-yard bombshell of a shot from full-back Brennan and is seen as one of the 'great' Burnley wins. This was Adamson's 'new' post-Dobson team with Noble in midfield and youngsters like Brennan and Rodaway (the outstanding player of the game) drafted in. One headline called it a champagne night to remember. What wasn't reported, however, was that this was a night when Jimmy Adamson sent Bob Lord out of the dressing room after the game. Lord had gone down to congratulate the team. Adamson had other things on his mind and did not want him there.

Colin Waldron remembers it, 'We had played so well and Bob Lord came down to the dressing room to congratulate us. Adamson too might well have been pleased but this was a night when Leighton James had kept well clear of Tommy Smith for most of the match and Adamson wanted to tear a strip off him. Lord was asked to leave the dressing room and Adamson let rip at James.'

Was this the 'new' Adamson determined that he would no longer tolerate the chairman's whims any further? There is no record of Lord's reaction.

If Lord was furious, as long as results were going Adamson's way, it didn't matter; and results continued to take Burnley into the top end of the table. If results were going Adamson's way, it was consolation for his grievances and silent suffering. There they are, handwritten on the letter pad in blue ink: the sacking of the groundsman for not watering Lord's tomato plants, the dreadful atmosphere in the ladies' room that May had to endure, Lord's power-mad ego, the incessant pressure, the way he wore people down, the loan to him of £4,000, Dobson's transfer, being at his continual beck and call even at the weekends, the directors' and staff parties that few people wanted to attend any more, the rudeness of Lord's behaviour towards others, never any admission that he was ever wrong, the way that everyone had to bend over backwards to please him; and now his insistence on Adamson filling in forms – such as lists of equipment. Adamson suffered in silence; not a player knew or suspected at this stage what was going on.

If his players and the training field were a relief and an escape there was a shattering result in the third round of the FA Cup in January of 1975. It had been a reasonable December with two wins, two draws (one of them a fine 2-2 draw at Leeds) and just one defeat. Burnley were seventh in the table and just two points away from top spot. They had just beaten Carlisle United 2-1 in front of nearly 20,000 people. What an easy afternoon it would be against non-league Wimbledon, a safe passage into the fourth round and extra income if there was a plum tie. Everyone, including me, all turned up never expecting for one minute the final crazy result.

Burnley's 45 goals so far was the highest total in the division. It was supposed to be a walkover, a stroll in the park, a gentle exercise – we thought. Leighton James was so far having a splendid season, though ironically he was far from popular with team-mates who grumbled that brilliant though he was, he never put total effort into any game. Imagine what he could do, how great he could be if he worked as hard as they did, they argued.

Adamson was aware of this undercurrent. As an exercise he asked all of them to list who they would have in their team, says

Colin Waldron. The only one of them to pick Leighton James was James himself. Adamson knew full well the players' feelings but after the exercise picked James for the very next game simply to show them all that it was he who picked the team, that he was boss. It was James that the Wimbledon boss Allen Batsford identified as the threat.

Burnley watched Wimbledon three times before the game and saw them lose twice. Batsford prepared a 15-page dossier to go through with his Wimbledon players. They practised their tactics on Saturday morning at a Burnley sports ground and what it basically boiled down to was stop James and stop the crosses.

Yet for all their preparation and pages of notes the final score was the result of two things: firstly the failure of Burnley to take their chances, and secondly a truly wonderful goalkeeping display from Dickie Guy. He was a clerk at London Docks (there were still working docks in 1975 in London). The Wimbledon side also contained Dave Bassett and he and his henchmen dealt with James superbly. For all the 15 pages of plans to contain Burnley, in truth it was Burnley who shot themselves in the foot by failing to score and when, four minutes into the second half, the unthinkable happened, the ground went totally silent when Wimbledon scored.

Scorer Mickey Mahon says he will never forget the look on the Burnley players' faces when he scored. I will never forget the silent drive home and then a Leeds inter-schools five-a-side football tournament in the evening at the university. I crept in but I was noticed. My Burnley support was well known and all I could do was gallantly say that Wimbledon had deserved to win and the longer the game went on simply outplayed Burnley.

The way we all felt, and probably the players and Lord and Adamson too, is perhaps best summed up by this piece from Tim Quelch:

> 'Oh God what can I say? I can't face work. I can't face anyone. The Khmer Rouge are besieging Phnom Penh. But those poor people have no idea what real suffering is. Ray Hankin says he's never going out again. Perhaps I should look him up. We need a Wimbledon survivors' group. I imagine Burnley to be as empty as Chernobyl (forgive the anachronism). Alright: Wimbledon are a Southern

League outfit for Christ's sake, but such organisation, such composure. They are the first side to shackle James this season. Burnley bombarded Wimbledon but it was all very predictable long ball tactics. Without James doing his stuff we looked poor. Sure there were enough opportunities to win.

'Thomson, Fletcher and James fluffed easy chances but keeper Dickie Guy was tremendous. Then, at the start of the second half, Mahon poked home a goal from 12 yards. Burnley pushed forward relentlessly but they couldn't break the Dons down. Jimmy said, "The players gave everything but their skills were off." I admired him for saying anything and became as mute as a Trappist monk.'

Prior to this disaster there had been the terrific game on Boxing Day at Elland Road with a battling performance by Adamson's men and a 2-2 draw; then the win over Carlisle United. Leeds had recovered from the Cloughie pantomime and Jimmy Armfield had taken over and calmed the troubled waters. I had been at Elland Road the night Clough was sacked with a group of lads and dads from the school where I was deputy head. We had booked a tour of the ground never expecting the circus that awaited our arrival with lights, cameras, press, TV and milling Leeds people. Our ground tour went ahead. Ever since then I've proudly announced, 'I was at Elland Road the night Brian Clough was sacked.'

I was at the Boxing Day game as well. Hunter, who had near-crippled Casper earlier in the year, was absent injured with cartilage problems. Filled with turkey and cranberry sauce from the day before and all the cold left-overs and Morecambe and Wise to look forward to in the evening, we saw a fabulous game filled with nastiness and bile. Seven players were booked, old scores were settled, carried over from the 4-1 win earlier in the year. The basic pattern was fight-goal-fight-goal until the 2-2 score was finally reached and then it was just the fights, the scuffles, the niggling, plus all the other off-the-ball stuff the referee never saw.

Jimmy was angered by what he witnessed, 'We were provoked and we retaliated. It has happened with Leeds for the past ten years.'

What was also clear was his increasing exasperation with the absence of any level playing field. As if having the despot chairman to contend with wasn't enough, he had to satisfy him with one hand tied behind his back in terms of availability of money and access to players. More than ten years on from the abolition of the maximum wage it was now impossible for Burnley to compete equally.

His frustrations were growing. Now it was freedom of contract that he turned against, 'Freedom of contract would be the end of British football. Many clubs would go to the wall; many players and many other people who work in football would be out of a job. It would only benefit a tiny handful of players who would improve their financial standing. But for the average player, not only in the lower divisions but in Division One as well, it would be a disastrous step.

'The most worrying thing is that the game would suffer too. Clubs would have to abandon their scouting systems and there would be no coaching at youth level. The home-grown youngsters who are the lifeblood of the game would no longer roll off the production line. The motorways would be packed with the managers of big-city clubs driving furniture vans full of money to sign players.

'At a time when the majority of clubs are experiencing severe financial strictures, the game would die. I leave you with that thought for Christmas.'

Around the same time, the great Spurs manager Bill Nicholson retired from management having had enough of the new-style footballer and money issues.

Immediately after the Wimbledon fiasco there was a win at Queens Park Rangers and then another against Luton Town. It made the Cup exit all the harder to take and understand. Peter Higgs had headlined his report on it with 'Hang your heads in shame' and proceeded to say what we all felt that this 'free pass' of a game to the next round was the most humiliating defeat ever in the club's history. Peter didn't know that seven years in the Fourth Division awaited the club in the 1980s with plenty more humiliations to come.

Adamson had just a year remaining at Burnley after the Wimbledon defeat. But his departure was still to come and none of us had a crystal ball. Lord, however, must at some point have started to think that Adamson was beginning to irritate him. If Adamson was no longer the willing 'yes man', not that he had ever been quite as compliant as the ever avuncular Harry Potts, then Lord at some stage must have begun to think 'either he goes or I go' and in such a situation it would not be Bob Lord.

Somehow, Burnley clung on to a top three spot as the year moved into February. And then astonishingly they were second in the table when Liverpool arrived on 8 March. Yet another player had been sold by then, this time the hard-working Geoff Nulty. He had been sold in December 1974 for a reported £120,000 so he and Dobson had generated an astonishing £420,000 between them.

It is not hard to imagine Adamson's private thoughts that here was another of his proteges, two players given a second chance in the game and moulded by him at Burnley, being taken away from him. It makes it all the more remarkable that he was still able to guide the club to second in the table. But it was a position they could not possibly maintain. It was the closest they ever got to being the 'Team of the Seventies'.

Burnley versus Liverpool, 8 March 1975, another game I was at. And like a handful of others it remains in the memory as being a defining game or moment in the club's story. Casper's injury at Leeds United, the FA Cup semi-final defeat against Newcastle, the sale of Dobson, the 1-0 defeat to Wimbledon and now the Liverpool game that ended 1-1. Had Burnley won that day and Everton lost they would have been top of the First Division. If they had still had Dobson and Nulty to call up, who knows how it would have ended up by May? Who knows if Jimmy Adamson didn't think exactly the same?

Funnily enough it was an earlier defeat when in my own head I saw the writing on the wall. It was a 5-3 home defeat to West Ham as early as September that season. My instincts told me then that the chickens were coming home to roost and player sales and a small squad would end all hope of any 'Team of the Seventies'. But then came three more consecutive wins. What did I know? But time would prove my instincts right. Today, there is the nagging thought that if that's what I was thinking, then in his heart of hearts maybe Adamson was as well.

Liverpool were also up at the top end and in contention for top spot. The press, ever realistic, gave little thought to Burnley as possible title winners. How on earth were they up so high these hacks asked? By and large they saw it as a tribute to Adamson's skills as coach and manager that Burnley were in this heady position. His reputation and standing was now at its peak. Magazines like *Goal, Shoot* and *Football League Review* featured the team regularly either with articles on the players or centre-page pull-out team pictures.

Football League Review was inserted into every club programme as a free extra for a number of seasons at this time. In this way, everyone knew about Burnley, this little town club that was working miracles. The stars of the team were frequently on the front covers – James, Hankin, Fletcher and Waldron. Lord enjoyed the limelight. Alas, it wouldn't last much longer.

I knew it was all over as the second half progressed in the game against Liverpool. It wasn't the greatest of games but Ray Hankin put Burnley in the lead in the first half in front of 32,000 people. The new stand had been opened earlier in the season and with the four sides now restored provided a fantastic atmosphere. But even in the 'home' area we seemed surrounded by Liverpool supporters. The burly Hankin was a damned good player but he was totally different to the out-of-action Frank Casper who fed off Fletcher using deft skill and finesse. In effect Burnley now had two centre-forwards, two Paul Fletchers in the side, and the balance was all wrong.

Nevertheless the 1-0 lead at half-time had us all on the edge of our seats. Could they go on and win the game? What would Adamson say to them at half-time? Would he encourage them to be bold and go for it against a Liverpool side that was hardly firing on all cylinders? Whatever he said, it seemed there was a clear change of approach. Burnley stopped going forward; they clearly went on the defensive and the initiative was lost. The inevitable happened and Liverpool equalised. I will forever point to half-time in this game as one of the crucial moments at Turf Moor.

After this game Burnley remained second but it was all downhill from that point onwards. Nine games remained. Just one was a win. Maybe Jimmy thought back to 1962 and the end of the season when Burnley and he had been heading for the double but won just one of the last ten games and won nothing. The slide down to the final tenth place was slow but sure and hard for us to watch and the season petered out with a 0-0 draw at home to Stoke City. Presumably the Sunday dinners at the Lords' house continued but if they did it was with the rapport slowly changing between the two men. The slide was so visible that by the end of March Burnley were described as looking like relegation contenders. It was a prophetic comment; that's exactly what would happen at the end of the next season.

Next up was a humiliating 4-2 defeat at Carlisle and by now Burnley were introducing young lads who would never make the grade – Mickey Finn, Richard Dixey and Derrick Parker among them.

'The season cannot end too quickly now,' we all thought and I have this image in my head of Sunday dinners with the Lords now eaten in total silence with Jimmy and May sick of them. The one remaining win was a 3-2 win over Tottenham at Turf Moor and it was on *Match of the Day*. Believe it or not Burnley after that were still in with a chance (in seventh spot) of a place in Europe. We forgot any hope of Europe in the next game with a defeat by Manchester City.

At the end of the season Adamson gave his opinion on how it had all ended. To a degree it was classic manager-speak as the reasons were rolled out. But he was right, saying, 'Circumstances combined against us and nothing came off from the moment West Ham equalised and then went on to win at Upton Park on 15 March. I sincerely believe that was the turning point. If we had won that match – and the chance was there, it could have been different. As it was, we fell out of the leading group. Then the knee injury to Paul Fletcher which needed an operation, and a less serious but troublesome injury to Doug Collins hit our hopes hard. It was asking a lot for the team to keep up the pace without such players as Fletcher, Collins, Frank Casper, Mick Docherty and more latterly Ray Hankin and Keith Newton.'

He went on to say it had been a good season but they were in no position to go into the transfer market to plug gaps and they had to look to the reserve side. What he did not say was that some of the gaps were self-inflicted. What he could not say was that the standard of the reserves was far below what it once was. He could not admit that the sale of Nulty had been a huge error because if he had said that publicly it would have been seen by Lord as criticism. And where had the sales-generated £420,000 gone?

Even though several players were allegedly earning £10,000 a year, that amount of money easily covered the wage bill. For sure it had also helped pay off the previous season's overspend as well but there had long been the suspicion that Lord managed to use club money to fund his own lifestyle via lavish expenses claims and having some of his bills sent there. If that sounds dreadful, maybe it needs comparing with the way in which today, directors or chairmen can be paid huge salaries thereby legally taking money out of a club.

When former player Les Latcham bumped into Lord as he played snooker with Adamson one Saturday night and Lord pointed to Adamson and said, 'There's my problem', it was clear that the rift was there and Adamson's presence was now gnawing away at him. Exactly when he became 'the problem' and argued with Lord and the differences and objections grew, we can only surmise.

Today I look back at that golden period and the 'nearly' team that Adamson created and all I can think about is how he came so close to his dream, but at the end was so far away. They were the golden boys and were one of the best collections of players ever assembled at Turf Moor. I emphasise collection because it was as a team not as individuals that they flourished. They were like a jigsaw that fitted together and gelled so beautifully, each dovetailing seamlessly, the perfect balance of the good, the very good and the outstanding.

Each one brought out the best in the others: Stevenson, Docherty (until injury struck him down), Newton, Waldron, Noble, Thomson, Dobson, Nulty, Collins, James and Fletcher. None of them really household names, but together as a unit they were outstanding. None of them were big money purchases, Fletcher being the most expensive at £60,000. Keith Newton was a free transfer, Dobson and Nulty were discarded by other clubs and were rescued by Burnley. James was the only outstanding flair player.

The link between the majority of them remains to this day and several of them, still living in and around Burnley, meet regularly for a Friday night drink and put the world to rights. Even Revie at Leeds was awestruck when they demolished his side 4-1. Just once every now and then a group of players come together be it by accident or design, and they are outstanding. But this group was no accident. They were Adamson's creation. But the problem was, exceptional though they were, they were not formidable. They were not unbeatable.

If they never won things or were fallible it was because it was Adamson's philosophy that going forward was a team's strength, rather than defending. Colin Waldron says that defenders were always encouraged to make runs into the opposition half. Training at Gawthorpe was always about getting players forward. Tactics were geared to being on the attack. Thus they were vulnerable and sometimes lost when they should have won. In games where they were outstanding and had even the most grizzled football writers drooling, they could still lose. Just such a game was the semi-final against Newcastle United.

At a civic reception for the 1973 champions, Bob Lord said, 'This team is capable of winning further honours.' His pride in them was tangible. Sadly they won nothing but they were a delight to watch. What they did win was the affection of an adoring crowd, and the respect of players, managers and newspapermen from all over the land.

They are why we still remember Jimmy Adamson and why he is still so often labelled the 'great' Jimmy Adamson.

Chapter 13

Horribilis, Blackpool, January 1976

'I thought our relationship was healthy ... we lived in each other's pockets ... I planned Burnley's future on the playing side and Lord did the rest ... until the day Lord retired from his butchery business and took up football as a full-time job ... then things started to go wrong ... I don't think it's right to devote the majority of the working day to the chairman's whims ... and he had many of those ... he ruled the club with an iron fist ... demanding attention most of the time ... to be fair Lord treated me well until I started disagreeing with him ... then our relationship went sour.'

Saturday 16 August: the opening game and a 0-0 draw at home to Arsenal. In five months Adamson would be gone. It is clear that those months were a period of frustration, irritation, conflict, ill-will and aggravation between Jimmy Adamson and Bob Lord. By now Lord thought Adamson was a problem and Adamson thought that Lord was interfering too much and increasingly cantankerous and demanding. There had already been one blazing row between them one Friday night before a game away at Ipswich when Lord had insisted that it was his club to run and not Adamson's.

The Sunday dinner ritual was an ordeal. May hated Saturday afternoons. If she was unable to attend a home game for whatever reason, she had to inform Hilda Lord and then Hilda Lord wanted to know why. Every scrap of angst that Adamson felt is there in the article he wrote:

> 'My wife used to dread weekends especially when we were playing at home ... sometimes she didn't feel like going to the game but it wasn't a case of just opting out ... she had to report to the chairman's wife.'

What Jimmy wrote is a damning indictment of a once sound relationship that was now heading towards complete break-up and was festering right up to the point where the final confrontation would surely approach.

> 'At one time I thought we were a great team ... and I thought our future was healthy ... expecting to be Burnley manager for a lifetime.'

Margaret Potts described a strange meeting she had with Lord while Harry was manager at Blackpool. They still lived in Burnley, at Read, and one of Margaret's habits was to take long walks round the country lanes and re-visit the places and cottage where she had been brought up. She would do these walks quite frequently and one of them she remembers was at a time when Burnley were not doing very well. It sounds like it could have been sometime in the autumn of 1975 when things were really beginning to unravel and break up. Other than that she could not accurately recall exactly when it was.

As she walked around Whins Lane one day and was getting down from a gateway, a car came along. It stopped and it was none other than Bob Lord. Down went the window and Lord asked her in his own gruff way and with some surprise as she clambered over the gate, 'What are you doing here?'

'Well Bob,' she replied, 'this has been my patch since as long as I can remember.'

Margaret recalled that Lord looked tired and weary as if he had all the cares in the world. He did not look a happy man at all and just sat there in his car and then said slowly, 'I made a mistake ... I made a mistake.'

'Well,' she told him, 'you won't be the first and you won't be the last.'

She was about to say more and was sure that he was going to confess to being unhappy with Jimmy Adamson. Alas, the conversation got no further as someone from a nearby cottage saw Margaret and came out to chat. For years she wondered what else he would have said, sensing that he was deeply unhappy and desperately wanted someone to talk to.

There was only one league win in the first ten games. Supporter Tim Quelch wrote that attending games was now like popping in to visit a sick relative just to see how they were getting on. He likened it to seeing if the patient was still breathing. Burnley were breathing – just – but while in the previous three seasons the Saturday fix had seen supporters in a happy mood through the working week, it no longer cast its optimistic glow.

Adamson had drafted in two new recruits, and most unlikely ones at that, Willie Morgan and Mike Summerbee. I can remember raising my eyebrows with surprise at the time when it was announced. Willie had once been the darling of the Turf Moor crowds but had fallen foul of chairman Lord. Now, Adamson, several years later, had brought him back. Despite the previous differences between Lord and Morgan, Lord must have approved his return; after all, it was he who signed the forms and negotiated wages and contracts.

Mike Summerbee recalled the day he joined and signed with Bob Lord, 'I was a bit concerned because Bob Lord had the reputation of being a tough guy. There was a large shiny desk in the room and there was nothing on it except the contract. I sat down and looked at it for the first time. It was a fantastic contract – and inflation proof. At that time inflation was going berserk, up by 25% a year or something. I said as much to Bob Lord. "You deserve that," he said. I asked him why, what he meant. "You've met Jimmy Adamson and Dusty Miller four times now and never mentioned money. That's your reward." I signed immediately. He was a superb man and Jimmy Adamson was brilliant.'

Adamson's programme notes for the first home game make poignant reading. He outlined what he would like to see in the game: entertaining football with teams going for goal; being positive not negative; better behaviour from players towards each other and referees; an end to football hooliganism with fewer pre-match provocative remarks from managers; players realising that we all, especially referees, make mistakes. He ended with a mention of his own optimism especially with the two new signings and he urged the crowd to be patient if things were going wrong.

Alas, things would go wrong; his players would let him down with too many bookings and in a game that really mattered after which Adamson would be axed, Hankin would receive a red card. Today, Colin Waldron wonders if Bob Lord, who had real desires of becoming president of the Football League, was unhappy about the number of bookings thinking it would reflect badly on him and harm his ambition; thus becoming one more reason to be dissatisfied with Jimmy Adamson.

Unfortunately even with the commercial and development section now bringing in a six-figure sum during the year, it was generous wages such as those paid to Summerbee, and no doubt Morgan as well, that were to be the ruin of the club. Adamson was pleased with the signings. He always maintained that even if and when money was available, he would only sign players who would truly improve the squad or were better than those he already had. But supporters knew that these two were well past their peak and there was a dreadful beginning to the season. By the time they had lost at Sheffield United and then at home to Leeds they were next to bottom.

Injuries and poor refereeing decisions played havoc with results. Other teams were awarded doubtful penalties and Burnley were denied certain kicks of their own. During the 4-0 defeat at Birmingham, Doug Collins broke a leg. Then full-back Ian Brennan broke a leg in a road accident. There were injuries to Fletcher and Noble. But the Sunday dinners continued:

'Most Sundays we were summoned to the Lord household for lunch and hours of chatter ... my wife hated it ... but we kept going, kept eating the roast beef and Yorkshire pud ... and swallowed the rest just to keep Lord happy ... but there's nothing worse than Lord when he's upset or angry. Conversation is restricted to a grunt or a blast and he seems to surround himself with a dark, depressive cloud ... the consequences can be disastrous as I know to my cost.'

Meanwhile Jimmy Adamson insisted that Leighton James was not for sale. James had other ideas and handed in a transfer request. In a Sunday newspaper article he said that Derby County were the only club he would sign for. Lo and behold he was signed by Derby County for £310,000. The match-winner was gone; the one player remaining truly capable of magic. Peter Higgs wrote in the local paper that apart from Georgie Best and Jimmy Greaves he was the best player he had seen. His team-mates such as Fletcher and Waldron thought he had the potential to be even better than Best but his flaw was that he took it all for granted, found it all too easy, and never got himself to the next level, which they felt he could have done with even greater application.

In November, Wolves came to Turf Moor, won 5-1, had three more goals disallowed and had two more efforts cleared off the line. If this wasn't a warning then nothing was. This was a side heading for relegation. By Boxing Day they had won just four league games. Young players in the reserves like Loggie, Bradshaw, Kennerley and Parker were just not good enough.

The end came with the third round of the FA Cup away to Blackpool, still managed by none other than Harry Potts. The press had a field day pointing out that this was a game not so much between Blackpool and Burnley, but this was Potts versus Adamson and a reunion with Bob Lord. With Burnley in such poor form it was anybody's game and Lord meanwhile was niggling away at Adamson.

'He started with me picking up on every point, scrutinising them, then trying to provoke an argument ... this went on for months until our FA Cup defeat at Blackpool ... this was the last straw in a disappointing season for Lord.'

Centre-half Jim Thomson, who for various reasons strongly disliked Adamson, nevertheless revealed clear sympathy for him. 'Much as I disliked him, I used to feel really sorry for him knowing that he had to work and deal with Bob Lord all the time, day after day. He was beginning to try and interfere with team selections and Jimmy was having none of it. Lord tried to insist that certain players played, and that one particular player didn't.

'Jimmy was a very private man but on away trips in the hotel just sometimes he'd open up a little and you'd see the strain he was under from Lord. Then there was the way Lord could try to make people feel small and intimidate them. I had first-hand experience of this. After a game in which I was sent off I was summoned to speak to him. He had this huge long table he'd sit at, him at one end and me at the other. Joe Brown sat alongside Bob and never said a word as Lord gave me the mother of all lectures. I looked at Joe every now and then for support but there was nothing. I don't think he dared speak.

'He never really wanted the manager's job when Adamson left; he was a good number two but he was frightened of Lord as many people were. I was fined £200, angrily got up and marched out but Lord shouted after me, "And when will we get our £200." I had the last laugh though. When a fine had to be paid, all the lads chipped in and helped out. It was Waldo who collected the money and handed it to me. But there was £210. I'd made a profit of £10.'

Thousands of Burnley fans followed the team to Blackpool on a dreadful day with wind and stinging rain driving in from the sea; the result and repercussions still remembered over 30 years later, yet another seminal moment in the club's history. It was a personal triumph for Potts and a disaster for Adamson while a joyful Margaret Potts probably danced around the house afterwards.

Only 12 months earlier there had been the Wimbledon humiliation and now this. Bob Lord must have squirmed and Adamson must have felt a sense of helplessness especially with the row in the dressing room that took place between the coach Joe Brown and skipper Colin Waldron. Adamson had suffered a dreadful few months in this awful season and the latest result was a hammer blow.

Frank Casper did not play in the game but remembers the dressing room flare-up. Adamson hammered on the door to get in. Joe Brown heard this. Adamson shouted to be let in. 'NO,' said Brown.

It was a game of argument and controversy as Blackpool scraped through on the strength of a solitary Bill Bentley goal in the 56th minute. Prior to this, Burnley's Ray Hankin had been sent off and the team was already missing four regular first-teamers. In a game full of blood and thunder tackles and spiced with aggravation and needle, Burnley accusations flew back and forth about players conning the referee and trying to intimidate each other. Blackpool were indignant and pointed to their own players' legs covered in cuts and bruises.

They had ridden their luck and held out and Burnley, even though they were weakened, still had players of the calibre of Newton, Morgan, Waldron, Summerbee and Flynn. Had Burnley taken their chances they would have beaten Blackpool easily. Towards the end, Waldron had what seemed a perfectly good goal disallowed when only the referee saw any infringement saying that Waldron had leaned on the opponent. Waldron was astonished and players and fans were open-mouthed at the decision.

Controversy continued after the game. Potts dismissed claims that Blackpool had been over-physical, saying it was not a game for namby-pambies. He pointed with pride to his 12 heroes. In the Burnley dressing room there was no such pride, only arguments and flailing arms. Waldron fumed so it was he that was involved in the scuffle with assistant manager Joe Brown while the door was locked so that Adamson could not get in after he had been to see the referee. Adamson's career at Burnley was vanishing in front of him while Potts, according to Bill Elliot in the *Daily Express*, had the air of a man who had just discovered the elixir of life and had a smile big enough to light up Blackpool Illuminations. Potts was naturally delighted but was too gracious a man to gloat or show pleasure at Adamson's discomfort – at least in public.

There was no game of snooker that night between Lord and Adamson and there was certainly no attendance by Jimmy and May at the Lords' house for Sunday dinner.

'Lord missed the Saturday snooker match for the first time in ten years. I spent the whole of Sunday in bed. I was shattered from working a 12-hour day and suffering from an overdose of Bob Lord ... I'd almost walked out on him 12 months earlier after an explosive bust-up at London airport.'

Margaret Potts well remembered the game. After it had finished, the Blackpool chairman, Frank Dickinson, came to the ladies' room and asked them all to stay where they were because of the noise and trouble in and outside the Burnley dressing room. 'We could hear the chants of "ADAMSON OUT, ADAMSON OUT".' It was obvious that things were far from well at Burnley Football Club.

The wheel had turned full circle. Something like four years earlier there had been shouts of 'ADAMSON OUT' ironically at the very same ground.

The headline was stark, 'SCRAPING THE BARREL, Clarets in dire trouble.' Peter Higgs's message was simple that Burnley were already three points adrift at the bottom end of the table and hopes of clinging on to their First Division place looked slim. Only the bare remnants of the first team squad remained. Injuries and suspensions would account for eight senior players in the coming games.

Jimmy Adamson had earlier summed up the situation, 'We always seem to be playing uphill. We've been waiting for the tide to turn in our favour for weeks but everything still keeps going against us.'

There was no easy solution. The team clearly needed strengthening but the odds on picking up good players at reasonable prices were slim. Plus which, clubs knew that Burnley had banked over £300,000 on the James deal so were in no mood to let anyone go cheap. Persuading players to join the unglamorous club was bad enough at the best of times. Now, in danger of relegation already, who on earth would want to come? And in any case, would Bob Lord release the cash? And who was there in the reserves that could step up? In short, no one.

Higgs was prophetic in his match report, 'Burnley's exit from the FA Cup in the Third Round for the second successive season may not have contained the immediate widespread embarrassment of last year's flop against Wimbledon. But the significance of Saturday's 1-0 defeat against Blackpool at Bloomfield Road could prove to have a far greater effect on the club's history.'

He could have had no idea of what was to come when he wrote that as part of his match report. He went on, 'The Clarets emerged from a niggling, untidy game with no credit and very little hope for the future – unless there is a dramatic improvement in their form ... When at last Burnley got the ball in the net in the final minute the "goal" was disallowed. Waldron's firm header from Docherty's free kick was ruled out for a foul, unseen by thousands in the ground (including me) ... the match underlined the Clarets' shortage of fit, available talent. If the lesson is learned and acted upon – in the buying of new players – then some value will be gained from it.'

I suppose there is a book to be written simply about decisions by referees that in one moment have fundamentally altered the course of a player or manager's life, be it at Burnley, or indeed any club.

At Burnley there were two in Adamson's time as manager. The first was by Gordon Hill at Sheffield when he allowed Malcolm Macdonald to make for goal even with Colin Waldron hanging on to him with a rugby tackle. In a moment that lasted but seconds Hill wrote in his book that he reasoned that Macdonald would shake Waldron off. Thus, he did not do what other referees might have done, and did not blow for the foul and halt Macdonald. He went on to score and put Burnley out of the Cup.

The split-second decision by referee P. Reeves at Blackpool to disallow Waldron's goal also had far-reaching effects for the club and disastrous consequences for Jimmy Adamson.

'It WAS a goal.' said Waldron. 'If I had fouled to get the ball I would be prepared to admit it, but I didn't. I followed the flight of the ball all the way from Mick Docherty's free kick and didn't even know there was a defender there with me.' If that goal had been allowed, if there had been a replay in prospect, would Lord have sacked Adamson?

Within 48 hours Adamson's life at Burnley was shattered by Lord's decision to dismiss him. Lord had two choices: to retain Adamson, with whom by now he was thoroughly fed up, and let him spend some of the James transfer money; or sack him and rid himself of the man he now saw as a problem. He chose the latter and let his replacement Joe Brown spend £100,000 on a new player. That didn't do much good either.

Lord had seen his opportunity to get rid of Adamson, with whom he was thoroughly uncomfortable and was now a thorn in his side. With fans clamouring by now for his dismissal, it was a decision that he knew would be applauded by at least one section of the supporters. But not all – those who had eyes to see saw that Lord was just as culpable – and were also able to recognise the terrible run of bad luck, injuries and suspensions.

'I was no better on the Monday morning and I decided to take the morning off, my first in 12 years. But I didn't get the sleep I needed. A director called, examined the facts, and then said, "Would you be willing to resign if Mr Lord paid up your contract?" Lord had the final word of course. The following day he sent for me to sack me for not reporting the Blackpool incident and not turning up for work. The pay-off of £25,000 softened the blow somewhat, as I became another of Lord's victims ... all my troubles seemed to come from tours or holidays ... I'd almost walked out on him 12 months earlier ... I didn't get far; another director stepped in and calmed me down. We thought Burnley was a family club, a place of spirit and warmth. It was until Bob Lord blew through and froze me out.'

'Who'd be in charge of Burnley this morning?' the media asked when they heard the news. The club was fighting for First Division survival, had no end of players injured, and was headed by the impossible Bob Lord. The job was a poisoned chalice.

Should the Turf Moor faithful have been surprised at the turn of events? The historians pointed to it following a familiar pattern – when things were bad, the axe fell where least expected. Lord once said that Jimmy McIlroy would not leave Burnley at any price. After a Liverpool Cup replay that was lost, he was sold. Harry Potts was part of the furniture. He too was dismissed as manager. Next up was Adamson of whom Lord had once said, 'He has a job for life.'

The press were realistic and knew the handicaps that Adamson had worked under and the miracles he had performed. The current form, they said, was merely one of his 'downs' and did not alter the fact that he had few equals in the game and any sympathy that morning should have been for the club itself, not Adamson, who would survive in the game and continue to make important contributions.

The doyen of north-west reporters, Keith McNee, who in fact bled claret and blue, wrote a moving tribute:

'I did not believe it when I first heard the news that Jimmy Adamson had resigned. It was the parting that could never happen. Jimmy Adamson, it was thought, was a permanent fixture at Turf Moor, part and parcel of an everyday scene. Everyone thought he had a job for life there. As both he and Chairman Bob Lord confirmed the biggest bombshell of them all from undoubtedly the newsiest club in the country, two famous Adamson occasions came so vividly to mind.

'The first was in April, 1962. On a dramatic night at Leicester, a brilliant Burnley side took a two-goal lead over Fulham on their way to Wembley in an FA Cup semi-final. Skipper Jimmy Adamson, in the number 4 shirt, and lining up after Jimmy Robson's second goal, shouted to the bench to find how long there was to go to the final whistle. I will never forget his "that's all we need to know" gesture when he was told just 10 minutes.

'He was not just a Burnley player, he WAS BURNLEY right through to the core and he remained so until those poignant moments on Tuesday when he shook hands with the players and then walked dejectedly out of their lives.

'Eight years after that game at Leicester, on February 27th, 1970, to be precise, I stood with the Burnley players and Jimmy himself to hear Chairman Bob Lord's announcement that he was their new manager. It was a memorable occasion for all of us and the new boss, already with well over 20 years' service to Burnley under his belt, looked a rock-solid certainty for another 20 years. But it was not to be and a few weeks under six years later, exactly 29 years to the day since he arrived as a junior player from the pits of Ashington, signed by Cliff Britton, he was out of a job.

'Life is full of irony of course, but how strange that after his playing career ended with a match at Blackpool through a back injury, his management career should end after another game at Bloomfield Road, and a dressing room argument in which the only part he played was to end it. In any history of Burnley FC Jimmy Adamson's name should be written in prominent lettering close to the top of the all-time list of those who made the club a part of English football out of all proportion to the size of the town in which it lives.

'The end came suddenly. It was a real knock-out for players and fans alike, just as much the man it hit straight in the face. I don't see the situation as one in which Jimmy Adamson suddenly decided one morning to pack in. The truth is that he was asked to resign because the board were not happy with him anymore. In falling in line with the request, he acted in what he thought were the best interests of the club. But there is certainly more to it in my view than has been suggested in print so far elsewhere.

One wonders whether a clash of personalities was involved on top of the on and off the field events which added to a final curtain coming down.

'The FA Cup defeat was the final blow and Burnley's league table position is very poor. Jimmy Adamson must obviously come into the firing line for that, while the bad disciplinary record with one booking following another, plus a sending-off last Saturday, does not make a pretty picture. There were, I suspect, a number of other reasons which privately built up into the Tuesday confrontation at Turf Moor and then the resignation.

'Apparently Jimmy was not at work on Monday and was summoned to Turf Moor at 10.30 on Tuesday morning. He is an exhausted and shattered man but he comes through everything with his very high reputation completely intact. One wonders what his potential would be at a club where he could link his coaching talents to a team he could keep together.

'The "Adamson Out" shouts have not been heard at Turf Moor for a long time which is another king-sized irony. As far as his own future is concerned he will swiftly find a top job but I am convinced he will never completely forget the events of this traumatic week and believe me he is not the only one.

'Personally, I remember Jimmy Adamson as a man with a tremendous sense of humour and big personality.

He has been approachable at nearly all times and many newspaper men have reason to thank him for the part he has played in keeping open the line of communication to them in very demanding circumstances at times.'

McNee probably knew full well what all the behind-the-scenes problems were between Lord and Adamson but was unable to put them into print. Had he done so he would undoubtedly have been banned from Turf Moor as so many other journalists had been over the years. But, he asked one question that we all still ask today – how would Jimmy have done had he not had to sell all the best players? McNee noted the absence of the 'Adamson out' chants but Margaret Potts mentioned they actually were evident after the Blackpool defeat. McNee felt he would find a top job swiftly. His tribute to him as a person in the final paragraph was heartfelt and generous.

'WHY I HAD TO QUIT' was the *Daily Express* headline. 'I feel I've let the Burnley fans down,' he said. 'I feel responsible for the club being in the lower reaches of the First Division and being knocked out of the cup. I don't want the players thinking I'm leaving a sinking ship. I don't think it is a sinking ship; we have players who can pull us out of this. I think I feel I have let the Burnley public down in one way. They expected greater things and I too expected greater things. We expected a good cup run. It has not materialised. I leave with no animosity to anyone. Chairman Bob Lord has been like a father to me. I have no recriminations or regrets. I don't regret anything I have ever done at Burnley. The chairman has supported me during my wrong-doings, and he has supported me through the good. And I have supported him.'

For now his sentiments towards Lord were publicly generous. As bitterness set in these would change. Nor did he want to jeopardise the generous settlement. He wisely kept his real feelings to himself and was probably, anyway, in a state of something approaching shell-shock. We all know the feeling when we have been in a traumatic situation; the words come out in a sort of blur.

In truth, he was utterly and totally shattered. And not only that, he was a victim. Ronald Crowther of the *Daily Mail* saw him as the victim of a relentless policy of selling players; a victim of the irresistible pressure that forced him to sell over £1m of the club's top players. The constant drain on resources had thus landed them in a situation where they were not able to cope in an injury crisis.

Crowther described Adamson as disconsolate with Adamson telling him, 'I thought when the season started that I had a good squad and the outlook was very bright but I leave Turf Moor with thousands of happy memories and even the heartbreaks will be memorable. I am sorry to leave, but I have been in the driving seat. I am the one responsible when things don't go right.'

In no interview did Adamson criticise the sell-to-survive policy, something that he might have done so easily. That would come years later. Chairman Lord meanwhile said the parting was amicable; that there were many reasons for the departure, but he would not discuss them. How could he? The plain fact was he'd had enough of Jimmy Adamson.

Adamson took Colin Waldron to one side at Gawthorpe to tell him first before the others. Waldron was stunned and in that moment knew that there would be a huge impact on his own life and career. 'In that moment I knew my life had changed and my happiness would be seriously affected,' he said. In football a player's security is only as good as his manager's. Waldron couldn't bear to accompany Adamson to tell the rest of the team. He went home and cried.

The players professed to being bemused, announcing that there would be player meetings to discuss what to do. There were mumblings of strike action, of some form of protest, of a petition. 'It has left us in shock,' said vice-captain Doug Collins. Colin Waldron said he would miss Adamson as he would miss his own father. Keith Newton said he was bewildered and that Burnley would not find anyone capable of replacing him. Peter Noble said it was the biggest shock of his life and asked where Burnley could find someone to replace the best manager in the game.

Bob Lord inevitably replied to all the criticisms in the local press. 'ADAMSON WAS NOT A SCAPEGOAT' was the header, and Lord said:

'I have often been reported to have said that when a football manager leaves a club, the reason is in many cases, but not all, because the Board of Directors have usually panicked, or wanted to find a scapegoat. That is not the case at Burnley this week.

'In all my 21 years as chairman I have always advised my fellow directors that when we have chosen our manager, he must be endowed with full and complete powers to carry out his job ... Jimmy Adamson cannot deny by any stretch of the imagination that he has enjoyed and used complete power, but I hasten to add, that for many months past he has not been anywhere near blessed with good fortune and luck. In fact he has experienced many troubles and fortunes which he could not resolve.

'Myself and my directors and all connected with the club in all departments, have always given every support and encouragement. In spite of all that has been done, the end came. There have been no rows over the matter; we parted on good and amicable terms.'

Adamson might have argued with Lord's claim that he had enjoyed full and complete power; in fact since Lord's retirement from his meat business he had meddled and interfered more and more. He might also have argued that if Lord was so aware of all the bad luck over which he had no control, then surely he did not merit being sacked and a perceptive chairman would have continued to support him. It is conjecture of course, but Lord might also have argued that Adamson was increasingly difficult to work with, brusque and uncooperative, moody and sullen. Whatever: Adamson and Lord both knew they had come to the end of the road in their decaying relationship.

Lord continued to churn out the platitudes. 'I won't quit,' he said. 'I wouldn't be a manager for all the tea in China but I believe I've done my side of the job looking after the business end. If I thought the staff was not fully behind me I would pack my bags. I've made lots of mistakes but I think I've done things that have repaid those mistakes. I had a father and son relationship with Jimmy.'

Talk of other directors being in agreement with and supporting him was hollow. Lord, in fact, WAS the board. Other directors were in fear and trembling of him. He ruled the place like a despot. What he wanted he got and the directors did as they were told.

'Nobody escaped the lash of his tongue ... he was the most feared man in football blasting his way to the top by a constant bludgeoning of people ... I'm not blaming Lord entirely for the lowly position the club were in when I left in January ... but his interference didn't help ... he ruled the club with an iron fist demanding attention ... he starts with what I call the pressure system forcing people to the limit until he gets the result he wants.'

Adamson knew full well that when Lord spoke of the board, he meant only himself.

The forecast was that he would get back into football quickly but Adamson said he wanted a good rest. One unnamed First Division club was thought to be a likely destination. Was it Manchester City? On one of the Basildon Bond writing-pad pages under the heading 'Evil', Jimmy wrote, 'Black-balled Manchester City'. Did Bob Lord tell him his compensation was dependent on not taking up the managership of any nearby Lancashire club? It is speculation, but did Lord scupper any possibility of the City job? Or had City tried to poach him earlier in his career at Burnley?

Other suggestions were that he would take up scouting roles. Arsenal and Leeds were named. The latter would have been a big surprise bearing in mind the stormy relationship between Revie and Adamson.

At the end of the traumatic week, local man Peter Higgs, who had never found Adamson an easy manager to get on with, wrote his tribute. 'ADAMSON MAN OF DIGNITY' it began. He described him as the club's greatest post-war servant and wrote, 'People in the game all over the country have been absolutely stunned. It's been likened to the collapse of Rolls-Royce. First Division managers have been saying, "If Jim's gone what chance have we got?"'

He asked if Jimmy Adamson could have done any more – with the inference that no he could not. He had been stripped of talent and was competing against clubs who could pay huge sums for players. He asked was it Adamson's fault that there weren't enough players fit enough to play and keep the miracle going?

He wrote that what Adamson should be remembered for were the great moments and the entertaining football he had provided over the past few years and he was one of the top coaches in football. The question now troubling Higgs was the same one that doubtless troubled many other fans. How could the Clarets afford to lose a man of such high soccer reputation whose heart was deeply embedded in Burnley Football Club?

Skipper Colin Waldron wrote for the *Burnley Express*:

'There can never be another week in my football life anything like the last seven days. I was shattered by the FA Cup defeat at Blackpool and there is no word to describe properly my feelings on Tuesday when Jimmy Adamson called me over to him and told me he had resigned. A morning training session on our all-weather pitch was halted suddenly and we all trooped into the conference room. Jimmy beckoned me over and gave me the knockout news.

'Then he lit a cigar and told the other players that he was no longer the manager. I am not ashamed to admit there were tears in my eyes as he shook hands with every player and then made a very, very sad departure from the scene. Jimmy has been a father to me since I arrived at Turf Moor in 1967 and he has taught me a lot about life and our game in particular of course. He is rated by hundreds of players as the best coach of them all. My phone has hardly stopped ringing with calls from players of other clubs, mostly former Burnley stars, wanting to know that the hell was going on.

'One said, "I honestly feel that a part of me has been ripped away. I didn't believe this could happen." He added that at his club, if they had a problem in a training session they would almost always say what would the Jimmy Adamson solution be?

'Why is Jimmy Adamson such a good coach? Basically, in my opinion, because, apart from having more knowledge about the game than anyone, he has outstanding vision allied to a knack of putting his views over in simple language. He isn't perfect but I like him very much indeed and quite frankly I am heartbroken over what has happened to him. Let me add for the record, and this is no secret to Jimmy, there are possibly three or four players at the club who don't like him quite as much as

I do, but that must be the case elsewhere in the league between players and bosses.

'It will seem very strange in the dressing room without Jimmy, a man of style and authority. What really niggles me more than anything else is the number of unfortunate adverse refereeing decisions in Jimmy's last few games as our manager. Without going into detail we have had some rough justice. That applies to some goals not given, some goals awarded to the opposition, and the number of bookings which give a false impression of our attitude towards the game under Jimmy Adamson.'

Waldron went on and pledged that he and the players would do their utmost to support the new man and battle on. They had to stand up and be counted in the grim struggle for First Division survival.

James Mossop asked what REALLY made Adamson leave Burnley? Mossop looked at things a week later, when the dust had settled just a little, and he could be just a little more objective. Emotions had run high in the thousands of words that had poured out in the preceding days. But he was still of the view, 'His decision to quit took some beating and he had been responsible for an astonishing story of football success.'

What Mossop did though, that no one else so far had done, was point to a fractured relationship between Adamson and his coaching staff. This was a new angle and something of a surprise to the outside world. Perhaps it explains why Joe Brown shouted 'NO' at him when Adamson was shouting to be let into the Blackpool dressing room.

'There is little doubt that problems have arisen between Adamson and the man who has succeeded him, his friend for 25 years, Joe Brown, and the coaches,' wrote Mossop.

'I will not make any comment that will be detrimental to Burnley,' said Adamson. 'I have no quarrel whatsoever with the chairman, the directors, the players or the office staff.'

When Mossop pointed out that he had omitted to mention the coaching staff, Adamson smiled a wry smile. It seemed that a gulf had developed between the men who did so much together and that on the unhappy ride back from Blackpool Adamson decided it was time to leave them to it.

There is no firm evidence that Adamson had decided to resign before Lord gave him the ultimatum; although maybe the idea flitted through his mind especially as he hammered on the dressing room door unable to get in. In fact, from what player Jim Thomson said years later reminiscing about the game, it seems very unlikely that Adamson had decided to resign that day. I had been to see Thomson and mentioned the Harry Potts book I had done with Margaret and how it was clear she intensely disliked Adamson.

'Yes,' he said, 'if ever she was in a room and Jimmy came in she'd get up and walk out.'

Then he grimaced as he remembered the terrible dressing room scenes after the Cup game, 'It was coach Joe Brown who was tearing a strip off Colin Waldron and when Waldron tried to make Brown look small with a remark, it was Brown who went for Waldron.

'As the scene kicked off assistant coach Brian Miller yelled, "Shut the door!" And then there was me yelling, "Get 'em apart, get 'em apart!" While all this was going on there was furious banging on the other side of the door and when it was eventually opened in came Adamson with a face like thunder. He was utterly fuming at the whole thing but to our amazement instead of having a go at Colin, he absolutely tore into Brown and Miller.

'What he told them was that it was his job, not theirs, to be telling players off after a game. He was always a great believer in waiting a couple of days to say what he thought, or go over a game. Still furious he ordered us all to be in for a meeting first thing Monday morning.'

At that point, therefore, the idea of resigning had never entered his mind. If Mossop was merely speculating on Adamson resigning, he did however reveal something that Adamson told him that was so far not widely known, 'From the flowers and letters that have flooded his home since he resigned, many of Burnley's fans understand the predicament. But some did not. For the last three months his phone has been ex-directory – for the first time in his life – because of abusive calls, some directed at his wife, in the early hours of the morning.'

But like everyone else Mossop gave no insight into the by now appalling relationship between Adamson and the man who mattered, Bob Lord. Poor results, the FA Cup defeat, injuries, suspensions, some players who didn't like him, differences with coaching staff, abusive telephone calls; the reasons stacked up to create a pressure and strain that was draining him. But the fundamental reason for his departure was the chairman. He was asked for his resignation.

> 'I started disagreeing with him ... our relationship went sour ... things started to go wrong ... his interference didn't help ... my wife used to dread weekends ... there's nothing worse than Lord when he's angry ... the consequences can be disastrous ... as I know to my cost.'

The new man would in fact be Joe Brown. He would oversee the release of players such as Doug Collins, Mick Docherty and Colin Waldron, allegedly ordered to get rid of them by Bob Lord. Frank Casper recalled that Adamson sometimes visited Gawthorpe after he had been sacked. On the last of them an angry Brian Miller, now assistant to Joe Brown, demanded that he leave.

Brown would oversee relegation by the end of the season. He would then be replaced by none other than Harry Potts during the following season. After Brown, Lord wanted a familiar face and to be able to retreat into a comfort zone where he had a manager who would not answer back.

Adamson's departure was the beginning of the relentless slide downwards to the Fourth Division where the club stayed for seven horrendous seasons. They are still known as the wilderness years. It took 33 years for the club to recover a place in the Premier League elite in 2009.

It lasted just one season and there had still been no reconciliation between the club and Adamson, but the promotion team played a brand of football that he would have been proud of.

Chapter 14

Genius but not everyone's cup of tea

I USED to be a headmaster. There are some hazy similarities between that and being a football manager. Both are jobs where there is constant interaction with other people. Both are jobs where you want people to do as you ask (or tell) them and both are jobs where the manager or the head must be motivators and have clear ideas of what they want and how they want to do things. A football manager has his players on the field; a headmaster has his teaching staff in the classrooms.

Whenever I talked to people about Jimmy Adamson and they might say he was not their favourite person I could empathise. Neither Jimmy Adamson nor I could please everybody all of the time. We could not be everybody's friend and certainly not everybody's favourite person.

In my little school I only had a staff of six teachers. Overall, two of them thought I was the bee's knees and bought into my style and the way I taught, two of them simply did their job and got on with things and I never really knew what went on in their heads, and two of them couldn't stand me. I can be the first to admit I could be cheerful one day and moody the next. I could give some people short shrift because they frequently irritated me, and towards others felt a constant warmth and affection.

I would imagine it was the same with Jimmy Adamson except on a larger scale with more people involved. He had his disciples, but also his detractors. I once joked with Stan Ternent that the essential difference between us was that while he could tell a player to fuck off, and they probably would, that was something I could never say to a teacher without being hauled before a grievance committee and probably suspended by the school governors. Mind you, this was in a tough little ex-mining village and there were occasions when the odd parent told ME to fuck off although they always said it politely and addressed me as Mr Thomas. If I did what Jimmy did and made a list of the good, the bad and the amusing, I guess I would put that on the amusing list.

A football manager can be respected but not loved and this was much the case with Adamson. It was perhaps the fact that Harry Potts was both respected and loved, that annoyed him so much as the years went by and he came to resent why Harry had been given so much credit for Burnley's past successes. Peter Higgs's impression was that he regarded Potts 'as a bit of a bumbling fool'. Peter's e-mail certainly made me realise the intolerable stress that Adamson must have been placed under by Lord. Lord's incessant demands and the pressure he was under from him, must have contributed massively to, and been inextricably linked with Adamson's mood swings and general manner towards others.

It must have been impossibly hard to come out of a room when you have just had an unpleasant one-to-one with Bob Lord, and then be immediately pleasant and chatty with the next person you meet. I can empathise with that as well. It was awfully hard sometimes to spend half an hour having a disagreeable meeting with an uncooperative member of staff, and then silently preoccupied, wrapped up in your angry thoughts, not to walk straight by the next person in the corridor, appearing rude and unfriendly.

Peter Higgs provided an illustration of how easy it was to fall foul of Jimmy Adamson and see his dark side, 'Adamson kept his relationship with Lord secret from me but I remember one example of how afraid he seemed of the chairman. This occurred at a time when Frank Casper went into hospital for a knee operation. Following the normal journalistic practices, I rang the hospital to discover how the operation had progressed, only to be told that Casper had not undergone a cartilage operation, as Adamson had told me, but an operation to correct ligament damage.

'Naturally enough I wrote what the hospital had told me (them being the medical experts) only to be given a public rollicking at the Gawthorpe training ground by Adamson. The theme of his rant was that I should have written what he told me (not what the hospital said) because he had not had any chance to tell the chairman.

'The inference was that if Lord read about the true extent of Casper's injury in the *Burnley Express*, it would be Adamson in trouble. Once again it was a case of you write what we tell you, not the truth. No doubt many a journalist at many a club experienced just the same thing.'

In 1988 Colin Waldron wrote about Jimmy Adamson. Waldron was and still is an Adamson devotee. He had rescued Waldron from a period of obscurity at Burnley when he had fallen out with Harry Potts. It took a lot to provoke the ever smiling Potts but Waldron managed it one day when he parked in the boss's parking space. Potts, says Waldron, shredded him:

'In 1969 I was 21 years old, captain of Burnley Football Club, and the youngest captain in the First Division. Even in those early days I was conscious of what would follow my career in football and I asked permission from the club to open a restaurant. It was turned down by Lord and Potts. On my second approach to the club, permission was granted by Bob Lord. He had the last word telling me that I was a bloody fool.

Within a month I had been dropped from the first team and stripped of the captaincy I had treasured. As my game or my leadership qualities had not deteriorated in that month, I decided that Lord or Potts had punished me for going against their wishes. I later found that many things (and people) that went against Lord's better judgement were quickly dismissed or over-ruled.

'Some years later I was given the club captaincy again but this time under the guidance of Jimmy Adamson.

He was without doubt the greatest coach or manager I have ever played under. His coaching techniques were outstanding and our tactics were so successful that over a three or four year period in the early seventies players who left the club often found themselves being asked during coaching sessions, "What would Burnley do here?"

'Adamson's coaching had a passing theme which was always reflected in our play and we became known as a passing side. On one occasion I spoke to West Ham and England captain Bobby Moore and he said to me that they always hated playing against Burnley "because we were always chasing leather".

'Part of Adamson's management technique was to allow me, as captain, to voice my opinion on many areas relevant to the club. I was once asked my opinion about one of the star players at the club. I told him honestly and bluntly that the player was not popular in the dressing room and that the players felt he was, more often than not, a liability. The following day this particular player was sold for an enormous fee.

'Adamson managed the club in "handcuffs". He knew that at the end of every season (and even during the season) he would have to balance the books by selling one or more of his players. A classic example of this problem followed the promotion year of 1973. Queens Park Rangers and ourselves both gained promotion to the First Division and by Easter were many points ahead of the pack. I felt we were a better side than QPR; we just needed to strengthen the side with a few players. In the summer QPR bought two top players. Burnley sold two. Back in the First Division, QPR finished second and we finished in tenth place.

'When Bob Lord's personal ambition and dictatorial rule began to destroy the empire he had built, he finally pulled the rug from under the club's feet by sacking Jimmy Adamson. The decision lacked any logic, as Adamson was the only man capable of keeping Burnley in the higher echelons of the league.'

Waldron might have been fully behind Adamson but it did not stop him from being furious with him on one occasion. Burnley had been in the capital, had played brilliantly but lost to West Ham. The press were in raptures, drooling over the Burnley style and passing game. Adamson was delighted with the accolades and in the dressing room told the boys how pleased he was, how well they had played, and how the press were praising them to the skies. But Waldron was incensed at losing and threw a boot at Adamson, furious that Jimmy was so delighted. Adamson remained calm.

'We'll speak on Monday,' was all he said and let the incident pass, recognising that now was not the time to respond.

Both Harry Potts and Jimmy Adamson had been to watch Waldron in a Chelsea reserve game. Potts was ready to leave at half-time as he was unconvinced by what he saw. It was Adamson who insisted they saw the second half and should sign him. He clearly saw something in the raw young player that was worth bringing to Turf Moor.

It took Waldron a couple of years to feel any affinity with either of them. He quickly realised that on the training pitch it was Adamson who had the knowledge and pulled the strings, while 'Potts just stood around looking like what a manager should look like'.

After he had blotted his copybook with Potts, as much to do with carrying on with his plans to open a restaurant as much as parking in Harry's parking space, he was totally sidelined. It was Potts who picked the team; Potts who dropped him; Potts who didn't give him any game in any team for three months; as well as having him in to train in solitude while the other players had their day off. And vice versa – when the other players came in, he was told to stay away.

All that changed when Adamson became manager. Not because Waldron was a favourite with him, in fact neither Adamson nor Waldron had warmed to the other at all, but simply because Adamson told him he could do a job for him and was ready to make changes. Waldron says he never noticed any of the changing relationship between Potts and Adamson while Adamson was coach, or Adamson was jockeying for the manager's job. That however, by his own admission, is probably because he was involved in his own problems at the club and for a lengthy spell simply wasn't a part of things. But he did realise that Jimmy had a job to do, sorting out the senior players, some of them past their sell-by date, releasing them one by one.

'You can call me boss or Jimmy,' said Adamson on his promotion to the manager's job.

Waldron called him Jimmy despite all the others calling him 'boss', his brash, youthful rebelliousness refusing to lie down. Within two months he says, he was an Adamson disciple and called him 'boss' from that time on. Adamson's taming of the centre-half was a defining moment in Waldron's career. From that point on he became very close to Adamson who allowed him, as captain again, to speak his mind, something that Waldron was never averse to doing when he thought it was in the interests of the team.

Yes, he too found him aloof but would argue that he was not arrogant, and Waldron realised what Adamson's opinion of Potts was, on the occasion that he overheard him with the coaches disparagingly calling him 'the mad hatter'. Soon he referred to him as 'the mad hatter' quite openly. From 1970 until 1972 he had no real idea what Potts did in his general role, largely because no one ever saw him.

He regards the three seasons from 1972 to 1975 as the greatest time of his career and the turning point he feels, in the story of the inevitable failure to achieve real success, was the Liverpool game of March 1975, when from second place they drifted down to a final tenth because with players being sold, there simply wasn't the squad to continue the momentum.

But, if Burnley went on the defensive in the second half of that game it was not on Adamson's instructions. Waldron can only remember one occasion when a deliberately defensive ploy was designed and this was to curtail the power of Joe Royle in a game against Everton.

Geoff Nulty, one of the players sold that season, was one of the two players Waldron deemed irreplaceable, the other being Frank Casper ('a gazelle with a rocket in each foot'). Nulty was simply one of the most insecure players he had encountered, but absolutely essential to the team's 'work for each other' ethic, and totally under-rated.

As things fell apart late in 1975 it was Leighton James who bore the flak from other players, particularly Waldron who by then saw him as someone who did not pull his weight. He made his feelings clear to Adamson on several occasions, in private and in team meetings. On one occasion he urged Adamson to drop him but Adamson replied how could he when he was the one player that had the ability to score a 90th-minute winner.

'It's the other 89 minutes I'm worried about,' said Waldron.

All of this eventually led to an extraordinary meeting. On the Friday night of the weekend visit to play a game in London, the players were organised to go to the cinema after the evening meal. As they were about to depart Adamson asked Waldron to stay behind. He asked him to go upstairs to talk to Bob Lord and the other directors who were with him that weekend. Waldron looked puzzled whereupon Adamson informed him that he wanted him to go in and talk about Leighton James.

James was about to be sold but Lord was afraid of fans' reactions and remembered the scenes and abuse when he had sold Jimmy McIlroy in 1963 and then Martin Dobson in 1974. But the bottom line was Burnley had to raise £300,000 a year from player sales to pay the wage bills and fund the lavish style in which the club operated.

Waldron went upstairs and entered the room where Lord and the directors sat in silence when he went in. Then Lord spoke to Waldron and was the only one to do so. 'Colin,' he said, 'we've had an offer for Leighton James but we are frightened of the reaction if we sell him.' Waldron says he gave Lord every reason he could think of for selling him and then offered to take the flak.

'You sell him,' he said, 'but I'll contact the press and tell them I have a story for them; and I can guarantee they'll react to what I say more than the sale itself.'

'GOOD RIDDANCE' was one headline and the story featured not so much the sale but why James was no great loss to the team. Lord got no flak for selling him. In fact, it was one rare occasion when he received a little bit of sympathy.

When the end came for Adamson, it was heartbreaking for Waldron. After Adamson had told him privately in a side room at Gawthorpe that he had been sacked, he could not bear to join the others who were assembled waiting, to watch and listen to the news again. Both he and Doug Collins went home to a small estate just outside Burnley, where they lived opposite each other. In the privacy of their homes each of them cried. They knew that with this dismissal their lives would change.

Together, on the Tuesday of the announcement, they visited Jimmy at his home. There was almost a queue of players waiting to see him, says Waldron. When it was Colin's turn Jimmy knew he was due to appear on Granada TV that night to speak about the dismissal.

'What are you going to tell them?' asked Jimmy.

'Everything,' replied Waldron, distraught.

'Look,' said Adamson, 'say the right things tonight but in 12 months I'll tell you what's gone on.'

Waldron duly appeared on TV and said the 'right' things but he never really did find out exactly what had gone on. It is reasonable to assume they were all the things that Adamson wrote in the unpublished article.

Waldron was correct about his life being changed, 'Joe Brown replaced Jimmy, but Joe never wanted the job. He was a good number two and was quite happy in that job. He was mystified to be given it and was totally in Lord's pocket.'

He was told to get rid of Doug Collins, Mick Docherty and Waldron himself. By the end of the season they were gone. Waldron pointed out an interesting statistic. In the promotion season Adamson used just 14 players, except for four others who appeared just six times between them. In the relegation season of 1975/76, 26 players were used.

He also remembered the mystery of the £4,000 loan that Adamson made to Lord. With Paul Fletcher he visited Adamson and Jimmy showed them a letter that Waldron thinks had arrived containing a £4,000 repayment cheque shortly after he was dismissed. 'He must have borrowed it because his business was going broke,' Waldron commented.

But if the money was borrowed sometime during the 1972/73 season which the Basildon Bond lists indicate, is the other story true – that Lord repaid it by increasing Adamson's salary? The letter has disappeared – or someone has it and is hanging on to it as a keepsake. In the cold light of day it seems astonishing that Lord should borrow money from his manager to prop up his ailing business. What would that £4,000 be worth today?

Waldron still watches football on TV and commented about Barcelona and their passing style, 'Dave, we were doing this here at Burnley 40 years ago with Jimmy Adamson. It may not have been as slick as Barcelona, we may not have been such big stars, but we were a passing side. Everything was done with the ball in training.

'Pre-season wasn't doing 20-mile runs over the moors; it was with a ball to get our touch back. We did one-touch training and two-touch, all the time. People rave about Barcelona but we were doing the same thing here 40 years ago – and THAT was down to Jimmy Adamson.'

Talk to every single player about Jimmy Adamson and they will all say he was a wonderful coach. Talk to them about him as a manager or his man-management and interpersonal skills, and a different picture emerges. Even his biggest disciple and admirer, Colin Waldron, once said of him, 'He was not everyone's cup of tea.'

Dave Thomas sees him now as someone who swaggered around with his staff entourage, all of them laughing at his jokes, nice as pie one minute, cut you dead the next. 'Jimmy Adamson was years ahead of his time with his free kick routines and his tactics. Maybe it was me; I've got a determined streak in me and stood up to him when he wanted his own way. He always thought he was number one, always thought he was right. He was a sort of "get your hair cut" bloke and he could be arrogant. Harry Potts if he passed you by always had something to say or a greeting. Adamson sometimes walked straight past you. You never knew what mood he would be in.'

Dave will readily admit to having the capacity to be awkward and his own man; perhaps he and Adamson were never meant to get on. Football is filled with relationships like this. It still angers him that Adamson once said to him that he lacked mental toughness.

Yet no matter how those who knew him regarded him as a person, all of them praise his coaching skills to the skies. Stan Ternent, who at Sunderland eventually might have had good reason to be disgruntled with Adamson because of an eventual contractual issue, simply said, 'He was a genius.'

In terms of his prickly personality he summed it up simply and without rancour. 'It's just the way he was,' he said matter-of-factly without an ounce of umbrage. He visited him regularly in his retirement years.

Martin Dobson speaks glowingly of him. If it was Harry Potts who agreed to Dobson's father's request to give him a trial at Burnley following rejection at Bolton, it was Adamson who rescued his career with skill and coaching.

Dobson described the coaching and the routines to Tim Quelch:

'Everyone was training with a ball: the internationals and the young players. There was "two-touch" and shadow football going on; players were going through pass-and-move drills ... What impressed me, immediately, was that so much of the training centred on developing ball skills. There was instruction in what to do, not only in technique but in making runs, positioning and so on. I had never seen anything like this at Bolton. And at the heart of all this activity was Jimmy Adamson. He seemed to know exactly what he wanted from his players, blowing his whistle to stop the play when the exercises weren't being executed as he wanted, praising the players when they got it right and demonstrating what was missing when they didn't.

'There was much practising of building attacks from the wings. Once again Jimmy was meticulous about the type of crosses that were supplied from the wings. We would go through a series of routines involving whipped or hanging crosses. He paid so much attention to detail which of course paid off.

'I can't recall Jimmy having the opposition watched prior to a game, not as they do today. Now, they have these Opta statistics to study. But Jimmy knew enough about other teams' strengths and weaknesses to devise good team plans. For example, we might have had a game against a team with a big, commanding centre-half, capable of gobbling up all crosses pumped high into the box. So, in order to neutralise his strength we would assign someone to pull him out of position. Centre-forward Paul Fletcher would sometimes be asked to do this. His primary job was to occupy the centre-half so as to create more space for his team-mates.

'He was outstanding. He commanded so much respect. Everyone knew what he'd achieved as a player.'

Ironically, one of the ways he did this irritated some other players on the occasions he reminded them of his Footballer of the Year trophy and that they might like to go and polish it.

Geoff Nulty talked at length to Tim Quelch and was another perfect example of the 'rescued' player, that is to say the player who found no success at a previous club but whose skills were then honed at Burnley to make him into an extremely effective and invaluable member of the team. At Stoke City he had struggled while at Burnley he shone and he too will still attribute his success to Jimmy Adamson, much as he disliked his habit on the training ground of beckoning him with his finger:

'What really impressed me was the training sessions were always very well planned. Jimmy Adamson and his assistant, Joe Brown, always worked out the training schedules in advance. This was quite unlike what I had experienced at Stoke.

'There, only the first team received any real attention from the coaches and even their training sessions didn't seem that well prepared. The reserves were largely left to their own devices. But at Burnley, the senior players, the reserves and youth team players trained together – at least for most of the week. Adamson and Brown would divide us into mixed groups and, typically, these groups would be made up of four first-team players, four reserves and four apprentices. Jimmy wanted everyone to be inducted in the Burnley style of play so that when anyone stepped up, say from the youth team to the reserves or from the reserves to the first team, they were ready to make that transition.

'The mixed group training sessions took place on Mondays, Tuesdays and Wednesdays. There was always a strong focus on ball work. This was a key part of the Burnley approach. But on Thursdays we started to train in our team units in preparation for the Saturday games. As first-teamers we practised 'shadow football'. This is where we played against imaginary opponents. This really helped tighten up our positional sense and interplay. Jimmy also introduced this routine whereby the first team would be reduced to four defenders and a midfielder. They would be tasked with taking on a full reserve side. The only concession was that everyone on the reserve side was expected to fulfil their normal roles. For example, the defenders couldn't become extra attackers.

'This exercise really helped improve our defending. You had to play as one. It helped sharpen our defensive instincts and organisation, our ability to cover for one another. We learnt how to spring the offside trap more effectively. We became better attuned to one another. Having no attacking outlet, the defender was under constant pressure – the ball kept coming back at us, so this training routine really helped us get our act together defensively. Once we got ourselves organised we found we could keep the reserves out for some time.

'We also used this other routine designed to improve our wing play. Burnley had a string of great wingers – John Connelly, Ralph Coates, Willie Morgan, Dave 'Ticer' Thomas, and Leighton James and so on. It was a key part of the club's success over the years. So, in order to make the most of these assets, Jimmy Adamson devised these practice matches comprising 15 players per side with no goalkeepers, in which we could only score with our heads. In order to get goals first we had to work the ball wide to the point where it became instinctive.

'We scored a lot of goals in league and cup games. I'm sure these practice sessions helped considerably. They also helped us in co-ordinating our attacks. When, say, Leighton James was attacking down one flank, the opposing defenders would be drawn to his side to deal with the threat, so we then pushed up our full-back on the other flank to help exploit the gaps that this left.'

Adamson knew that he needed every ploy and strategy he could think of to gain an advantage. Martin Dobson remembers:

'When Jimmy was a player at the club, he and Jimmy McIlroy were the tactical brains. The club were so fortunate to have two such tactical thinkers, let alone two such brilliant players. We used to have this near-post routine at corners. My job was to reach the near post at the precise moment that the ball arrived at just above head height. I would be at the back of the 18-yard box on the opposite side of the corner taker. From here I would make a curved run taking me along the goal-line to reach the near post before anyone else could. But having got there I had to judge my jump just right, letting the ball just kiss the top of my head – no more than a deft flick – so that it would fall into the goalmouth at an unexpected angle. If a team-mate didn't get on the end of it, the resulting scrum could result in an own goal. It was really hard to get the required delicacy of the flicked header. Hour after hour went into this drill until we were really proficient.

'In 1973 we played Manchester City twice. The first game was staged at Maine Road in the Charity Shield. Here, we used a set-play routine that worked to perfection. We had a couple of lads standing over the ball – Dougie Collins was one. There was a bit of shuffling about – a false start – as if there was confusion as to what the plan was. In fact, the two of them started a mock argument, blaming one another for fouling up the routine. That caused the City defenders to relax and lose concentration. They thought our guys didn't know what they were doing.

'Just as City dropped their guard, Dougie suddenly clipped a lofted ball to the back of the six-yard box. Waldron, our centre-half, had anticipated the move. Unseen, he ran around the back of the City defence and met Dougie's chip with a diving header. It was the Charity Shield winning goal.

'A few months later we were due to play City again. This time it was in the league at Turf Moor. Jimmy said to us before the game, "Remember that free kick routine that worked so well at Maine Road?" And we said: "Yes boss but we can't pull that stunt again. They won't fall for it twice." But Jimmy replied, "But they might if we change the players involved. They might be fooled into thinking it's a different set-play."

'Well, we did as he suggested. This time Fletcher was the target. He too scored with a diving far-post header, and we won easily by 3-0. That was typical of Jimmy's brilliance as a tactician.

'It was so easy fitting in at Burnley. I owe so much to Jimmy Adamson. He saved my career. I was going nowhere until I arrived at Burnley and he saw something in me that others hadn't. He could see I had some skill but he thought I might benefit from having more time in possession. It wasn't as if I was slow but he thought I might progress better in a midfield role rather than up front where there was so little time. He'd started off as an inside-forward but had been converted into a magnificent wing-half. He really should have played for England, he was that good. He was right. Midfield did suit me better. No one else had seen that.'

If Jimmy Adamson groomed and coached Martin Dobson with cleverness and care, he was not averse to 'teaching him a lesson' either, of the 'short sharp shock' kind. There came a point early in his career when Dobson was demoted down to the A team in order to get him back on track and better focused. Something similar was done to Geoff Nulty, except that in Geoff's case it was even more draconian as he recounted to Tim Quelch:

'I felt well-looked after at Burnley ... but while I was helped to develop my game; they certainly weren't soft with me. One week I found my name missing from ALL the team sheets. I wasn't even down to play for the reserves or the A team. So I asked a team-mate what I should do. He said I should speak to the "boss" Jimmy Adamson. I went to his office under the Cricket Field Stand. After knocking first, I put my head round his door and asked, "Why am I not playing in any of the teams this week, boss?"

'His answer was curt but to the point, "Not fucking good enough."

'The next week I was really wired, fighting and scrapping for the ball in our practice matches. Jimmy Adamson confronted me with, "How much do you really want this? I mean, is it everything to you? If it isn't everything to you, you're not going to make it. You are not as naturally talented as some of the other lads. This means you're going to have to work that bit harder."

'I took that advice to heart.'

Paul Fletcher will always maintain that Jimmy Adamson had a love affair with Burnley Football Club and that afterwards when he went elsewhere, it was never the same for him. He could never re-create the almost perfect team he had once had at Turf Moor. Everything else was perhaps an anti-climax, certainly in terms of achievements. 'He loved the place but when it went wrong he became so bitter. He wanted to build a team but Bob Lord wanted to build a stadium. We had our star players and our bread and butter players but most of us were in the latter group. The problem was that as the star players went, all that remained were the bread and butter guys.'

In conversations with Paul Fletcher and in his book *Magical*, Fletcher pays glowing tributes to Adamson. Fletcher's attitude towards his old boss is based on one simple premise, 'He changed my life.'

Adamson might well have been difficult, prickly, brusque and a hard man to love, but I never heard Fletcher refer to that side of him once. He recalls that the players never saw anything of the differences between Lord and Adamson. When Fletcher (and Waldron) first saw the draft article that Adamson had written about Lord they were astonished.

'The 1972/73 season was magical,' said Fletcher in his thoroughly entertaining book.

'It was in the three golden seasons we had that Jimmy's reputation as coach and manager was cemented. He would never surpass them and I suspect that when he left, football was never the same for him. We came so close to success and maybe even greatness with him but it was all based on teamwork, and that a team was a sum of its parts, not 11 individuals. But, he never had a prayer of sustaining the work he did in building that team of which I was a part. If he was a great manager in that period there was one simple reason. He was in love at that point with Burnley Football Club.

'When he left, wherever he went, it was never the same even though he tried to surround himself with familiar faces. He maybe wasn't the greatest ever manager at Burnley, but there, he got the mix right. It's an essential football secret, in fact it's no secret at all; if you get the right blend of players, youth and experience, flair and workers, you'll fit a team together and it will gel. Owen Coyle did it at Burnley in 2009. Jimmy Mullen did it in 1992 although they were mainly Frank Casper's players. Stan Ternent did it in 2000. Jimmy didn't want 11 star players; he just wanted 11 people who could play together. The team ethic came first. It still binds us together even today.

'Several games have left great memories and one of them was at Chelsea. It's what Jimmy said that left an indelible impression. We were losing 3-0 at half-time to a good Chelsea side. A hammering seemed on the cards and as we trooped off we expected Jimmy to go mad with us for the way we had played and goals we'd given away. To our amazement he was calm and simply said not to worry and to go out for the second half as if it was just a practice game with our training boots on.

'Quite stunned by this, but also put at ease at the same time, we went out for the second half quite relaxed, thinking oh well, let's just do what we can and enjoy it. Remarkably we came back to draw the game 3-3 with me scoring the equaliser. Absolutely delighted we came back in at full-time and asked him why he hadn't bollocked us earlier.

'He grinned and just as pleased as us said, "I'd have been relieved if it only been 6-0 at full-time. Chelsea were outstanding in the first half. What else could I say other than to try and relax you?"

'When I arrived at Burnley I didn't score until my sixth game but got great support from Jimmy in this time. I could have got really worried but he didn't let me. He'd say what Nat Lofthouse used to say to me, that supporters didn't expect me to be brilliant every game, but they would expect 100 per cent at all time and would expect me to give everything for a Claret shirt. He'd tell me that all supporters would give anything to be in my place.

'To be dropped from the team back then if it happened was a massive blow. There was no squad rotation in those days when you expected to be left out sometimes and accepted it. Week in and week out the team was the same but there came an inevitable spell when I was not playing well and I expected the worst especially when coach Joe Brown came over to me to say that Jimmy wanted a word with me. It could only mean one thing, I brooded; I was out.

'I can still remember the beautiful, sunny afternoon and when I met Jimmy he was standing in the middle of the wooden bridge that spanned the river between the Gawthorpe training area and the changing rooms. He was deep in thought and throwing dandelions into the river below, clearly contemplating the news he had to give to me that I assumed was the worst. I looked glum and despondent. To my surprise he began by asking about my wife Sian and the kids. He chatted away about them and how the kids must be growing up. He chatted about the weather and how pleasant it was so that I assumed he was just relaxing me before giving me the bad news. But there was no bad news.

'What he told me was that of all the players he'd brought to Burnley he regarded me as the best. He loved every aspect of my game and that I never gave less that my best in any game. Then he went on to the game that was coming up and assured me that he knew I'd give everything. Then he said he expected me to have the best ever game; that if I didn't score it was his problem. He picked me so that if I had a poor game it was his fault, not mine. He told me to stop worrying, to keep trying, and on the way home to pop in the changing room where I'd find a bunch of flowers for Sian and some chocolates for the kids. He told me to give them his love and that he'd see me on Saturday.

'How's that for man-management? Can you imagine how I felt as I drove home? There I'd been expecting a bollocking and the axe but there he was telling me I was his best signing. If at that point he'd asked me to jump off the Town Hall roof, I'd have done exactly that. I couldn't wait for Saturday, to get on that field and play my heart out. It would be nice to say I'd gone out and scored the winner but I honestly can't remember what the next game was. I do remember I was only dropped once in ten years.'

Frank Casper initially had to work hard to convince Adamson to keep him at Burnley even though Frank was one of the most gifted strikers at the club. Frank's problem was that he had been a Potts signing in 1967. Frank recalls that Adamson had little to do with it other than driving him back home to Barnsley after the signing. At that point Casper had no car. The journey to Burnley, driven by Harry, he remembers well. As they neared Burnley Harry drove him from Hebden Bridge up the incredibly tortuous Mytholm Steeps and then over the moorlands.

Anyone doing this drive for the first time soon begins to wonder just where the hell they are. At one point after a few miles of driving across what seems like the top of the world you come to a small hamlet of cottages set around a now demolished old mill. Drivers could be forgiven for thinking they were in the middle of nowhere. The inhabitants had the habit of stringing their washing across the moorland road on washdays so if the bus came along the driver would stop, honk his horn and the women would move the washing.

Casper remembers Harry Potts simply driving straight through it and muttering about why on earth was washing strung across the road.

When Adamson became manager, however, Casper was summoned to the office. Assuming it was for some kind of 'geeing-up' session, he was astonished to be accused by Adamson of being a Potts man. 'I don't think you can do a job for me,' Adamson told him bluntly. It was clear he wanted to shift the old brigade out and get his own players in.

'I was told that Bristol City wanted me and the deal would bring John Galley to Burnley. Anyway, I said I wasn't moving there and was determined to stay and prove him wrong. I told him I didn't play for Potts, I didn't play for him; I played for ME and my family and then the club. By the end I'd proved him wrong.'

Casper wasn't sold and received coaching from Adamson to hone his striking skills. This involved individual work after training, or work with another player, Billy Ingham, and then sometimes a second player, Colin Waldron, was added to the routines to produce situations where he would have to receive and control, and then beat the defender. If he managed to score it was the other two who got the roasting for not preventing him.

He said, 'He had his finger on every button and knew everything that was going on. When I was out injured for a long spell there were weeks and weeks of weight training in a small concrete room that by the end was utterly depressing. Day after day this was nine until 12 in the morning and two until 4.30 in the afternoon and every afternoon he came down at 4.30 to check on things.

'I was so utterly depressed and miserable so one day I begged physio Jimmy Holland to let me go early, which he did at 4.15. Adamson was furious when he came down, rang me at home and ordered me to return. This I did whereupon the only thing he said was that he'd given Jimmy Holland a bollocking and now I could go back home. He could be like that. If Adamson was tough on those who were injured there were in fact echoes of his mentor Alan Brown who was particularly harsh with Brian Clough after his severe injury; so inflexible in fact that Brown later acknowledged that "I was too hard on him".

'On one occasion Jimmy was slightly late for training and Joe Brown had taken the players out on the pitch. He tore into Joe for doing this before he'd arrived. He had me and Paul Fletcher in the room with him when he did this; it was as if he simply wanted to show he was in control.

'He'd have no hesitation in telling players to get their hair cut. He definitely based himself on Alan Brown. But, when I did tell him that I needed a break from all this endless and monotonous weight training, and was feeling like a stranger at the club, then he got me back to the training ground to mix with the other players again and he had me refereeing the practice games and the five-a-sides.'

Jim Thomson, centre-half for much of that golden three years when things went so well was one of the quiet, unsung players, never in the limelight like Leighton James, Paul Fletcher or Colin Waldron, but nevertheless a key team player. When he first arrived in 1968 he says it was clear that even though Potts was manager, it was Adamson running the show, 'manager in all but name'. 'It came as no surprise to him when he did become manager and it is correct that he didn't want Potts at the training ground any more. He just didn't want him near the place. We found that out from Colin Waldron. He and Adamson were very close.

'On the training field at Gawthorpe it was Adamson doing all the coaching and organising. Eventually we rarely saw Harry in his tracksuit and he was never in the same league as Jimmy as a coach. Jimmy was so clever, an unbelievable tactician. If the cameras were there filming a game it was as if they were waiting for something special to happen. He had this expression and he'd say, "We'll double-thunk them, we're gonna double-thunk them."

'It meant that all our free kicks involved a lot of doubling back especially in the one that won us the Charity Shield. City's Francis Lee was open-mouthed by it and when in another game we did it a second time he just stood there and said, "I don't fucking believe it." We just used different players to make the runs. Adamson was such a clever, clever man and other managers copied him.'

It was then that Jim took me aback a little when he firmly revealed that he hated playing in the first team and described team-mate Geoff Nulty as having similar thoughts. He explained the strange feeling they had that whilst never enjoying being first-teamers, nor did they want to be dropped into the reserves. But on they went week after week, knowing that on a Monday morning it would always be their heads on the block if things had gone wrong, even if they had won on many occasions:

'I hated training. It was a strange feeling. I hated being in the first team but at the same time not wanting to be demoted to the reserves. Me and Geoff Nulty knew every Monday morning what was coming and made every effort to hide from him. He had his nucleus of favourite players and we still talk about it when we meet up most weeks. There were four of them, Paul Fletcher, Colin Waldron, Doug Collins and Martin Dobson. We'd joke it was always them that got the biggest Christmas turkeys. Training might begin with a jog and Geoff and me would make sure we were in the middle of the pack so he couldn't see us.

'And then it would happen. His habit was to blow a whistle and we'd stop. Then the finger would beckon. The group would separate to reveal us and the others knew what was coming, particularly Waldo and Fletch. They'd think it was hilarious and even point to us and say, "There they are boss." And then we'd be summoned over by the wagging finger.

'Over you went and he had this habit of standing next to you with his arms folded. Then he'd ask quietly, "And how do you think you did on Saturday?" I might have had a good game and I'd reply, "Well I think I did OK boss." He would say nothing and turn to walk away with a simple "hmmm" whereupon you'd follow him to find out what was wrong. In all the time I played for him I don't think I ever got one word of praise or one pat on the back.

'Geoff was sold to Newcastle and about a month later rang me to say he'd never been so happy away from the Adamson treatment. Looking back I'm sure it was all mind-games on his part, doing it to keep me on my toes and stay focused. If that was the case then I suppose it worked but it made me thoroughly dislike him. It always seemed to me he wanted to make me feel small. Maybe it was his way of not letting players get above themselves.

'There was an occasion I went to see him in his office and I remember he had a day-at-a-time calendar on his desk, one of those where you tear off each day. On each day there was a slogan and on the day I went it read, and I've never forgotten it, "The biggest asset a woman has is a man's imagination." He asked me if I'd read it and I told him yes. Next he asked me if I understood it, "Er yes boss," I told him. "And do you understand it?" he asked. "Er yes boss," I said.

'"Well think about it and keep it in mind," he said.

'Today I've worked out what it means but then I'd no idea how it applied to me and I think it was just his way of being superior, putting me on the spot, testing me, trying to make me think he was clever and that I wasn't.

'There was a time when I was so fed up of him that I asked for a transfer. He asked me why on earth I would want to leave when I was in the first team and then explained he would have to put it to the board; that it wasn't his decision to make. I'd ask him again and get the same answer. In the end I just gave in.

'Many years later when the Adamson Suite was opened at the club in 2011 we met again. I knew he wasn't well and wondered just what and who he would remember. But he saw me and gave me the biggest hug and just said, "Ah Jim." I was really taken aback. Until that moment I had truly believed he had always disliked me but in that moment realised it was all just psychology. For years he made me feel so bad I used to hate even talking about him, he left such indelibly poor memories in my mind. But that hug changed things.

'But his psychology didn't work all the time. Leighton James was a wonderful player and Jimmy would treat him in the opposite way to me. He'd praise him much of the time; but the praise that Leighton got and all the press accolades seemed to us to go to his head after a while. Jimmy, feeling that he was slacking, decided he needed to do something to get Leighton focused again so in his absence one morning he told us all to give him a good kicking every time he had the ball in the five-a-side games. One or two players who weren't too fond of him relished the idea.

'Colin Waldron led the treatment and James must have been kicked several times in what were always quite serious games. But the psychology, if that's what it was, backfired. After four or five minutes of this treatment, James just walked off. "I'm not putting up with this," he said and headed for the dressing room. What we did was cruel and quite wrong. Three weeks later he was sold.'

'It is a crime to lose the ball' was one of Adamson's basic mantras. It was that which he began to try to instil into the players as soon as he became coach in 1965. That was the fundamental difference between him and Harry Potts; since Potts always encouraged his players to take a man on, to try and beat him, and to dribble and use initiative. Both were committed to teams that went forward but with Adamson it was with possession, passing, passing and more passing with just Leighton James as the only flair player.

Eddie Gray and Peter Lorimer's opinions of Adamson at Leeds United are elsewhere in this book as are those of Sunderland's Gary Rowell. There is no question that Adamson was an enigmatic and deeply private man, able to inspire great respect but little affection. His understanding and teaching of football was exemplary and his ability to get the best from players second to none. Some he hurt along the way, others he irritated, and yet more were angrily indignant. He could inspire the deepest loyalty in some and strong dislike in others. He changed peoples' lives, some for the better, and some for the worse. Such is football management. Perhaps it is simply what all managers have to do.

Chapter 15

Sunderland via Rotterdam

T HE PERIOD that Jimmy Adamson spent in Rotterdam was intriguing if only for the fact that no one on this side of the North Sea, other than Jimmy himself and local Burnley reporter Peter Higgs, knew much about it.

Until now the football history books simply state he coached briefly at Sparta Rotterdam. Players who I talked to knew nothing about it; his grandchildren knew nothing. But there was one item in his memorabilia, another notebook, this one a tiny pocket book, filled with notes of his spell there.

This was a club that was in Holland's First Division and without actually winning anything had occupied a top-end position in the table for many years until 1975/76 when they were tenth in a league of just 18 teams.

From 1971 until 1973 Ajax had dominated Europe. In 1974 Holland were runners-up in the World Cup in Germany. The roll-call of illustrious Dutch players at this time was a lengthy one with the greatest name being that of Johan Cruyff. Dutch Total Football was what other teams aspired to. In its simplest terms it was any player being comfortable with the ball in any part of the field and if any player moved to a different part of the pitch, someone just slipped into his place to cover. Rinus Michels had been given the credit for this 'invention'.

Like many Dutch teams Sparta enrolled young players from the age of eight with junior teams and youth development a key foundation at many clubs. Adamson's attraction to Sparta officials was therefore an obvious one. His reputation in this area was still sky high despite his exit from Turf Moor. His notes indicate that he was there in May planning for the new 1976/77 season.

I had looked at the Sparta Rotterdam official site and found a section in English where I could contact the club. There was a quick reply; alas it was in Dutch but even speaking no Dutch at all I could figure out that it said 'we will contact you within 48 hours'. A week later I was still waiting.

'Does anyone speak Dutch?' I asked on the Claretsmad website. There were two responses. Cliff Hacking had a Dutch business colleague he could contact. Then, Alfons Meijboom, a Burnley fan, responded from Holland itself and volunteered to contact Sparta. He came up trumps:

> 'On 9 May, 1976, Sparta treasurer Floor Bouwer went to Burnley to arrange the contract. He would be the new trainer/coach of Sparta for the 1976/77 season. On the 14th of May, Adamson went to Rotterdam for the preparation of the start of the new season. On the 15th of May he went for a visit to watch Sparta play Maastricht. Sparta lost 1-0. On May 23 he went back to Burnley to arrange business at home. On the 26th of May he decided not to join Sparta due to private circumstances. This was a big setback for Sparta. His wife and daughter didn't want to leave.'

But was he to be appointed as manager or coach? Clarets fan Tony Scholes dug out the relevant newspapers in Burnley library; in them Peter Higgs wrote that he was to take over as manager. He reported that Adamson had received a fabulous offer believed to be in the region of £20,000 a year. Having been out of football since January and desperate by now to be back in the game he had just spoken to the directors of lowly Southport Football Club. Sparta, however, presented a real challenge and what Adamson described as an offer 'that was too good to turn down'.

The talks lasted almost a full day but it was agreed that he would visit Rotterdam to evaluate the job and then take up the position in July for a minimum of one year. Adamson told Higgs that he had given his word to Sparta and the contract would be a mere formality. Ironically, the first ever manager there had been an Englishman and not only that, he was from Burnley. David Walders had played for Burnley from 1903 to 1906 and then spent a year as Sparta coach/manager. Adamson described it as an amazing coincidence and then went on to say:

'I look upon this as a tremendous opportunity to prove myself as a coach. Sparta are a famous club with very strong traditions but they have not had much success lately. They have been overshadowed by local rivals Feyenoord. It is my job now to launch a revival. In addition to taking charge of the playing side of things I shall also be attempting to build up the club's youth system through the many amateur teams they run. Sparta players have expressed their delight that I am joining their club which means a lot to me. The whole venture is going to be a wonderful challenge.'

In his pocket book he noted that the dressing rooms needed re-painting, the stadium was in need of better maintenance and that he would need to develop 'a new and bright image with a better environment'. His comments on the team were severe, 'Drastic work needs to be done. The forwards are unable to score, the defence wide open.'

He would look to improve the team with English players. The whole scouting system would need reorganising. He would need money to buy players if necessary. His recommendation was that Dave Blakey would join him. He was the best scout in England and would earn his salary in one year. His contacts included every manager in England and he was part of the fraternity of scouts in England. All that, plus he was an excellent salesman.

Regarding any foreign players brought to the club he, Jimmy Adamson, would insist on assessing their ability before buying. Hans Sommerveld would have authority to buy young players if Adamson was unable to see them first. At the foot of one page he jotted that he looked for guts, ability, speed and temperament. He would assist at all levels including juniors.

Other pages have jottings relating to problem players (the number seven was a barrack room lawyer apparently), discipline, pre-season preparation, the medical department, players' characters, dossiers on opposition teams, pre-season games, equipment, relationships within the club, how the club was structured, duties and responsibilities, travel arrangements, the press, radio and TV, training times, and 'any other problems or snags I should know about'.

Other pages have notes on who he is to meet and what time, lunch with this person, dinner with that person, a meeting with the board (it lasted four hours). He notes the occasions when he takes a stroll in the city centre and tellingly when he telephones May at home. The final entry notes that he inspected his new flat, met the players and there was an invitation to attend the British Embassy.

On 23 May he returned home. Three days later he made his decision not to sign the contract and informed the Sparta directors by letter. Jimmy's wife May had no intention of leaving Burnley for London in 1962 when he had been offered the England job. The prospect of her leaving Burnley for Rotterdam was even less. Nor would she later leave Burnley for Sunderland. The first sentence of his letter seen all these years later is poignant and touching. At home in Western Avenue, Burnley, he still had daughter Jayne with him; close by lived his other daughter Julie who had a baby girl, his granddaughter Katie.

> 'We find as a family after the recent visit that it is impossible for us to live apart. The need to take this important factor into consideration was the reason I came to Holland last weekend to see how we would cope as a separated family. We found that being together as a family was a far more important thing than financial considerations, or the satisfaction I would have achieved from the job.
>
> 'We have always been a close family and that's the way we want to stay. After I had been in Holland for six days I began to realise I would not be able to stay.
>
> 'It would have been no use to me being there worrying about my family and them being back here worrying about me. I suppose you could call it homesickness. Now, my family are delighted that I'm stopping here.'

Adamson had received no other offers from any English club that changed his mind, he stressed. He assured Sparta it was simply a family matter and nothing more. Vacancies at Wolves and Arsenal might have looked attractive but there was no contact; it was as if in England he was on the shelf with an uncertain future.

He told Peter Higgs, 'I have received no offers from English clubs and at the present time I have no idea what the future holds. Obviously I want to stay in football but if the right offer doesn't come along I will take a job outside football in order to work.'

Maybe he knew that his old boss Harry Potts had eventually signed on the 'dole' and the officials at the office where he signed on were so embarrassed they did their best to see him in a private room. His old illustrious team-mate Jimmy McIlroy had gone back to bricklaying for a spell when he finished playing. Football is cruel to the out-of-favour.

Predictions that Adamson would be snapped up quickly by another club were wide of the mark but for the moment, without money worries, he could afford to sit and wait. The £25,000 settlement in January on his dismissal at Burnley had been generous and in addition he had been repaid the £4,000 that Lord had borrowed. It would be many months before he did return to football. It was 1 December when he was appointed as Sunderland manager and by then he had been out of the game since January and had received no firm offers from any other league club.

His notebook reference, however, to 'Manchester City – blackballed' is a curious one. City had their last success of a golden period in 1976. Malcolm Allison had left them in 1973. Was Adamson approached in 1976? Did Lord somehow block the move? It is pure conjecture but Lord's influence was far-reaching; within football circles he was a powerful man, albeit disliked. Manchester City managed by Jimmy Adamson would have been an intriguing partnership with their then chairman, Peter Swales, very ambitious for his club. Bob Lord had no great love for Peter Swales so the thought of Jimmy going there would have been intolerable.

The eight-year-old Jimmy Adamson who first went to Roker Park could never have imagined that he would one day be Sunderland manager just about 40 years after that visit. When he joined Sunderland in December it was towards the middle of what had become a difficult season for the club. His hero Alan Brown had been there until 1972, remembered vividly by the players if not by supporters.

Adamson however, had the near-impossible task of replacing 'The Messiah' Bob Stokoe. It was also a time when supporters were still hopeful of the return of another favourite – Brian Clough, who had set scoring records at the club and had once said that he would be prepared to walk back to Sunderland to manage it. A consortium of local businessmen once tried to persuade Clough to lead them in a takeover of the club and when Clough was manager at Nottingham Forest, 100 Sunderland supporters followed him to a game at Leyton Orient and begged him to take over. When Adamson eventually left, again Clough was linked with the job.

It was 'The Messiah' who had sparked an astonishing revival at the club that rejuvenated everyone. With a couple of shrewd signings, and through his own personality galvanising what was basically the same under-performing team, he guided Sunderland to a memorable Cup Final against Leeds United after beating another two top sides on the way there. One of them was Manchester City, the favourites, and the replay, after a draw at Maine Road, was voted the best ever game at Roker Park in a newspaper poll. Stokoe thus became a Wearside immortal along with Ian Porterfield who scored the single Wembley goal. Even selling two key players, Dennis Tueart and Dave Watson, neither of whom he wanted to sell, Stokoe took the club to the Second Division title in 1975/76 for the first time in the club's history.

Football is filled with ironies; Stokoe's first game in charge had been in 1972/73 at home to Adamson's Burnley. It was a 1-0 defeat as Burnley notched up the wins that took them to the Second Division title but Stokoe did something that endeared him immediately to all Sunderland fans. There had been no prior announcement but they ran out in the old style black shorts instead of the white ones that they had worn for the last ten years or so.

The return to the First Division was not a good one, however. There was no win in the first nine games; there were reports that Stokoe was not in the best of health and rumours that he was losing his grip with some of the players. In October 1976 he resigned. Ian Macfarlane was caretaker manager for just six weeks and won two of his seven games in charge. It meant that Sunderland had won just two of the first 16 games.

All in all then, Adamson took over at a club in the First Division that was not quite in turmoil, but almost. Relegation was already a word being used and he had the two shadows hanging over his head, Stokoe and Clough. Nevertheless Adamson was regarded as one of the top thinkers in the game; Sunderland fans were well aware of his achievements at Burnley, his skills with young players were much admired, and his reputation was still unsullied. It all looked promising and there was a measure of optimism among supporters.

Like all managers he began to bring in his own people and Macfarlane was immediately dismissed. Bringing former Burnley commercial man Jack Butterfield to Sunderland was a strange move on Adamson's part. There had been a huge bust-up between them at Burnley when Adamson felt that Butterfield was beginning to have too much influence with Bob Lord and was even encroaching into playing matters. Butterfield was part of Lord's Saturday evening snooker clique.

'The green bit is mine,' Adamson had angrily told him. Adamson informed Lord bluntly, 'He goes or I go,' such was the depth of ill-feeling. Adamson even told his staff they had to stop drinking with Butterfield after a game, a habit that had developed at the Park View pub across the road from the Burnley ground. At least one of the staff informed Adamson that he would not be told where he could and could not drink. Butterfield left the club after a row with, ironically, Bob Lord not Adamson. The jokers at Burnley, Paul Fletcher and Colin Waldron, used to jest with Butterfield that they knew enough about what was going on and what he was up to, to put him in jail.

But here he was back with Adamson again at Sunderland, one of several ex-Burnley people with whom he surrounded himself; Dave Merrington, Dave Blakey and Stan Ternent although Ternent was already there. His former player, Dave Thomas, still refers to them as 'the Adamson entourage'. Adamson stayed much of the time with Fred Stewart, a Sunderland director, and his wife Jenny, the irony being that they were just a few doors away from Dave Thomas's wife Brenda's mother and father.

On occasions Dave and Brenda visited and stayed with her parents and Dave thought it quite amusing that there a few doors away was the man who had sold him. Occasionally Dave would see him though they never actually met and spoke, although Dave wonders if Adamson had seen him would he once again have beckoned him with the irritating finger.

On his dismissal at Burnley, Adamson had recommended to Bob Lord that Merrington would be a good appointment to replace him but Lord's preference for the less forceful Joe Brown had been a disaster. Adamson would later refer to this in his Sunderland programme notes with an almost wry satisfaction. Merrington had a strong personality, a firm mind of his own and was quite aggressive in his approach to football. It is reasonable to think that he and Lord would soon have been at loggerheads, something that Lord would have been well aware of.

'I recommended Dave Merrington. Bob Lord in his wisdom selected his own man, but is now not too happy with the outcome,' wrote Adamson. The tone, beautifully understated, is almost mocking.

George Forster of the Sunderland Supporters' Association was certainly no fan of Jack Butterfield, 'We had a thriving association and were raising as much as £4,000 a year for the club which we handed over to them. That was a fair sum back in the mid-seventies. Butterfield came in and said he would be taking over all the fund-raising and wanted to see our books. I remember he arrived in a big Ford Granada, had plans to fill the shop with all kinds of sports gear including golf equipment, and then eventually left to join Yorkshire Cricket Club.

'Jimmy Adamson called in at the Supporters' Club office one night for a chat. He'd seen the light on and it was very late so he came and chatted away with me. I'd actually lived and worked near Burnley for four years from 1958 to 1962, seen him play many times and could still name all the players. Then one night at the Black Cat Club I persuaded him and Dave Merrington to get up and sing a few north-east folk songs with our organist and drummer. They had good voices too.'

Adamson's Sunderland memo pad, a spiral-bound Northumbria 160-page reporter notebook, begins on 9 December 1976. If only there had been something similar for his torrid time at Leeds United. If there was, it has obviously disappeared.

The Sunderland notebook, in the first month, reveals all of the minutiae that he faced and had to deal with; appointing Merrington and Blakey, players to review, a pay rise for the scouts, a meeting with Stan Ternent, ground-staff matters, the training facilities, injuries to several players, a possible move for Billy Hughes to Charlton, the mountain of correspondence, the need for a gymnasium, office furniture, arrangements for his first game in charge, player signings, players' behaviour, a package deal for the departing Ian Macfarlane, Bob Stokoe, the Merrington contract, solicitors' matters, security, internal problems, general maintenance, travel arrangements, disciplinary appeals, termination of the consultation committee, Jackie Ashurst's transfer request, adjustments to the players' rule book, press room drinks, Doctor Scott, directors travelling with the reserves, executive staff meetings, dreadful conditions at Washington, player suspensions, scouts' expenses, Christmas turkeys, a player on loan to Sheffield United, possible transfers for Malone and Gibbs, signing Mick Docherty from Burnley and his basic wage and medical report, possible move for goalkeeper Montgomery to Chelsea, state of the players' lounge, trainers' room and broken equipment.

Perhaps the most significant heading is simply 'Noble and Flynn latest position'. Another one is 'players not in my plans'. The reference to Noble and Flynn is repeated. There is a separate list of possible outgoings – Montgomery to York, Towers to Stoke, Lee and Guthrie to Sheffield United, Train to Carlisle and Holton to Walsall. Incoming possibilities were Armstrong from Arsenal, Noble and Flynn from Burnley, Martin from Carlisle and Waldron from Manchester United.

The list of tasks and needs was daunting and this was just the first month. The attempt to bring Brian Flynn and Peter Noble from Burnley incensed Bob Lord and Harry Potts; they accused Adamson of deliberately trying to unsettle the two players. Were they tapped up? Did Adamson actually speak to them? I would find that out later. By February 1978 the notebook was filled.

Adamson eventually brought three Burnley players in (Docherty, Waldron and Collins) so that supporters joked he would be changing the strip next and would have Sunderland playing in claret and blue. In addition he reappointed Billy Elliott, one of his old team-mates from the mid-1950s, to the coaching staff. Elliott was already a legend at the club and known for being one of the hardest players in the game. He was a winger who played in an age when full-backs kicked wingers into the stands week after week at every opportunity. Elliott reversed the process. His crosses were so hard that forwards often dodged out of the way because they came across at bullet speed. This used to incense Elliott, says Jimmy McIlroy, who would stand, glare and yell angrily, 'Which of you fuckers ducked?' and would have decked them all if he had been close enough.

McIlroy also tells the story, apocryphal perhaps, that he found him with a mouth full of blood one day before a game, filing his teeth down so they would fit better. The mid-1950s were the days of the legendary full-backs, Roy Hartle, Tommy Banks and Willie Cunningham, all of whom he kicked mercilessly. It was Elliott who was coach to the Wembley team of 1973 and he is credited with the conversion of England international Dave Watson from centre-forward to centre-half. Today Billy Elliott is revered at Sunderland Football Club and it is a standard joke on Wearside that when the *Billy Elliott* film came out, Sunderland fans thought it would be their football hero's life story.

On the playing field Adamson had a disastrous beginning that fully tested the town's motto of 'Nil Desperandum', his debut game as manager being at Birmingham and a 2-0 defeat. It was the first of a truly dreadful run of seven consecutive defeats without a goal being scored. On and on went the goalless games so that even though, next, there were two draws, they were both scoreless.

During this run of games Adamson dropped big Jim Holton, brought in by Bob Stokoe from Manchester United. The giant Holton was popular with the fans. He was no Dave Watson but was rugged, never shirked a challenge and always gave 100 per cent. Ivan Ponting described him as the quintessential 'rugged defender', near-unbeatable in the air and abrasive in the tackle. He exerted a formidable physical presence although when it came to the game's finer points he was undeniably clumsy. All this made him into an instant cult hero so that one of the memorable chants of the age was designed for him: 'Six foot two, eyes of blue, big Jim Holton's after you.'

His omission did not go down at all well with many fans so they got up a petition for his reinstatement and sent it to Adamson. Adamson dropped it in the bin. 'That's where petitions belong,' he announced.

A staggering eight players played their last games for Sunderland during Adamson's first season in charge; Foggon,

Gilbert, Malone, Gibbs, Train, Towers and Hughes, plus Holton of course. Malone and Hughes had been members of the great Cup Final team and Adamson's alleged lack of recognition of that achievement was strongly resented. The exit of all these players might have seemed draconian but new managers everywhere do the same; getting rid of the old guard and bringing in their own players. But what Sunderland players of the time say echoes that of Adamson's old Burnley players, 'Great coach but poor man-manager.' Adamson's poor interpersonal skills were always his Achilles heel.

It was the 0-0 draw against Stoke City that stopped the rot after all the defeats – nine in all including the two in the Macfarlane period. Stoke produced nothing as an attacking force and were simply defensive with goalkeeper Peter Shilton having a superb game. Sunderland simply could not find a way past him. Against any other goalkeeper that day Sunderland would have scored at least once. If there were many reasons for relegation at the end of the season, Shilton was one of them. Time and again Shilton intervened and Sunderland could not find a way past him, or when he was beaten the shot went inches wide.

Stoke had scored just 12 goals in 22 games with good players injured. Waddington apologised for their negative display, saying, 'There are times when you have to do what you have to do. I can only apologise for the lack of football.' It was of no consolation to the frustrated Sunderland fans or Jimmy Adamson who by now must have thought the football gods were against him.

'We were unlucky not to win,' he said. 'We were better organised than we have been. Stoke never got through to have a shot and we could have had a goal or two.' The draw lifted them to nine points from 23 games but they were still bottom, four points adrift of Bristol City and West Ham, and six points away from safety.

The first win did not arrive until 11 February with Sunderland bottom of the division and their supporters in despair. It came with a 1-0 victory against Bristol City. It was only the third of the season so by now relegation looked a certainty.

But despite the gloomy prognosis, there was jubilation and relief. Adamson continued with Gary Rowell who had already made his debut, and then gave first games to Kevin Arnott and Shaun Elliott and what happened next was a near miracle as

Sunderland almost avoided relegation, a feat very much enabled by Arnott, Elliott and Rowell. Arnott was a Glenn Hoddle-type player who never really hit the heights that he should have done. The three of them were known as 'Charlie's Angels' after the Sunderland scout, Charlie Ferguson. It was Stan Ternent who urged Adamson to include the three of them on a regular basis having worked with and developed them for some time.

By the end of his tenure at Sunderland, some supporters might well have been ambivalent about Adamson's departure, but many of them also appreciated how close he had come to saving them from relegation. Supporters had given him tremendous flak during his initial run of winless games and demanded that he played the club's best players. Adamson looked at Rowell, Arnott and Elliott and answered that he was playing the best players. Rowell went on to become one of only three Sunderland players to score more than 100 goals for the club, including a hat-trick against Newcastle United. Ironically he played 19 games to end his career at Burnley where Jimmy Adamson had by now turned his back on football. The win against Bristol City was the first of nine and five draws in the next 16 games. In the three games after Bristol there were terrific wins by the astonishing scores of 4-0 against Middlesbrough, 6-1 against West Brom and then 6-0 against West Ham United. Supporters saw superb football and through the remainder of the season, form that if not title-winning, would have comfortably seen them at the top end of the table.

Adamson had been back to Burnley to relieve them of Colin Waldron, Dougie Collins and Mick Docherty. Waldron was dependable in defence but would eventually leave for Tulsa when he found himself out of favour and in the reserves. Collins, alas, was not the same class player he had been at Burnley and received short shrift from supporters. The two players he wanted to sign from Burnley, Peter Noble and Brian Flynn, did not materialise. Bob Lord made sure they stayed at Burnley and along with Harry Potts was furious at the attempts to unsettle his players. Whilst Lord had given instructions that Collins, Waldron and Docherty were to be sold, Flynn and Noble were still valued members of the team.

Years later Waldron thinks that Adamson dropped him, Collins and Docherty when he realised that supporters were critical of him favouring all the Burnley players. He saw what he described as the 'cold side of Adamson' when he told him he would be leaving to play in the USA. Here was a player who had given years of totally devoted service to Adamson, had left Manchester United to re-join him, had been his captain and shared confidences with him. They had enjoyed what Waldron felt was a very special relationship, so it was reasonable to expect more than just the almost dismissive 'oh OK then' that he received as Adamson more or less walked straight by him.

Harry Potts referred to the attempt to poach his players in his programme notes for the Sheffield United game in March 1977. It was rare for Harry to publicly castigate anyone but he was incensed at the blatant attempts to 'steal' two players. He did not name Adamson but everyone knew who he was referring to:

> 'What really does annoy me, however, is some of the off-the-field happenings in this game. I want to place on record the fact that I totally resent it when the manager of another Football League club makes 'transfer' references to two of our players, in a manner which creates an unfair situation. In my opinion this sort of thing is wrong. Therefore I am pleased to be able to officially inform the very many loyal supporters of this club that despite what has been wrongly said by one Football League club manager, Peter Noble and Brian Flynn will be remaining as Burnley players.'

Relationships between Adamson and the Turf Moor hierarchy were now dreadful and would remain that way for as long as he remained in football.

The only Burnley player who really established himself in the team was Mick Docherty. He became well respected not as a full back but as team captain and midfield ball-winner until injury ended his playing career at the age of just 28. Jim Forster, of the Supporters' Association, was clearly impressed with Docherty in his spell as acting manager in 1981. Whenever there was a request from Jim to Docherty to do something for the association, he obliged, saying it was all part of his job.

One of the four wins had been against Manchester United on 11 April. Sunderland had already drawn 2-2 against bitter rivals Newcastle United. The performance against Manchester United was superb with a flying start seeing them almost score after just 80 seconds, and then they took the lead in the fourth minute. Stepney failed to hold a ferocious shot and Arnott slipped in to score neatly. In an end to end game United came back with a vengeance and when McCreery was brought down in the box, Gordon Hill levelled for Manchester United with the penalty.

In the 19th minute Sunderland took the lead again after two defenders sandwiched Mel Holden and referee Hackett pointed to the spot, whereupon Towers rammed home his third penalty of the season. This by now was a simply stupendous game and although there were no more goals, the action was incessant. Sunderland held out against relentless pressure although they themselves continued to have good scoring chances. Waldron and Ashurst were outstanding at centre-back. Tommy Docherty paid Sunderland a huge compliment saying that they were 'the team of the future'. He had great respect for Adamson having sent his son Mick to Burnley some years earlier because that was where Adamson turned good kids into good players.

Adamson was understandably jubilant especially as the game at Newcastle had seen Sunderland throw away a two-goal lead. It was another point lost that fans could later point to, saying, 'If only ...' The win against Manchester United, however, took Sunderland from second-bottom to seventh from bottom. Six clubs were all on 27 points and Sunderland had the better goal difference.

Five games remained before the very last game of the season away at Everton. The last Saturday of the season had seen Bobby Kerr come off the bench to snatch a late point for Sunderland with thousands of supporters going wild at the end. It meant that if they won the very last evening game they were safe, having pulled off the proverbial 'great escape'. In the previous nine games Sunderland were unbeaten with four wins and five draws. An astonishing 18,000 fans made the journey to Everton, producing an electric atmosphere inside the ground and it was reasonable to think that Sunderland in such good form could pull off the impossible.

Had Sunderland beaten Everton away in that game they would have survived, but it was not to be. There was controversy at Coventry when the game there against Bristol City began seven minutes late allegedly due to crowd congestion. Oddly enough,

Sunderland fans noted, in a previous game there had been over 36,000 when Liverpool played at Coventry. There was no crowd congestion and no delay to that particular kick-off.

As they reached the final minutes of the game both teams knew that Sunderland had lost and therefore knew that a draw would see them both safe. In the final stages, Coventry and Bristol simply went through the motions of playing a football match. Coventry chairman Jimmy Hill had the Sunderland score displayed on the scoreboard and the last minutes of the game petered out ending in a goalless draw. Such is football. Adamson's Burnley and Preston had done just the same at the end of the 1972/73 season. The complaints flew back and forth but Coventry received only a simple reprimand from the unsympathetic Football League.

Jimmy Hill is still reviled by Sunderland fans of a certain age that were there at the end of this traumatic season and know the story. Their bitterness was still evident at a Fulham versus Sunderland game in 2008 when the statue of the great Johnny Haynes was unveiled; a player of whom Pele once said was the greatest passer of the ball he had ever seen. At half-time the great and good paraded in front of the fans and who was there but Jimmy Hill, a one-time team-mate of Haynes. The Sunderland fans were incensed by him, even 30 years after the Coventry versus Bristol game. When Hill did a Mr Universe pose to wind up the Sunderland travelling supporters, Rob Mason, the Sunderland historian, remembers that police had to hold them back such was their fury.

Fans will always try to analyse how and why relegation happened whatever club they support. It is true that you can point to any draw and argue that it could have been a win; or any defeat and say it might have been a draw. The fact that Sunderland went down by such a narrow margin made it all the worse. Adamson pointed to one particular 1-0 defeat away at Manchester City, a game in which he felt that there had been two diabolical decisions:

> 'I think that we could be forgiven for moaning. The first one came in the first half when a ball was crossed from the left-wing on the goal-line and reached Mel Holden on the edge of the six-yard box. Mel promptly put the ball in the

back of the net only to see his effort disallowed for offside. It was probably the worst decision I had seen up to that point but worse was to come. Just on the stroke of half-time Jackie Ashurst took the ball away cleanly from Garry Owen who then rolled over in the penalty area, got up, and was running away to play on. But to his amazement and everybody else's at Maine Road the referee awarded a penalty. Former Sunderland man Dennis Tueart converted it and City went on to hold their lead. Those two dreadful decisions put us one-down when we could just as easily have been one-up.'

Relegation might have been heartbreaking but much of Adamson's strength came from his family and marriage. That summer he and his wife May headed to Majorca to unwind, for Jimmy to recharge his batteries, and to celebrate their silver wedding anniversary.

The attempt to stave off relegation had been a gallant one and at this stage few, if any, Sunderland supporters had cause to be dissatisfied with Adamson. The ship had been in rough waters when he had arrived; his initial run of games was dismal, but the recovery in the second part of the season was excellent. There was no reason not to be optimistic for the new season if the form could be continued so that the return to the First Division could be immediate.

It began with Adamson confident, 'Our prospects for promotion are better than any other club in the Second Division.' He was prepared to go into the transfer market if necessary but while at Burnley his top price had been £60,000, here at Sunderland he would have no hesitation in spending £150,000 on just one player, he said positively.

Adamson was particularly pleased with the progress of youngsters Arnott, Elliott and Rowell but there were others in the pipeline. He was optimistic but cautious. Football in the Second Division was different with teams coming to defend ruggedly resulting in frustration and supporters had to be patient. The fantastic roars of support that had waved down the terraces in the previous season's final games had acted like a 12th man. Now he was worried that the fans' impatience would transmit to the players on the field.

Striker Billy Hughes, who had never really got on with Adamson, was sold for £30,000. Bobby Kerr was now the only player left from the 1973 FA Cup-winning side. Two new men came in, Wayne Entwistle from Bury for £30,000 and Wilf Rostron from Arsenal for £40,000, but neither was a 'big' signing and they would make only average contributions to Sunderland.

The first game of the season was a resounding 3-0 defeat away at Hull City. A section of supporters were groaning already. The first home game with supreme irony was against Burnley and Jackie Milburn asked if it would be a grudge match. Adamson was diplomatic. It is not rocket science to suppose that he was praying for a win but he answered that the last thing he wanted was a grudge match and all he wanted was a good performance and a good win. He got it, 3-0. The crowd was an impressive 31,405; alas by the end of a mediocre season they would have sunk to half that.

The Burnley win was the only one of the first ten league games and to add to those were two League Cup games against Middlesbrough, one a draw and one a defeat. It is reasonable to say that as far as supporters were concerned by mid-October the writing was already on the wall for Jimmy Adamson. By the end of the season Sunderland would finish in a respectable sixth place but that was only because of the five wins from the last six games. Without that final flourish it would have been a decidedly mediocre season. Of 42 games they had won just 14, and five of those had come in April. Fans, well before this time, had made their decision. Adamson was not the new Messiah.

And yet in the programme in November Dave Merrington was writing that confidence was high, that skill levels were higher and they had a formation that suited them. He described them as having no midfield, but six forwards, so interchangeable were the players. He answered criticisms that the club now had too many chiefs and not enough Indians by trying to justify the number of coaches and assistants. Yet another coach had been brought in – Syd Farrimond. Adamson was described as the man who had his finger on all the buttons.

An article, however, in the Sunderland fanzine *A Love Supreme*, gave an insight into how supporters felt about the manager and how there seemed to be little respect for him. It referred to the

Blackburn game away at Ewood Park in December 1977. It began almost cruelly:

> 'One particular trip we took to Blackburn was in the heady days of Jimmy Adamson, who, when he wasn't driving round the Whitley Bay area full of drink, was trying his best to sign the entire Burnley team. Could Doug Collins have been done under the Trades Description Act for putting Professional Footballer on his CV? I think so. This was a Christmas fixture in the good old days when we used to play games on consecutive days and we had played Blackpool at home on Boxing Day the day before. Two goals from Lord Rowell had ensured a 2-1 victory. At the time Blackpool had a particularly foolish forward who was daft enough to cross swords with Joe Bolton. The forward's face came in contact with Joe's elbow; Joe set off for the bath without giving the ref time to get his book out. Two minutes later the forward wakes up.
>
> 'It was when we stopped for a pre-match pint at a big pub near Burnley that we found the reason for Joe's exclusion from the team bus. Both the Sunderland and Blackpool teams had stopped there for dinner and Joe's presence may well have dented the entente cordiale that was evident between the two sets of players.
>
> 'There was also a bus in from Bishop and one of their lads began to berate Mr Adamson about the amount of money he was allegedly earning and telling him that he should get a round of beers in for the whole bus. Jimmy looked uncomfortable but the tension eased when he surprisingly agreed to this quite moderate request. This only went to prove that we were paying him too much, or, that he was very generous. Whatever the reason, it lightened the mood and gave Mr Adamson a better reputation than he deserved in certain parts of Bishop.'

The 1978/79 season started in sunshine but with most fans resigned to another season of mediocrity. The previous season was regarded as a complete anti-climax; a season that had trundled along with little to look forward to and nothing at stake in the final few games. Fans everywhere will recognise when their club is simply treading water and those at Sunderland were as astute as any. Disenchantment had set in with Adamson; that was clear enough, and optimism was low.

At least there was a 1-0 win against Charlton in the opening game but it was a poor performance with football that was scrappy and unimpressive. The one thing of note was the beautifully worked goal that was the result of a classic Adamson free kick scam. In fact it was pretty much a carbon copy of the one that had worked so well at Burnley. This time it was Rowell scoring. Bobby Kerr ran in to take the free kick but then stopped before shooting and pretended to argue with his team-mates. While Charlton were wondering what to do, Docherty stepped up and chipped the ball to Joe Bolton who, having run round unnoticed, was completely unmarked on the left and from his header Rowell nodded the ball home. It was however, the only thing of note in an error-strewn game in which supporters saw that Charlton could easily have taken both points having missed some glaring chances.

If the 20,000 crowd were not pleased, neither was Adamson, 'We did not play well and the anxiety complex which hit the players and crowd had a destructive effect. Football is meant to be played with a chuckle in the boots, but there was no way that Sunderland could relax enough to play that way.'

His comment that football was meant to be played with a chuckle in the boots he had heard many time before – from Harry Potts. It was a Potts mantra and Adamson in using it must have forgotten his dislike of the man. What the fans disliked was Adamson already pointing his finger at them and blaming them for the anxiety in his players. This, after all, was only the first game of the season and already he was using them as the reason for a poor show. Now, there was not just disenchantment, but resentment.

But he was delighted with the free kick, 'We have been trying this for some time and I was pleased to see that it worked like a dream. In fact it worked better than it normally does in training.'

At this point supporters had no idea that Adamson would be gone within a few weeks. He too might have been surprised to hear that by the end of October he would be in situ at Leeds United. But in the meantime there was one game to come that would go down in Sunderland folklore as the 'Battle of Turf Moor'. The two games during the previous season had gone by without incident and when Sunderland visited Burnley for the first time with Adamson as manager, his name did not even appear in the programme other than as part of the team group captions.

The Harry Potts 'welcome' simply said, 'Today we welcome the Chairman, Mr K I Collings, his directors, manager, players and supporters of Sunderland FC.' But the welcome to him was hollow; there was no way that Adamson's was a welcome presence.

But the second time Sunderland came with Adamson the game was a horror show. 'A kick in the teeth for soccer,' wrote Keith McNee. 'Football reached a new low ebb in this nasty, niggling grudge confrontation which gave the game a dreadful kick in the teeth.'

'Professional,' responded Mick Docherty, by now the only one remaining of the Burnley players Adamson had brought to Sunderland.

'I am proud of my lads, I was sacked by Burnley so I get a special satisfaction from winning,' added Jimmy Adamson after what McNee described as one of the most disgraceful masquerades of a match ever at Turf Moor.

Even with two players sent off and three booked, Sunderland hung on to their 2-1 win. It was presumed that the aggravation resulted from the anger felt by Docherty and Adamson towards the Burnley they had left two years earlier against a background of great acrimony. It was seen as a grudge match but Adamson, in fact, had made no attempt to wind his players up or to treat it as anything but an ordinary game. But the events that took place during it made it seem like a deliberate vendetta was in force.

Burnley's Harry Potts was incensed by everything he saw, although he missed the bitter confrontation between Bob Lord and Adamson in the stand. 'No team of mine has ever, or will ever play like that,' he said. 'I would rather pack in with the game completely than sink to Sunderland's level. Sunderland just went for the man. As a match it was a shambles and I was disgusted by the way Sunderland went about it.'

He claimed that one of the Sunderland players had even spat at a Burnley player. A graphic description of the game appeared in the Sunderland magazine *A Love Supreme*:

'The history of Sunderland Football Club, in modern times, has often seen episodes when emotional "highs" were immediately followed by desperate "lows", and vice versa. A fine example of a single match that reflects this was the "Battle of Turf Moor", Burnley, in late September 1978. The connection between the two clubs in terms of ex-Burnley men on the management, coaching and playing staff at Roker park suggested a possible "grudge" match, but certainly no indication that the match was destined to end with nine bookings, including Sunderland's coach, and two sendings off.

'Both sides had made a modest start to the season, lying mid-Second Division after six games. Both had injury problems on the day and were forced into making several team changes. Sunderland had four teenagers in their line-up, including the highly promising Mick Coady at centre-half.

'The match started well for Sunderland and, after a bright but quiet opening it ignited after 23 minutes. Mick Docherty, former Burnley man, and playing a blinder, was involved in an incident with the unsavoury Leighton James. James was booked. Two minutes later Sunderland right-back, Mick Henderson, flattened James and became the game's second booking. Sunderland continued their early enterprise and Gary Rowell hit a post after Wayne Entwistle had created an opening. The name of Joe Bolton had entered the ref's notebook for a foul on Burnley winger Tony Morley.

'Joe Bolton will be remembered for never making a half-hearted tackle. Regular inhabitants of the Paddocks would testify that his opening snarl to any dainty wingers as he launched his first tackle of the match would invariably be "eat cinders". Picture the winger trying to "run" him on the outside. Joe would connect and his victim would career through a cloud of dust into the hoardings between the tunnel and the corner flag. Such a tackle had befallen the unfortunate Morley.'

It is quite easy at this point to imagine the 'Mad Hatter', Harry Potts, going apoplectic on the touchline at what he was seeing.

Nice man that he was, a change came over him during the 90 minutes of a game as any player will testify. In his time he had jostled linesmen, run on the field during a European game to put a ball in the correct position for an opposition free kick, had thrown cushions at a referee and grabbed hold of opposition players (one of them being the legendary Dave Mackay in the tunnel at White Hart Lane). The top of his head was frequently covered in cuts and bruises, the result of him jumping up and down in the dugout when he was enraged.

'A yellow card for Shaun Elliott followed within minutes as the game "came on the boil". Observers would, of course, recall that Burnley had started the aggro and a particularly weak "homer" of a referee had let the game get out of control when the lads had begun to assert themselves. Rowell then hit the bar, before disaster struck almost on half-time. Henderson's second booking of the game led to him being sent off. He had barely had time to muddy the invigorating waters of the proverbial early bath when he was obliged to shuffle towards the "tap-end" in order to accommodate his fellow full-back Joe Bolton. Joe had followed him moments later.

'On the pitch, Burnley's veteran winger Steve Kindon was cautioned for a tackle on Docherty and then Ken Knighton, on to tend the injured, was shown the yellow card for enlightening the referee with his observations of the proceedings. At half-time it was Burnley (with 11 men and two bookings) 0, Sunderland (nine men and several bookings including the coach) 0.

'The second half, without full-backs, and considering that Burnley included effective wingers James, Kindon and Morley, was surely destined to end in tears. A particularly unwelcome "low" appeared to be in prospect. In fact during the contest with the ball, Sunderland continued to take the game to Burnley and great work by Alan Brown incredibly created a goal for Gary Rowell after 60 minutes.

'1-0 Sunderland!

'Mick Docherty was then booked for a possibly over-enthusiastic challenge on Leighton James just to keep the alternative entertainment going. Burnley's Billy Rodaway was next to be shown the yellow and then, after 69 minutes, a Rowell penalty made it 2-0.

'Unbelievable!

'The bookings stopped, Burnley pulled one back and it was backs to the wall for the last ten minutes. The Lads actually finished the stronger and even had a goal disallowed in the last minute. This would have been Rowell's hat-trick.

'Final score: Burnley 1 Sunderland (canny bairns) 2 and heights of ecstasy!'

One account of the day says that a seething Adamson burst into the dressing room at half-time only to shout at them all what a 'useless set of bastards' they were and then immediately stormed out, with him assuming they would now lose and his big day back at Turf Moor would end in an embarrassing humiliation. When he left, the players then sorted themselves out. Of course when they unbelievably won, having decided to go on the front foot because the last thing Burnley would expect would be for them to come out and attack, Adamson was delighted and in fairness to Sunderland, it could be argued that the 'battle' had been initially kick-started by Burnley man Leighton James with his foul on Docherty.

Harry Potts's reaction to the defeat did not go unnoticed by Adamson and he referred to Potts's grumbles in his next programme notes. The Jimmy Adamson who was utterly livid at half-time in the dressing room was a very different person a week later:

'Thanks to a certain manager in Lancashire and the remarks he has been making, Sunderland Football Club's image has not been enhanced these last seven days. I should have been a happy and contented man after our victory at Burnley last week. Is there a manager who would not be proud that nine of his players could beat 11 of someone else's? There are good losers and bad losers in this game and when I read that our 2-1 win was gained because we were a dirty side I was saddened and could only conclude that the bad losers are growing in number.

'There have been some damaging charges made against my players and I cannot stay silent when I know full well that they are untrue and totally without foundation. I believe the gentleman at Turf Moor has been searching for an excuse to account for what for him must have been an embarrassing defeat. Had the circumstances been reversed I would have been embarrassed but I would not have thrown up this sort of smokescreen. I would not have produced such a lame excuse; I would have held up my hands and admitted that, one the day, we had been beaten by a better side. It was a game that did have some needle in it; but violent – certainly not.'

Adamson provided nothing else of note in his remaining time at Roker Park and he departed in October 1978. He left by mutual consent as the saying goes but knowing that the Leeds United job was his to go to. In a magazine article shortly after he joined Leeds he talked about the ghost of Brian Clough driving him out of Sunderland:

'He's their big hero up there and when they got me they weren't satisfied. I couldn't stop them going down in my first year and when I didn't get them straight up again the fans started chanting "Adamson out, Adamson out". As a manager I expect criticism when things go wrong but it had a terrible effect on the young players. They became afraid to play at Roker Park. They froze at home. They say the Sunderland fans are worth a goal start which is true when things are going well. But at other times, they can be worth a goal start to the opposition.

'If Clough ever does go there, they'll get crowds of 40,000 to 50,000 and if things go wrong they won't blame him. They'll blame the players, the directors, the staff, anyone but Clough. Until the Sunderland supporters forget Clough no other manager has much of a chance at Sunderland. I would like to have stayed and finished the job but when the Leeds job came up, I decided to leave.'

Those Sunderland supporters who saw and read this article were not best pleased. In it they saw a man who was bitter at his failure, blamed everyone but himself, and in particular made fans the scapegoat. Some of them questioned his commitment and they had certainly noticed his drinking. Few Sunderland fans, if any, were sorry to see him go.

But one of those sorry to see him depart was Gary Rowell and he gave several insights into Adamson's time at Sunderland. Rowell today remains a Sunderland goalscoring legend and ironically as his career drew to a close he played 19 games for Burnley, where he now lives in the suburbs at Reedley. Born at Seaham near Sunderland, he played for Sunderland from 1972 to 1984, scoring 102 goals and being voted their best player of the 1980s by Sunderland supporters, and his hat-trick against Newcastle United is part of Wearside folklore.

'What a gentleman' were the first words he said about Adamson, echoing those of Eddie Gray at Leeds United. 'He was such an influence on me.'

'I'd already made my debut for Sunderland before Jimmy arrived so I'd had a taste of things but in no way was I a regular then; just in and around the first team. He came with a big reputation as a coach and as someone who did well with young kids. I found that to be absolutely true the more I worked with him. He was, quite simply, the best coach I have worked with. What I found was that he knew how to get the best out of players by challenging us ... "Here's your first team chance ... prove me right ... if you can't ... there's always the reserves." Some managers today will see it as their job to protect young players. But Jimmy if he saw young talent had no hesitation in using it.

'When he arrived we were already on a bad run and that continued as he looked at the place and looked at the players, looked at those with potential, and then eventually identified me, Shaun Elliot and Kevin Arnott as three young players to be given a regular place. We were not doing well; he had to do something radical and he threw the three of us in at the deep end. Suddenly we were winning with me the up and down, box to box goalscorer, Kevin the passer, and Shaun the destroyer.

'He kept Bobby Kerr of the old Cup Final team on the right of midfield for his experience. Of course a few noses were pushed out and some of the older players were not too fond of him. But that's football. Every manager leaves players out and those players will be none too pleased.

'It looked like he was going to turn things round and suddenly we had what I still remember as the best week of my career when we had three wins and scored 16 goals. It was just amazing. They were three home games; that was because the middle one was a re-arranged game played in the midweek. The first was a 4-0 win over Middlesbrough, not quite a big derby but almost, and it wasn't so much the four goals it was the terrific way we played. Next it was 6-1 against West Brom in the re-arranged game. Supporters couldn't believe what they were seeing; we were winning with such style and confidence. They were thinking a miracle was on the way and we could avoid relegation because that was something that had looked well possible before Jimmy arrived. The fact that I scored four of those 16 goals made it all so special for me.

'By now Jimmy was really pulling everybody together and what he'd done with me still makes me smile to this day and makes me appreciate how clever he was and how he saw things in players and new things that they could do, that the players themselves didn't think was possible. What he did with me was see me as a left-sided midfield player which is not at all how I started. I played in centre-midfield, an old-fashioned inside-left, if you like, which is a different role altogether. But he took me on one side and explained what he wanted me to do; that he recognised what a good engine I had and could get up and down. So he set me this new challenge and pushed me hard and pushed me further still, told me I had an eye for goal and that I had to get in the opposition box ten times in each half.

'It was such a simple challenge but nobody had ever said that to me before. He told me that if I did this every game then the ball would drop for me, more often than I realised, and I'd get the chances to score. So, that was the challenge and when I said that I'd never played there before he just told me well OK then there's always the reserves I could play in. So that was it; take the challenge, take it on, or stay in the reserves. I never looked back.

'Anyway, next up in the three home games was West Ham. They had some great players in that side and we scored another six goals. That was 16 goals in one week and we only conceded one. It was maximum points from three games. We went out there fearless, filled with confidence thinking, God this is easy.

'For the rest of the season we picked up more good results, but not to the same degree as that fantastic week. Then it all came down to the last game of the season; a game that is still so controversial. We lost at Everton but then sat in the dressing room afterwards with little or no idea of what was going on in the other game that mattered, Coventry versus Bristol City. They were the two other relegation candidates. This was before mobile phones in our pockets, texting and Twitter, plus Sky Sports News with its instant updates on the wall of the dressing room.

'We had no idea they were still playing; no idea they were just kicking the ball around without trying to score because they knew we had lost. So there we sat in the dressing room and it was probably an hour before we heard for sure what had happened and they'd just played out the game keeping themselves safe.

'Even today it causes bad feeling. I was there at Fulham co-commentating when Jimmy Hill was abused by the Sunderland fans for what he did all those years ago displaying our score at Coventry. Sunderland fans will always think he deliberately contrived to delay their kick-off.

'We went down, but what a roller-coaster season it was and we almost did the impossible. The margins are so fine. Had we done that Jimmy would be a Sunderland hero today. After the three games we won one after the other, we only lost three more games that season. It was sod's law that one of them was the very last Everton game. If there is such a thing as a glorious relegation then this was one. Trouble is, the fans thought we'd go straight back up the next season. Alas we didn't.

'Slowly I saw changes in Jimmy in his second season. At first he was never off the training ground, always in his tracksuit, always coaching and right in the middle of things but bit by bit that changed. We began to see more of Dave Merrington than Jimmy. Perhaps he was getting sucked into all the problems that all managers have to contend with. I sometimes wonder if he would have been better remaining as simply a coach and concentrated on that and left all the managerial stresses and problems to someone else.

'And then came the "Battle of Burnley". It was just before Jimmy left Sunderland. The previous season we'd drawn at Turf Moor 0-0 and won 3-0 at Roker Park; they were games that went off with no trouble at all. Of course we knew there was an edge to these games because of Jimmy's past history there so you could always tell when a Burnley game was getting closer although nothing was ever said.

'For the game coming up Jimmy said nothing at all to wind us up, and he certainly made no attempt to make it into a grudge match as has sometimes been suggested. He did not like crude play, would never condone it and would never tell any player to deliberately rough anyone up or be extra physical. Truth is, he was a hard man to read much of the time and whatever thoughts he had about Burnley or Bob Lord we never knew them.

'But it was Burnley and there was a huge following from Sunderland and for that alone we were pumped up as well as knowing that there was a bit more to a Burnley game. But there were never any special instructions from Jimmy, or bad intentions on our part. Some games just take on a life of their own; something sparks things off and in this case there was certainly some bad feeling between Mick Docherty in the Sunderland team and Leighton James on the Burnley side and bit by bit it became the most violent game I have ever played in. Nobody gave an inch; the ball might be on one side whilst players were kicking each other on the other side. Clatterings were common and the ball became an irrelevance – but not because of Jimmy. It's just the way it happened; it just degenerated and the more the crowd got riled the worse it got.

'When Mick Henderson was sent off, the fall guy, it could have been anybody, it didn't end there. Before half-time Joe Bolton was sent off as well. However, because it was so near half-time coach Dave Merrington had gone back to the dressing room with Mick Henderson. So, he had no idea that Joe Bolton had been sent off as well. We all followed in at half-time and Merrington just assumed that Joe had come off with us as per normal for the half-time break.

'The next couple of minutes were amongst the funniest I can remember as Dave began to give Joe new instructions for the second half and Joe kept trying to interrupt to say he'd been sent off as well. Dave just didn't listen until at last he stopped, looked, mouth open, eyes wide and was utterly speechless. Then he spoke, "Well how many fucking men do we have left then?"

'Next, Jimmy Adamson stormed in from his seat in the stand. The door burst open with a slam and I have never seen such anger in a man anywhere. He was rarely a man to swear or lose his rag ever, but this time he did and proceeded to give us the biggest rollocking I can ever remember. He absolutely slaughtered us for our conduct. He said he was ashamed and that we were a disgrace and now for all he cared we could go out and lose because we had a ready-made excuse for the impending defeat. He stormed back out, gave us no instructions, no tactics, no re-shuffle, just slammed out and vanished.

'We were stunned and silent. And then Mick Docherty stood up. Mick was great and was just a natural leader. He told us he wasn't having any of that; he wasn't going to be told to go out and lose and by the time he'd finished we'd decided to go out there, never mind we were missing two men, and give it a real go in the second half. We quickly reached the conclusion that the last thing Burnley would expect would be for us to take the game to them in the second half. We decided to go all out in the first 15 minutes and see what happened. We'd do the unexpected; they'd expect us to sit back and just hang on.

'We went for them – and scored! The Burnley back four came out thinking they were in for an easy 45 minutes and couldn't believe it when we set into them. Adamson's words were still stinging and ringing in our ears even as we scored and the Sunderland fans went mental. Unbelievably I got a second with a penalty. This was just astonishing to be winning 2-0 with just nine men and only then did Burnley wake up and from then on threw the kitchen sink at us. The violence had stopped as it so often does at half-time and teams come out in a different mindset. It had become a proper football match so that when Burnley pulled one back they did everything but score as we hung on and amazingly won 2-1.

'Of course Jimmy came down into the dressing room with the biggest grin on his face I had ever seen and since that day I have often wondered; was Jimmy's rant and explosion of fury just that? Or was it a deliberate clever ploy to wind us up by telling us OK now you can go out and lose? Was it a great psychological masterstroke to make US angry and go out and prove him wrong? Managers do that all the time. We'll never know – but what I'll never forget is that massive grin all over his face.

'I was sorry he left Sunderland. For me he was brilliant. But yes, in the final few months he was absent from the training ground more and more. You noticed it because he had previously been such a regular on the pitch. You did wonder what was going on. At his best he was a great innovator, finding new ways of doing things and finding new ways to stretch players. But, maybe the tragedy for him was having to deal with all the clutter of management – wages, contracts, travel, directors,press and supporters. So for me his move to Leeds was a disappointment; others not in his plans might well have been pleased. But that's football. A manager makes decisions that affect people's lives.

'For a short time while he was at Sunderland things were very special. You think back to a point lost here, a point lost there, a missed chance that might have been the goal and the win that kept us up in the relegation season. But it wasn't to be. I never had any idea that he had such a bad time at Leeds in his final year, and regret never visiting him seeing as we both lived in Burnley. I never had any idea that he finished with football after his time at Leeds. It was a sad end for him. But he was the man who made me into such a successful Sunderland player, and made me the man that I am today.'

Chapter 16

Leeds United

O N 25 October 1978, when Jimmy Adamson took up his post at Leeds United, I was the deputy head of a primary school in Leeds. By then we had lived in Leeds for something like ten years, had a house in Headingley and on a clear day from the upstairs rooms could see Armley Jail across to the south and the Elland Road floodlights when they were lit, further to the east. I could never decide which was the most iconic.

His arrival at Leeds United as manager seemed strange; I couldn't quite work out how he would fit in at a place that was so unsettled and still longing for Revie. And those Leeds fans – they were a hard, hard lot. To me, even though he'd had a couple of years at Sunderland he was still synonymous with Burnley; he had been there so long and had been an integral part of my younger days, and then for both me and my wife they were such special times when we saw all the games of that golden period of the 'Team of the Seventies'.

When I saw the headlines, it didn't quite register that he was to take over the club that had battered Burnley so often over the years since the 1960s and where we had seen that marvellous game when Burnley astonishingly won 4-1 in Revie's own back yard. Even having lived in Leeds since 1968, we only have a passing interest in Leeds United, even though we're still there, except not in Headingley.

The only tangible links to them was that when I first arrived at St Margaret's Junior School in Horsforth's leafy suburbs and resurrected the school football team, the school had no kit so the lads all brought their own white Leeds shirts for the first game seeing as they and their fathers were all Leeds fans. Then, in 1972, Leeds had won the FA Cup and the ruddy-faced, cantankerous old headmaster I worked for arranged a trip for the football team to see the FA Cup when it was on display in a local Sunday school. The lads and dads cheered while I sat there unmoved. Then in 1974 there was that memorable visit to Elland Road where we stood in the home end and Revie went incandescent as he watched the demolition of his finest by Adamson's men.

And finally and perhaps best of all, for sheer drama and unexpectedness, there was the night some of the lads and dads visited Elland Road for a guided tour of the place. It was the last of Brian Clough's days there. Revie had gone, the directors had made a mess of what they should have done and did not appoint Johnny Giles, so instead Brian Clough arrived, Adamson's invisible nemesis at Sunderland.

To our astonishment when we arrived in the car park by the West Stand the place was filled with Yorkshire TV cameras, lights, reporters and a milling crowd. It became clear that something big was happening and as we approached we saw Brian Clough emerge from the building, struggle his way through the reporters to get to his car, on the way saying a few words, and then drive away with a large pay-off and his new motor. We had no idea he had just been sacked. The memory of that night is still as clear as yesterday. Some things remain indelibly imprinted. I still say to people almost as my party piece, 'I was there the night they sacked Brian Clough.'

Adamson arrived just about four years after that and of course it was known to all and sundry that I was a Burnley supporter so my opinions on him were keenly sought. Alas most of the people who asked also seemed to remember the occasion when Wimbledon beat Burnley in the cup at Turf Moor when Adamson was manager. My only reply to that was had they forgotten that it took a replay for Leeds to beat Wimbledon in the next round.

One member of the St Margaret's staff was the wife of a particularly fanatical Leeds supporter and knew United's Paul Madeley quite well. 'What's Adamson like?' she asked, as if she somehow thought I knew him personally. She and her husband had noted that he hadn't done too well at Sunderland

and were two of the many Leeds supporters who viewed his appointment with some scepticism. News seems to travel fast in the football supporters' world from one club to the next and the suspicions of Adamson's fondness for a drink or two were soon communicated.

* * *

Leeds United were still recovering from Don Revie's departure. Clough had been a disaster; Jimmy Armfield had calmed the place down but fell victim to directors' impatience; Jock Stein had lasted just a few weeks, the same as Brian Clough, and next up was Jimmy Adamson who had clearly been approached and agreed to the move while he was in situ at Sunderland so sudden was the move. His wife May had remained in Burnley whilst he was at Sunderland but agreed to move to Leeds and an area, Roundhay, that was one of best parts of the city.

Revie had left a legacy of a fine collection of superb players. Unfortunately several were beginning to approach the age where a manager planning for the future begins to replace them but Revie hadn't even started to do this. So Clough arrived to what really was a rebuilding job, despite the fact that Leeds were champions and in the European Cup.

The teacher I knew at St Margaret's, Rilla Blagg, used to tell me of the tales she had heard via Madeley, that Clough's name on his door was pulled off, notices he put up would disappear and yes they were aghast at the things he had said to them regarding their medals and how they had won them. Yet prior to his accusations, according to the books they have written, or interviews since, most if not all were fascinated by him and were willing to give him a chance. Eddie Gray said as much when we met. Clough really did shoot himself in the foot.

Armfield arrived and did a magnificent job that season even if he was regarded eventually as someone 'whose indecision was final'. He was thoughtful and careful to the opposite extreme of Clough. As a player he was known as 'Gentleman Jim' which is pretty much how he was as a manager so he smoothed the ruffled feathers, got the place back in some semblance of order and although unable to rescue the league season, he guided these veterans to the Paris final of the European Cup. This ironically was something that had eluded Revie. So, it was still 'Glory Days' at Elland Road but the luck (and a competent referee) deserted them in the final and they lost to Bayern Munich against a background of rioting fans.

Leeds fans, and rightly so, still talk of the decisions that robbed them of victory so that the result provided one of those turning points in a club's story when the effects determine what happens next, not for just a couple of games, but for several years. The rioting saw them banned for an initial four years, although this was reduced to two and Armfield began the job of breaking up the great side. Out went Cooper, Giles, Hunter, Bremner and Yorath. In came Tony Currie and from Burnley came Ray Hankin and Brian Flynn, products of the Adamson coaching manual. In the midst of his re-building job Armfield took Leeds to the semi-final of the FA Cup in 1977, and the League Cup Final the following year. This was no mean achievement but not good enough for supporters and directors, so out went Armfield.

I can still remember the amazement in the city when Leeds appointed the legendary Jock Stein next. It was seen as a magnificent capture to tempt him away from Glasgow. He was a giant figure in the world of football with an enormous reputation. If anyone could galvanise the place, then surely he could. Here was a man that players could truly look up to, and with him Celtic had been the first British club to win the European Cup. He jumped at the chance to join Leeds, now unhappy in his new role as general manager at Celtic.

Alas, it was as if the football gods were now toying with Leeds United as some sort of punishment for their years of kicking and intimidating other teams and winning trophies with what most thought were less than scrupulous methods on the field. Stein lasted just 45 days. He had not signed the contract, his wife did not like Leeds or want to leave Glasgow, so he accepted the chance to replace Ally MacLeod and manage Scotland. Had he done the same good job with Leeds as he did with Scotland then Leeds might well have been back up there at the top of the tree. The suspicion was, however, that Stein had always known it was likely he would be offered the Scotland job and his acceptance of the Leeds job was simply an insurance against the unlikely possibility that he would not be approached by the Scottish selectors. Leeds fans were not pleased.

It was against this unstable background and as the next part of the post-Revie story that Adamson arrived with Leeds in mid-table, a sense of deflation that Stein had left, a club still in the process of a rebuilding job, and with fans still harking back to the Revie days. On top of all that the place was run by a group of directors not quite in tune with each other. While Stein had been a stellar appointment and his mere name lifted the place, Adamson simply brought a sense of anti-climax, that here was a manager who had achieved nothing in football over the last two and a half years, and Sunderland fans seemed happy with his departure. All in all, save for a small number of fans who were vociferously angry, most were not vehemently opposed to this appointment, but they did find it disappointing and uninspiring.

Of Revie's men there still remained Peter Lorimer, the two Grays, Frankie and Eddie, Paul Madeley, David Harvey and Trevor Cherry. Armfield had added the gifted playmaker Tony Currie, Arthur Graham, John Hawley, Paul Hart, Ray Hankin and Brian Flynn. Add to these some decent fringe players, and Leeds had a good squad of players even taking into account that Madeley, Eddie Gray and Lorimer were almost in the 'veteran' category.

If Adamson had been plagued by the memories of Brian Clough at Roker Park, then here at Elland Road he was plagued by the memories of Don Revie. Revie was an icon, a legend, hero and cult figure all rolled into one. Leeds United, being in a rugby city, had never possessed a football history until Revie had made it into one of Europe's top clubs. It was his creation and it was now disintegrating, although no one knew this at the time because of the blinkered belief that the good times would be resurrected as a matter of course and there were still good players there. But it was an illusion and Adamson would be only one of a procession of managers who oversaw decline.

Adamson was bold in his initial pronouncements in an article in which he announced his admiration for Revie. Perhaps in this he was being diplomatic. Clough had made it quite clear that he disliked Revie and his methods, and look what had happened to him. Prior to joining Leeds there was no evidence at all to suggest that Adamson was a Revie admirer, in fact quite the opposite. Adamson along with Bob Lord had always blamed Revie for unsettling winger Dave Thomas at Burnley and there had been some vitriolic exchanges in the press with Lord suggesting that it was time Revie 'kept his trap shut'. Now here was Adamson praising him:

> 'There have been a few managers at Leeds United since then [Don Revie] so I don't see I'll be compared to him. I rate Don Revie as one of the most successful managers we've had in the British game. So much of what you achieve as a manager can depend on what you inherit when you take over a club. When you come here, as I have, and inherit players like Tony Currie, it's a bonus. But Don inherited badly when he arrived at Leeds United and the club were struggling at the foot of the Second Division. But in no time at all, he had them in the First and winning things.
>
> 'Don was the sort of man who, if he badly needed a result away from home, he'd put up the shutters and feel no qualms about it. In the same situation Ron Greenwood would be more likely to say, "If we're going to be defeated let's lose playing entertaining football." These days though, people don't always want entertaining football. They want to win. And a lot of them would rather see their side play badly and win 1-0 than play well and get beaten.
>
> 'It's sad but the game is more of a business now. As a professional, I have to go along with that. I want to see Leeds win first, and entertain second. I have a philosophy of my own. Attack if you can; defend if you must. In other words, you do the positive, attacking things first. But you can't neglect your defensive duties.'

He went on to say that three years was long enough for any manager to prove he was capable of building a winning side. That was the length of his contract at Leeds. If at the end of it he had a successful side, he might get another contract. If not, he might expect to be shown the door.

He would be shown the door in just two years.

How much of what he said in the article was genuine belief, or honeyed words simply designed to bring the Leeds fans onside is debateable. In his golden three-year spell at Burnley defending was always the second option, shutting up shop was an anathema; Colin Waldron was often in despair at the cavalier approach. And Revie's name was mud.

As he attempted the job of rebuilding the ailing Leeds club, over the Pennines at Burnley the situation there at Turf Moor was even worse. Adamson still had close ties to the Burnley area. He still had a house there. His wife, May, was a local girl born and bred; his two daughters and their families lived there. He had friends in the town and some of 'his' players were still in the Burnley team. But by now Burnley Football Club were penniless and struggling in the Second Division; by the end of it they would be relegated to the Third Division.

There is no question that Adamson was still hugely emotionally attached to the club. Peter Higgs suspects that he never wanted to work anywhere other than Burnley. He had never recovered from the sacking and the bitterness towards Lord was deeply embedded. Lord had just blamed the players for an embarrassing 7-0 defeat at Queens Park Rangers that was shown on *Match of the Day*. Adamson, only just appointed at Leeds blasted Bob Lord, clearly bridling at Bob Lord's criticism of the players, 'In my opinion there is only one man to blame for the position Burnley is in. Anyone with any interest in the club will realise to whom I refer. I said that Burnley would be the "Team of the Seventies" and to this day I believe they would have been if someone else had not sold the best players. The list of those who went was endless and the sales ruined the team we had built.'

Adamson's opinions when they appeared in several newspapers resulted in an unseemly public slanging match in the press with Lord taking umbrage at the now Leeds United manager, 'What Jimmy Adamson says is simply untrue. The principle at Turf Moor has always been that the manager says who goes and who stays. I have never insisted on somebody being transferred.'

On reading that, Adamson's eyes must have bulged with astonishment and he must have thought back to the time, one Friday night in London, when with tears in his eyes he had told a small group of players that Lord had informed him he had to sell Martin Dobson.

The debacle at Queens Park Rangers and Adamson's comments acted as the catalyst for renewed attempts by the Supporters' Group to oust Bob Lord with pickets and petitions and angry letters in the local newspaper. It seems reasonable to assume that Adamson must have felt some satisfaction at seeing

Lord in such an uncomfortable position although Lord himself continued to bluster his way through the crisis.

'I believe that this time the whole town is against him and when he goes it will be like VE Day all over again in Burnley,' said Adamson.

Lord, insisting he was not a dictator, continued to ignore the existence of the Supporters' Group and as he hung on to the chairmanship, rebuffed them, 'Providing I don't drop down dead, I'll never give in.' It would be another two years before illness struck him down and he passed away.

A report that was then commissioned by new chairman John Jackson and completed by director Derek Gill described the administration as 'an untidy shambles' and a situation of 'general inefficiency' after 'years of malfunction'. What had been long suspected was confirmed; that Lord was using the club to subsidise his own lifestyle. Over his final year it was reckoned that he had claimed something approaching £6,000 from the club under the heading of travel and hotel expenses but without adequate invoices and receipts to support the claims. It is pure conjecture but maybe explains why he was determined to hang on to the chairmanship come what may.

At Leeds as at Sunderland, Adamson began to bring in his own men; the familiar faces of Dave Merrington, Stan Ternent, Syd Farrimond and the inevitable Dave Blakey arrived, along with a couple of young Burnley fringe players, Tony Arins and Marshall Burke. Brian Flynn and Ray Hankin were already there. The same joke that had amused Sunderland supporters rose to the surface; he would fill the place with Burnley people and have them playing in claret and blue before long.

Merrington was a fiery character, a one-time member of the fabled Burnley half-back line of Merrington, Waldron and a wild player by the name of Colin Blant whose style was somewhat gladiatorial to say the least. The three of them together put the fear of God into most opponents with Peter Osgood before one game at Turf Moor, allegedly deciding he couldn't face coming out to play against them and 'injuring' himself in the warm-up.

Dave Merrington spared no one, not even his own team-mates, and on one occasion he even set upon Colin Waldron. This was when Waldron was at Sunderland and Merrington was coach. When Merrington went mad at the back four in the dressing room after a game, Waldron interrupted him. When he interrupted him a second time Waldron recalled that Merrington hit him. John Wray, in his time as reporter for the *Bradford Telegraph and Argus,* was certainly one who felt Merrington's ire and wrote of when he was pinned against the wall one day for something he had allegedly said or written.

Lorimer tells the story of himself, Adamson and Dave Merrington in his superb little book *Leeds and Scotland Hero,* describing that when Adamson came into Elland Road from Sunderland Lorimer knew he was in trouble. During Adamson's time at Sunderland central defender Jackie Ashurst kicked Lorimer, so he went over the top on him in retaliation. There was no break but Ashurst was carried off. Sunderland were in trouble at the time and Adamson's assistant, Dave 'Mad' Merrington, whom Lorimer used to taunt during his playing days at Burnley, made his feelings known towards him.

With Merrington assisting Adamson at Leeds, he went round the players and Merrington told Lorimer that he didn't bear any malice. It confirmed to Lorimer that he had remembered the tackle and Lorimer thought it ironic that he never played in an Adamson team. He felt that Adamson wanted him out. This may well have been correct as Adamson and Merrington had identified a number of players they felt should be moved on. To Lorimer it was quite obvious with Adamson that the club were going nowhere and were struggling. In fairness to Adamson, Lorimer's description of Leeds as 'struggling like hell' was certainly inaccurate in Adamson's first season when he took them to fifth spot and a place in Europe. This was the best season they had enjoyed since Revie's time.

By contrast to Lorimer, Eddie Gray, who attended Adamson's funeral, found him to be 'a thoroughly pleasant, decent person' and his appointment 'seemed sound enough'. He thought his initial impact was impressive. From looking no more than an average middle-of-the-table team for the third season running, a 16-match unbeaten run pushed Leeds to fifth in the table which gave them a UEFA Cup place and saw them reach the League Cup semi-final.

However, he found Adamson was laid-back in his approach to the job and felt that this was one of the reasons why it all went wrong for him. He took too much of a back seat during the week, leaving a lot of the responsibility to Dave Merrington and this led to confusion. The way Merrington got Leeds to play did not always tie in with Adamson's instructions. Gray was puzzled by this; it seemed strange to him that this should have happened because they knew each other so well. Gray initially believed Adamson was a tracksuit manager, but at Leeds found him on the periphery of the training work. Bearing in mind his coaching reputation, Adamson's coaching role was less than he expected.

In his tactful, diplomatic way, Gray had hit the nail on the head. The bottom line was, in blunt terms, the longer he was there, the situation was confusing with one guy saying one thing in the week and the other guy something else on a Saturday and if there is one thing any professional footballer wants it is clarity. Today Gray describes Merrington as 'being in charge but not in charge'. Were he and Jimmy 'banging from the same drum?' On occasions no one knew where Adamson was and being dubbed 'Howard Hughes' possibly spoke volumes for the lack of respect from some of the players. This was maybe not the same Jimmy Adamson who had lived on the training field at Burnley with his finger on every button. At Leeds did he leave too much to Dave Merrington, Gray asks today.

Gray remembered Dave Merrington had been a fiery player. He was a strong-minded character who seemed to see things in black and white so that Gray felt he wanted you to do things his way or not at all. He couldn't accept the manner in which it seemed he tried to impose his beliefs on people. These included his belief as a born-again Christian. One day Merrington called a meeting of the players. Two huge leading American football players gave them what seemed to be a lecture on how the Bible and Jesus helped achieve success. There might well have been a lot more to it than that but Gray did not stay to find out. He told Merrington that this line of approach to his job as a professional footballer was not for him and left.

When I met Gray at Elland Road he commented that, in any case, should it not have been Jimmy Adamson calling player meetings?

The picture is one of eventual disharmony and a lack of common purpose. Gray is guarded and diplomatic in the picture he paints; Peter Lorimer is blunt, and his account of the rift between him and Adamson paints a picture of breakdown of all respect between the two of them. If such a thing then eventually communicates to other players the standing of the manager might be undermined. Add to that the growing supporter dissatisfaction with player sales and their replacements; then there was only one eventual conclusion. After that first reasonably successful season, Adamson was on borrowed time.

Then came the Saturday when Adamson didn't turn up to announce the team. All the players were in the lounge awaiting news of the team selection. The manager's car was in the car park, but he never came into the lounge and at 2.15pm there was still no indication of the line-up. One of the players asked Maurice Lindley what the team was going to be.

Lindley explained that there was no sign of the boss. The requirement was for the team sheet to be in by 2.30pm, and just in time Lindley and Merrington came rushing in with a line-up that they had quickly thrown together. Those selected went off to change and when the lounge had emptied Lindley was asked exactly what was going on.

He then explained that it was in the best interests of the club that he and Merrington picked the team. They were worried about the manager's health in view of the state he was in. It is reasonable to suppose that Adamson had had a few drinks too many and was incapable of selecting the team.

Although several players called him 'Howard Hughes' on account of his disappearances, one day he appeared on the training ground. He shouted Lorimer off, saying there was somebody on the telephone from a club that wished to sign him. He took the call in Adamson's office. He had become so rude to him by this time that he asked would there be a £40,000 fee involved and asked Adamson to leave his own office as he had no intention of discussing his future while Adamson was present. Lorimer says Adamson fumed but was so desperate to get rid of him that he turned and left.

Lorimer then writes a curious thing; that he was prepared to go back to Leeds for another campaign and that he knew Adamson would be on his way in the close season. Was this just an educated guess on his part or did he know something? As it turned out Adamson was hounded out although it was not in the summer; it was several games into the new season.

One person who was delighted, however, to see Jimmy Adamson at Leeds was Brian Flynn. Today Flynn regards him as the most influential person in football he ever met. Flynn's father had actually done some scouting work for Adamson in Wales.

Flynn said, 'He was the man who set all the standards I aimed at. I never had any grumbles about him. He wasn't quite the same Adamson that I knew at Burnley though. His knees were bad and he was really struggling on his legs so that he didn't spend the same time actively coaching as he did at Burnley. But he'd be on the sidelines watching at the training ground although that did tail off towards the end and he was absent more and more as he possibly thought his time was up.

'But until then I'm pretty sure he was involved in all the coaching decisions and had meetings with the coaching staff regularly. Losing Tony Currie was a huge blow and was not Adamson's fault. We missed Tony in the dressing room as much as on the field. He was a big loss.

'He still influences me as a coach and a manager. I never had any grumbles with his man-management either. He was a great believer in waiting until the Monday before he ever said anything to a player. When he gave praise he meant it and he always spoke to you on a one-to-one basis if there was any aspect of play he wanted to improve.'

Flynn illustrates perfectly the way that Adamson divided opinion. There were those who disliked him intensely, and those who appreciated him and how he improved personal performances, with Flynn clearly belonging to the latter.

How ironic it was that Adamson and Flynn were reunited at Leeds after the aborted attempt to take him and Peter Noble to Sunderland. Adamson had indeed approached them both to sound them out before making a bid. They met face to face in Whalley, not far from Burnley, and Flynn would certainly have agreed to join him. Now, circumstances had brought them together again. The irony was perhaps not lost on Harry Potts and Bob Lord who had been so incensed at the attempts to 'tap up' the two players.

Paul Harrison, an author of three Leeds United books who followed and reported on Leeds for many years, met Adamson several times and was hugely sympathetic towards him, graphically outlining the problems he faced and the situation he inherited. This was indeed a club that was still haunted by Revie, with one group of directors even at this stage still wanting Johnny Giles to take over and a smaller group Billy Bremner. This was a club that appeared unhealthy, beset by undercurrents and factions at all levels and with Adamson the stopgap appointment, desperately wanting to do his best but bowed down beneath a crippling yoke of pressure that was almost impossible to cope with.

Yet all of them were united in one area; they wanted instant success and a return to the glory days. But there was no instant fix and despite Adamson's first near-success, the fifth place the best since Revie and not bettered until Howard Wilkinson arrived, it was not enough. He had them playing decent football again, says Harrison (so did Currie), but the exit from Europe in his second season was a disaster and from that point on he was as good as bullied out of the club.

Harrison described a situation that seemed to him never gave Adamson any chance of re-structuring the club in the way he might have wanted, because he was pulled in all directions by different directors working, it seemed, against each other. It was clear, thinks Harrison, having often spoken to him, that Adamson knew what was needed and what needed to be done. But what he didn't have was time and unanimous support from the board, even though it was they who had appointed him. Nor did he know exactly who he could trust. With all this as the background, what chance was there of having the time to establish a youth policy and get a production line rolling? In a word – none.

Harrison saw both sides of Jimmy Adamson; there was the one who did enjoy a drink and after a few drinks would be none too careful what he said. Sometimes they met and Harrison knew he had already had a few. The landlady at The Peacock opposite the ground knew exactly what drink to pour the minute he walked in. One time they met there to talk, Harrison had barely begun his drink before Jimmy had downed his second pint and a whisky. The other Adamson was the measured, sociable person at Fullerton where they sometimes met on Tuesdays and Adamson would go through team matters, selections, his worries for the coming game and who would not be playing. His football brain was fully evident; his knowledge of the game was unmistakable.

But one scene he witnessed in the car park before a game was thoroughly unpleasant. It was during the second season when things were going wrong and the abuse aimed at him was frequent. As Adamson walked from his car, he was approached by a fan and was subjected to a barrage of vehement criticism. Instead of walking on and ignoring it, or just acknowledging with a simple answer and a smile, Adamson let himself become involved in an unseemly slanging match; again, thinks Harrison, having already had a few drinks. Eventually someone from the club hauled Adamson away and into the club with by now, a large crowd gathering round this unpleasant scene.

If Adamson was under this constant pressure, unsure who were his allies and who was not, senior old-guard players who maybe were not in tune with him, and supporters subjecting him by the end to endless cries of 'ADAMSON OUT, ADAMSON OUT', is it any wonder that Harrison says he could see the man visibly wilting? Just how does anyone deal with this on a daily basis?

The result, by the very end, was a man who was slowly having his own confidence undermined and had lost much of his assertiveness; a man who was nowhere near the same Jimmy Adamson of just a few years earlier whose word was law. Was this a man who now played the players he felt he could trust rather than the best players? But if this seemed a place filled with subterfuge, unrest and disharmony, then nevertheless the terraces were still filled with the 'we are Leeds' siege mentality. But this was no longer a club 'marching on together', this was a place that behind the scenes was thoroughly unhappy and the marching was now out of step.

It fell apart on the field in his second season, says Eddie Gray. 'His bid to build on what he had achieved in the 1978/79 season provoked a number of fans to claim that he had lost the plot. One reason for this view was that two of the players sold by him, Tony Currie to QPR in the 1979 close season, and John Hawley to Sunderland in September that year, were great favourites with the crowd. The antagonism towards Jimmy because of this was a bit harsh, considering that Currie had asked for a transfer on the grounds that his wife had become unsettled in the north.'

Hawley, who went to Sunderland for a reported £200,000, was far from pleased to be sold and later said, 'Jimmy Adamson and Dave Merrington didn't like me at Leeds so the deal was done involving a Sunderland player whose name escapes me but sounded as if it was a Welsh veterinary disease.'

Currie had been bought by Jimmy Armfield and was already an icon for what was allegedly the first football kiss. In a match shown on *Match of the Day* he and Alan Birchenall collided and fell to the floor. They decided quite literally to kiss and make up. The image went round the world, was printed on t-shirts and he and Birchenall both became gay icons in Germany.

Blessed with pop-star good looks, a huge skills repertoire and the ability to make sweeping passes, Currie was supposedly on Tommy Docherty's radar to replace Bobby Charlton at Manchester United. He had been at Sheffield United for eight years before his move to Elland Road. He was hero-worshipped at both Sheffield United and Leeds and it was simply Adamson's bad luck that his wife after 11 years in the north wanted a return south. Currie himself revealed that this was the only reason, as well as suggesting that while he was there at Leeds, from the ages of 26 to 29, he played his best ever football.

In 1995 in the *Leeds United Monthly*, he was quoted as saying, 'I would have stayed at Elland Road. We were playing some good stuff and I had a great relationship with the crowd. I only left for family reasons.'

It was firm evidence that Adamson was desperately unlucky to lose the player, yet with a section of the supporters he became the scapegoat.

Eddie Gray's opinions as to how and why it went wrong were straightforward enough, 'What harmed Jimmy Adamson's cause [even more than Currie's sale], was that none of his major signings made a big impact. Kevin Hird (Blackburn), Gary Hamson (Sheffield United), Jeff Chandler (Blackpool) and Wayne Entwistle (Sunderland) were always going to struggle to convince the fans that they had the ability to take the club forward. Of the others, Derek Parlane (Rangers) was past his best; Alan Curtis (Swansea) and Brian Greenhoff (Manchester United) were hampered by injuries; and Alex Sabella (Sheffield United), the last arrival, the costliest of the group at £400,000 and the one who excited me the most, suffered by not having enough players on his wavelength.'

Sabella was a midfielder Gray rated very highly. He worked hard in training and his dribbling and passing skills were typical of a top player from Argentina. But, while he brought great individual flair to Leeds, the team was not good enough to give him the right support. With Leeds going steadily downhill Sabella was unlucky to be in the wrong place at the wrong time.

Another who was sold was full-back Frank Gray to Nottingham Forest. According to one of Brian Clough's autobiographies, Gray was shocked and upset to be sold but Jonathan Wilson tells a different story in his Brian Clough biography *Nobody Ever Says Thank You*. Maurice Edwards, who was scouting for Nottingham Forest in an unofficial capacity, was spending an afternoon watching the planes taking off and landing at East Midlands Airport. Who should he bump into but Frank Gray who was heading to Tenerife? Edwards asked him if he would be interested in joining Forest and when Gray said he was, Edwards got in touch with Peter Taylor. When Gray returned, a £400,000 deal was sorted.

A rampant Forest came to Elland Road on 5 January 1980, in the third round of the FA Cup. Forest won 4-1. One of the goals came from Frank Gray to make life even more uncomfortable for Adamson. But if the Wilson version of the transfer is correct, it was hardly Adamson's fault that Gray left.

Talk to any Leeds supporter today who was there during the Adamson years and they will all say the same, that both Tony Currie and Frank Gray were huge losses. But those losses alone were not the reason for Leeds' consequent struggles. The problems were the replacement signings that Adamson made. The classic was maybe Wayne Entwistle who said of himself years later, 'I wasn't good enough. I played in some games and hardly ever got a touch.'

It wasn't just Entwistle however. Too many were simply not good enough and for this, supporters could not forgive Adamson.

Chapter 17

Goodbye football

E VERY CLUB has at least one supporter who is there at
every game come what may, rain or shine, distance no
object, and in some cases their unfailing attendance record
goes back 30 years and more. These are the guys who travel
thousands of miles and their support is unconditional. At Leeds
there is Gary Edwards. I had seen Gary's name on Leeds blogs
and had actually bought one of his books some years ago. From
the blogs, I knew that Gary was one of the original and founder
members of the 'ADAMSON OUT' brigade. Getting in touch was
done via Leeds website message boards. Gary answered the next
day. He immediately agreed to go through his collections of old
Leeds material and see what he had that I could look at. It was
one of his e-mails that I thought really touching:

> 'Like I said Dave, I was part of the demonstrations and a
> number of pictures of me appeared in the national press
> with my "ADAMSON OUT" banners. I was 26 or so when
> this happened. I'm now 56 and I don't look back with a
> great deal of pride over what took place. It was just a sign
> of the times I'm afraid. It is only in recent years when
> I have been writing my own books that I have begun to
> realise how much dignity Jimmy had in the face of this
> torment and abuse. Even in pre-season games in France
> and Switzerland Adamson was followed by the "Adamson
> out" chants. There was no hiding place.'

And back in 2009 Gary had written about Adamson:

'In the late 70s Leeds were managed by a certain Jimmy Adamson. To begin with, there was slight unrest amongst the Leeds fans but this was to escalate at a very fast pace. I was part of this rebellion.

'Jimmy Armfield was the manager in the mid-70s. He took Leeds to the 1975 European Cup Final. It must be said that the board of directors has never been particularly impressive at Leeds United and this era was no exception. Don Howe was "Gentleman Jim's" assistant and they made a great team. Armfield was the tactics man and Howe kept the players in check. However, when Howe left to take the manager's job at Arsenal, things began to worsen, as certain players were less attentive to Armfield as they were to Howe. This was definitely apparent to supporters although admittedly we didn't have the full details to hand. Unfortunately for Jim, the board became impatient and sacked Armfield.

'On the face of it, Jock Stein looked a good appointment but it was common knowledge that Stein was only interested in the Scotland job. Enter the Geordie, Mr Adamson.

'The Leeds fans were furious with the board and vented their anger. After the home game against Coventry in March 1980 had ended in a goalless draw, hundreds of fans gathered outside the back of the West Stand and mounted police had to break up a demonstration that had reached fever pitch.

'This was the norm for weeks to come. The "Adamson out" brigade was out in force at every game and I was present at every demonstration outside the ground at both home and away matches.

'At the time the Yorkshire Ripper was on the loose. Everyone thought the Ripper was a Geordie because of the famous hoax tape, and the police would come in to the pubs in the city playing this tape of the man reputed to be the Ripper to see if anyone recognised the voice. At every pub the police would be met with the shouts of, "That's Jimmy Adamson, lock 'im up please."

'The start of the following season, 1980/81, wasn't any better either. The first game was at Elland Road against Aston Villa. A few of us had decided to take the protest inside the ground and we made a large banner saying simply, "Adamson Out". At the start of the game, a mate, Butter and me got onto the barrier and unfurled our banner. Understandably it received a mixed reaction and when Leeds went ahead through a Byron Stevenson penalty, some abuse was hurled our way. We stood firm and got back on the barrier and showed the flag once more. This time a number of coins and other objects were thrown in our direction.

'I hated going "against" the club but we firmly believed that what we were doing was the right thing and we weren't going to take it lying down. So Butter and me jumped from the barrier and went off in the direction of where the coins seemed to be coming from to vent our anger. Others from the group followed. Minor scuffles broke out here and there, but just then, Villa equalised. The mood changed slightly and then almost immediately Villa went in front. We jumped back on our barrier and once again the flag was raised aloft. After a very short time, thankfully, the rest of the Kop seemed to be behind us and loud chants of "Adamson out" rang out; this was then echoed in the South Stand, and then all round the ground.

'Eventually, in September 1980, Adamson bowed to public pressure and resigned leaving full-time football behind him for good. Unfortunately, in my opinion, irreparable damage had already been done, and worse was to happen a couple of years down the line.'

'Fell on his sword,' said Peter Lorimer.

The margins of success and failure are so close. In season 1978/79 Leeds had a 2-0 lead in the semi-final of the League Cup at Elland Road against Southampton but the game ended 2-2. It was Jimmy's first season in charge. 'If only', the two words again that we say so much in football. The away leg was lost 1-0. When the home game was played on 24 January, Leeds had played 25 league games and were fifth in the table five points away from top place. Over 36,000 had watched the previous home game against Manchester City. John Hawley was leading goalscorer with 11 goals followed by Eddie Gray with nine. Just two weeks earlier they had beaten Hartlepool 6-2 in the FA Cup third round. Since losing to Arsenal 1-0 on 11 November, Leeds had enjoyed an unbeaten run of 13 games, one of which had been a 4-0 win over Southampton. Jimmy Adamson could be forgiven for feeling that things were on the up.

In his first programme notes at the beginning of the 1978/79 season much of what he wrote was the usual spin that most managers write at this time of the season – about the optimism that exists and the belief that they could be challenging for honours at the end of the season. He asked for encouragement from the supporters and that they would enjoy the football of the next eight months. He also emphasised that the sale of Tony Currie had been beyond his control and that Currie had made it clear he needed to return to London for domestic reasons. Then he pointed to the three things that all sides need but over which a manager has no control:

> 'I have always considered that while you can prepare your players to peak fitness and get the right kind of balance there are still three factors over which you have absolutely no control – injuries, a lack of confidence in the side, and the part that lady luck plays. If we can stay clear of injuries, maintain that touch of confidence that is so important, and luck is with us; then I believe we can be challenging for the major honours.'

It is reasonable to think he must have been genuinely optimistic. However, the comment about having no control over 'confidence' was a strange one. It is true enough in football that confidence is a key factor in any player's performance. But other managers would argue it is their job to instil that confidence, to make a team feel that they are unbeatable, to make a player feel 'ten feet tall'. The players' confidence, or lack of it, was something that Allan Clarke would refer to when he took over from Adamson.

The opening game was against Everton. Adamson's former players, Dave Thomas and Geoff Nulty, were Everton players though not on the team sheet. One of his favourite players, Martin Dobson, whom he had once said was like a son to him, had just moved back from Everton to Burnley. Leeds won 2-0 but it was the only win in the first ten games of the season. One of them was a horrendous 7-0 defeat in the League Cup at Arsenal. At the very end of the season there was a 2-0 win over hated rivals Manchester United at Elland Road in front of just under 40,000 people but it was of little consolation for a lacklustre season.

It was a season of several attendances of below 20,000 with a serious loss of revenue; Adamson had once remarked that when income suffered he knew he would be shown the door. Against Aston Villa, there had been just 15,840 and against Stoke City only 15,541. This was a club in serious decline and even if the directors were split into factions they were united in their alarm at these declining attendances. The average for the season was just 22,788 in a ground where attendances had once rarely strayed below 30,000, and for many games were almost 40,000. Fans were now voting with their feet; those that stayed were angered and frustrated by the continual mediocrity. The only bright spot was the introduction of young lads from the youth system – Carl Harris, Terry Connor and John Lukic.

It was the defeat against the Romanian side University Craiova that as good as sealed Adamson's fate with supporters. There had been previous demonstrations but now they began in earnest and make no mistake, some of them were vicious. Leeds fans will themselves recognise they were among the most hostile and intimidating in football; it's been said that no manager, before or since Adamson, has ever provoked such depth of feeling at Leeds. If that is true then it is harsh; he was one of a line of managers unable to stop the downward trend.

The demonstrations were also aimed at the directors but in time-honoured tradition, as at every football club, even though it is the chairman (in this case Manny Cussins) and the directors who appoint the manager, when things go wrong it is the manager who suffers the worst and most sustained abuse. Such is football. As Edwards suggests, the Leeds board did not escape scot-free, but nevertheless it was Adamson who became the easier, sitting duck target in the dugout at a club where the troubles went far deeper than just him. Nor was he the target only at the end of his time there; it had started early and went on and on, preceding his departure for months in a fashion that was sustained relentlessly every Saturday, be it home or away.

When the Romanian side came to Elland Road on 7 November 1979, they had already established a 2-0 lead. This was a virtually unknown side so Leeds, having already disposed of Maltese club Valletta, were expected to make further progress. Sadly, two goals down, Leeds – in spite of valiant efforts – never looked like pulling those goals back. The basic tactic was one of left wing crosses aimed at the big men in the middle but Craiova and a ten-man defence stood firm and waited for the breakaway opportunities. They had some fine players including the best of the national team.

Before the game began the ground announcer asked for silence while a police message was read over the tannoy. Even the notorious Gelderd Road End fell silent. Then came a plea that if anyone recognised the voice they were about to hear, they should contact the police. It began with the sound of a familiar voice: 'I'm Jack; I see you're still having no luck catching me. I have the greatest respect for you George, but oh Lord, you are no nearer catching me.'

Mercifully the Gelderd Road End did not respond with 'It's Jimmy bloody Adamson'. Instead, shamefully, they sang 'One Yorkshire Ripper, there's only one Yorkshire Ripper'.

Who knows what would have happened if Paul Hart had taken a good heading opportunity in the first minute instead of putting it wide, and then three minutes later the goalkeeper saved at point-blank range from Arthur Graham?

What made the whole thing worse, in true football fashion, was that the first Craiova goal was the result of a horrible deflection. Football is cruel; a 25-yard shot hit Byron Stevenson and turned the flight of the ball from one corner of the net to the other where it gently arced in. Shots from Graham and Eddie Gray went close but then came the clincher, scored by the man who had missed a penalty in Romania.

The first half had been goalless but the crowd was stunned when Craiova took the lead. It was no surprise when they scored again with just minutes to go leaving supporters utterly dejected and at the same time furious. Adamson, having done the hard work in the previous season and got the club into Europe, was now seen as the reason for the ignominious exit. The second goal from the Romanians rubbed salt into the wounds; a blistering 30-yard pile-driver that went past Lukic before he could blink.

Prior to that, Leeds had piled on the pressure but to no avail, resulting in chants for the resignation of Adamson and the return of Don Revie. After the game there were the inevitable demonstrations outside the main offices that were broken up by the mounted police.

This was the third consecutive home defeat and the third time there had been a demonstration – and it was still only November. The worst, during and after the Coventry game in March the following year, was still to come.

John Wray was the Leeds United football correspondent of the *Bradford Telegraph and Argus*. He had constant daily access to all that went on. In the Revie days he had travelled on the team bus in an era when it was common for players to telephone the reporters. Trevor Cherry once rang him at 11pm when he was in bed asleep catching up on a 12-hour day. Football reporting is a far from glamorous occupation.

Like many others, Wray found Adamson a hard man to fathom, charming and co-operative one day, aloof and uncommunicative the next. 'There were some days it was as if he didn't know me, but other times when he always made himself available and looked after the local reporters,' he said.

He remembers too that director Bob Roberts was a regular 'leak' and source of unofficial information. At Burnley he encountered Bob Lord on a number of occasions and recalled how the press box area at the back of the stand was always covered in bird droppings from the innumerable pigeons that congregated there. 'He didn't much like us press guys and I'm sure Bob Lord arranged the pigeons deliberately,' laughed John.

Discovering that John lived only a couple of miles from me in Leeds was a real bonus. When I went to see him, now the head of Gosnays Sports Agency, at his home he had organised all his press cuttings for me to look at, season by season. Some of them stood out from the rest: an early one in which Adamson stated that he was at Leeds to change the opinions that they were no longer a top club; another where striker Ray Hankin headlined that 'Adamson is the best' when Adamson took over.

Adamson couldn't have raised his popularity level when for one game he dropped the fans' idol, Tony Currie. 'I only want players who are willing to sweat blood to win a match,' Adamson explained. For him Currie didn't fit that bill in every game.

Halfway through the first pile of cuttings, November 1979, it was clear that the rot had already started for Adamson. There had been a particularly drab, goalless draw at Brighton and several hundred fans were chanting 'Adamson out'. His transfer dealings were being questioned and he himself acknowledged that they were unpopular. He fell back on the mantra he had used at Burnley, that he had a thick skin after so many years in the game.

'United must buy,' wrote John Wray, adding that Manny Cussins and the directors were in no mood to tolerate more performances that were driving supporters away. The anti-Adamson feelings were now growing to epidemic proportions and Leeds 1 Bristol City 3 was described as a shambles of a performance. 'Blame me not the board,' said Adamson, beginning to adopt the role of martyr and scapegoat.

There was already conjecture in November 1979 that he would be replaced after being 'hauled before the board ... but who would replace him?' wrote Wray. There were even rumours that Revie might return. Everton 5 Leeds 1 was a 'night of shame'. At this point he refused the offer from a hypnotist, Edwin Heath, to help the team. 'If anyone hypnotises the team – it will be me,' he responded. There were reports of an attempt to sign Kevin Keegan.

'The rumours were true,' e-mailed Dave Merrington. 'Dave Blakey our chief scout was in negotiations with his agent and Jimmy was also in discussions with Peter Withe who was at Newcastle at the time. The intention was to pair them together as a strike force which on paper looked lethal. Jimmy put the pairing to the board and told them this could change the direction of the club.

'But he hit a brick wall as the board would not sanction the transfer money and the players' contract costs. Keegan went to Southampton and was a great signing and Withe went to Aston Villa and he too proved a great signing. We thought they would have had a great impact and would have whetted supporters' appetites, had the directors sanctioned it.'

Keegan at that time was Europe's leading footballer. He was only 28, ready to move, and Leeds could have signed him for £500,000, a release figure that was in his Hamburg contract. In terms of fame and celebrity he was the Beckham of his day (but a far more influential player), a match-winner who drew the crowd wherever he went, twice the European Footballer of the Year, inspirational and charismatic. He went on to play some of his best-ever football at Southampton where increased attendances and related income as good as paid his costs. The impact of his move was simply stunning.

The same directors at Leeds who later sanctioned Allan Clarke's purchase of Peter Barnes for £900,000 could have signed Keegan for not much more than half that. Not only would Keegan have galvanised team and club, his signing would have also injected new vitality and energy into Adamson himself. Frustrated and disillusioned, he confided to Merrington that the directors lacked vision and desire and he was wasting his time at Leeds because the club would simply stand still and eventually go backwards. How right he was.

Those same directors would eventually oversee relegation but in the meantime the abuse for Adamson grew ever louder from supporters who had no real idea that the directors had baulked at this massive but affordable signing. It would have transformed not just the club, but the whole city.

Another fine player Adamson wanted to sign was England international Martin Dobson, then at Everton. At Burnley Dobson had been one of Adamson's key players, someone that he had nurtured and moulded into the elegant, influential player that he became. At Everton he was offered only a one-year extension to his contract and was contacted by both Harry Potts at Burnley and Jimmy Adamson at Leeds. Potts got his bid in first and Dobson agreed to join him. Before the contract was signed Adamson telephoned him.

Dobson remembers the conversation. 'Dobbo I want you to come to Leeds,' he said and offered him a two-year contract. But Dobson had already met Potts face-to-face in Southport and they shook hands on the deal at a time when there were few agents involved and Dobson had given his word. It was still a time when the shake of a hand was important so it was to Burnley that Dobson went.

Years later Dobson has some doubts that he did the right thing when he re-joined Burnley, finding a club that was nothing like the one he had left in 1975. Who knows the effect that he might have had at Leeds and how important it would have been to Adamson to have had a real ally in the dressing room and someone he could trust.

'Adamson survives shareholders fury' wrote John Wray following the AGM that Manny Cussins managed to miss, owing to a dose of illness. 'I'm still the man for the job,' he fired back after criticisms of him, his coaching staff and the scouting system. Doctor Aubrey Share called for his dismissal. 'His record is as appalling as the balance sheet and I ask that he is replaced,' he announced angrily.

And then in the deep pile of clippings heaped up on John's carpet, two small ones turned up that told a huge story. The shadow of Revie darkened and lengthened with the revelation that he had an astonishing £90,000 consultancy agreement with Leeds to be paid at £9,000 a year for ten years. At what point did Adamson learn of this? What must he have thought? He must have been stopped in his tracks by the news.

Wray thinks that it might only have been a way of paying Revie what the club owed him, but within the arrangement was the contractual obligation to attend four board meetings a year. The whole thing in fact beggars belief. Revie was subjected to a ten-year ban by the FA but appealed against it and it was overturned.

'Cussins says there will be no conflict between Don Revie and our own manager Jimmy Adamson,' wrote Wray, and then in a further piece he said that Adamson had broken his silence on the matter and said he would be prepared to listen to the former boss but stressed he would make his own decisions.

'I wouldn't shut the door in his face,' said Adamson, 'but you can't have two women running the same kitchen.' You can only surmise what Adamson was thinking privately especially with the lifting of the ban on Revie. He must have been horrified. Consequently, the possibility of having Revie back grew bigger in supporters' and in some board members' minds.

After a season-long campaign to get Adamson out, and now the more strident mentions of Revie's name, he was still there at the beginning of the new 1980/81 season. But the summer break did nothing to ease the dissatisfaction. Adamson tried to deflate things with a little humour. 'I haven't been shot,' he joked, 'but I've told my wife to take out more insurance.'

In *Shoot* magazine there was an Adamson feature. For the new season he was pinning his hopes on the £1m trio, Curtis,

Sabella and Parlane. He confessed that the season just gone by was best forgotten and he was aware that fans felt let down. Tellingly he said, however, 'Some of the players did not show the commitment a manager has the right to expect.'

He again referred to the departed Currie; that it was Currie who had insisted on returning to London, and that they had struggled without him. Eddie Gray was another to be singled out. On joining Leeds, Adamson had thought Gray would have little to offer. But after they were trounced 7-0 by Arsenal in the League Cup, Gray had been brought back and was now a fixture in the team. What Adamson also mentioned was the need for a successful youth policy.

Shoot, the most neutral and harmless of magazines, forecast that only a climb up the table would satisfy the success-starved supporters and save Adamson from all the verbal lashings from the terraces. If things didn't improve, it wouldn't be the team going anywhere, it would only be Adamson. Its prediction turned out to be correct.

The first game of the 1980/81 season was at home to Aston Villa and was a 2-1 defeat. The banners were there waiting for him. Then there was a 3-0 defeat away at Middlesbrough. Feelings were running high but next up was a game away at Norwich and at last a win, 3-2. Again, the 'Adamson Out' banners were waiting for him.

His heart must have sunk when he saw the placards yet again and he certainly knew that after the two defeats so far, his job was on the line. But his appearance, save for the one unseemly lapse in the car park, was always calm, his demeanour always composed. He seldom betrayed his emotions in public but in this game he did allow himself a rare moment of joy. By the final whistle the ecstatic fans were shouting loudly and defiantly, 'UNITED ARE BACK'.

For this game Adamson brought back Paul Madeley for his first game of the season and the defence, that had been so disorganised in the previous matches, looked so much more settled and confident. Leeds took the lead in the sixth minute with a Paul Hart goal. The second goal came in the 55th minute, scored by Arthur Graham from a Terry Connor cross. Adamson always looked to give good young players a chance and Connor was one of them having made his debut aged just 17.

Justin Fashanu pulled one back. There was no sitting on the lead however and Connor scored a third with just a few minutes remaining. Alex Sabella had a fine game and it was he who created the Connor goal with a brilliant run taking him past four defenders and then getting the cross over. Adamson was utterly elated not just by the goal but by Sabella, one of his signings who so far had hardly been a roaring success.

Norwich made it 3-2 but Leeds hung on to the win with supporters agreeing that this was a team with balance and commitment with a greater degree of sharpness. The score could have been even greater for Leeds if a penalty had been awarded for a foul on Gary Hamson in the box. A Sabella scoring attempt, after a moment of individual magic, could have added another. He beat his man in the centre-circle and then raced half the pitch but was thwarted by a Hansbury save.

Adamson permitted himself a few smiles after the game, 'I have nothing but praise for the attitude of our players. Madeley played like he did ten years ago and Sabella provided the match-winner with the kind of magic you don't get from English players. But Graham was my man of the match. He was tremendous. For us, the season starts here and we are hoping we can go from strength to strength.' It was a forlorn hope.

It was back to earth when Leicester were the next opponents at Elland Road. A poor crowd of just 18,530 saw Leeds lose 2-1. By now Adamson was committing the cardinal sin of blaming the fans, saying that their abuse was getting through to the players.

By 1 September director Rayner Barker had to ask for police help to contain the demonstrations outside the ground by the angry mobs. Three days later he announced he was not going to quit, 'I can take as much as they can throw at me and will carry on until the directors decide otherwise.'

It was as good as a challenge to them to dismiss him and pay him off. This then was a tricky dilemma for the directors, wrote John Wray, who would then have to stump up a sizeable compensation settlement.

The Norwich game was Jimmy Adamson's last taste of a victory in football. It was his final experience of that great moment of any kind of euphoria when a goal is scored that wins the game. He punched the air like any fan when Leeds' third goal went in. He must have gone home on that long bus journey back to Leeds thinking all was not yet lost. But, if there was hope, it was the hope that comes with delusion.

By now he had already expressed the view that he was tired of football. What he was probably more tired of was all the subterfuge that went with it behind the scenes and the thought that Revie might re-appear as adviser. His four years at Sunderland and Leeds and all the accompanying abuse had drained him. He wanted out; it is amazing that he endured it for as long as he did. But even then, the worst was still to come. If he thought he could just slip away, mend his wounds and re-establish some sort of life free of football and stress, he was mistaken.

On 6 September there was a 3-0 defeat away at Stoke City. 'The End of the Road' headlined the *Telegraph and Argus*. It was Adamson's final game as a manager and the end of his involvement with football. He was only 51. The five-man board of directors met at Manny Cussins's home in Alwoodley and made their decision to give him an ultimatum, resign or be sacked. He would be the fifth manager to leave in the space of just six years. He would not resign, he told them.

He saw Cussins at the chairman's home on Sunday 7 September and announced his resignation on the Monday. At this meeting it was agreed that if Adamson left the club it would be on amicable terms. Public comment would be kept to a minimum, with neither side criticising the other. This was an important agreement and was key to the decision taken later by Adamson to seek compensation for what he considered to be defamatory remarks made following his departure.

After seeing Cussins he announced he was indeed resigning as it was in the best interests of Leeds United and the club was bigger than any individual. He had in fact decided to resign having agreed that the remaining period of his contract would be paid up, a figure of something between £25,000 and £30,000 according to John Wray.

Following Maurice Lindley's spell as caretaker, Allan Clarke was Adamson's replacement after his success at Barnsley where he had guided the club to promotion from the Fourth Division at his first attempt. On his appointment he declared that he was a winner and stated that he would consider himself a failure if he could not produce a trophy in three years. His first game was a 0-0 draw against Manchester United in front of a crowd of 32,539 people; the Leeds contingent hoping that Clarke, their former hero, could get the club back on track.

Alas he did not and under his management Leeds United were relegated at the end of the 1981/82 season. It is reasonable to think that this might just have given Jimmy Adamson some measure of quiet satisfaction following the comments that Allan Clarke made when he took over at Leeds and the incessant abuse he had received from the Leeds fans.

In the boxes of papers and memorabilia that Adamson left behind there was a collection of old 1981 editions of the *Daily Mirror*. None of them mention Adamson himself, but all of them contain articles relating to Clarke and Peter Barnes, a player who was signed by Clarke for a then club record fee of £930,000. Barnes then did very little at Leeds United and the fee was remarkable considering that at this time the club was haemorrhaging money. Bearing in mind that one of the supporters' accusations aimed at Adamson was that he had bought a number of players who contributed little to the club, Clarke's Barnes purchase was ironic and Adamson must have collected the cuttings with a measure of wry satisfaction.

In January 1981, still living in Leeds at Park Avenue, Roundhay, Jimmy Adamson contacted his solicitors. As a result, Allan Clarke was informed that he had made what were seen by Adamson to be defamatory allegations in the national press. John Wray reported what Clarke had said on 18 September in the *Bradford Telegraph and Argus*, 'The biggest lesson I have learned is that the players are not as fit as they should be.'

On 20 September 1980, the *Daily Mail* published an article, 'You're not fit to play, new manager tells panting Leeds'. 'I'm shocked by the standard,' he stated. 'I have been shocked by the standard of the team's fitness.'

Adamson felt there was an implication that under his management the Leeds players were so unfit that they were in no position to play professional football. The allegation also appeared in the *Daily Mirror* under the heading 'Unfit says Sniffer'.

In an edition of the *Sunday Mirror*, an interview was published under the heading 'The truth about Leeds, shambles at Elland Road'. Adamson felt that this article repeated the allegations and implied that under his management the players became sloppy, undisciplined, lazy and overweight. Adamson felt there was an implication that he as manager had reduced what was once a great club to a disgrace.

Clarke appeared on the TV programme, *The Big Match*, and it was felt he implied that Adamson was guilty of bad management in that he had bought players out of panic rather than on ability. The allegation was repeated in the *Daily Express*, 'Some of the players here have been bought to keep the fans happy and that is bad management.'

Whether these allegations were well-founded, whether they were fair comment, is not the point. It is what Adamson felt that was the key. True or not, they made him feel like the scapegoat for all the troubles that Leeds had experienced, and that his reputation was being damaged. Furthermore he had the agreement with Cussins that there would be no public criticisms. He therefore asked for an apology from Clarke and all the newspapers involved; an undertaking not to repeat any similar statements, a substantial sum by way of damages, and all legal costs.

Manny Cussins was informed that Adamson was sad and astonished that Clarke had been allowed to make defamatory and scurrilous attacks upon his character. He was informed that at no stage during his managership had the board suggested that he had allowed the players to become so unfit that they were in no position to play professional football, that the club was undisciplined, and that Adamson had allowed it to become reduced from its former glory.

The allegation that Adamson was guilty of panic-buying was a particularly strange one Cussins was informed, in light of the fact that all transfers and purchases had to be done with board approval. In other words, if Adamson was culpable then so were the board.

Cussins was further reminded that at his home on Sunday 7 September, there had been an agreement that neither side would criticise the other and public comment would be kept to a minimum. In view of all this Leeds United were asked to join in making an apology; to agree not to publish, or cause to be published, further similar defamatory statements and to pay a reasonable sum by way of compensation and legal costs.

The editor of the *Daily Mail* was informed that the article in their newspaper clearly implied that Jimmy Adamson had no right to be regarded as one of the top coaches in the game because under his management the Leeds players became so unfit they were in no position to play professional football, let alone for a club in the First Division. The allegations, it was made clear, were entirely unwarranted and extremely damaging to the prospects of Adamson's future employment. Sadly, no attempt had been made to contact Adamson for his views before the article was published, the letter continued.

The Leeds versus Brighton programme of 29 November 1980, was viewed by Adamson as continuing the attack on his character. Reading it years later, however, it is hard to find anything in the programme piece that is anything other than fair comment. Presumably the final paragraph was the one in question. In it Clarke explained that it was now just over two months since he had taken over and he believed that progress had been made with player fitness. The players had responded even though this was not the ideal time to be concentrating on getting players fit with midweek games and players away on international duty. He ended by writing that, 'It's a job that should be done in the pre-season.' Adamson felt it was aimed directly at him and his pre-season work.

Had anyone mentioned Adamson's drinking they might have had a fair point but football seems to close ranks and protect its own when the subject of a manager drinking excessively comes up. It could be argued that it did eventually harm Adamson's capacity to carry out his job at Leeds and if that was the case, the directors must certainly have been aware.

Perhaps Brian Clough gave the best explanations of how drink can take over, 'Booze is part of the managerial scene. Drink is readily available. It is always there if you want it. It is provided and it is free. You have a drink with the chairman. The occasional journalist may be invited to join you. Friends and colleagues, particularly after a match, will sit and share a glass. Because of its availability, if you are not careful, drink becomes a habit which is extremely difficult to break.'

The culture of football 'encourages you to have a drink because of the strains and pressures you're under. You get a point away from home and you put your feet up and have a drink. You enjoy your success and you drown your sorrows. Because you lose too many times in this game, when you win you enjoy it.'

What football managers also found hard, said Clough, is being hard-faced and doing the horrible things that need doing.

You have to tell people things that you know will break their heart – and it breaks your heart as well – but that is something a manager must never show. What you do afterwards is see if there is a drink available.

If by the end Adamson was increasingly remote and paranoid, Dave Merrington, Adamson's assistant at both Sunderland and Leeds, had one uncomplicated explanation for Jimmy's 'failure' if that is what it was, at Leeds United. He said that by the end, he was just utterly battle-weary and worn out. Quite simply he had had enough of player problems, in-fighting and boardroom politics. On his arrival at Leeds the departing Jock Stein spoke to Adamson and told him what a difficult job he had on his hands. We might presume from this that Stein was thankful and relieved to be leaving.

Merrington explained that Adamson had never signed a contract at Sunderland so it was easy for him to leave that club. Therefore it was easy for Leeds to offer him their job. He had not bought a house in the north-east so that was one complication he did not have to contend with. While he had been at Sunderland May had been quite ill so Adamson spent a considerable time back in Burnley, leaving more and more of the daily work on the training ground to Merrington. May's health may well at that time have been a major influence on his decision to move especially as she agreed to join him in Leeds.

One of the first things that Adamson did was ask Merrington to join him at Elland Road. On his arrival he spent several weeks preparing a report on the playing side of the club. It covered the youth set-up, scouting programme, coaching and playing staff, training programme requirements including the need for afternoon sessions and projections of where money was needed and why.

Having done that they went through the problems they faced. Firstly they realised that they had a transitional job on their hands and such jobs take time, at least two years they estimated. The likelihood of Leeds' fans understanding that need was as good as nil. As long as there were still Revie's players in the squad fans could hark back to the glory days all too easily.

Fans and directors, fed on the earlier diet of success, wanted an impossible instant fix. Adamson and Merrington identified 11 players in total that they needed to move out. On top of that they quickly realised that the directors were divided into factions bringing a whole new raft of problems into the equation. Some of them had never wanted Adamson in the first place so he clearly had no support from them.

Gary Roberts remembers Manny Cussins becoming reserved about the appointment as soon as he realised at a supporters' meeting that feelings were running high and that this was not a universally popular appointment. By the end he had totally distanced himself from it.

'He shifted allegiances very quickly as I recall,' said Roberts. He had been the same with Brian Clough. 'When he saw the reaction from supporters (and players) he soon became publicly anti-Clough.'

Adamson, faced with attitudes and support in the boardroom that shifted as quickly as the sands in Morecambe Bay, and a chairman who seemingly changed colours depending on which way the wind blew, on some days must have had no idea if he was coming or going.

On top of all that, recalls Merrington, some senior pros were not exactly co-operative, although Eddie Gray was an exception to this. 'A superb professional,' Merrington described him. The idea of introducing afternoon training to iron out what they saw as glaring deficiencies was a totally unwelcome idea.

They found a club where wages for some players were surprisingly low and they wanted to do something about this. It led to battles with members of the board who controlled the finances. Such was the distrust between Adamson and some board members, Adamson insisted that everything be minuted at every meeting. It was a huge problem that he had no budget of his own to work with and for everything that involved finance he had to approach the board. He wanted one key player in particular to have a much better salary and it took three difficult meetings to achieve this.

And then he found the same problem Brian Clough identified in management, that you have to take on board all the emotional baggage of so many players in an attempt to provide not just moral support but real, practical solutions. Merrington mentioned several players at the club who all had different kinds of worries; drink, debt, domestic issues, gambling, and all of them impacting on performance levels. Some days, Adamson went home drained having had to deal with them one after the other.

Unfortunately, bit by bit succumbing and throwing in the towel in the face of all these obstacles, none of them known or appreciated by supporters who clamoured for his head, Adamson was absent from the training ground for longer and longer periods. On some occasions it was all too clear he'd had a few drinks including on match days. The notebook he had at Sunderland gave an insight into the constant demands on his managerial time and energy. They are filled with the bricks and mortar of running a club and that's before you even mention team selection, coaching, confrontations, setbacks, and matchday tensions. I don't doubt for a minute he would have kept the same kind of memo pad at Leeds and its contents would have made for fascinating and painful reading.

Merrington certainly knew about the legal action against Allan Clarke, the club and the newspapers. In fact, he relates, of course he knew, it was he himself who took the initial offence at the suggestions that the fitness of the players had been neglected. He brought it to Adamson's attention and Adamson informed him that he would sort it out and take action on both their behalves. Merrington still had his planning notes on all his training sessions as evidence that fitness was of the utmost importance. Eventually it was all settled out of court. What the amount was, Merrington never knew and it was Jimmy, he says, who was the beneficiary with Merrington receiving nothing.

Adamson most certainly endured enormous strains and pressures. At Burnley they came from Bob Lord; at Sunderland from the shadow of Brian Clough; and at Leeds from the directors, supporters, and the elephant in the room that was Don Revie, along with the frustrated longing for the old glory days. Revie had described the club as a 'family'. Brian Clough described that family as more Mafia than Mothercare.

Director Bob Roberts, known as 'Pearhead' to the fans, was widely cited as the man who provoked Don Revie into leaving. Manny Cussins, it was alleged, could change his colours like a chameleon. The name might have been Leeds United but in truth the place was far from united. Perhaps it was a poisoned chalice Adamson should never have touched.

In his obituary for Jimmy Adamson in 2011, Brian Glanville described the post as a kind of Sargasso Sea for managers trying to follow in Revie's giant footsteps. But how tempting it must have been for Adamson to join them when it was so much closer to his family in Burnley and when his beloved May agreed to move to Leeds with him. His granddaughter Katie today vividly remembers the regular trips they made across the Pennines to see them and what a lovely house they lived in.

Adamson's move to Leeds was doomed to failure. 'It just never happened for him,' said Eddie Gray. But then you wonder just what might have happened had the board of directors sanctioned the signings of Kevin Keegan and Peter Withe; the history of Leeds United might well have taken a different turn. Did Leeds supporters realise just how serious an attempt it was by Adamson and that it was the directors that vetoed it? If there was one moment that convinced Adamson that he would not make progress at Leeds, then that was it, and from that point on he must have wondered 'just what am I doing here?'

Finale

FOR TWO years until early 2011 I would make the journey once a month from Leeds up the A1 to Acklington in the north-east to visit someone I knew in the prison there. Just north of Newcastle there's a sign for Ashington. When I drove by I would say, 'Ah that's where Jimmy Adamson came from.' After the second time my wife politely asked was I going to say it every time we drove by; so after that I just said it to myself. There never seemed time to turn off and take a look, much as I would have loved to, and anyway a morning walk along the beach at Druridge Bay seemed more appealing at that time, before entering the locked doors of Acklington.

Ray Pointer was from Cramlington, Alan Brown from Corbridge, Jimmy Robson from Pelton, Harry Potts from Hetton, Stan Ternent from Gateshead, Brian O'Neil from Bedlington, Dave Merrington from Newcastle, Dave Thomas from West Auckland, and John Angus from Amble. You could spend a week in the north-east and the list would go on and on.

Twelve months after we stopped the visits, I started the Jimmy Adamson book and thought I would have to get back up there again if only to take a look at the famed Laburnum Terrace. Plus, if I went on my own I could say 'ah this is where Jimmy Adamson was born' as often as I liked. I had planned to drive up on Saturday 10 November and stay overnight with Alan Parker who had done so much to help with the early research in and around Ashington. By this time too, Laburnum Terrace's Sir Bobby Charlton had agreed to provide the foreword.

Truth is I never actually got there. But one day...

Once a week many years ago, as a spotty 15-year-old at Todmorden Grammar School, we had football on one of the mudbath pitches at Centre Vale Park. We would head down the steep Ferney Lee Road from the school to the park (we were knackered before we got there), and spend an hour taking on the roles of our Burnley heroes. There would be Ed Cockroft, John Helliwell, Jammy Fielden, Colin Walker, Winston Sutcliffe, Bernard Horsfall, Philip Brown, Harold Ashworth and many more clattering down the hill in our boots and studs. We would pretend to be the dashing and handsome John Connelly, Ray Pointer or Jimmy McIlroy. But oddly enough, great players though they were, nobody would bother being John Angus, Brian Miller or Jimmy Adamson. They just didn't have that same appeal or glamour. It was the forwards that generated the excitement and goals.

So much had changed during the almost 30 years between Jimmy's first appearances in the Burnley first team in 1951, and turning his back on football in 1980, aged just 51. Football styles, tactics and methods, kits, boots, balls, haircuts and training were unrecognisable. The age of a manager putting out his best 11 players week after week, injured or not, was over. When was the last time anyone had played the old-fashioned two full-backs, three half-backs and five forwards? In 1950 a player could command a wage of just about double figures; in 1980 the best players were on £500 a week and more. Players in 1950 walked to the match or used the bus side by side with supporters. Thirty years later few did not have a car, many of them owning luxury models.

It was now a time of Keegan-esque football stars, many of them celebrities. Football wasn't quite global, the Far East was still untapped, but nevertheless it was an expanding and developing phenomenon. Football in general was light years away from the parochial greyness and serfdom of English football in the early 1950s.

When Jimmy started as a player supporters from rival teams walked to the game side by side, and even stood at the game alongside each other. It was an era that was now well and truly over. Violence and rioting at football grounds was common place. Travel and communications were easier. Rival gangs were almost tribal and football was the vehicle by which they could meet up and cause mayhem.

The game was about to become more of an industry than a sport but all this was pre-Hillsborough so football grounds were still, more often than not, unsafe and uncomfortable. While the actual football might have progressed and changed, stadiums with poor facilities by and large had not and were still Spartan places. Meanwhile Brian Clough, cast aside by Leeds, was about to win a second European Cup with Nottingham Forest.

Jimmy might possibly have sat in his very pleasant and well-appointed house in Roundhay, Leeds, and shuddered at the memories of the cramped two-up and two-down that he had once shared with his large family in 1940s Ashington. But he might have found it difficult to decide if he was a happier man. Life and football were now so much more complicated. Such was the unhappy way that Adamson walked away from football, he might well have yearned to turn back the clock to those simpler, if austere times, when he was still a newly-married player.

The gawky, fresh-faced young man with so much talent and so much to achieve as a player ahead of him, by the end was a weary and dispirited figure fighting losing battles in both boardroom and dressing room and then becoming involved in a demeaning litigation battle with the press, Leeds United and Allan Clarke. Little wonder he turned his back on football totally. And all the while, the dislike he felt for Bob Lord still ached and festered like an unhealed wound.

That his mother's suicide, the father he disowned, and all his managerial troubles should be followed later by the heart breaking deaths of his two daughters might well have made him wonder if much of his life was doomed to be tragic and unfulfilled. Just as a Thomas Hardy novel in which none of us are really in charge of our lives but are subjected to the whims and vagaries of forces and people beyond our control, in Jimmy's case it was the autocratic Bob Lord.

From Roundhay he returned to live in Burnley where the football club, once his pride and joy, was teetering on the edge of insolvency. Bob Lord was seriously ill with just a year of his life remaining. He died in 1981 and Jimmy did not attend his funeral. Lord and Jimmy hadn't spoken for the previous five years. Harry Potts was no longer manager of Burnley and had been replaced by Brian Miller. Harry continued in football, undertaking scouting work until the mid-1980s for Chelsea and his good friend Ron Suart. By then he was beginning to suffer from Parkinson's disease and dementia. He died in January 1996; he and Jimmy hadn't spoken since 1972. Margaret Potts passed away in 2009 still bitter and angry about how she felt Harry had been manoeuvred out of his job by Lord and Adamson. But Harry was Harry and when he learned how ill Lord was, he went to visit him.

So when did it all begin to go wrong for Adamson? Clearly it was some time before the infamous FA Cup tie at Blackpool in January 1976, as the relationship with Lord became one of increasing antipathy. Possibly it was indeed when Lord retired from his business and the football club became his only focus and where he spent all his time to Adamson's increasing frustration. Certainly it was when Martin Dobson was sold.

And what is his legacy?

'There are two schools of thought,' says Paul Fletcher. 'The first sees him as a great coach and manager who should never have been sacked at Burnley. The other sees him in a less kindly light, that while as a coach he was a genius, as a manager "he was not everyone's cup of tea" to quote Colin Waldron.'

As a general rule those players who revered Harry Potts at Burnley did not have the same feelings for Jimmy Adamson. But is that not human nature? If a manager does not retain or play you, are you likely to have warm feelings towards him? Brian Flynn to this day looks up to him but his wife Elizabeth remembers that not all players were saddened by his Burnley dismissal.

'What I think is simply this,' added Fletcher. 'That he was a great coach and that for me personally he was a good manager, and I had the best years of my career under that management. I visited him every Christmas until he died. The Jimmy Adamson Suite at Turf Moor is a wonderful tribute to him with the glass cabinets filled with memorabilia and pictures. And, whereas some managers from the club's past will barely be remembered, if remembered at all, Jimmy's achievements will be there forever.

'On the day of Jimmy's funeral the cortege drove along Harry Potts Way passing pavements lined with people paying their respects and appreciation. There was loud applause as is the custom these days. For me it was a hugely personal day as images and memories of great games with him flooded back. At the game against Leeds United on 19 November 2011, we stood on the field before the game started and joined in the applause that rang round the ground.

'How ironic it was that it was the game against Leeds that was the next home game after he passed away, for that is where his managerial career ended and his connections with football. Like many players, I can say, he changed my life for the better.'

Players like Gary Rowell, Colin Waldron and Martin Dobson would certainly echo Fletcher's words.

Stan Ternent to this day sees him as the best coach he knew and was a regular visitor to see him, 'I was an admirer then and still am. When I'm coaching today I still think of things he did and said. I liked him as a guy even though he used to bollock me up hill and down dale but that was because he wanted me to do better. He was always keeping you on your toes; he'd find out what made you tick inside and treat you accordingly – an arm round the shoulder or a kick up the backside.

'He was hugely influenced by Alan Brown. If he said it was dark, then it was midnight, just like Brown. He encouraged me to take coaching certificates and to go round the schools coaching. He'd want to know what I was planning on doing each day at Sunderland and Leeds and then make his own suggestions. He'd do the most unusual things like telling striker Frank Casper to mark Bobby Moore. Since when did strikers mark defenders, Moore wouldn't be expecting it, but Jimmy knew that Moore made West Ham tick. Stop that and you stopped West Ham.'

And his record: as a player he appeared 486 times for Burnley and scored 18 goals. He was one of only two players to lead the Clarets to the ultimate success of winning the league title. He was a man-of-the-match Cup Finalist and played in Europe and was the 1962 Footballer of the Year. He was the assistant England manager in Chile and was regarded as the best uncapped player in football for many years. Players like Tommy Docherty, Jimmy McIlroy, Danny Blanchflower, Dave Mackay and Jimmy Greaves were baffled that he never played for England. He played just one game for the England B side against Scotland in the mid-1950s. Between 1972 and 1975 he produced one of the most 'beautiful' teams seen in league football. His coaching was exemplary; he took cast-offs and made them into first team regulars. He took good young players and improved them even further.

Of course he upset people along the way, what manager doesn't, but he made so many players better and brought young players into his teams whether it was Burnley, Sunderland or Leeds, and they will not forget him. At Sunderland he was within a point of saving them from relegation. At Leeds, at a time when the club was in serial decline after the Revie years, it is seldom mentioned that he achieved their best season since Revie with a fifth position and a place in Europe. If he 'failed' at either Sunderland or Leeds, it should be remembered that at the former he had to replace the incomparable Bob Stokoe. At Leeds, where Revie's shadow still blanketed the place, he was simply one small part of the inexorable slide to the years of mediocrity and where the directors of the club bore a huge responsibility for its grim decline.

Being a football supporter at a time when Jimmy played for Burnley made him a strong part of my own life. I saw him play many times. Writing this book began in 2012, exactly 50 years after Burnley's 1962 FA Cup Final. In one of the boxes of his memorabilia I brought home after a visit to Katie, there were some treasured items. Underneath the folders of pension schemes and tax returns lay the silver salver presented to him when he was the Second Division Manager of the Year. I lovingly polished it until it glistened.

In later life Jimmy opened up just a little and often spoke with his grandchildren but only occasionally about his past; a past that he kept very much to himself other than his wife May. Perhaps it was just old age that made him reminisce; perhaps it was the untimely deaths of his two daughters Jayne and Julie; perhaps it was just something inside him that happens to all of us when there is more time to think and remember what might have been and how we might have done things differently.

Paul Fletcher and Colin Waldron tried their hardest to encourage Jimmy to talk about his past. They played bowls at Towneley with him and May often cooked dinner for them all. But try as they did, they learned little. When they saw Bobby Charlton's elegant tribute to him in his England book it made them even more determined but they still could not draw anything from him and persuade him to tell them all his football stories. Slowly the visits dwindled to just Christmas Eve.

Katie remembered how, when they were children, Jimmy spent his time in the garden, or at Towneley Park, bowling. Jennie remembered that the name of the Scottie was Sandy and that Towneley Park became a special place for them when she was small. They would visit frequently; her brother Sam kicked a ball around with Jimmy. Jimmy collected her from school and taught her to read and write and learn all her tables. He never needed a calculator. He loved the outdoors and at Towneley taught her to throw and catch and they spent hours swimming at the local baths. 'There's no such word as CAN'T,' he told her over and again.

In May 1987 when the final Fourth Division game of a humiliating season was played at Turf Moor and a defeat would have meant a sorry exit from the Football League, the ground was packed with top sports writers, supporters and former players all as good as ready to read the last rites on a day that had the whole town collectively fearing the worst. But not Jimmy, he was at Towneley Park playing bowls such was his disregard for the club that had once been part of his life and that he had once represented with such distinction.

On some days he used to help his daughter Jayne in the Burnley newsagents shop that she and her husband Ken ran near Hawthorne Road. David Binns remembers getting his newspapers there sometime during the 1980s and would always chat to Jimmy about the results of the previous day, but rarely Burnley FC. Jimmy was always smartly dressed, polite and pleasant but Binns does remember that he always seemed reserved in his manner.

He remembered too that his friend spoke to Jimmy in the shop about a week before the fateful Orient game, trying to engage him in conversation, mentioning Orient's danger man, Alan Comfort. There was no profound reply, no interest, just a casual 'oh OK' as he handed him his change. Jennie, his granddaughter, remembers how he would lift her up when she was a toddler so she could reach the jars of chocolate raisins on one of the high shelves.

Towneley Park was some distance away from his final home on Brunshaw Road but from there he used to take a wheelbarrow down the hill, fill it with the rich soil that the Towneley moles dug up, and then push the wheelbarrow all the way home again. His former neighbour testifies that he had an immaculate garden and as his aches and pains worsened, a gardener kept it neat and trim.

Old team-mate Jimmy Robson remembers how both Jimmy and May used to sit in their front garden on a summer's day and chat to passers-by. Jimmy would walk by on his way to the shops and stop and talk; but not once did they ever talk about football.

In winter it wasn't the wheelbarrow he pushed up and down the hill, it was the sledge he pulled the grandchildren on, all of them laughing and giggling. Whenever they visited there was always music – Frank Sinatra, Dean Martin and Neil Diamond. Jimmy's favourite was Neil Diamond's 'Hello Again'. Their favourite film was the 1980 remake of *The Jazz Singer*.

The memories of holidays with grandma and granddad remain strong. He loved his holidays in Spain using the villa of a good friend when he had finished with football. Boxes are filled with old colour pictures of those happy times. You can feel the delight and the strength of the bond between him and May. Nobody could begrudge him those long holidays in the sun. He'd had a tough early life, and his final years of management had drained him; his mother's suicide must have been devastating after he had brought her to live near him in Burnley. Her problems, much to do with depression and the debilitating years spent as a miner's wife, eventually overcame her.

If he talked of 'mental toughness' it was something that he had clearly learned in his early difficult life. It was only mental toughness that helped him cope with the death of his mother. It was his sister Florence, then just 18 and living in the little terraced house on Mitella Street very close to Turf Moor, who found her mother early one morning by the gas oven in the small living room. She had inhaled coal gas through the tube fastened to the gas tap 'whilst the balance of her mind was disturbed' said the death certificate. Mary died later in hospital. Jimmy played in the first game of the season just a few days later.

From the early 1990s onwards he was plagued by ill health and immobility. He suffered from osteoarthritis in both knees. The pain on some days was unbearable. He found leaving the house extremely difficult and with May could drive just a couple of miles to the supermarket once a week. But on the day I visited him when they had just returned from a shopping trip, though chair-bound, he was bright, talkative and jovial, and had a pin-sharp memory. But what upset me was his size and how swollen his legs were.

Age and illness can be so cruel especially to sportsmen, once so supremely fit and agile. By now, he weighed over 17 stones and could barely walk 20 yards. For some time he had been unable to enjoy holidays in the sun, go bowling at Towneley or tend to his garden, things he loved dearly. He had received a doctor's warnings that his drinking would kill him if not curtailed. The problem with his right knee he traced back to an injury in September 1955, during a game following which he was out of action for nearly five months and ever afterwards needed cortisone. His final years became reclusive. His eventual public appearance at Turf Moor to open the Jimmy Adamson Suite was extraordinary.

Gary Edwards, in another e-mail, wrote, 'I have to say that looking back Adamson showed immense dignity and restraint throughout the torment and abuse hurled at him at Leeds – he never once sought to apportion blame on anyone else or condemn anyone else. And I was certainly full of remorse when I heard of his death a short while ago.'

Gary is one of many Leeds United fans who all those years ago thought so little of him, but if this book does one thing it might just show something of what Adamson had to battle with at Elland Road and that he was simply one part of a continuum that took the club to eventual relegation.

It is ironic that Allan Clarke, who eventually oversaw that relegation, suffered only a fraction of the criticism hurled at Adamson. And, on top of that it could be argued that Clarke's purchase of Peter Barnes for a reported £900,000 was just as great a waste of money as anything that Adamson ever did. And what did Billy Bremner achieve after Allan Clarke and Eddie Gray? In short, precious little. There is a school of thought that would suggest that Bremner, by disbanding the young and promising team that Eddie Gray was carefully nurturing, and that with just one or two experienced additions might have brought back success, failed just as miserably.

Yet it is Adamson that folklore sees as one of Leeds' 'most controversial' managers. If fingers point at Adamson then they should surely too point at a group of directors that history says made wrong decisions from the minute that Revie was allowed to leave.

While the great Jimmy McIlroy, Adamson's partner in so many great games and seasons, had embraced and been able to enjoy his 'ex-footballer' life as he grew older in the town, Adamson had not. McIlroy has never sought out the limelight, but at the same time he has invariably accepted invitations to dinners, presentations, charity functions, or requests to help people, but Adamson kept well away, declining any invitations to attend reunions of the great title-winning team of 1959/60 and the Cup team of 1962. Nor did he ever attend any of the reunions of the beautiful team he created in the 1970s.

McIlroy too had a period when he felt the club was showing a measure of ingratitude for his achievements, while at the same time 'using' his name, but that was resolved some years ago and he now attends most games and is club president.

Other than the aborted cup tie he attended in 2005 with Paul Fletcher and Colin Waldron, Jimmy Adamson maintained his distance from the club for nearly 30 years until at last he attended the opening of the Jimmy Adamson Suite bringing some measure of closure to his years of estrangement. Adamson was not so much the 'son' the town forgot; it was simply that he presumed it had forgotten him.

Sometimes there is unexpected luck involved in writing a biography. I had been away in Australia for most of February and the book was drawing to a close. Meeting Terry Ridout in Tasmania and hearing him say, against a background of screeching cockatoos and parrots outside, that he had once worked for Bob Lord, had been quite surreal. Then he had joined the police force and had been on the beat in Burnley and on duty at Turf Moor on several occasions.

It is funny the things that leave indelible memories. I can still picture Jimmy's loping running style as if it were yesterday. Terry's memory is the sight of hundreds of Everton supporters all lined up at half-time urinating against the back wall of the Cricket Field Stand when he was on duty.

Frustrations remained with pinning down the last couple of people for the final interviews but at last we got them done. Then there was the totally unanticipated e-mail that was waiting for me when I got back from Sydney. It came from Jimmy's nephew Mark who had seen mention of the book on the internet. He only provided the barest of details about Jimmy but what he did reveal was hugely significant showing the huge burden of responsibility and family obligations that Jimmy must have carried throughout his life, of which he said so little to anyone and that made him such a deeply private man. This was a family beset by so many difficulties and upsets, and it was Jimmy who had broken the mould, had become the family 'success' and that his siblings looked up to.

Mark's father was Bill Adamson, the brother born in 1921 and nine years older than Jimmy. He was one of twins but Mark, the other twin, died at birth. Bill was the one who had joined the RAF during the war but on his return to Ashington resumed his life down the mines. Then, sometime before 1955 he left Ashington and deserted his wife and daughter, somehow finding his way to Rochdale. It was at nearby Littleborough Cricket Club that Bill met Alice Law and Mark was their son, named after the twin who had died.

Divorce in the 1950s was uncommon so such a thing in a close-knit community like Ashington and the desertion might well have brought a sense of stigma and shame on the Adamson family. At the very least they would have been the victims of finger-pointing and accusatory gossip in the world of terraced rows where news of scandal travelled quickly from doorstep to doorstep. It is not unreasonable to think it would have hit Jimmy's mother hard, a woman who already suffered the indignity of being expected to take her husband William's dinner to the pub on a Sunday; this the man that Jimmy eventually disowned. Mark thinks that his grandfather actually took his own life, 'It was just something my mother said.'

Sometime around 2003, Mark, by then a very successful businessman, tried to contact Jimmy via daughter Jayne. Jimmy declined to see him he says with Mark receiving the message that it was because of the bad memories of his father Bill who had never repaid Jimmy any of the money he had borrowed. But, it was also a time when Jimmy's health was failing more and more and he was reluctant to see anyone.

The victim of a difficult childhood, deserted by his alcoholic father when he was 11, Mark remembers having his first ever bath when he was seven years old at Jimmy's house in Burnley when he and his father had visited and stayed overnight. He still remembers seeing the proper bathroom, a table tennis table where the girls were playing and he saw Jimmy's Footballer of the Year trophy. He remembers too that his father was given money.

Maybe Bill was proud of Jimmy and looked up to him, 'living in his reflected glory' says Mark. Or did he simply see Jimmy as a source of handouts?

In 1963, travelling from Aylesbury where they then lived at the time, they went to see Burnley play at Chelsea and afterwards met up with Jimmy. In 1974, Bill, by then penniless, tried to find Jimmy again in Burnley but Jimmy was away. As a result, out of the blue, Bill turned up on Mark's doorstep. Jimmy paid his debts, put him on a train to London, and that was the last time he saw him.

But that wasn't the last Jimmy heard of his brother. Somehow during 1974 Bill found work as a domestic porter at Radley College, Oxford, and lived in a small Radley cottage.

Whilst there he was assaulted by a co-worker and received injuries to his head when he fell. The following day he was admitted to Radcliffe Infirmary with brain injuries.

He subsequently died on March 20 aged just 52. Jimmy was given the news and paid for the funeral but did not attend. It was just another thing that Jimmy kept to himself.

None of his players ever knew.

You can't help feeling that there is a strand of tragedy that runs through the whole Adamson family.

The little lad who today confesses that because of the constant changes of address he rarely attended school, whose father was not just a drinker but violent with his mother when drunk, a man that would travel to Burnley if they lived near enough to 'borrow' money from Jimmy, whose mother suffered so many desperate years with her husband, who saw a proper bathroom for the first time when he was seven at Jimmy's house, was determined to escape the poverty trap. In 2004 he sold the business he had built for many millions. It would be reasonable to think that Jimmy would have been proud of him had he met Mark in later life and been proud of his success.

As all this communication with Mark was established, fellow Burnley author Mike Smith found register records of the names of Jimmy's family. The five grandchildren had struggled to remember but with the book almost completed there in the records were the names of his mother and father, Mary and William. Jimmy's mother and father had married in September 1921, with Mary already six months pregnant with the twins,

William and Mark. There too were the names of Jimmy's brothers and sisters – William, Roy, Jane, Doreen and Florence.

They must have been somewhere in Katie's subconscious as the names slowly came back to her. In one of the huge boxes of old photographs there in an album was a faded picture of Bill and the girls in their 20s. How smart and attractive they looked. How old and tired their mother looked sitting in front of them. When I went to see Stan Ternent for one of the last interviews, it was his wife Kath who leapt in with an unexpected contribution, 'My mother, she's 90 now with a sharp memory, knew Jimmy's mother Mary.'

I was quite stunned; Kath was as hooked on finding out more as I was and immediately rang her mother (Stan calls Kath 'Miss Marple'). From this we learned that Jimmy as a youth had been in digs with a couple called Lill and Bill May on a street very near the ground. He came to see them almost as a second mother and father as time went by.

On that same day I had been to Burnley Crematorium to ask what records they had of Mary Adamson. There was just one Mary Adamson with a year of death recorded as 1954. Katie's sister Sarah also went, found the actual grave and confirmed the headstone date as 1954. Kath Ternent's mother remembered that both his mother and one of the sisters had come down to live with Jimmy and look after him. He then bought her a house on Mitella Street very near Lill and Bill May.

She took her own life in 1954, just two years after Jimmy's marriage and the year that Jimmy played for Young England against England at Highbury. She was only 57. Mitella Street, a name I knew well, was one of the streets where my father used to park the car, a little old Ford Prefect, on match days in the late 1950s and early 1960s. All of this was like the bits of a jigsaw finally coming together especially when an e-mail arrived from John Ramsay up in the north-east with the story that Florence had eventually married Edwin Purbrick, had two children, Lynn and Ted, and lived in Abingdon for the rest of her days.

It was on 4 May 2013 that Mark and the grandchildren met at Turf Moor for the first time. It was the final game of the season and a table had been arranged next door to the Jimmy Adamson Suite. Mark had seen the cabinets of memorabilia and had been shown round the ground. For Mark it was a moving moment, it was the first contact with anyone from the family for decades. And things couldn't have gone better; the football gods smiled. Burnley won 2-0.

After living in their own home for so many years, for their final months Jimmy and May moved together to a care home in Burnley but were at last separated when May was taken into the Royal Blackburn Hospital. How both their hearts must have ached at the parting. They had been together for almost 60 years. Jimmy then moved to a specialist care home in Brierfield. Just like Harry Potts there were many days when he had no real idea where he was.

The grandchildren were apprehensive about telling him of May's death. He had good days and bad days. Perhaps, mercifully, he wouldn't comprehend what had happened. Or perhaps it would be a clear day when he would be all too aware and he would be consumed with grief. Jennie remembers that he understood perfectly. He cried and over and again repeated, 'Oh that's a shame, she was such a lovely woman, she was such a lovely woman.' It was all he could say, 'Such a shame, such a shame' over and again while they sat with him sharing his anguish.

They worried how he would be at her funeral but he was perfectly alert and focused, says Jennie. It was afterwards that he declined rapidly without the stimulus of May to talk to him and keep his mind alive. Jennie still has the mink coat that Jimmy brought back from Chile for May all those many years earlier. All of the grandchildren emphasise how private he was, how there were depths to him that lay hidden, how he never talked of his father, and rarely spoke of his earlier days of hardship and the mines, although he did tell Sam that one reason he turned down the England job was that he was too young; that with a tennis ball he had played football in the Ashington streets with the Charlton boys and that he loved all the travelling he had done.

On his own final journey the funeral cortege drove by Turf Moor for the cremation and service at Burnley Crematorium just a few miles away. The pavements at the club were lined with staff, players and fans paying their final respects. There was an irony in that this final drive took him down the road named after Harry Potts, the man he had not spoken to for so many years and whom he came to disdain. Nevertheless this enigmatic man died having made his peace with the club and the supporters.

The service was attended by many of his former players, by Eddie Gray, Stan Ternent, Sir Bobby Charlton, Alex Elder and Jimmy McIlroy. In the rich story of Burnley Football Club he will not be forgotten, especially by those who saw him play so elegantly, or were privileged to have seen the team that so nearly did become the 'Team of the Seventies'.

They say time heals but it never healed his rifts with Bob Lord and Harry Potts. What time did heal however were the views and opinions of Leeds United supporters who gave him such a torrid time at Elland Road.

'Hey rock and roll, Adamson's on the dole,' sang the Geldard Road End with unfeeling cruelty on his dismissal. But on his death their fans' message boards contained many wishes that he might rest in peace and it was significant that many of them now acknowledged that he was a victim of internal problems at Leeds and unrealistic expectations.

Some of them were the very same people who had loudly demonstrated against him. Their applause for him before the Burnley game in November 2011 was heartfelt and sustained. The Leeds chapters in this book will perhaps make them even more forgiving. Just think what a team they would have had that included Martin Dobson, Kevin Keegan and Peter Withe. But it was not to be.

Jimmy Adamson died on 8 November 2011, aged 82. His wife May died before him in August 2010, aged 78. They had been utterly devoted to each other. Theirs was a love that stood them true in trying times and through all manner of difficulties. Their daughter Julie, whose children were Katie, Sarah and James, died aged only 44 in 1998. Daughter Jayne, the mother of Jennie and Sam, died in 2005 aged just 45. These were personal tragedies of a magnitude that might have destroyed anyone else without the same strength and fortitude that Jimmy and May Adamson gave to each other. Jennie confided that when her mother Jayne died, that was when Jimmy and May shut themselves off from the world.

Jimmy and May chose one of the flower gardens nearest to Towneley Hall to scatter first their daughter Julie's ashes and then seven years later, Jayne's. In a poignant and emotional gesture the grandchildren chose that same flower garden to scatter Jimmy and May's ashes. There they were re-united at last, in the next world, if not in this. It means though that there is no headstone or any kind of memorial anywhere to mark their last resting place. During their lives he had put a protective wall around his family, a direct result of his own early hardships when it was mental toughness that got him through. It was why he always looked for mental toughness in others and they were words he frequently used.

In the very early 1970s, at a time when things were not going well for him at Burnley, he attended a function at Burnley Cricket Club. Someone who wasn't particularly interested in football approached him and smiled. 'Never mind Jimmy it's only a game,' she said.

'It's rather more than that,' he replied.

It certainly was. And in the end it was a game that just about broke his heart.

References

A 1950s Childhood; Paul Feeney, History Press 2009

A Rock 'n' Roll Years Diary of Burnley Football Club; Tim Quelch 2000

Ashington Images of England; Mike Kirkup, Tempus 1999

Burnley – A Complete Record 1882–1991; Ray Simpson & Edward Lee, Breedon 1991

Burnley – A Season to Remember 1959/60; Bill Evans, Tempus 2002

Burnley Corporation Official Handbook 1950

Burnley – The Glory Years Remembered; Mike Prestage, Breedon

Cissie Charlton – Football's Most Famous Mother; Cissie Charlton, Bridge Studios 1988

Cup Final Story 1946–1965; David Prole, Robert Hale 1967

FA Cup Giant Killers; Geoff Tibballs, Collins Willow 1994

Fighting Back; Jimmy Armfield, Stanley Paul & Co 1969

Football And All That; Norman Giller, Hodder and Stoughton 2004

Football Gentry – The Cobbold Brothers; Brian Scovell, Tempus 2005

Football's War and Peace, Season 1946/47; Thomas Taw, Desert Island Books 2003

Harry Potts – Margaret's Story; Dave Thomas, Sportsbooks 2006

Jack Charlton – The Autobiography; Corgi Books 1996

Jimmy Armfield – The Autobiography; Headline 2004

Jimmy McIlroy – Prince of Inside Forwards; Dave Thomas, Hudson and Pearson 2009

Leeds And Scotland Hero; Peter Lorimer, Mainstream 2005

Leeds United – A Complete Record 1919–1986; M. Jarred & M. Macdonald, Breedon 1986

Leeds United And A Life In The Press Box; John Wray, Vertical Editions 2008

Magical – A Lifetime In Football; Paul Fletcher, Vertical Editions 2012

Marching On Together – My Life With Leeds United; Eddie Gray, Hodder and Stoughton 2001

My England Years; Sir Bobby Charlton, Headline 2008

My Manchester United Years – The Autobiography; Sir Bobby Charlton, Headline 2007

Never Had It So Good – Burnley's 1959/60 Triumph; Tim Quelch, Know the Score 2009

Nobody Ever Says Thankyou – Brian Clough The Biography; Jonathan Wilson, Orion 2011

No Nay Never – A Burnley Anthology Volume 1; Dave Thomas and published by Dave Thomas 2004

No Nay Never – A Burnley Anthology Volume 2; Dave Thomas, Burnley Football Club 2008

Northern Life; Frank Atkinson, Select Editions 1991

Northern Soccer Annual; Edited by Eamonn Dunphy & Peter Douglas, Pelham 1969

Ron Reynolds – Life Of A 1950s Footballer; with Dave Bowler, Orion 2003

Simply The Best; David Ross, Yore Publications 1995

Soccer's Golden Nursery; John Gibson, Pelham 1970

Stan The Man – A Hard Life In Football; Stan Ternent, John Blake 2004

Sunderland – The Complete Record; Rob Mason, Breedon 2005

The Autobiography; Brian Clough, Corgi Books 1994

The Clarets Chronicles 1882–2007; Edited by Ray Simpson, Burnley Football Club 2007

The Double – Spurs' 1960–61 Season; Ken Ferris, Mainstream 1999

The Football Man; Arthur Hopcraft, Simon and Schuster 1988

The Footballer Who Could Fly; Century 2012

The Glory Game; Hunter Davies, Mainstream 1972

The Sixties Revisited; Jimmy Greaves, Queen Anne Press 1992

Time On The Grass An Autobiography; Bobby Robson, Weidenfield 1982

Willie Irvine – Together Again; Dave Thomas, Sportsbooks 2005

World Cup 1962; Donald Saunders, Sportsman's Book Club 1964

Underdog: 50 Years Of Trials And Triumphs With Football's Also-Rans; Tim Quelch, Pitch 2011